THE CAMBRIDGE
PIERS PL(

Piers Plowman has long been considered one of the greatest poems of medieval England. Current scholarship on this alliterative masterpiece looks very different from that available even a decade ago. New information about the manuscripts of the poem, new historical discoveries, and new investigations of its literary, cultural, and theoretical scope have fundamentally altered the very meaning of Langland's art. This *Companion* thus critically surveys traditional scholarship, with the aim of recuperating its best insights, and it ventures forth into newer areas of inquiry attuned to questions of social setting, institutional context, intellectual and literary history, theory, and the revitalized fields of codicology and paleography. By proceeding through chapters that offer cumulatively wider views as well as stand-alone analyses of topics most crucial to understanding *Piers Plowman*, this *Companion* gives serious students and seasoned scholars alike up-to-date knowledge of this intricate and beautiful poem.

ANDREW COLE is Associate Professor of English at Princeton University.

ANDREW GALLOWAY is Professor of English at Cornell University.

A complete list of books in the series is at the back of the book.

THE CAMBRIDGE COMPANION TO

PIERS PLOWMAN

EDITED BY

ANDREW COLE AND ANDREW GALLOWAY

CAMBRIDGE
UNIVERSITY PRESS

CAMBRIDGE
UNIVERSITY PRESS

University Printing House, Cambridge CB2 8BS, United Kingdom

Published in the United States of America by Cambridge University Press, New York

Cambridge University Press is part of the University of Cambridge.

It furthers the University's mission by disseminating knowledge in the pursuit of education, learning and research at the highest international levels of excellence.

www.cambridge.org
Information on this title: www.cambridge.org/9781107401587

© Cambridge University Press 2014

First published 2014

Printed in the United Kingdom by Clays, St Ives plc

A catalogue record for this publication is available from the British Library

Library of Congress Cataloguing in Publication data
The Cambridge Companion to Piers Plowman / edited by Andrew Cole
and Andrew Galloway.
pages   cm. – (Cambridge Companions to Literature)
Includes bibliographical references and index.
ISBN 978-1-107-00918-9 (hardback)
1. Langland, William, 1330?–1400? Piers Plowman.   I. Cole, Andrew, 1968–
editor of compilation.   II. Galloway, Andrew, editor of compilation.
PR2015.C27   2013
821'.1 – dc23   2013039685

ISBN 978-1-107-00918-9 Hardback
ISBN 978-1-107-40158-7 Paperback

CONTENTS

CONTENTS

ILLUSTRATIONS

CONTRIBUTORS

ROBERT ADAMS is Professor of English at the Sam Houston State University. He has published many scholarly articles on Middle English literature, most of them concerning various aspects of *Piers Plowman*, and is former Director of the International *Piers Plowman* Society as well as one of the senior editors of The *Piers Plowman* Electronic Archive. He is the author of *Langland and the Rokele Family: The Gentry Background to Piers Plowman* (Four Courts Press, 2013).

SUZANNE CONKLIN AKBARI is Professor of English and Medieval Studies, and was educated at Johns Hopkins and Columbia. Her research focuses on the intersection of English and Comparative Literature with intellectual history and philosophy, ranging from Neoplatonism and science in the twelfth century to national identity and religious conflict in the fifteenth century. Akbari's books are on optics and allegory (*Seeing Through the Veil*), European views of Islam and the Orient (*Idols in the East*), and travel literature (*Marco Polo*); she is currently at work on *Small Change: Metaphor and Metamorphosis in Chaucer and Christine de Pizan*. She is volume editor for *The Norton Anthology of World Literature* (Volume B: 100–1500), co-editor of the *Norton Anthology of Western Literature*, and editor of *The Oxford Handbook to Chaucer*.

HELEN BARR is Fellow and Tutor in English at Lady Margaret Hall, University of Oxford. She has edited the poems within the *"Piers Plowman* tradition" (Dent, 1993), and is author of *Signes and Sothe: Language in the Piers Plowman Tradition* (Brewer, 1994) and *Socioliterary Practice in Late Medieval England* (Oxford University Press, 2001). She has also co-edited, with Ann M. Hutchison, *Text and Controversy from Wyclif to Bale* (Brepols, 2005). Her recent work includes an edition of the Digby poems (University of Exeter Press, 2009) and a book entitled *Transporting Chaucer* (University of Manchester Press, 2014).

ANDREW COLE teaches in the Department of English at Princeton University. He edited the *Yearbook of Langland Studies* from 2004 to 2011 with Fiona Somerset and Lawrence Warner, and has written many articles on late medieval literature, including essays on *Piers Plowman* and the politics of late medieval labor, as well as papers on Langland and Wycliffism or "Lollardy." He is author of *Literature and Heresy in the Age of Chaucer* (Cambridge University Press, 2008) and *The Birth of Theory* (University of Chicago Press, 2014), and editor (with D. Vance Smith) of *The Legitimacy of the Middle Ages: On the Unwritten History of Theory* (Duke University Press, 2010), as well as editor of a special cluster of essays for the *minnesota review* entitled, "The Medieval Turn in Theory" (2013).

ANDREW GALLOWAY, Professor of English at Cornell University, has published diversely on the works of the medieval writers John Gower, Geoffrey Chaucer, William Langland, and Ranulph Higden, as well as other writers and their contexts. His monographs include *The Penn Commentary on Piers Plowman, Volume One* (University of Pennsylvania Press, 2006) and *Medieval Literature and Culture* (Continuum, 2006). He co-edited with John Alford the *Yearbook of Langland Studies* from 1997 to 1998, and edited it from 1999 to 2003. Other edited volumes include *The Cambridge Companion to Medieval English Culture* (Cambridge University Press, 2011) and *Answerable Style: The Idea of the Literary in Medieval England*, co-edited with Frank Grady (Ohio State University Press, 2013).

MATTHEW GIANCARLO is Associate Professor of English at the University of Kentucky. He is author of *Parliament and Literature in Late Medieval England* (Cambridge University Press, 2007) and articles on William Langland, Geoffrey Chaucer, and John Gower. He has also published on topics such as the historiography of philology, medieval English romance and genealogy, and the intersections of medieval English institutional politics and literature. Currently he is working on fifteenth-century literature and the poetry of Peter Idley, and on the literary intersections of late medieval and early modern genres of legal writing, constitutional theory, and handbooks for princes.

RALPH HANNA is currently Senior Research Officer in the Faculty of English Language and Literature, University of Oxford. He was previously Distinguished Professor at University of California – Riverside and Professor of Palaeography at Oxford. His research covers a variety of insular texts and their transmission in medieval English, French, and Latin, mainly in the late thirteenth and fourteenth centuries.

SIMON HOROBIN is Professor of English Language and Literature at the University of Oxford and a Fellow of Magdalen College. He is the author of books on Chaucer's language and texts and on the history of the English language. He has published widely on the manuscripts of *Piers Plowman* and on the scribes who copied literary manuscripts in the fifteenth century. He was co-investigator (with Linne Mooney and Estelle Stubbs) on the Identification of the Scribes Responsible for Copying Major Works of Middle English Literature Project, funded by the UK Arts and Humanities Research Council (www.medievalscribes.com).

STEVEN JUSTICE is Professor of English at the University of Mississippi and formerly at the University of California–Berkeley. He is author of *Writing and Rebellion: England in 1381* (University of California Press, 1994) and editor (with Kathryn Kerby-Fulton) of *Written Work: Langland, Labor, and Authorship* (University of Pennsylvania Press, 1997). Among his recent publications are essays on the historical study of belief and on the literary properties of literary history.

JILL MANN is Emeritus Notre Dame Professor of English, University of Notre Dame, where she taught from 1999 to 2004. Previously she taught in the University of Cambridge (UK), where from 1988 to 1998 she was Professor of Medieval and Renaissance English (C. S. Lewis's Chair). Her books include *Chaucer and Medieval Estates Satire* (1973), a dual-text edition of the Latin beast-epic *Ysengrimus* (1987), *The Cambridge Companion to Chaucer*, edited with Piero Boitani (2003), *Feminizing Chaucer* (2002), an edition of the *Canterbury Tales* in Penguin Classics (2005), and *From Aesop to Reynard: Beast Literature in Medieval Britain* (2009), which won the Sir Israel Gollancz Prize in 2011. She has published over fifty articles and essays on Middle English, medieval French and medieval Latin literature, and is a Fellow of the British Academy.

JAMES SIMPSON is Donald P. and Katherine B. Loker Professor of English at Harvard University. He was formerly Professor of Medieval and Renaissance English at the University of Cambridge. His most recent books are *Reform and Cultural Revolution*, being volume 2 in the *Oxford English Literary History* (Oxford University Press, 2002), *Burning to Read: English Fundamentalism and its Reformation Opponents* (Harvard University Press, 2007), and *Under the Hammer: Iconoclasm in the Anglo-American Tradition* (Oxford University Press, 2010).

LAWRENCE WARNER is Senior Lecturer in Medieval English at King's College London, and Director of the International *Piers Plowman* Society. He is author of *The Lost History of Piers Plowman: The Earliest*

Transmission of Langland's Work (University of Pennsylvania Press, 2011) and *The Myth of Piers Plowman: Creating a Medieval Literary Archive* (Cambridge University Press, 2014), and, with Andrew Cole and Fiona Somerset, was co-editor of the *Yearbook of Langland Studies* from 2004 to 2012. He has also published and taught on many non-Langlandian topics, ranging from a twelfth-century autobiography by a convert to Judaism to Shakespeare's *Othello*.

NICOLETTE ZEEMAN is Fellow of King's College, Cambridge and Lecturer in the Faculty of English. She is author of *Piers Plowman and the Medieval Discourse of Desire* (Cambridge, 2006) and has published on medieval Latin, English and French literature, including authors such as Gower, Chaucer, and Langland; her interests include medieval psychology, literary theory, commentary, allegory, song and scepticism. Currently, she is working on a number of theoretically or psychoanalytically oriented projects and writing a book on *Piers Plowman* and the history of allegorical narrative.

Locales in London may be found on the map (Figure 1)

1327–77   The reign of Edward III.

c. 1337–1453   Edward III claims crown of France by hereditary succession; Hundred Years War.

c. 1340   Geoffrey Chaucer is born.

1348–9, 1361, 1369, etc.   Plague in England (between one-third and half of the population killed).

c. 1350s–c. 1420s   Efflorescence of alliterative poetry: *Wynnere and Wastour*, *Morte Arthure*, *Parlement of the Thre Ages*, the works of the *Gawain* poet, *Saint Erkenwald*, *Siege of Jerusalem*, *Destruccioun of Troye*, and others.

1360s   Langland works on the A text.

1360 (June 14)   Treaty of Brétigny signed by Edward III, relinquishing claims on the French crown for large tracts of Normandy and a ransom of 3 million gold crowns for the release of John II, king of France (captured during the battle of Poitiers in 1356, imprisoned until 1360 in London). See B.3.189–208.

1360 (October 24)   Treaty of Calais, ratification of the Treaty of Brétigny, first payment of 400,000 écus paid on the ransom of John II of France.

1362 (January 15)   Great southwest wind on Saturday (see A.5.14, used to date the A text).

1362   Tournament at Cheapside, London, with the challengers arrayed as "The Seven Deadly Sins."

1362   Pleading in English Act (36 Edw. III c. 15), mandating all pleas in courts to be in English and enrolled in Latin.

1370s   Langland works on the B text.

1373   John of Gaunt, fourth son of Edward III and Duke of Lancaster, leads an invasion of France.

1374   John of Gaunt returns to England to assume leadership of the government during the dotage of Edward III and the illness of his older brother and heir apparent, Edward the Black Prince.

1376   (June 8) Death of Edward the Black Prince.

1376 (April 28–July 10)   "Good Parliament," in which the Commons, appointing a Speaker for the first time, impeach some royal officers and counselors for financial mismanagement and illegal profiteering, including the wealthy and flamboyant Alice Perrers (reputed to be mistress of Edward III). See B.Prol.146–208, and passūs 2 and 3, used to date the B text.

1377   John of Gaunt reverses most of the convictions in the Good Parliament (not reversing that of Alice Perrers), imprisons the first Speaker of the Commons, Peter de la Mare.

1377   Death of Edward III (June 21); coronation of Richard II (July 16) at age ten, son of the Black Prince and grandson of Edward III. Richard's coronation celebrated in London at Cheapside with a castle pageant with four virgins (the Daughters of God?) and a mechanical angel that descended to offer Richard a golden crown. See B.Prol.128–45.

1378   Papal Schism; two popes elected, one at Rome (Boniface IX) and one at Avignon (Benedict XIII); restoration of the western church achieved at the Council of Constance (1414–18). See B.Prol.107–11; 13.174–76, 19.431–51.

1381   "The Rising": widespread rebellion of laborers, some clergy, and others, destroying many legal archives and killing some church officials. Archbishop Simon Sudbury was decapitated by the mob outside the Tower of London.

1382 (May 17–21)   Blackfriars Council (also called the "Earthquake Council") held at the Blackfriars house in London, publicly condemning twenty-four conclusions on such topics as the Eucharist and church endowment drawn largely from

John Wyclif's works (though Wyclif was never named in the published proceedings).

1380s	Langland works on the C text.
1380s–90s	Wycliffite Bible translation; English Wycliffite sermons and other writings.
1384	John Wyclif, doctor of divinity, dies at his living (benefice) in Lutterworth, Leicestershire, after leaving the University of Oxford in 1382.
c. 1385–93	John Gower works on the *Confessio amantis*.
1388	Cambridge parliament, reissuing the Statute of Laborers (possibly alluded to in *Piers Plowman* C.5.1–105, thus perhaps dating the C text to after 1388).
1390s	Chaucer works on the *Canterbury Tales*.
c. 1390	John But "finishes" the A text (A.12), mentioning how Death "drove" Will "a dint."
1396	Richard II marries Isabella of France, who is seven years old at the time.
1399	Deposition of Richard II; coronation of Henry IV, son of John of Gaunt.
c. 1400	Death of Chaucer.
1400	Richard II murdered at Pontefract Castle.
c. 1401	*Richard the Redeless*.
c. 1401	*Pierce the Plowman's Crede*.
c. 1409	*Mum and the Sothsegger*.
1550	Robert Crowley (in the Holborn area of the Inns of Court, outside the walls of London) first prints *Piers Plowman* (glossed as prophesying Protestantism).
1561	Owen Rogers (near Aldersgate, London) reprints Crowley's *Piers Plowman* (not printed again until 1813 by T. D. Whitaker).

ABBREVIATIONS

Piers Plowman editions:

Athlone editions:

K   Kane, G. (ed.), *Piers Plowman: The A Version. Will's Visions of Piers Plowman, Do-well, Do-better and Dobest*, London, Athlone, 1960; cited is rev. edn., London, Athlone, 1988

K-D   Kane, G. and E. T. Donaldson (eds.), *Piers Plowman: The B Version. Will's Visions of Piers Plowman, Do-well, Do-better and Dobest*, rev. edn., London, Athlone, 1988

R-K   Russell, G. and G. Kane (eds.), *Piers Plowman: The C Version: Will's Visions of Piers Plowman, Do-well, Do-better and Dobest*, London, Athlone, 1997

Schmidt   Schmidt, A. V. C. (ed.), *Piers Plowman: A Parallel Text Edition of the A, B, C and Z Versions*, 2 vols., London, Longman, and Kalamazoo, Medieval Institute, 1995–2008

Schmidt B Schmidt, A. V. C. (ed.), *William Langland: The Vision of Piers Plowman: A Critical Edition of the B Text*, 2nd edn., London, Dent, 1995

Other abbreviations:

EETS   Early English Text Society

e.s.   extra series

MED   *Middle English Dictionary*, ed. H. Kurath, S. Kuhn, and R. E. Lewis, 22 vols., Ann Arbor, University of Michigan Press, 1952–2001; online edition http://quod.lib.umich.edu/m/med/

OED   *The Oxford English Dictionary* [electronic resource; by subscription], 2nd edn., prepared by J. A. Simpson and E. S. C. Weiner, Oxford, Clarendon Press, 1989

o.s.   original series

SAC   *Studies in the Age of Chaucer*

YLS   *Yearbook of Langland Studies*

References in notes with * are given in full in Guides to further reading.

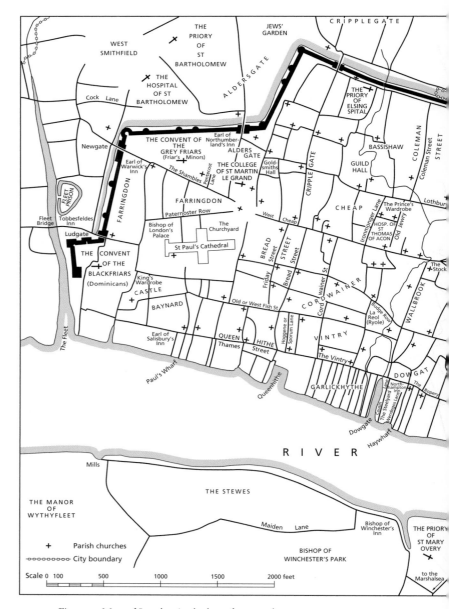

Figure 1 Map of London in the later fourteenth century.

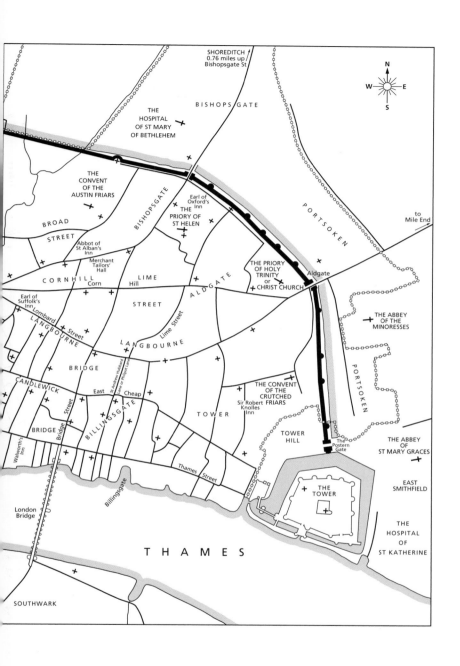

SHOREDITCH
0.76 miles up
Bishopsgate St

N
W   E
S

BISHOPS GATE

THE
HOSPITAL
OF ST MARY
OF BETHLEHEM

THE
CONVENT
OF THE
AUSTIN FRIARS

BISHOPSGATE

Earl of
Oxford's
Inn
THE
PRIORY OF
ST HELEN

PORTSOKEN

to
Mile End

BROAD

STREET

Abbot of
St Alban's
Inn

Merchant
Tailors'
Hall

CORNHILL
Corn

LIME
Hill

ALDGATE

Aldgate

THE PRIORY
OF HOLY
TRINITY
or
CHRIST CHURCH

THE ABBEY
OF THE
MINORESSES

Earl of
Suffolk's
Inn
Lombard

Street

LANGBOURNE

STREET

Lime Street

LANGBOURNE

BRIDGE

Street

CANDLEWICK

East

Cheap

St Andrew Hubbard

Lane or Philpot Lane

THE CONVENT
OF THE
CRUTCHED FRIARS

Sir Robert
Knolles
Inn

PORTSOKEN

BILLINGSGATE

TOWER

BRIDGE

Bridge

Street

Walworth's
Inn

TOWER
HILL

The
Postern
Gate

THE ABBEY
OF
ST MARY GRACES

Thames   Street

Billingsgate

THE
TOWER

EAST
SMITHFIELD

THE
HOSPITAL
OF
ST KATHERINE

London
Bridge

THAMES

SOUTHWARK

ANDREW COLE AND ANDREW GALLOWAY

Introduction

Studying *Piers Plowman* in the twentieth and twenty-first centuries

Scholarship on *Piers Plowman* in the second decade of the twenty-first century looks very different from that available when the first academic journal devoted to the poem, the *Yearbook of Langland Studies*, arrived on library and personal bookshelves in 1987, soon followed by the first "companion" to *Piers Plowman* in 1988.[1] The quantum of new research, editions, commentaries, and monographs presents a poem and a range of approaches to it that would hardly be recognizable to scholars twenty years ago. New information about the manuscripts of the poem and their affiliations, recent historical discoveries, and important chartings of the literary, cultural, and theoretical scope of the poem, have all emerged. We have reached a point that rewards our taking stock of knowledge about this perennially intriguing poem, and encourages us to highlight some of the most important and promising terms for current teaching, criticism, and research.

The need for a consolidation of current prospects (emphatically in the plural) is hardly surprising, given the many complexities and mysteries that have always made *Piers Plowman* a moving target. Even basic issues are hardly "settled" in the way they are for Chaucer or Gower – after all, there are real reasons why scholars feel it necessary to reaffirm, repeatedly, that one poet named Langland wrote the three (or perhaps four) versions of the poem we call *Piers Plowman*. Both the choice of what edition of the poem to use and the question of how to understand the relations between the different versions – both matters that Ralph Hanna considers in his chapter here – have long remained intriguingly open, and in some respects do so to the present. On the matter of editions for citation, for example, contributors to this collection have chosen either the compendious "Athlone" texts edited by George Kane, E. Talbot Donaldson, and George Russell, or the more student-friendly volumes more recently edited by A. V. C. Schmidt, and of the latter, authors have chosen either Schmidt's parallel-text "full" edition, including the controversial "Z" text, or his paperback edition of just the B text. Insofar as this question of "which edition?" is at once a question of "which version?," our contributors might have chosen C as the "final" version of the poem, or they might have used all the versions for comparison of every point. But the warp of research meets the weft of practicality when it comes to publishing scholarship, and in the case of this volume the discussions below are generally based on the B text, as the version most commonly studied and taught (citations not otherwise identified can be assumed to be from that version). These matters can be tedious and thorny, but they need no longer either stifle other discussion or be dismissed from any notice. They simply need to be made visible. For we have reached a time of necessary and productive pluralism of considerable depth and range, which is why now is also the time for a new "companion" to the poem, its contexts, and the wide range of responses it has elicited since its inception.

In fact, more surprising than how much innovation and how many new discoveries have appeared in the last two decades is how durable were the foundations laid down in the late 1980s. The "companion" edited by John A. Alford is a collection of essays that are permanently valuable. Yet it is the product of a different moment in our knowledge of the poem and in the discipline of medieval literary studies itself. In this regard, it is worth briefly reflecting on that earlier moment in the field, in order to appreciate that "companion's" contributions and set in relief what makes the present volume different and, it is hoped, helpful for its moment. It is seldom remembered that for two decades before the publication of Alford's "companion" there were three collections available to guide readers through the poem, helping create something like a discipline called Langland studies: *Interpretations of Piers Plowman*, edited by Edward Vasta in 1968; *Style and Symbolism in Piers Plowman: A Modern Critical Anthology*, edited by Robert J. Blanch in 1969; and *Piers Plowman: Critical Approaches*, edited by S. S. Hussey in 1969.[2] Appearing at roughly the same time, each of these nonetheless tells a quite different story about Langland studies, presenting divergent points of view of the once-dominant critical topics of "exegetical" criticism, the "authorship controversy," and more formalist and aesthetic literary assessment. Each also tells us something different about Middle English studies in the mid twentieth century.

Mid-century Langland criticism: a window onto Middle English studies

Edward Vasta was the first to offer readers a way through not only *Piers Plowman* but its long history of criticism. He sought to tell the story of Langland studies over the eighty years leading up to 1968 (xviii), from the debates about authorship that arose after "the publication of Skeat's parallel text edition of 1886" (ix) to "matters of form and idea" in the 1930s, in which it is thought that new editions of the poem were desperately needed, to the "outpouring of interpretive studies" (x) in the 1950s. But when one reads Vasta's volume today, a sense about *Piers Plowman* studies rather different from his stated purposes seems to inform the selection of essays – namely, a concern about how scholars should approach the poem as an allegorical and literary work, in which every rift was loaded with ore for interpretive controversy. Does one follow D. W. Robertson and Bernard F. Huppé, who reasoned that if the Church Fathers and medieval clerics read the Bible according to the levels of allegory (tropological, allegorical, anagogical), then authors like Langland wrote accordingly – thereby prescribing a modern method of reading *Piers Plowman* that asks you to scan timelessly through centuries of exegetical meanings supporting the pursuit of "charity" and the condemnation of "cupidity"? Or do you adopt the equally learned methods of T. P. Dunning, using the same Church Fathers and later exegetes (especially Aquinas) to read the poem not in relation to the *lingua franca* of medieval allegorical criticism, but in light of the poem's penchant to think in threes and prescribe forms of living in a graduated fashion? Or do we, with E. T. Donaldson, read the allegory out of the interstices separating the different versions of the poem? Might readers instead – or as well – adhere to Morton Bloomfield's program of study, in which allegory is seen to indicate larger patterns of history that will end in apocalypse, requiring the individual, in turn, to gain "perfection" or suffer catastrophe?[3] Or does one read the allegory of *Piers Plowman* in the manner of Robert Worth Frank, who proposed that the personifications in this poem should be read literally and in accordance with the poem's own internal logics that frustrate tidy triads or any imposed organization?

These are rhetorical questions now, since the apparent wider and more programmatic issues they referred to in historical and literary understanding have long lost their sense of momentous importance, replaced by more socially, culturally, and economically specific historicism, on the one hand, and more self-conscious pursuits of the idea of "the literary" as such in medieval culture, on the other. As close consideration of two near book-end chapters here shows, Steven Justice's and Lawrence Warner's, there remain fundamentally different ways of thinking about the "literary" or the "cultural," as either recurrent memes or more direct textual transmissions of ideas and literary materials. Intellectual history remains crucial, as is suggested below in a chapter by the editors, but it has come under closer scrutiny for its contradictions and its hidden debts – including the debts of later theory and philosophy to the idea and the thought of the Middle Ages. And important studies have emerged proposing more comprehensive answers about how we are to read medieval literary allegory (see also Chapter 4).

All these later developments are useful for thinking about what is *not* articulated in Vasta's *grand récit* of Langland studies. One such point is not only to say, with Vasta, that "a large number of scholars remain unconvinced" by Robertson's "exegetical" proposals (xvi). Rather, it is to emphasize that what Robertson did for Chaucer studies, in *A Preface to Chaucer*, he could never do for Langland studies, even when teaming up with Huppé. It is true that, as Justice observes in his chapter here, *Piers Plowman* has always been seen to display a desire "for poetry to be more than poetry," offering "an interesting challenge to literary history because it has regularly convinced its readers that it has no part in such a history, that it is something more than art." Yet something about *Piers Plowman* has always resisted systematic allegoresis, a fact acknowledged by Robertson's most vigorous defender, Robert Kaske, who admitted that the "most significant weakness" of the exegetical method was "its tendency to proceed from general assumption to the explanation of particulars, instead of vice versa"; "[n]ot every exegetical image or allusion is most fruitfully interpreted by direct recourse to *charitas* and *cupiditas*" (324, 321; see 320). Moreover, although some have claimed otherwise, the Christian allegorical tradition emphasized by Robertson was never the only way in which scholars in Middle English studies approached historical contexts, or for that matter the allegorical tradition. Nor was it the only way of reading Langland within intellectual history. Unlike scholarship on Chaucer, in scholarship on *Piers Plowman* there was no strict dichotomy between historicism and formalism, or History and Literature. That facile distinction was overcome well before Robertsonianism, when work in the late nineteenth century and early twentieth century that customarily read *Piers Plowman* as a social "document" fell out of favor: Dorothy Chadwick's *Social Life in the Days of Piers Plowman* (Cambridge, 1922) is the apex of such a documentary reading practice. Thus although Vasta's presentation of the range of options for approaching *Piers Plowman* helped create the sense of a "field" for studying this poem, his selections imply oppositions in approaches to Langland's allegory that obtained more in studies of Chaucer in his period than in work on *Piers Plowman*.

Robert J. Blanch's collection crystallizes a moment in Langland studies in a different way. Surely all critical history is "transitional," but Blanch's volume captures a period when the "authorship controversy" was waning but innovative methods of textual editing were just beginning to emerge, promising fundamental changes in the possibilities for understanding the poem's forms, although these textual studies had not yet advanced far enough to influence in a significant way interpretations of *Piers Plowman*. Eclipsed though it now is, the authorship controversy is still worth thinking about, because it is a critical moment referenced to this day. In the early twentieth century, scholars of Langland began to wonder whether one person wrote all three versions of the poem, or whether in fact up to five different authors contributed to each version. Why scholars started asking questions about authorship is easy to see: W. W. Skeat's editions of the poem made the comparative study of the versions relatively efficient, especially when his parallel-text editions were printed. As soon as John Manly published in 1906 his "The Lost Leaf of *Piers the Plowman*," which challenged the single-authorship theory endorsed by Skeat, the authorship controversy was off and running, and (as Hanna remarks in his chapter here) persisted through sustained rebuttals by Donaldson, George Kane, and others. Bloomfield's essay in Blanch's volume remains essential reading on the authorship debates, an excellent point of departure for reconsidering the critical atmospheres of these disputes and rethinking their issues. But the essay itself embodies the belatedness of Blanch's volume, and the futility of collecting papers published across a rapidly changing span of criticism as a way of giving shape to something that could be called "Langland studies." Entitled "The Present State of *Piers Plowman* Studies," Bloomfield's essay is tasked to summarize Langland criticism up to 1969, but the bulk of the essay was written thirty years earlier and received only minor updating. That Blanch thought it was a good editorial decision to include this essay can only be explained by his sense that the field had not changed substantially in the interim. But more fundamental change was underway, as Blanch indicates in a footnote about Bloomfield's essay: "Since the appearance of Bloomfield's essay, the definitive edition of the A-text has been published" by George Kane (vii).

Kane's edition of the A text, and especially the Kane–Donaldson edition of B, produced new, often heated debates about editorial methods; about the poetics – from meter to anything else – that were being reconstructed; and about the unity of the poem's project. The Athlone editorial project supported a further study by Kane himself of some familiar old topics in his *Piers Plowman: The Evidence of Authorship*, which sought to end any suggestion that more than one person wrote this poem – at least in the three "versions" that Kane, following Skeat, accepted as authorial (a contention that, in having excluded Z, has been vigorously resisted by Charlotte Brewer who traces this critical history and who produced with A. G. Rigg an edition of the Z text, which has attained in Schmidt's parallel-text edition at least careful presentation and commentary if not universal acceptance as Langland's). The "life records" that Kane presented there are quite minimal by necessity, since only one record (quoted at the outset of Robert Adams's chapter below) can be said to offer a local and early identification of the poem *Piers Plowman* with the poet William Langland, son of Eustace de Rokele. To be sure, there is evidence enough to support a speculative biography of Langland, including the materials that Hanna has collected,[4] as well as a unique contemporary reference to "long Will" recently discovered by Michael Bennett.[5] But speculative that biography remains; all we can say is that Langland was probably born sometime between 1325 and 1335, and died evidently between 1385 and 1395, probably soon after 1388 – if indeed the C-text "autobiography" refers to the reissued Statute of Laborers from that year.[6] A more precise sense of the poet's range of worlds, however, is becoming clearer by indirect as well as direct means, especially in the important new collection of the poet's more widely extended and longer family history offered here by Adams.

Even these hazy vistas were not possible just a few years ago. But Blanch's collection displays the origins of something else in Langland criticism. Readers were ready to give "literary appreciation" new emphasis, after some previous assorted attempts (especially by Lawlor; see Vasta, xvii). In Blanch's words, it was time to realize "the *desideratum* for *Piers Plowman* scholarship – the importance of turning away from authorship and textual problems to the literary merits of the poem" (viii; see vii). At first, this turn to literary matters was motivated not by scholars' great passion for literature qua literature. Unlike Chaucer criticism, as noted, Langland studies never saw a belle-lettristic movement pressing back against the historicists. Rather, scholars began to appreciate *Piers Plowman* as a poem, with affective and sensuous appeal, because so much clinical attention had been previously paid to its author in the authorship controversy. Those embroiled in any aspect of the authorship controversy necessarily read the poem as indexers and catalAoguers of poetic effect and development, isolating passages and juxtaposing their variations among the versions of the poem; in the early criticism on this topic, scholars looked keenly for differences of poetic temper, meter, argumentative clarity, theological sophistication, and political adventurousness. Such studies were obliged to do many things at once – cups, saucers, tilting chair and all – but chiefly to decide how much discrepancy of opinion and fineness of craft might fit inside the head of one author before one can determine that all of these data points represent either multiple personalities or multiple authors.

The authorship controversy was a necessary phase of Langland studies and gave the field a significant hermeneutic still used to this day. It was also the moment when scholars were finally coming to terms with the poet's perspectival and often polyvalent form. Yet it was a phase that many scholars were from an early point ready to move swiftly beyond – or at least, they were ready to discuss the poet's complex ideas and dialectical, exploratory forms under some rubric other than authorship. More recently, however, versions of this issue have reappeared. Provocative new work requiring such close attention includes detailed cases supporting the authenticity of the Z text by Rigg and Brewer and Schmidt's modern commentary on Z, as well as research that unsettles earlier assumptions by arguing that the origin of the popular B text itself is in large a scribal confection modeled after C.[7] Even a recent student edition of the A text – the last version to be given a student edition – is framed with the assumption that that text, and indeed all the versions, should be treated as distinct poems, best understood outside of the idea of unified authorship.[8] These modern claims have brought scrutiny back to the material and historical evidence of the poem's (or poems') extremely complicated genesis and development, and that topic is of continuing importance even within the transformations of what is usually understood to have made B into C.

Turning now to the third "companion": in the late 1960s, S. S. Hussey's collection succeeded in moving *Piers Plowman* scholarship as a whole beyond the early forms of the "authorship" debate, but almost by accident. For Hussey was compelled to assemble a different kind of anthology of *Piers Plowman* criticism, finding "little point in reproducing what has been made conveniently available elsewhere" (vii) by Vasta and Blanch. Instead, he commissioned authors to write essays for the volume itself. Although Hussey expresses this editorial endeavor with a hint of frustration – that is, with the sense that he was beaten to the punch of anthologizing pre-published papers – the results of his alternative program are important and can be regarded as the first experiment in seeing what would happen if authors worked up original essays exemplifying "Critical Approaches," as the subtitle to the volume reads. Hussey's is the first attempt to conceptualize "Critical Approaches" as something other than a museum wherein is collected important scholarship from the previous thirty years. This project has obvious importance for the history of Langland studies (as well as of "companions"). To be sure, Vasta's and Blanch's volumes emerged at a moment when no overall school of interpretation could be declared for Langland studies, but Hussey's was the first to make something of this fact, practically cornered into acknowledging the impossibility of assigning to the poem any single meaning or theme. Most of the articles contained therein admit that the poem offers contradictory points (Russell, 27; Woolf, 51; Kean, 108; Elliott, 226; Evans, 246). Two papers make contradiction – or uncertain knowledge (Burrow, 112, 123) and incompatibility of meanings (Jenkins, 125) – a theme of the poem itself. If this means that Langland studies was fissiparous, it was so in a productive way that opened up the field, introducing new scholarly variety – not the variety that offers different takes on one overarching topic, such as the authorship controversy or allegory (as above), but a variety that supplies within the same collection an essay on text and manuscripts (Russell), one on place and locality (Elliott), one on genre (Knight), and one on Chaucer (Bennett). A version of Langland studies we can now recognize, with its multi-faceted thematic, manuscript, and contextual approach, begins to emerge in Hussey's collection. It was there all along, to be sure, but the other two anthologies were not able to show it, much less conscientiously document it. Even Hussey's volume limns the outlines of what was only a nascent "field," and does so more by happenstance, more visible forty-four years later than in its own time.

Langland today

John Alford's *Companion* was the first properly modern set of commentaries on *Piers Plowman*. That volume showed, by its collection of essays ranging from history, literary influences, alliterative poetics, reception, dialect, and text, that those earlier "moments" of Langland criticism so documented by the previous anthologies were in large measure an exhibit of how disciplines wax and wane over the decades – textual scholarship for one period, interpretive scholarship in another, and historical work on the poem every now and then. Alford's volume, in other words, realized in full the directions opened up in Hussey's collection, which, like the anthologies before it, had not argued the case for Langland studies as a discipline *in the present* pursuing in one moment a diversity of fundamental approaches. To reap the full benefits of a volume like Blanch's required knowing already what was going on in the field over the last few decades; one had to be enough in the thick of the scholarly debates on "one author or five?" to yearn for something else: namely, the questions of literary value, poetic merit, and formal and symbolic quality. Alford's volume, by contrast, starts in the now, and assumes no specialization in the field; it was intended to be an education in the field, almost in the manner of a *Bildungsroman*. "[T]he book," Alford writes, "is arranged to facilitate a linear reading. Each chapter builds to some extent on its predecessors. The earlier parts are more general; the later, more specific and technical" (xi). Whether readers approached the *Companion* in the prescribed way is hard to know – and such readers would inevitably be those new to the poem. The upshot of Alford's program is that some chapters made for great reading assignments in the undergraduate classroom, while others were better suited for devoted, longtime readers of the poem.

It is now time to take stock of all we have learned about *Piers Plowman* – the poem and the field – since the publication of Alford's volume. Our goal is to offer a *Companion* evenly suited to beginning and more experienced readers – a text that does not require sequential reading and instead invites the reader to start anywhere and choose his or her own adventure. Indeed, one thing that has changed substantially since the publication of Alford's *Companion* is the sense of how some methods and materials that have historically been kept distinct are, or should be, closely related to a range of others. A single essay on "the text" of the poem, for example, no longer seems desirable in view of the scholarly consensus that textual issues should always be a factor in reading Langland. Thus here, textual issues are discussed across a set of essays that are all textual, historical, and linguistic: Hanna's, Simon Horobin's, and Warner's. We have not included chapters on Langland's alliterative meter or dialect, since excellent overviews of current understandings of the poet's meter have recently appeared,[9] and since the foundations for assessing the poet's dialect have also recently been both surveyed and unsettled.[10] Even so, two chapters below touch on some matters of meter and dialect (Justice and Horobin, respectively).

So, too, recent research dealing with the spiritual, visionary, theological contexts in which Langland wrote suggests that the religious and theological elements of the poem cannot be conveyed in a single chapter. Instead, two chapters are needed – one on scholastic theology and the poem's elusive redefinitions of "philosophye" itself (Cole and Galloway), another on "everyday" church institutions (especially the range of medieval religious orders) and the values such as "conscience" that both sustained and later shattered them (Simpson). Other chapters have subtler connections and may be read in various combinations. Justice's discussion of the poem's relation to "literary history" involves an analysis of how the poem's effect of "art shipwrecked on reality" shows how central are its imaginings of ecclesiastic and political institutions, thus directly resonating with James Simpson's account of how "religious institutions" are shown to construct the poetic "I." The assessment of medieval allegory and *Piers Plowman* by Jill Mann speaks to some of the "theoretical" readings surveyed in the final chapter on "*Piers Plowman* in theory" by Nicolette Zeeman. The "versions and revisions" of the poem that Hanna treats merge readily into the early history of medieval copies and copyists of the poem surveyed by Horobin.

Readers will also find that the volume offers a logical linear progression, each chapter building on the last all the way to the volume's end, where they will discover a list of 'further reading' keyed to each chapter (except Zeeman's, which uses secondary sources as its main focus). The volume is divided into three sections, beginning with "The poem and its traditions," which presents the poem in terms of its most "literary" contexts and properties. An initial chapter by Helen Barr offers a thematic and dramatic summary of "major episodes and moments in *Piers Plowman* B," in order to provide an overview of the poem's most crucial passages and topics. This section then moves through the versions and their revisions (Hanna) to the poem's peculiar place in "literary history" (Justice) to its complex modes of allegory (Mann).

Each of those chapters looks out upon a wider medieval context, but Mann's chapter especially does so, thus offering a bridge to the next section, on "Historical and intellectual contexts." That section opens with a summary of the latest understanding of the poet's family lineage (Adams), allowing us for the first time to chart the poet's social origins by way of the kinds of figures that his family included, emerging from the basic documentary materials summarized and listed for further exploration. This section of the volume continues with, first, the "religious" (Simpson) then the "political" (Matthew Giancarlo) "forms and institutions" found in and around the poem – readings that display the potency of wide historical contextualizing for understanding the poem's unusual attention to its contemporary world. As Giancarlo observes, "more than any other poem – indeed, perhaps more than any other work of art from its era – *Piers Plowman* is suffused with the language and sensibilities of contemporary institutions." As Simpson further notes, the idea of those institutions precedes even the poem's idea of what we would call an individual "self." This second section continues with the editors' chapter on "Christian philosophy in *Piers Plowman*," which, like the other contextual chapters, seeks both to lay out some of the pertinent contexts (here, of intellectual history), and to pursue the poem's resistances to and endorsements of those.

To be sure, all the essays in the second "contextual" section also treat *Piers Plowman* as a poem, offering its own reimagination of preceding and surrounded contexts and discourses. This is no less true of Adams's discussion of how Langland's family history leads us to see the artificial nature of the poet's persona, than it is of the final essay in this section by Suzanne Akbari, on the non-Christian entities within the poem and considered through the range of other late medieval imaginings.

The final section, on "Readers and responses," takes up the issue of the interpretations of the poem, as figured in multiple ways. The section begins with Horobin's essay on Langland's scribes that details the geographic and social setting of these first readers of *Piers Plowman*, about whom there have been major discoveries and reassessments in recent years, including a number by Horobin himself. Next is an essay by Warner, addressing perhaps the most common question that beginning as well as more advanced students of the poem raise – concerning the history of the "plowman" figure. Warner surveys this history as both background to and reception of the poem; yet he emphasizes that the history of that recurrent plowman figure should not be seen strictly as a narrow lineage of interpretations of *Piers Plowman* alone. Rather, he argues that this figure recurrently emerges in response to wider cultural changes in religious, political, and economic contexts. The final chapter, by Zeeman, follows the contours of the most influential theoretical approaches to the poem. Since the early 1980s, Langlandians have become increasingly attuned to questions of social identity and (to a lesser extent) gender in the reading of *Piers Plowman*; so, too, have they examined the problems of the "subject" in this poem as well as the airier issues of language and meaning. Not all of these studies overtly draw from the work of modern theorists, but they have nonetheless been influential owing to their level of conceptual sophistication and even abstraction, their "theory." The volume thus closes with a discussion of the kinds of theoretical criticism that have shaped the interpretation of this poem over the last few decades.

By these strategies and features *The Cambridge Companion to Piers Plowman* is intended to shepherd students and scholars toward an initial or renewed understanding of the poem, surveying its features, contexts, and scholarly questions at present and the further prospects to which those point.

PART I

The poem and its traditions

I

HELEN BARR

Major episodes and moments in *Piers Plowman* B

Almost literally, the narrative of *Piers Plowman* takes the ground from beneath the reader's feet. Within six lines, the Malvern Hills of the Prologue suddenly become a wilderness in which Will, the dreamer/narrator, is lost (lines 5–11). The apparently neat allegorical topography of heaven, hell, and middle earth that comes to geographical rescue dissolves into a shape-shifting carousel of human beings (and some rodents), going about their worldly business, and evaporates at the end of the Prologue into a cacophony of traders' street cries in Cheapside. With the entrance of Holy Church, and her sermon in passus 1 we might expect a return to order and clarity. Instead, her worthy exposition of truth, love, and charity prompts Will to demand knowledge of the opposite: the false (2.4). Instructed to look to the left, a direction moral rather than spatial, Will sees the characters False and Favel (Deceit) with a marvellously dressed woman: Meed (2.6–7). Who she is, and what her name means, are questions which dominate the action of the next three passūs and pulse consistently throughout the whole poem. While the narrative in individual episodes is dizzyingly mobile, one feature of *Piers Plowman* that remains constant is the question of what is to be done with Meed.

Meed

Meed's marriage provides the overarching structural metaphor for the episodes in which she appears. This is not marriage in the romantic sense of an exchange of pledged love between two individuals. Through gendering the personification of reward as female, worldly exchange is aligned with the transaction of women and social procurement. When Will is ravished by Meed's first appearance, what has taken his fancy is not her body but the aristocratic display of commodities she models: crown, jewels, fur (2.9–17). Save the red gown that has connotations of the whore of Babylon from the Book of Revelation (2.15), Meed's sexual attraction lies in the precious objects that are her trademarks and cause her to be in trade. Meed is proposed to several husbands. Favel is the "brocour" (broker) who brings Meed to be enjoined to False (66): a suggestively incestuous union given that Holy Church has told Will that Meed is a bastard and False is her father (2.24–5). Theology protests against the impending union: Meed is the legitimate offspring of Amends and God has granted her to truth (2.115–32). As these competing accounts of her family history show, Meed is never the active subject of the verb "to marry"; always its passive object: "was maried" (2.40) or "ymaried" (2.53/76). She is fetched by Favel (2.65), given either to truth or a deceiver (2.120), fastened to False (2.124), led to London (2.135), dominated by False Witness (2.148), or set on a sheriff (2.164). No marriage ever takes place, but in the serial plans for her disposal, Meed is in the "middes and alle thise men after" (2.185).

Meed is circulated between men from all estates of society. The entourage that sets out to accompany her to London before they flee for terror at the news that the king purposes to hang them for making an illegal marriage includes beggars, representatives of the law, both civil and ecclesiastical, archdeacons, bishops, merchants, apprentices, pardoners, physicians, friars, and minstrels (2.142–88). Meed is an object of desire because, in a perverse version of how marriage sustains the community by producing legitimate offspring, she traffics, and is the traffic, of the riches and goods that sustain the social system. At the end of passus 2, Meed is under the king's arrest, weeping and wringing her hands, but at the start of the next, she is welcomed courteously to court, and with a cleric's arm around her waist, led to a private chamber. While the King might protest at a wedding arranged without his permission, once Meed is within his power, he plans, like those other men before him, to dispose of her to his best advantage: to marry her to Conscience, his knight and counsellor.

In the court of Westminster, we see that Meed is not only what is given but also a giver herself. No longer a passive, non-speaking object in a commercialized world that sucks all and sundry into a recursively transacting immoral vortex, she is a gracious aristocrat, bestowing gifts and largesse, seducing those around her with her bounty and her voice: chamber knights, clerks, lawyers, and, predictably, a friar (3.13–35). The ease with which Meed is received, and her poise in directing operations, dramatizes aristocratic dependence on mercantile exchange: the fair Meed of Cheapside comes to court. All those who transact business with her do so "courteously," including the king, when he appears to defer to her wishes in asking her if she is willing to marry Conscience (3.99–111). At this point in the poem, Conscience is a figure responsible for public pronouncements on matters of policy and ethics. In defiance of the king, he refuses to marry

Meed, and denounces her fraudulence to the court assembly. That he does so with a viciously misogynistic attack on Meed as a woman, denouncing her as a garrulous, lying whore whose "tail" (3.131) (accounts tally / vagina) is treacherous public property, serves only to show how much a figure such as he has to fear from association with profitable exchange.

It is often suggested that Conscience's attack on Meed's pernicious influence over the king carries a topical reference: to the manipulation of an increasingly dotard Edward III by his mistress Alice Perrers. Topically personal or not, Conscience's charge is clear: Meed usurps the king's authority through perverting the course of justice through financial favor. In one month, she is able to do more with the private seal of royal authority than the king "in sixe score dayes!" (3.146). The whole realm is in jeopardy and it is the poor and the needy who suffer. A less challenging poem than *Piers Plowman* would stop there. Financial corruption in the most powerful institutions in the land is an easy topic to demonize. But Meed is given right of reply. She points out that Conscience has launched a personal attack while covering up his own role in material exchange, especially in the conduct of war. A recent truce in the wars between England and France, arranged for financial profit rather than to realize England's military claims against the French, has sacrificed the reputation of king and nation:

> Cowardly thow, Conscience, conseiledest hym thennes –
> To leven his lordshipe for a litel silver,
> That is the richeste reaume that reyn overhoveth.

(3.206–8)

Her remarks chime with contemporary criticism of the campaigns against France, and in particular of the Treaty of Brétigny concluded in 1361, in which the English relinquished their claims of "lordship" of France for a sum that was never fully paid, whereby after the deaths of both kings who had crafted the treaty, the war resumed. Meed outlines a different policy of war, one in which military aggression would enrich the land financially and help those poorer members of society that Conscience has accused her of destroying. Having accused Conscience of a craven use of transaction to secure financial gain, she defends commerce as a social necessity: "[m]archaundise and Mede mote nede go togideres" (3.226). No person can live without Meed (3.227). All members of society – priests, members of professions, entertainers – need to be paid for their services. Artisans and craftsmen need to pay their apprentices. In effect, she redefines her role; Meed is not extortion or corruption but the essential means to ensure subsistence (3.211–24).

Whether the king's granting of victory to Meed shows his vulnerability to flattery and favor, or his grasp of economic sense, the reader is left to decide.

Still defiant, Conscience attempts to change his mind. In a long and tricky speech (3.230–330), the grammatical complexity of which is intensified in the C text (3.343–435; see Chapter 8 below), he distinguishes between two kinds of reward: "Meed" which is appropriate recompense for honest work, and "Meed" which is immoderate reward given in order to secure favor, or improperly to influence duties that must be performed. (In the C text this is renamed "mercede.") The first kind of reward is necessary; the second attracts God's vengeance. Were the country to work only in line with the first definition, Conscience argues, a golden age would dawn. No lawyer would wear a silk coif, law would work like a humble laborer, swords turn into plowshares, peace and moral rectitude prevail, and even the Jews grow wise and acknowledge Jesus Christ as the Messiah (3.299–330). Academically precise though Conscience's lexical analysis may be, his rapturous conclusions overplay his hand: Saracens will sing "Gloria in Excelsis" and both Muhammad and Meed shall be destroyed. Meed's first appearance in the poem shows her wearing sapphires from the Orient; she and her gems carry the allure of exotic treasure. Conscience flips the orientalist coin. Converting her into a demonized alien Muslim, he casts Meed out from the race of Christians and condemns her to perdition: clinching his tirade with a quotation from Proverbs 22:1: "better is a good name than great riches" (3.330).

Furious, Meed counters Conscience's use of Latin texts to support his case, and offers up her own countertext from the same book of the Bible: "he that maketh presents shall purchase victory and honour" (3.335a; Proverbs 22:9). Biblical texts are exchanged back and forth, the probity of Conscience's arguments weakened by his readiness to play skittles with Latin quotations and by his retreat into misogynistic scorn for female learning. Sated with Latin squabble, the King orders Conscience to kiss Meed and the pair to be reconciled. Both shall serve him: a directive reminiscent of the king's judgment in the alliterative poem *Wynnere and Wastour* that both eponymous principles are necessary for the health of the realm. But in *Piers Plowman* the King's problem of how to use material reward ethically is solved not by debate but by the example of a dramatized legal case. Conscience begs the King to refer the matter to Reason, a character who stands for natural justice and rationality. The episode shifts ground, both topographically and discursively.

In a session of the King's Chancery Court, Peace presents a petition to the King which indicts Wrong with rape, theft, and murder (4.47–60). Wrong is shown to be in the wrong. More problematically, Wrong then persuades Wisdom and Wit to involve Meed in the case (4.61–2). When Peace reappears with a bleeding head (4.75), it is clear that an out of court settlement has been reached in which thugs have been paid to beat up the plaintiff to deter him from prosecuting his case. Langland gives us an allegorical dramatization of the practice known to his contemporaries as "maintenance." Economically powerful members of society who were forced to answer for criminal offences in a court of law used bribery and corruption, and often physical violence, to buy their way out of trouble. With a moral decisiveness that belies countless contemporary complaints to the king about maintenance that appear to have gone un-redressed, Langland's King orders Wrong to be thrown into prison for seven years. When Meed pleads for mercy for the prisoner, and offers Peace a present to join her in arguing for clemency, it appears that Conscience's view of Meed is vindicated. In a speech of legal summing up that revisits, but with more restraint, some of the utopian topoi of Conscience's recent rhetoric, Reason explains very clearly that the law has no room for mercy and pity on Meed's terms. Wrongdoing must be punished; criminals must be humbled to acknowledge their faults. Financial bribery has no place in law (4.113–48).

The King puts on legal record that Reason has prosecuted his case correctly. Meed is defeated. With her unscripted exit, order is restored. The courtroom declares her a whore (4.166). Summary judgment may have been reached, and Meed never re-enters the poem as a character, but this is not the end of the issues around exchange and reward in the poem. During the hearing, Wisdom argued that if Wrong could make amends, he could be bailed, with Meed standing as "maynpernour" – as legal guarantee (4.87–90). The diction reprises Theology's argument in passus 1: that Meed is the daughter, not of False, but of Amends. Making amendment in the form of extortion and violence clearly cannot be tolerated, but Reason's triumph, and the alacrity of the court to pronounce Meed a prostitute proceeds with a relish for strict justice that does not provide the poem's final verdict. If correct amends are made, is there a role for Mercy? And if so, what social and religious forms might it take?

Pilgrimage, plowing, and pardons

Almost immediately, two social and religious forms for that reconciliation are attempted: pilgrimage and plowing. Both catastrophically fail. The medieval religious practice of pilgrimage was organized around widespread worship of localized saints whose bones, wells, footsteps, or other relics oriented Christendom around particularly potent holy places. In England, Canterbury, Walsingham, and Durham, for instance, became part of a spiritual geographical itinerary that took in St. James of Compostella, Rome, and of course Jerusalem. Pilgrimage to one of these shrines as an act of penance incurred spiritual merit and "amends" for sins. Profitable not only for the soul, however: the regions in which these shrines were located, and those responsible for tending them, became exceedingly wealthy from spiritual tourism. The treatment of pilgrimage in *Piers Plowman* is part of a powerful surge of criticism of the practice that is visible in fourteenth-century writings even before the full-scale critiques by the Lollards or Wycliffites (followers of the teachings of the Oxford academic and reformer John Wyclif).

Already in the Prologue, readers of Langland glimpse "Pilgrymes and palmeres" who "temper" their "tonge ... to lye / Moore than to seye sooth" (46–52), and "Heremytes on an heep" who bring their "wenches" with them to St. Mary of Walsingham (53–4). And yet after a brilliantly satiric "confession of sins" (passūs 4–5), the poem attempts to mount a full-scale pilgrimage. It turns out to be one that is glaringly misguided: they "blustreden forth as beestes over baches and hilles." They meet a professional pilgrim, festooned with badges and trinket-relics from the shrines he has visited (5.514–24), who turns out to be no help at all. It is at this point that Piers the Plowman first enters the poem from an adjoining hedge (5.537) and dismisses the entire venture of an actual pilgrimage. He directs the pilgrims instead through a wholly allegorical landscape toward "a court, cler as the sonne," whose "moot is of Mercy the manoir aboute" (5.585–6). Only if they abandon the physical pilgrimage, and take instead this inward allegorical journey, will they see in themselves "Truthe sitte in thyn herte / In a cheyne of charite, as thow a child were" (5.605–7). This reorientation of the pilgrimage proves to be beyond the crowd's abilities or will, even though Piers the Plowman "poked hym to goode" (5.634–8). Having embarked on a literal pilgrimage with great eagerness, the pilgrims' collective failure even to begin one that is more spiritually efficacious shows an ecclesiastically sanctioned mode of meritorious activity to be bankrupt.

So the poet tries again, and through a different form. When the crowd complains that they still have no guide for the "wikkede wey" that Piers the Plowman has sketched out, he turns them toward plowing his "half acre" (6.5–6). With this move, the poet turns to another system of endeavor and reward that is foundational to the medieval economy, only this time one that is secular rather than sacred. The poem enters the domain of agrarian labor, a system in which merit and reward are supposedly balanced. Problems multiply. Although Piers the Plowman (with the help of a Knight) manages to cajole some reluctant recruits into hard labor, and actually makes headway on maintenance of his piece of land, his venture founders in the face of the resistance from "faitours": slackers and shirkers. Confident in their own status, like the "wastour" who challenges Piers the Plowman to a fight (6.152–3), they refuse to work to Piers's orders. Only when the ravening Hunger arrives is a temporary order and recommitment to hard work restored, and then only through fear. While Piers initially welcomes Hunger he then comes to recognize that his attempt at discipline is inexorable and undiscriminating. Starving bellies prove to be no better at balancing merit and reward than pilgrimage. A temporary period of terror provides no lasting morality. More, it still gives no answer to the role of Mercy.

This challenge to the labor system parallels major tensions in fourteenth-century England. After the Black Death of 1348–9 drastically reduced the numbers of agrarian laborers, the threat of the growing independence of those remaining (whose labor was all the more valuable) led to a series of ever more draconian laws to control their ability to demand higher wages or seek competing employers. Pressures between the land-owning and law-imposing estates and the lower laborers contributed to the social unrest of 1381. The tensions in this scene may be said to dramatize the poem's difficulties in retaining a basic orientation to the managerial classes while committing to the worth of agrarian humble labor. Laborers need to be managed, but the value of their work rests on fragile social and ethical foundations. The poem cannot comfortably manage the logic of the medieval secular economy.

But the poem still keeps trying to find an answer to the relationship between merit and mercy. When Hunger fails to provide a solution, the poet turns to the contemporary practice of pardons. No dramatic episode in *Piers Plowman* has proved more baffling than what happens in passus 7 when Truth sends a pardon to Piers as he is still standing in the field. There is no consensus amongst readers as to what the pardon means, and why, after an altercation with a priest, Piers tears it up. Neither the pardon's destruction nor the detail of the quarrel appears in the later C version of the poem. The pardon episode results in narrative implosion. One reason for this is that the premise of the poetic vehicle is too simple. The document that Truth sends to Piers categorizes roles and persons within society who are good or bad, or could do better. Those who work honestly in society – Piers, kings and knights who protect the church, holy bishops, and true laborers – are stated to have the pardon that the document promises (7.9–17). Merchants are placed in the margins (7.18) unless they give aid to the poor, and members of the legal profession who practice for "mede" receive scant pardon at all (7.39). Able-bodied beggars are excluded (7.64–5). Langland has already used a document to classify the good and the bad in society. In preparation for Meed's first marriage, False draws up a deed of endowment that grants the couple all the deadly sins in perpetuity and an eternal dwelling place in the torment of hell (2.69–107). A devil's charter provides a vehicle to satirize corrupt exchange in the legal profession, but as the Meed episode as a whole demonstrates, profitable exchange cannot be so starkly condemned.

Especially when theological reward enters the equation. In contrast to the consistently devilish deed in passus 2, the terms of the document in passus 7 are bewilderingly fluid. Truth purchases a pardon for Piers, and his heirs in perpetuity "*a pena et a culpa*" (7.3). Leaving to one side for a moment the problem of what Truth could figure, a keyword here is "purchaced." Why is money exchanged, and from whom does Truth buy this pardon? As critics have observed, the Latin tag suggests that the document is a papal pardon, or indulgence. Papal pardons, however, were not meant as a substitute for the sacrament of confession. Only a truly confessed penitent should buy an indulgence: to fulfill part of their satisfaction – making amends – for sinning. Penitential payment contributed to the work of the church; it did not buy forgiveness.

How can Piers be sent a pardon when he has not been shown receiving the sacrament of penance? Even allowing for the narrative ellipses with which the dream visions of *Piers Plowman* teem, how can this document remit not only punishment (*pena*), permitted within the terms of an indulgence, but also guilt (*culpa*)? Only God is in a position to absolve human beings from guilt, and, as I shall discuss below, to equate Truth with God serves to compound, not to solve, the narrative slippages. That the pardon is sent to Piers and "his heires for everemoore after" (7.4) makes an exemption that no contemporary indulgence could promise. Terms appropriate in a legal charter that is granted to a group of people are inapplicable to a pardon sent to an individual. The legality of a document depends not only on what is written in it, but on its material form. We are told that the Pope would not grant merchants pardon "*a pena et a culpa*" (7.19), but that Truth, under his personal seal (claiming a legal prerogative wielded only by a king), has sent them a letter which promises to protect them from the devil and despair as long as they use their money for good social causes (7.23–35). Merchants weep and cry for joy at this news, praising Piers Plowman "that purchaced this bulle" (7.38).

In fewer than forty lines a document that is something between a pardon, a deed of endowment/grant and a royal prerogative has been purchased both by Truth and by Piers Plowman. Whether both, or neither, bought the document from the Pope remains unclear. And whose is the narrative voice that tells its contents? Only when Piers unfolds the document to show it to the priest is Will able to see its wording. The long English exposition of who is, and who is not, in the bull is shrunk to two Latin lines from the Athanasian Creed: "*Et qui bona egerunt ibunt in vitam eternam; / Qui vero mala, in ignem eternum*" (7.111–12). Logically, it cannot be the dreamer who has narrated the pardon's terms. The priest is also quite right that he can find no pardon in the wording: those who do well shall have eternal life; and those who do evil shall proceed to an eternal damnation. This is not a pardon; it is a judgment. Nothing in this document adds up: its source(s), its material form, its wording, or its purpose. There is no consistent reading, on either a literal or an allegorical level that can paper over its narrative cracks. As such, while it is a shock that Piers should tear it in two (7.115), his response attends honestly to the complete muddle, socially and theologically, that this episode enacts.

Like the pilgrimage and the plowing that precede it, the pardon fails. It has to. Only God is in a position to determine who shall be saved. Whatever the human assessment of social position, or the worth of one's works in the community, a commentator, however morally upright (moral probity is one of the available senses of Truth), who makes judgment on eternal reward compromises God's absolute power. If readers, like characters within the poem, expect a piece of paper to single out roles or persons destined for heaven, purgatory or hell, especially a document associated with the pope, given that the corrupt practice of trading in indulgences has already been dramatized in the poem (Prol.68–82), then they have fallen for a poetic wrong-footing. If the description of the pardon and its furious destruction by Piers has any single dramatic point, it is to expose the presumption of trust in easy (ab)solutions. The episode reworks, in part, the dilemma of Meed, but adds a spiritual dimension which braids the issue of temporal worthiness with spiritual reward. It is too early in the poem to provide even an answer, never mind a solution to this issue, but the episode provides the first serious acknowledgment that temporal reward cannot be considered without reference to spiritual destiny and to the relationship between justice and mercy. Piers tears up a paper that contains impossibly competing narratives; a gesture that is applicable not only to the document in his hand but to the poetic vehicle that contains him.

It has been argued that Truth, the sender of the document, is God. In tearing up the pardon, Piers signals the limits of a covenant with God that depends on strict justice alone, and opens the way for the necessity of mercy in determining spiritual reward. This is an attractive response to the transitional force of the pardon episode; the narrative does shift into more abstract discussion after this point, debating with considerable theological heft the place of justice and mercy in the doctrine of the atonement and the relative merits of faith and works in salvation. But to equate Truth with God in passus 7 charges Him with sending a document that contains misleading terms and whiffs of papal corruption. While it is not impossible that Langland chose narrative confusion to dramatize God's inscrutability, Truth is not God at other points in the poem: in passus 3, Theology affiances him to Meed; in passus 18, she is a principle of justice or uprightness. Truth is the failed destination of the pilgrimage in passus 5. To equate Truth with God "saves" the episode, but at the expense of the poetic honesty of the poem.

When God is explicitly associated with documents at other moments in the poem, they are articulated with much greater clarity. In passus 17, Moses/Hope shows Will a writ that contains the Ten Commandments which God gave him on Mount Sinai. Hope seeks:

> hym that hath the seel to kepe –
> And that is cros and Cristendom, and Crist theron to honge.
> And whan it is asseled so, I woot wel the sothe –
> That Luciferis lordshipe laste shal no lenger!   (17.5–8)

Crucially, the seal of the open letter is not yet fixed; human beings have to keep the commandments, but Christ's death on the Cross is necessary to validate the document. A material document is imagined in which a seal hanging from the letter figures Christ's bleeding body fixed hanging from the Cross. Documents were often sealed with red wax. Written on the letter patent are words from Matthew 22:37, 39, 40: "Thou shalt love [the Lord thy] God ... and thy neighbor [as thyself]; On these two commandments dependeth the whole law and the prophets." Explicit here is the transition from the Old Law to the New, and the necessity of human beings to keep the commandment of love so that "nevere devel hym dere, ne deeth in soule greve" (17.18). In contrast to the pardon in passus 7, the material form of the document and its allegorical terms are congruent with God's promise to human beings to redeem them from sin. Moses/Hope seeks the keeper of the seal because the poem is still not ready to dramatize Christ's death on the Cross and the doctrine of Atonement. Passus 17 reformulates the impossible promise of reward in passus 7 in theologically consonant documentary terms. With hindsight, the only end to the poetic vehicle in passus 7 is impasse.

But why then omit the tearing of the pardon in the C text, and the details of Piers's quarrel with the priest? External factors may have played a part. In the uprisings of 1381, legal documents were a target of insurgent anger. Records of the hated poll tax and charters that legalized the rights of owners over workers were destroyed; those associated with legal and clerical writing were attacked. Coded letters circulated between John Ball and other leaders of the revolts implicate the figure "Piers Plowman" in dissent and appear to quote catchwords from Langland's poem. To have an apparently illiterate plowman challenge the clerical literacy of a priest (that Piers is "lettred a litel" [7.132] draws explicit scorn), and to show him tearing a legal document in two, may have chimed rather too uncomfortably with the events of 1381 when Langland came to revise his poem and he removed elements that could have been seen to have been inflammatory.

What replaces the tearing and the quarrel, however, is far from socially anodyne. In revising his text, Langland does not alter the problematic details of the pardon and its source, nor is there substantial revision to those who are rewarded, marginalized, and excluded, apart from two long and passionate passages that speak out for the poor, the crippled, and the mentally unstable (C.9.69–97, 105–38). A crucial line is added: "woet no man, as y wene, who is worthy to haue" (C.9.69). No one (even Truth?) can adjudge who ought to receive reward, but those who have most need are the poor folk in cottages, encumbered with children and the rents of mighty lords; women waking in winter nights to rock the cradle with hands that have been chillingly employed in spinning, carding wool, patching, and washing. These are not beggars, but those who attempt to clothe themselves through their menial work, and live on scarce resources with barely sufficient to eat. Or those that cannot work, though able-bodied, because they lack their wits. The frustration of matching social and spiritual reward in the B text boils over in C to fierce denunciation of those who are able to work, but feign excuse, and, through begging, siphon off the alms that ought to be given to the deserving needy. There is no poetic vehicle. Bare of device, the narrative voice declaims in the starkest and most moving terms the plight of the most vulnerable members of society who are excluded from support. These additional C passages overweigh the import of the troublesome pardon poetic vehicle; they carry the momentum of the episode away from an attempt to align social and spiritual justice through an unwieldy written document. Instead, the poet appears to speak in his own voice.

Nonetheless, in both texts, Will emerges not much the wiser. What he has seen and heard leads him to distrust the whole business of "songewarie" (B.7.159), dream interpretation itself. Significantly, however, he does conclude that pardons and patents are worthless (7.195). His conclusion may be over-emphatic, but it does foreground the futility of attempting to redress social inequalities through institutionalized pieces of paper. But the poem is not yet finished with lost causes. Will becomes fixated on the words of the Athanasian Creed that both Piers and the priest agreed were no pardon at all. The poet sends his dreamer, and his readers, off on a search for a definition of Dowel, suddenly elevated to a proper noun (7.220). We are, at the end of the *visio* in all versions of the poem, still some way off from any encounter or episode that may provide lasting insight into how to reconcile the messy worldly lives of humankind with God's eternal truth.

Atonement

One episode only in *Piers Plowman* provides hope of any such reconciliation: the account of Christ's Crucifixion and the Harrowing of Hell in passus 18. The move into scriptural history, begun by the Tree of Charity episode in passus 16 and followed by Will's meetings with Abraham, Moses, and the Good Samaritan, comes to fruition in passus 18. That in itself is significant; a narrative chain of events is sustained over several passūs without the abrupt serrated transitions characteristic of earlier visions of the poem. And while earlier episodes are played out in disoriented time and place, the dream logic of passus 18 provides temporal harmony. The events of Holy Week in first-century Jerusalem unfold in scriptural history, *and* in recognizable fourteenth-century English social practice.

Christ's entry into Jerusalem on an ass is dramatized through the liturgy for Palm Sunday. Will wakes from his dream to the sound of glory and praise and "osanna" sung to the sound of the organ (18.7–8). Latin quotations score the narrative with snatches of liturgy woven into the drama of the fourteenth-century alliterative line. Liturgical performance already made present and dramatic to the assembled church congregation the scriptural events of the day that the service commemorates. Langland's Latin-English verse recreates a sense of that presence. The singing church also welcomes a nobleman, barefoot on a donkey, coming to be dubbed a knight (18.11–15). Inspired perhaps by the traditions of mystery plays in which the entry of Christ into Jerusalem modeled the royal entry of a king into a city, the poem conflates scripture, liturgy, and secular social spectacle. Christ's entry is also a jousting tournament. Langland draws on an established allegorical and exegetical tradition witnessed poignantly in the *Ancrene Wisse* and in devotional lyrics: Christ's crucifixion is likened to the willingness of a chivalric knight to wound himself in battle to show his love for the human soul.

Abraham as Faith, first introduced in passus 16, is present in the episode as a herald for the joust. Standing in a window from an overhanging street like a character from a mystery play, or a figure in stained glass, he announces the name of the anonymous jouster with words from Matthew 21:9: "cryde '*A fili David!*'" (18.15). Christ is not just an adventurous knight, however; he is also Piers Plowman:

> This Jesus of his gentries wol juste in Piers armes,
> In his helm and his haubergeon – *humana natura*.
> That Crist be noght biknowe here for *consummatus Deus*,
> In Piers paltok the Plowman this prikiere shal ryde
> For no dynt shal hym dere as *in deitate Patris*. (18.22–6)

Through the mystery of the Incarnation God becomes man and takes on human flesh and is both God and man. Here, Christ is both a knight and a plowman. Christ rides both in knightly armor and in a plowman's jacket. In the supreme moment at which Christ demonstrates his love for human beings by dying on the cross to redeem them from sin, Piers Plowman is not only indistinguishable from a knight, but his simple "paltok" is a defence against the wounding of the Godhead. In C manuscripts "paltok" is replaced by "plates" (knightly armor). Either Langland or his scribes can be seen to have quailed at the social audacity of the poet's imaginative rendering of church doctrine. While the knight in passus 6 was unable to help Piers in plowing the half-acre, here a "prikiere" on a donkey, in defiance of sumptuary laws which regulated very precisely what could be worn by knights and peasants, rides to a fight which, as Faith tells Will, is a joust against the devil (18.28). God as man as knight as laborer join forces to conquer sin and to dramatize the promise of redemption.

Barefoot like a poor laborer, the knight comes to earn "gilte spores on galouches ycouped" (18.14). The gilt/guilty spurs on the slashed shoes are the nails of the cross that will pierce the feet of a knight hung like a criminal. Langland's dense punning produces a theological vision in which social abjection and ennoblement dramatize unbearable pain and triumph. Writing at a time in which the imagery of the crucifixion stressed compassion with Christ's suffering through focus on blood, gaping wounds, tendons stretched and forced in a body twisted with pain, Langland's clerkly wordplay stiffens the sinews of affective piety to express stark theological truth. Compassionate suffering and doctrinal significance are as indivisible as God's human and divine nature.

Not content with writing a scene in which church, street, tournament, and field occupy one and the same place and time, Langland moves his cast to Hell, and to a disputation whose terms are those of a legal court. In passus 7, two lines from the Athanasian Creed contribute significantly to the failure of the poetic vehicle; in passus 18, the citation of *"descendit ad inferna"* (111) from the same text takes us not only to a legal argument that resolves what the pardon failed properly to articulate, but to the heated exchanges between the participants in the Meed episode. The debate between the daughters of God – Truth, Righteousness, Mercy, and Peace – has its own moments of insult. At the point when Peace produces documentary evidence of God's promise to show mercy to human beings, Righteousness accuses her of being either mad or dead drunk. What Peace (significantly, the plaintiff in passus 4, though now female) shows her sister is a patent letter to show that God has forgiven human beings. It is a "dede" (18.186), that is, a letter of authorization, which grants Peace and Mercy to be "mannes maynpernour for everemoore after" (18.184). "Maynpernour" is the role of legal surety that Meed attempted to assume for Wrong in a system of corruption. Here, Peace and Mercy are authorized by God, through Christ's freshly dramatized death on the cross, to act as brokers for sinful humankind. Like Moses's document in passus 17, and unlike the pardon in passus 7, the material form of the document is congruent with the theological promise it articulates, and, significantly, this is a piece of paper which reprises what the narrative has just shown us: Christ's suffering on the cross as surety for humankind.

Complete authorization, however, comes not from one of God's daughters, or any other spokesperson, but from Christ himself: "*Attolite portas!*" (18.261). Proclaiming the words that a priest would have used in the liturgy for Easter Saturday as he banged with his staff on the west door of the parish church, Christ calls upon the devils of Hell to open up the gates. Christ comes now as a gloriously crowned king (18.264), and he forces Lucifer to defend his legal right to the souls he has wrongly imprisoned. Precise legal diction, drawn from contemporary fourteenth-century practice underpins the exchange. While Lucifer claims legal right ("seisin") to possession of the souls (18.283), Satan anxiously points out that he gained possession fraudulently: Eve ate the apple in the Garden of Eden because Lucifer deceived her into Original Sin through "gile" and through "treason" (18.285–91). Goblin corroborates his story: we have no "trewe title" (valid claim of possession through title deed) to the souls because they were damned through treason (18.293). Christ repeats these charges in his accusations to Lucifer; he has committed theft, treason, and felony. Matching guile with guile according to the principle of the Old Testament law of an eye for an eye and a tooth for a tooth, Christ quites Lucifer's claim. Just as through Adam and a tree all were condemned to death, so through a new Adam (Himself), and the tree of the Cross, guile shall be beguiled and the death sentence overturned (18.328–61).

Christ comes not to break the law but to fulfill it (18.350a). He reminds Lucifer that, according to human law, one cannot hang a felon twice, and that the power of a king's prerogative can pardon a condemned criminal. Grace can rescue humankind convicted of sin by upholding the law. Mercy can avenge Lucifer's "untrewe title" of possession through righteousness; souls imperfectly cleared of temporal sin through contrition will be washed clean in God's prison of "Purgatorie" (18.380–93). Through Langland's insistent punning, earthly justice matches up to the doctrine of Atonement. God as Christ as lawgiving king as humble laborer provides the resolution lacking in Reason's triumphalist courtroom sentence in passus 4, not just through legal amends, but through merciful love for human beings based on common kinship: "I were an unkynde kyng but I my kyn helpe" (18.399).

Paraphrase completely undoes what Langland has fused through his poetic "makyng": Grace, nature, common humanity, kingship, and kinship are co-inherent. When Langland added those passages to the C text imploring compassion on the poor and needy, perhaps he had in mind lines he had already penned in Christ's kingly appeal to common humanity:

> For blood may suffre blood bothe hungry and acale,
> Ac blood may noght se blood blede, but hym rewe.
>
> (395–6)

God suffers seeing his own blood going both hungry and cold; suffers in two senses: endures it and feels it. Moved to compassion by the unbearable bleeding of his own family, He mingles His own spilt blood with theirs. Blood for blood through bloodruth. Rhetorical commutation of sense and syntax chimes the doctrinal exchange that seals forgiveness for human beings. Not money, not favor, not gift. Legally transacted blood transfusion is the "meed" that promises redemption.

Lucifer is bound in chains and passus 18 resounds to the music of angels, tuned to the lyricism of the four daughters of God singing in harmony. The kiss that Conscience refused to bestow on Meed is here exchanged in sisterly concord (18.410–26). This is the first occasion on which Will wakes up in time with the poetry of his vision. Summoned by the Easter church bells of the Resurrection, he becomes a figure in a parish community, worshipping the cross as a jewel with his wife and daughter at the Eucharist of Easter Sunday (18.427–34). So why does the poem not stop here? Because human beings should already know the truth that Langland's poetry has dramatized so thrillingly. God's mercy is possible only through strict justice. God has paid more than he owes through Christ's death to pay back the debt of Original Sin. Humankind must pay back their ongoing debt of temporal sin through penitence and contrition. The unity of time, place, and persons in passus 18 demonstrates God's immanence in the contemporary world, but it does not destroy the free will of humankind to continue to sin. God cannot force human beings to pay their debt of contrition; the knowledge that He has paid a debt that He did not owe through this love for mankind ought to make them want to honor their own obligation through love in return.

Dissolution

When, in the final passus of the poem, Will is in despair at the attack on the pristine apostolic church that Piers builds in passus 19 – a church founded on both testaments of the Bible, worked through the words of the gospels and the Church Fathers, and sown with seeds of the cardinal virtues – he asks Kynde what craft is best to learn. "Lerne to love," says Kynde, and abandon all other practice (20.208). In a rare moment of heeding advice, Will travels through confession and contrition and is able to enter the Barn of Unity (20.231–4). Surely all shall be well? But Langland's contemporary world is ruled not by love, but by money and contention. With his army of the seven deadly sins Antichrist can attack the Barn of Unity, because its allegorically simple construction has already been breached by a brewer who refuses to work in accordance with the Spirit of Justice (19.399–400), and an uneducated vicar (19.412) who inveighs against the worldliness of the Pope and his Cardinals, and declares that for the common people the Spirit of Justice means guile. Each man devises stratagems to cover up his sins and disguises them as acts of virtuous living to continue life intent on worldly gain (19.460–1).

The institutions that ought to regulate sinful behavior collude with its continuation. When Conscience herds the folk into the Barn of Unity, the attacks thicken. All the social abuses castigated thus far in the poem – those of the Meed episode, and later – reappear in the wiles of Antichrist's army. Incurable diseases rain down from the skies. What proves even more deadly, however, is what happens inside the Barn itself: Contrition is destroyed by a friar. Friars have been a target of criticism since the start of the poem. In the *Prologue*, the narrator warns of the looming destruction to Holy Church since they have turned the business of confession into mercantile transaction. The final scenes of the poem realize the danger that has haunted the poem almost from its inception.

As his name suggests, Friar "Sir Penetrans Domos" ("Sir Invader of Homes," 20.341) usurps a social position (knighthood) and a place (the Church of Unity) to which he has no legitimate access. His success depends, in part, on the naivety of Conscience. Fearing that the Barn is about to collapse because of the threat of "inparfite preestes and prelates of Holy Chirche" (20.229), he calls for help from Clergie. The Friars swarm to his aid. Initially, Conscience will have nothing to do with them. Need warns him that they "come for coveitise to have cure of soules" (20.232–3); that is, motivated by money they come to compete with parish priests for the right to minister the sacrament of confession. This is exactly the practice to which Wrath, a friar, lays claim when he makes his confession as one of the deadly sins in passus 5.133–79. Need tells Conscience why the sacraments are vulnerable to fraternal assault. Because the friars live in voluntary poverty, they are reliant on those with money to support them. He advises Conscience that he should leave them to live the life they have chosen as beggars, or else let them live on angels' food. Conscience, however, thinks he knows better, and invites the friars to enter Holy Church on condition that they live in unity, show no envy to learned or lay, and keep to their rule as laid down by St. Dominic and St. Francis. Conscience offers to be their "borugh": their guarantee (20.248). If they keep to their promise, he will ensure that they have sustenance. Like Meed, and Christ, before him, Conscience offers himself as a broker. Even though he is aware that the friars have swollen in malpracticing numbers from their founding ideals, Conscience makes the very place he is supposed to guard vulnerable to fraternal malpractice. Despite his condemnation of Meed earlier in the poem, the consequences of his offer to be "borugh" have more in common with the woman he condemned as a whore than with the Son of God.

In response to those inside the Barn who complain that the confessional practices of their "surgeon" are too harsh (20.310–11), Conscience falls prey to the hypocritical lying words that have launched a last wave of attack. Friar Flatterer comes armed with a letter from a bishop that licenses him to hear confession (20.325–9). Clerical corruption destroys the Barn from within. The easy plasters of contrition that the Friar supplies produce an allegorical effect that is opposite to the confession of the sins in passus 5. Having paid the Friar for granting easy penance, Contrition "clene" forgets to weep (20.370). In the bleakest moment of the whole poem Contrition is hollowed of meaning. The cleanliness of soul that ought to accompany confessional healing is reduced to an empty adverb. Without contrition for sin, humankind cannot pay back to God the debt that they owe Him. With the friar's entrance to the Church and to the frailty of the human soul, the means of redress for sin are severed. Improper exchange, practiced by an interloping member of the institutionalized church, imperils redemption.

Conscience is left denouncing the friar who hoodwinked him, crying in an enigmatic line that he wishes that friars had some kind of stable support "fyndyng" (20.384) to prevent such abuse. The end of the poem abandons the Church of Unity it has so carefully built up with its pristine allegory. It is hard not to read Conscience's striding out of the Barn and into the world as a gesture of defeat: Langland's turning his back on his contemporary church; its corruption a danger to the very souls over which it ought to exercise pastoral care. But while trust in institutions is as shattered as the Barn itself, Conscience is not in despair. A new search begins. Conscience seeks Piers Plowman and his cry for God's Grace wakes the dreamer (20.381–7). At the end of the Pardon scene, left baffled by events, Will pondered upon Piers Plowman "ful pencif in herte" (7.146). The thought of Piers impels the dreamer to keep asking questions; it initiates a new direction in the poem. Then, as in these final lines, the memory and the promise of Piers are an affective touchstone in the poem that the surrounding turbulence is unable to dislodge or engulf. Conscience goes in search not just to *find*

Piers, but to *have* him (20.386). The figure of the enigmatic plowman who has emerged and disappeared with equal abruptness at some of the most dynamic moments of the poem carries an emotional charge that belies his narrative containment in any one figure or essence, be that social, historical, or theological. The re-call of Piers Plowman has an affective resonance that holds back the poem at the brink of the abyss. If, at the end of the poem, Langland gives up on his church, he does not give up on the memorial hope of Piers transacted between plowman as knight as man as God: made from the poetry of his reformist imagination.

2

RALPH HANNA

The versions and revisions of *Piers Plowman*

Piers Plowman, like all medieval poems, comes to us in manuscript, and these fifty-odd surviving medieval books present us with nearly all the primary evidence available for discussing Langland's biography and his poem. In this context, one might begin by invoking the subtitle to Charlotte Brewer's impressive study of the poem's editorial history, with its citation of the word "evolution."[1] The manuscripts provide "raw evidence"; scholars select some portion of this material and their interpretation transforms this data. Only within the context that interpretation provides does it evolve in certain directions. Consequently, all we think we know about *Piers Plowman* rests upon inferences, hypotheses predicated upon various selections from and interpretations of the manuscript record.

However, investigating the manuscripts of *Piers Plowman* introduces a sequence of problems that strikingly challenges the experience, and thus interpretative procedures, customary among those who first approach the poem. Most English medievalists have, as their basic grounding, an experience of Chaucer. But the security that this experience gives does not well accord with interrogating *Piers Plowman*, where one might be excused for believing that everything is in flux. Chaucer's text is not particularly problematic, nor are the manuscripts, at least the early seminal examples, exceptionally diverse in content.

In this context, perhaps the most salient introductory statement to make about the manuscripts of *Piers Plowman* is that something like fifteen to twenty copies of the poem possibly, or very probably, were copied before 1400. This showing probably indicates that Langland's poem was the single most popular verse text disseminated in the fourteenth century, only rivalled by the circulation of *The South English Legendary*, a collection of saints' lives from the southwest Midlands. In contrast, circulation of Chaucer's poems may have begun in the very late fourteenth century with the "Hengwrt" copy of the *Canterbury Tales*, but, as an industry with a volume comparable to Langland's, is identifiable only from the second decade of the fifteenth.

This bit of manuscript demographics is important, because of what intervened between the frequent provision of *Piers Plowman* and that of *Troilus and Criseyde* and the *Canterbury Tales*. As Doyle and Parkes showed in a magnificent influential study, between the circulation of Langland's poem and of Chaucerian texts intervened the development of a reasonably organized London book-trade.[2] Moreover, this was a trade devoted, in the main, to supplying copies of two local poets, Chaucer and Gower (and eventually, Hoccleve and Lydgate as well). Rather than what succeeded – some continuous access to source-texts to use as models for the copying of literary works, and an apparently continuous audience demand for such copies – *Piers Plowman* emerged in a distinctively un- (or maybe dis-) organized book-world, and the relative stability and consistency familiar Chaucerian texts received does not seem to have been possible for Langland's poem within those conditions. (Indeed, this instability, in company with superior techniques of trade organization, may be a factor behind the gradual eclipse of *Piers Plowman* through the fifteenth century, until it was rediscovered by Protestant reformers, who found in its poet a kindred spirit, in the mid sixteenth.)

Unlike Chaucer, who was conceived as a real authorial personage by about 1405, during the Middle Ages there was simply A Poem called *Piers Plowman*, and, one with an exceptionally various and variable history. Part of that variety is due to its poet's peculiarly idiosyncratic view of his authorship. Part of it was occasioned by his partners in the poem's promulgation and consumption, his readers and those book-trade individuals who responded to their orders. (Unlike modern conceptions, which distinguish book-producers from their [mass] audience, in the Middle Ages these need not have been entirely separate groups, for many literate people copied books for their private use.)

There are quite substantial difficulties in explaining to beginners either the author's or his writers' and readers' contribution to this situation. To begin with Langland's own activity: those beginning to address the poem know it, most usually, through the helpful student editions of A. V. C. Schmidt (1995) or Derek Pearsall. These essentially offer texts predicated upon a single copy, and the actual evidence for the poem's diversity is largely silenced. To discover that plurality, the student must abandon his or her helpful text and turn to large and expensive volumes, usually kept in university (rather than personal) libraries.

Here there are several immediate places of first recourse. However, the most authoritative of these, "the Athlone edition," covers several volumes, and it is notorious, even among scholars, for eschewing ready explanation and for confusing organization. Considerably more useful for assessing Langland's activity is the pair of "digested" presentations of the poem, Skeat and Schmidt (1996–2008). These two-volume works present a variety of textual forms in parallel columns. This page-format allows ready visual signaling of both similarities and discrepancies between various forms of Langland's poem. However, even in the most helpful situations, confusing glitches lurk; no two editions of *Piers Plowman*, for example, have ever agreed in their lineation.

Piers Plowman as revision

I begin presenting Langland's various text by citing that first moment in *Piers Plowman* where one would discover that it was not a single poem. Any copy one might pick up would generally agree with any other for nearly ninety lines. From that point, however, a student with access to more than one edition would find various materials. (For a carefully organized presentation, on the same pages, of the following passages, the reader might want to have to hand the parallel-text editions of Skeat or Schmidt [1996].) And although the textual forms and their numerations I cite initially concur with those elsewhere in this chapter, in being drawn from the Athlone editions, I also, in this one instance, refer to the more commonly used student editions (in this unusual instance, lineation across all editions is identical).

As I have said, about the first ninety lines of the poem in any edition one reads will be more or less similar. But then, if one is reading a copy like Knott and Fowler's, one will find:

> Archideknes and denis þat dignites hauen
> To preche þe peple and pore men to fede
> Ben ylope to Lundoun be leue of hire bisshop,
> And ben clerkis of þe Kinges Bench þe cuntre to shende.
> Barouns and burgeis and bondage also
> I sauȝ in þat semble... (A.Prol.92–7)

On the other hand, Schmidt's paperback edition reads:

> Bisshopes and bachelers, boþe maistres and doctours,
> That han cure vnder Crist, and crownynge in tokene
> And signe þat þei sholden shryuen hire parisshens,
> Prechen and pray for hem, and þe pouere fede,
> Liggen at Londoun in Lenten and ellis.
> Somme seruen þe kyng and his siluer tellen,
> In Cheker and in Chauncelrie chalangen hise dettes...

[followed by six more lines]
I parceyued of þe power þat Peter hadde to kepe,
To bynden and vnbynden, as þe book telleþ...

(B.Prol.87–101)

And a final complication, readers of Pearsall's paperback edition will discover:

Bischopes and bachelers, bothe maystres and doctours,
That han cure vnder Crist and crownyng in tokene
Ben charged with Holy Chirche charite to tylie,
That is lele loue and lyf among lered and lewed,
Leyen at Londoun in Lenton and elles.
Summe seruen þe kynge and his siluer tellen,
In Cheker and in Chancerye chalengen his dettes...
[followed by three more lines, largely as the first three added in
   the preceding excerpt]
Conscience cam and accused hem – and þe comune herde hit –
   And seide, "Ydolatrie 3e soffren in sondrye places manye...

(C.Prol.85–96)

However diverse these renditions of similar materials on priestly irresponsibility, following some forty years of wrangling,[3] it has become accepted that, leaving aside matters of detail to which we will turn shortly, Langland is responsible for all three of them. He appears to have written his poem three times, and all three forms had public currency, available to be recorded by copyists. The poet seems to have been at work for an extended period, composing and recomposing. During this period, he promulgated, by means not entirely clear today, the work at various times. But in a situation where anyone who could acquire a copy might make yet another one, Langland had no control over his text, once it had become public. Consequently, second (and third) thoughts required some renewed act of promulgation, and, as a result, substantially differing versions of the work were "public property" – and thus variously available to scribes and readers.

The three versions of the "same" passage I have presented above exemplify the poetic procedures that distinguish various states of the poem. First, one must be struck by disparities in length and elaboration. In the first passage, the discussion of parish priests occupies four lines, in the second thirteen (with another 116 lines added after it concludes), in the third forty-five (with a further ninety-five, most of them more or less identical with those added in the second passage, at its end). This expansion is achieved by intruded elaborations of the discussion, initially the seven or eight lines that passage 2 has added to the first, of which I have quoted only the first two – not to mention extensive succeeding materials. The technique is extended in passage 3, where a further thirty lines now appear between the fourth and fifth of the lines the poet had added in passage 2. This technique, which Langland perhaps considered "interposition" (the Latinate term used to describe Will's poetic activity at B.12.22a), should be familiar, since Chaucer uses the phrasal verb "in eched" ("augmented by insertion") to describe his original materials intruded within the translation of Boccaccio's *Il Filostrato* that forms most of *Troilus and Criseyde* (3.1329; also "make in" [5.1788]). Of course, since for Chaucer the phrase refers specifically to non-inherited commentary, he learned this technique from Langland, who is the supremely commentative poet.

But expansiveness is not the only variation between forms of the poem on offer here. Consider a line from the first passage cited above: "To preche þe peple and pore men to fede." In the second passage, this has been reformulated as:

> þei sholden shryuen hire parisshens,
> Prechen and pray for hem, and þe pouere fede.

The line of what we may now by anticipation call version 1 is still a ghostly presence in this second rendition, where it has been recast within a more precise and inclusive statement of clerical responsibility, particularly evoking the poem's great theme, the ubiquity of human errancy and the consequent need for pardon. The third and fourth lines of (let us say) version 3 revise this into a more general (and quasi-allegorical) statement. Along with "interposition," Langland persistently attends to the local evocativeness of his verse. (Another pregnant example might be the transformation of the vigorously willful "Ben ylope to Lundoun" in passage 1, line 3, into the other versions' "Liggen at Londoun," the depiction of clerical indolence in a season of intense spiritual need.)

This stretch of the poem, which provides the first extensive such conundrum in reading *Piers Plowman*, could be taken as exemplary. The poem has always, from the late fourteenth century, been available in three basic states, what are known as its A, B, and C versions. The example under discussion cites from each the analogous passage, in this alphabetical sequence. Overall, A is considerably shorter and less developed than the other "long versions"; most emphatically, it stops, amidst its third vision, after about 2,500 lines, at some (debatable) point around the opening of its passus 12 (a moment roughly equivalent to B.10.470, C.11.295). The B version, whilst including many elaborations of the sort already apparent in this stretch (for example, B.5.385–441 and 477–509), also subjects A to often extensively meticulous local rewriting, and it includes a further seven dreams, two of them "inner dreams," dreams within dreams, in B passūs 11 and 16. Eventually, this text runs to about 7,700 lines. In those portions also represented in A, it is about a third longer, an expansive 3,300 lines. The C version follows the outline of B, although as B had done in revising A, with some redivision of material between Langland's structural divisions, his passūs; it has considerably less local tinkering than B, although a great many passages have been carefully reworked, and it includes, as the example above indicates, perhaps half a dozen substantial pieces of further "interposition." (The most prominent of these is the famous "autobiographical" episode at C.5.1–104.) In overall length, the C version is comparable to B; as the initial example shows, while this effort is frequently more extensive than its predecessor, it also excises material, about twenty lines in the Prologue, for example.

Versions and variations of *Piers Plowman*

From early in the B-version extension of A (B passus 11), *Piers Plowman* presents itself as "a life," the life of Langland's poetic surrogate, Will. Equally, the various versions of the poem represent nearly the totality of our surviving biography of William Langland. Generally, scholars believe that the various states of the poem were composed in the alphabetical order the great Victorian scholar Walter Skeat assigned them.[4] And generally, scholars have tended to see the poem as effectively Langland's life and have tried to assign the versions of the poem to fourteenth-century dates within the poet's (largely hypothetical) lifespan. A rough dating can be achieved on the basis of the poem's allusions to historical events. Most typically, A is placed in the later 1360s (certainly after 1362), B around 1377 (and before 1381), and C after 1388 and perhaps so late as 1390. Most normally, scholars believe that the three versions are exclusive – that Langland revised twice only, and that the diverse manuscript evidence for the poem might be reduced to these three versions.[5]

Unfortunately, this remains, at best, a gross statement, and editions of *Piers Plowman*, which provide the basis on which one can discuss Langland's versions – and thus his ongoing poetic creation, his revisions – have to cope with overwhelmingly diverse detail. Here, one might consider three closely related copies, the B-version manuscripts identified by the abbreviations Bm, Bo, and Cot. These books were produced side by side, probably in London, *c.* 1400–30; two of them (Bm and Bo) are virtual page-by-page twins, generally corresponding in their content leaf by leaf throughout. Both are probably providing exact imitations, the closest medieval texts ever come to photographic reproduction, of the single copy of the text that served all three manuscripts as their exemplar, or source for readings.

Yet although the three books provide a text distinctive when compared with all other manuscripts communicating the B version, they are scarcely identical. On several hundred occasions throughout the poem, the copies differ from one another, and it is not even clear that the two "facsimile reproductions" (Bm and Bo) resemble each other more closely in their local readings than they do the copy not in facsimile (Cot). Quite simply, variation, here mostly a mass of inadvertent scribal misapprehension, does not admit any easy sorting out.[6] The books raise pressingly the question of how one would determine what represents Langland's deliberated revision of his text and what conveys only variation that has accrued in the course of its transmission between the author's promulgated copy and the surviving manuscripts.

This is not a difficulty limited to a consideration of BmBoCot, but a general one in assessing the poem. And it is not clear that any of the available editions have entirely solved, or thoroughly addressed, the issue. A further feature shared by BmBoCot (and inherited in them from their common source) will adduce a further complication. I have described the three books as B-version copies, but, were one to consult their rendition of the Prologue passage at the head of this chapter, one would find that all three books reproduce the third version I have cited. At this point, they are not B-version books at all, but copies of C. The source underlying all three books started as a copy of B that lacked its opening. The scribe who was faced with this obvious gap tried to fill it in from what appears to have been an eight-leaf fragment, without any apparent awareness that this was a C-version copy. However, copying this source in full did not entirely fill the lacuna at the head of the fragmentary but extensive B copy. Consequently, the scribe sought – an indication that, before copying, he already was aware of the parameters of the text – yet a third manuscript to provide a whole text. From this, he acquired a relatively brief bridge, equivalent to B.2.90–212, to join up the C fragment with the scribe's extensive copy of B. But in this activity, the manuscript laid under contribution was neither a B nor a C copy, but one of A (its materials read as A.2.61–170). As a consequence, BmBoCot all present, within the single covers of each book, samples of all three versions.

With BmBoCot, one observes a problem endemic across the manuscripts. In the situation in which our evidence was produced, many book-producers knew only that there was an important and stimulating poem called *Piers Plowman*, and they reproduced it from copies at hand, without necessarily having any mechanism for distinguishing Langland's various textual promulgations. As a result, a great many copies show signs that scribes knew more than one version – and thus potentially, whatever textual version the text from which they were copying represented in gross terms, might unpredictably intrude readings from some other form of the poem.

The pre-eminent example of the procedure, and the one widely shared "versional awareness" in the Middle Ages, concerns the text of A. This was, if only by brevity and its absence of any conclusion, a clearly recognizable "incomplete" rendition. There are eighteen copies of *Piers Plowman* A, and among them seven scribes "faithfully" represented A, but equally, with some consciousness of its "incompleteness," when A ended, filled it out with a "longer version," always C. This procedure, in most instances (the copies called Z and K are exceptional), respects the integrity of the earliest version, even in a situation where the scribes knew another extensively revised version of the poem. The universal choice of a C manuscript to complete "the A fragment" may only attest to that version's popularity at the end of the fourteenth century. C spread immediately like wild fire, apparently in "pre-Chaucerian" London. The several extant pre-1400 C copies represent, at the very best, a third generation of copying, all the earlier examples that helped spawn them having disappeared.

Matters are more complicated in the case of those few scribes who could actually recognize the differences between individual versions. They knew that any one was only a partial rendition, and they sought to provide omnibus accounts of Langland's work, selectively fusing what had been for the poet separate engagements in his task. Paramount among discussion of these eccentric and exceptionally interesting volumes has been "the Z text" (originally designated text Z of the A tradition). But Z is scarcely an isolated instance; similar efforts occur in Ht of B (materials comparable to it form a marginal contribution to J of the C tradition) and, as Simon Horobin has indicated, H of B.[7] F of B, in addition to rewriting portions of the poem, and in places including substantial passages of this scribe's own composition, incorporates materials from both A and C.[8] A further example of readerly/writerly participation in the poem occurs at the end of A, where three manuscripts provide a variously extensive twelfth passus. In this case, the enthusiast responsible for at least portions of this material gives his name, "John But."

But Langland's text and, consequently, versional affiliations are potentially obscured by a variety of other, more commonplace disruptions. Editing the text, following George Kane's interventions, requires identifying commonplace types of errors (and thereby eliminating them from consideration as Langland's text). But *Piers Plowman* may be a singularly unpropitious text on which to exercise this otherwise useful tool. Given the great similarities of substantial portions of all versions (they are, after all, forms of the same poem), and given that Kane's editorial principle identifies spurious readings because they are "commonplace" and thus infinitely repeatable, readings of any version may accidentally converge with those of another.

Further, in the "bespoke book-trade" in which all the manuscripts were made, all new books constituted special orders. No one who wanted a personal copy of the text did not already know it, perhaps in considerable detail, and, correspondingly, the scribes employed to work for them might predictably be those chosen precisely because of their experience with the poem (and access to potential sources for copying the text). Thus, the readings of the manuscripts are often frequently unlocalizable, and never necessarily from what might appear the scribe's main source.

In the bespoke trade, both readers and scribes might remember a version of the line from elsewhere and "correct" whatever they had formally received. They might, as I have already indicated, consult another manuscript in cases of difficulty – sometimes just for an isolated reading; sometimes more pervasively, as in the N2 copy of the C tradition, which is most basically related to W of the common splicing of A completed with C, but with extensive use of an unrelated C copy and another of B. And like "John But" and the copyist responsible for F of B, the scribes demonstrate a strongly participatory impulse. For example, at B.4.38, all B copies add a line, extending a reference to foodstuffs; similarly, at B.5.369, they all provide a double oath, rather than the single one widely attested in the poem. (In these cases, with unanimous agreement, both readings come from a single scribe early in the B tradition and have been accurately transmitted by his successors.) Simply because a reading occurs in a manuscript of any given version does not necessarily mean it is a reading of that version, much less Langland's reading of the version. And the many manuscripts that include corrections by medieval scribes complicate this various access to the poem yet further.[9]

Obviously enough, conversion of this state of affairs into editions (which are necessary to ascertaining problems of revision) is deeply problematic. Editions began with Robert Crowley in 1550 as representations of single copies – and thus, broadly, of single versions (in Crowley's case B, in Thomas D. Whitaker's edition of 1813, for example, C). Walter Skeat's great contribution to the study of the poem was to sort the manuscripts and to assign them to appropriate versions, largely on the basis with which this chapter began. Skeat edited the entire poem, but originally as self-contained separate volumes, one for each version, and his lead has been followed ever since. This partitioning of the evidence, as I have tried to indicate, is not necessarily helpful, and future editors will need to be a great deal more conscious of ways in which versions of the text might be seen as intermittently in convergence, at least in the manuscript record. And any effort to discuss

Langland's practice of revision needs to be offered within this introductory caveat.

"Revision" provides a particularly provocative term for considering *Piers Plowman* because of its multiple implications. On the one hand, the term customarily refers to the act of revising one's work, that is, Langland's continuing effort over at least two decades to achieve a presentation appropriate to his chosen subject, the spiritual condition of England. But of course, etymologically, the word "revise" means "to look [over] again." In a poem unique in European tradition in being given over to repeated feats of "visioning" (finally ten dreams in all, two of them symmetrically disposed "inner" dreams), re-visioning what has already occurred, re-opening, commenting upon, and qualifying earlier discussions, is the very metier of Langland's poetics. (And the two inner dreams, the doubling of the device, a technique Langland learned from contemporary romance, the poetry of knightly quests, offer yet another formal mechanism, and one persistent in the poem, for providing re-visions of ideas earlier discussed.) Not for nothing does the dreamer, late in – if not at the end of – his career describe himself as "romynge in remembraunce" (C.5.11). What Langland found as his normal mode for pursuing a spiritually incisive narrative is simply writ large in the procedures by which he engaged in successive refinements upon what he had already written.

From *Wynnere and Wastour* to *Piers Plowman* A, B, C

Viewing versional difference as an extension of the poet's usual practice – further commentary upon an already commentative text – helps undo one oversight endemic in the poem's critical history. Concentration upon interversional "revision" has nearly always relegated *Piers Plowman* A to a form of silence. (It is, for example, the last version to have been made available in an edition designed for student use.[10]) With a few honorable exceptions, A has always stood as that undeveloped foundation upon which Langland constructed greater poetic glories. Thus, this has always been the most ignored version, although in certain respects it might be construed the most important.

First of all, in the customary account, the A version speaks to the origins of Langland's conception. More than the longer versions, it emphasizes how the poem began as a traditional single vision, and in a received mode. Langland's commitment to the alliterative tradition (which should be seen as a motivated choice, rather than as inevitable) might be more manifest here, as well, for his inspiration was the alliterative debate poem *Wynnere and Wastour* (cf. the poet's marked, yet differently charged, allusion to this title at A.Prol.22). This is a poem that, like Langland's opening, takes up topics of contemporary decline – in *Wynnere and Wastour*, that of provincial ("westren") great-house culture. *Piers Plowman* generalizes this view into an account of a broader decline affecting all England "siþþe þe pestilence tyme" (A.Prol.81). Langland responds to a vertiginous turn in national fortunes, particularly military ones (cf. A.3.176–95), that had occurred between the English triumph over the French at the battle of Crécy in the early stages of the Hundred Years War (1347) and the inception of his poem in the mid/late 1360s. And certainly a significant portion of the character that Langland constructs for his persona Will has been derived from *Wynnere and Wastour*'s dark thoughts on the fate of provincial sons sent off to London and inexperienced poets who can only "jangle als a jaye" (cf. A.Prol.35).

In genre, *Wynnere and Wastour* is a debate poem (and thus, by its nature, about doubled alternatives), a slanging match between the title figures. They clash over that topic that consumes Langland's first vision, how to use the wealth of this world (cf. A.1.42–3). As debate, *Wynnere and Wastour* seems to presuppose an all or nothing resolution, a ratification of either conspicuous consumption ("wasting") or hoarding to build an imperishable, if rather dour, estate ("winning"). Yet perhaps surprisingly, the poem breaks off (although a fragment, it appears nearly complete) in an aporia, an absence of decision. The poem's judge (a figure for Edward III, also "the king" in Langland's first vision) ratifies equally the views of both contestants, but as differing functions – and significantly, ones allocated different spheres of operation.

Any variety of features in *Piers Plowman* A reflects the earlier poem, from Langland's initial dream landscape onward. *Wynnere and Wastour* opens with a procession of estates types (in this case adversarially on the brink of warfare), before passing to a representative argument between opposites, succeeded by a scene of judgment. Affinities with Langland's prologue are obvious enough, just as are those with the subsequent confrontations in the opening vision of *Piers Plowman* A: Holy Church v. Meed *and* Meed v. Conscience (yet another conspicuous doubling of the device, implicit contrast explicated through formal debate). Although "Edward III's" judgment appears definitive in *Piers Plowman* A, and, just as in *Wynnere and Wastour*, produces a spatial disjunction (Meed banned from the court, other figures – Conscience and Reason – intruded), it actually is not so. Meed remains implicit in the royal voice that controls his new counsellors (A.4.146–7, substantially clarified by B.4.174–6), and the banished Meed remains loose and unsupervised in the realm outside Westminster.

This description might imply "by-the-numbers" appropriation. But in moving past this point, the A version introduces Langland's greatest formal innovation, the decision to extend materials received and, by doing so, to recast them into a dream sequence. The poem fails to rest at the perfectly adequate, if cynical, resolution *Wynnere and Wastour* provides (the king opts to pillage, "win" from, his continental enemies so Englishmen can party, "waste," at home). The full received A extends to three visions, and, in the second of these, Langland offers his first address of the problem *Wynnere and Wastour* declines to take up: how to reformulate diverse imperatives into a morally acceptable communal life. Yet the afterlife of *Wynnere and Wastour* within *Piers Plowman* A is pervasive. All three A visions open argumentative vistas, and all end (A.4, A.8, A.11) in aporia or enigma: the second, with Langland's abidingly central scene, Piers and the priest arguing over the pardon; the third, with Will's confusion and anger, when he cannot understand the grounds of salvation. In A, Langland deliberately evokes contentious and problematic issues, yet never offers an overt solution to them – and, at least in the first two instances, promptly begins a "re-visioning" predicated on the unresolved events and issues that had occurred in the preceding dream.

This, too, is an important and continuous feature of Langlandian poetics, discovered in composing A. Quite self-consciously, Langland writes what might be described as an "unsignaled" or "unsignposted" poem. This feature is emphasized for readers at almost the exact center of A, at the poem's moment of greatest ostensible clarity, Piers's pathway/pilgrimage to Truth (a sort of child's garden of Christianity). However clear, Piers's effort is greeted as "a wikkide weye, but whoso hadde a gide" (A.7.1). Although it is an ahistorical analogy to propose, yet useful given the poem's persistent reliance on dialogue, *Piers Plowman* has affinities to drama, where the playwright never steps out of the wings to affirm or deny any speech. The A version, for example, makes no effort whatever to invite one to contemplate the affinities – as well as the real differences – between Holy Church, Conscience, and Reason. As a further example, an attentive reader should notice that, were Will – or any of the figures he debates in the third version – able to conceive of a concept like "God's grace," he would not fall into the near-despair with which A ceases.

The conclusion of A raises more problems, however. Historical references in the earliest written portions of B imply that Langland was already rewriting A in the early 1370s. The interval between composing the first version and converting it into B seems absolutely minimal. Thus, it may be that A represents only a stage of a quickly superseded draft. If so, although the earliest in composition, it remains possible (and features of the transmission may affirm this) that A was not promulgated as the other versions were. It may represent a quickly superseded engagement that escaped into circulation, owing to the popularity of longer versions.

When Langland came to revise his first version into B, he appears originally to have extended his poem to its "full dimensions," i.e., written B passūs 11–20. He then returned to the standing text of A and subjected it to intense and detailed scrutiny, bringing his earlier work into some alignment with what was now intended to follow it. A great deal of this writing involved extensive "interposition," as a return to the passage from the A prologue, with which this chapter began, will indicate.

That example shows, at the end of the presentation in the A version, that the poem originally had no passage corresponding to B.Prol.99–216. Half of this new initiative is generated as a "back-formation" from Piers's response to the "wikkide weye" complaint I have just quoted (A.7.3–52), and thus forms a major piece of structural/narrative doubling. In the original passage in A passus 7, Piers acts as a reeve or "strawboss," arranging communally sustaining tasks in the half-acre. The mirroring passage in the revised prologue (B.Prol.112–45) offers a much more conventional account of founding a commune, royally governed (incidentally re-enforcing A.1.92–111, retained as B.1.94–113, not to mention the newly written B.18 and 19.10–198). Although Piers manages, at least temporarily, to bring querulous interlocutors within a single voice and a single program of just action, the new "interposition" in the B Prologue, perhaps more typically "Langlandian" (cf. B.19.396–20.50), ends in a bilingual cacophony of voices, undifferentiated by any overt commentary, lunatic/poet, angel, "goliardeis," and populace all offering their opinion.

This first intervention is completed by a second, again of a sort typical to the poem. With only an adverbial transition, and no further explanation at any point ("Wiþ þat ran þer . . . at ones," B.Prol.146), there ensues a short fable, the story of the rats' plan to bell the cat (146–210). This episode, which doubles monitory example with political *roman à clef*, concludes with what one might recognize as Langland's signature technique, an ironic invitation:

> What þis metels bymeneþ, ye men þat ben murye,
> Deuyne ye . . .   (B.Prol.209–10)

Langland chooses to make the device explicit, and then with some irony, only at the conclusion of this first long insertion into the poem. Discussion of how to moralize a fable is the proper work of ten-year-olds, from whose grammar school text this tale has been drawn. Such study forms, in the biography of any literate medieval person, an introduction to sophisticated commentary. Thus, the first B intervention into A demands that a reader understand, not simply the literal and propositional referents of language, but the implications of often convoluted and contested formulations of argument. The fable concerns, after all, disputes about what might, in a certain situation, constitute good counsel. Langland's imagined ideal reader, encouraged to a form of non-Chaucerian "solaas" ("ye . . . murye"), should be commentative, an image of the poet, whose words themselves offer commentary across a range of issues, social, textual, biblical. After all, in a passage unique to B (12.20–4), Will affirms such an interest in poetic "gaudia" (joys), perhaps surprising to soberly pietistic and theological readers, through another citation of a grammar school text familiar to all.

In addition to provocative "interpositions" like this, the B-version copiously rewrites A in detail. A small instance from the portrait of the deadly sin Envy may illustrate the process. At A.5.69–72, Langland follows up the customary introduction to his sins, a physical description of Envy laden with quasi-symbolic material, indicative of the distortion of the "human face divine" by errant propensities, with:

> Venym, or verious, or vynegre I trowe,
> Walewiþ in my wombe and waxiþ as I wene.
> I miȝt not many day do as a man auȝte,
> Such wynd in my wombe wexiþ er I dyne.

In the B revision, Langland found the four lines otiose and eliminated this passage. He apparently saw that the description replicated another he had written later in the portrait (A.5.98–102). This he retained – and he supplemented it with two lines from the now cancelled earlier passage (cf. B.5.119–25, where 121–2 rephrase A.5.71–2). The portrait no longer offers simply a description of the State of Envy, the sour spirit responding to the success of others through self-harming physical discomfort. Rather, as the belated second A discussion (now the sole surviving one of B) had done, Envy's dyspepsia appears, not as state, but as the result of a process. This is not the process of committing the sin, but simply recalling and confessing it. As the figure immediately admits, to the thorough detriment of penance itself, "I am sory . . . I am but selde ooþer" (B.5.128). Quite shockingly, the constructive (and salvationally necessary) aegis under which Envy has been brought to voice here concludes by reinforcing, rather than eradicating, his sinfulness. This represents "romynge in remembraunce" indeed.

Generally, beginning students are exposed to Langland's B version, as a fully formed and imaginatively realized state of the poem. In contrast, C has long suffered from the claim that it is "unpoetic." Traditionally, scholars were fond of citing as a litmus of such views, "the liȝt" that "*blewe* alle þi blessed into . . . blisse" (B.5.494–5), where C.7.134–5 replaces the surprisingly kinaesthetic verb with the colorless "brouht." While it may be difficult to argue with this particular example, one might, more constructively, find in C a persistent attention to structural clarity and an attentiveness toward explication of the enigmatic. This version is frequently more insistent upon what issues are at stake, and C is thus a poem more overt in its intellectual engagement than earlier versions had been. In particular, Langland most persistently attends to problematic portions of the poem, the end of the second and the third visions, and he removes from the text a major bit of narrative repetition, consolidating his presentation of Seven Deadly Sins in the second vision. (B.13.271–459 becomes dispersed among the parallel materials of C.6.1–7.118a; cf. the major excision at the parallel C.15.232.)

One could point to one example, the recasting of the important speech at B.11.184–319. In many ways, these lines are the fulcrum upon which the poem's later development turns, the unsigned, implicit recognition that Piers's gesture of tearing the pardon is imitative of a model established by Jesus, and constitutes "patient poverty," i.e., that poverty of spirit enjoined in the first beatitude. However, in the B version, the status of this utterance is remarkably murky. It is preceded by yet another sudden intervention, that of the Roman emperor Trajan (11.140–53), who resumes speaking, at least briefly, at 11.171. No further speech-direction occurs in B until 11.320, when, following an excuse for digression, appears the thoroughly unspecific "þus wiþ me gan *oon* dispute." This confusingly seems to indicate that the intervening speech does not communicate the dreamer's understanding of spiritual affairs, as the earlier 11.153–70 may well do.

C defuses this enigma – although scarcely without adding its own intellectual complications. In revising the text, Langland eliminates Trajan's second explosion into the text (C.12.93, although the line remains in that voice with which Trajan usually speaks in B). Moreover, the praise of patient poverty now proceeds at great length, not simply to end of C passus 12 (line 247), but through to C.13.128. There its speaker is firmly assigned, "Thus Rechelesnesse in a rage aresenede Clergy," and any equivalent to the enigmatic B.11.320 is excised.

While this eliminates one problem (who speaks?), as my citation suggests, it raises another: who *is* this speaker? Recklessness, whose name connotes spiritual negligence (the willful failure to perform necessary responsibilities), appears only briefly in B, at 11.34–6, where he "st[ands] forþ in raggede cloþes." He appears here to applaud the despairing dreamer's decision to abandon spiritual pursuits in favor of Fortune and worldly delights. C insistently identifies the speaker as some form of double for Will (and presumably the person who, in both versions, has been speaking in praise of poverty).

RALPH HANNA

C.11.193 draws the connection explicitly by identifying the figure as akin to Will's state of despair, and Will's worldly sweetheart Covetise-of-eyes addresses him as "Recchelesnesse" in C.12.4.

However, this clarification does not address other difficulties, which I simply enumerate. At C.11.198–301, Recklessness suddenly absorbs the B dreamer's speech. But this includes a substantial excess over what Will says overtly in B. Recklessness takes up, not with the exactly parallel B.11.184, but with Will's despairing speech (identical with what had earlier ended A), B.10.378, and the narrative order of C passūs 11–12 has been substantially readjusted from what had stood in B passūs 10–11. Moreover, the now swollen speech includes not simply local rewriting (e.g., the intrusion of a bit of Lollard cant at C.11.205–6) but a very substantial "interposition" – all of C.12.155–247, 13.1–99. In the course of all this, the nature of Recklessness (and of his double Will) may be elaborately redefined. But the whole allegorical movement in both texts can only be completed more than a vision later (B.13/C.15), with the appearance of Patience, another doubling figure, in this case a model available for the dreaming figure to follow, and one who faces his own destitution with delight, not despair.

As I have indicated, C does not simply provide major structural clarifications like this one. It also removes many things from the B text. Most perturbing to readers has always been the complete suppression in C of the poem's signal passage of enigma, the tearing of the pardon (see also Chapters 1 and 4). Here (C.9.281–94, cf. B.7.107–45), one sees only Truth's brief message, the priest's (proper) rejection of it *as pardon*, and Piers entering (here an unreported) argument with this adversary. Yet, just as in the case of the praise of poverty, there is a major bit of "interposition" here, the immediately preceding C.9.71–280. While this passage still presents some only lightly and locally revised B materials (e.g., B.7.88–106 = C.9.162–86), it introduces a variety of issues at least reminiscent of those raised by tearing the pardon, lunatic *lollers* and God's minstrels, those who live in involuntary destitution, for example. The destructive gesture that underscores Piers's exact response to the priest is absent, but revision may represent a different way of discussing the same issues, although now no longer present in their original formulation.

These examples of revision actually problematize some types of argument I have engaged in above. All of them result from reading the poem in its most organized, parallel text form. Within this practice, the examples I have chosen stand out as local interruptions of difference. Yet in each case, as I have tried to suggest, Langland's revision does not appear "backwards motivated," that is merely a correction of something earlier amiss; each represents a constructive intervention that creates poetic meaning anew, and

48

this is a new poetic meaning that extends across the full text of this particular revised version. Parallel texts present the poem, as it were, vertically, as a successive sequence of "levels" erected on the same site. The poem, however, in any of its three versions, has a projective horizontality, a movement toward an end, a process to which each individual intervention presently contributes.[11] In these terms, the three versions may not actually be, as they seem in parallel, "more of the same," but the longitudinal and incrementally additive sequence by which Langland seems always to have composed, and in whose poetic – they constitute, after all, the poet's visible life – each occupies a specifically assigned position. Ultimately, getting to grips with the poem requires beginning with A, and (with whatever relevant help that the aides-mémoires parallel-texts provide) reading through all its versions in succession.

Piers Plowman manuscripts cited

These are grouped according to the customary versions, as used, e.g., in the Athlone editions and Hanna, *William Langland*, pp. 38–42; for shelf-marks and basic information about all manuscripts of the poem, see the latter.

A

K = Oxford, Bodleian Library, MS Digby 145
Z = Oxford, Bodleian Library, MS Bodley 851

B

Bm = London, British Library, MS 10574
Bo = Oxford, Bodleian Library, MS Bodley 814
Cot = London, British Library, MS Cotton Caligula A.xi
F = Oxford, Corpus Christi College MS 201
H = London, British Library, MS Harley 3954
Ht = Huntington Library, MS 114

C

J = University of London Library, S.L. v.88
N2 = National Library of Wales, MS 733B
W = York, Borthick Institute Archives MS Add.196; *olim* Duke of Westerminster

3

STEVEN JUSTICE

Literary history and *Piers Plowman*

Literary history examines how works emerge from the conditions they inherit from older works, and how they in turn set the conditions of later ones; it is a history internal to literary composition and notionally distinct from its place in cultural and political history. Any work is conceivable only against a background of context and expectation, established by works already extant, which shapes style, structure, form, and conceptual presupposition for literary performances – that, indeed, defines what is "literary." Such expectations can be constraints, but also questions or provocations, embodiments of what has already been accomplished and therefore starting-points for what has not: ambitions already realized imply and help formulate others. So it is useful to regard every literary work as an answer to questions implicitly posed by what preceded it and a source of new ones posed to what follows. These questions and answers, like all real questions and real answers, are partly open, undetermined (if they were not, the questions would answer themselves). To write such a history means discerning the questions and the answers; this effort requires interpretation, which includes doubling or repeating the interpretation of predecessors that later authors have undertaken.

Thus described, literary history may sound trivial almost by ambition; while one of literature's claims on the attention is its ability to evoke and embody what lies beyond its mechanisms – to make another life, another time, seem drastically present – this inquiry worries about the mechanisms' internal history. But these mechanisms are instruments of practical and speculative reason, by which experience can be construed for thought and thoughts rendered available to experience. To understand them is to understand something about understanding itself, about how it is derived, packaged, communicated, and used; it is also to appreciate how complex is the enterprise of apprehending things past. This may still seem thin gruel. But if literature can add anything to what can be known of history by other means, it does so by virtue of being literary. Understanding what its properties entail, discerning their internal logic, is prerequisite to grasping what they do and do not communicate. Clarity on that distinction can provide new material for studying the past; it also offers some indemnity against swallowing its fictions.

Piers Plowman and earlier literary history

A full account of *Piers Plowman*'s literary history would trace all the filaments of literary accomplishment that funnel into it and all of those that diffused back out, and would be unbearable to writer and readers both. In so short a space as this, even a superficial survey is impossible (and Chapters 10 and 11 below on the poem's reception make it partly redundant). Instead, this chapter outlines the central problem of its literary history and the logic that makes it so.

This problem touches upon the very desire, just mentioned, for poetry to be more than poetry. *Piers Plowman* offers an interesting challenge to literary history because it has regularly convinced its readers that it has no part in such a history, that it is something more than art. Almost from the moment of its appearance, the poem was treated more often as a document than as a literary artifact, and in some ways still is. One of the work's first interpretations was that of English rebels against the organization of justice and of agricultural production in 1381; letters originating among them counted "Pers Plouȝman" among their number, and bade him "go to his werk." (If the account offered in Chapter 11 is correct, then this conclusion is wrong, and vice versa.) Like many readers who followed, theirs was not a failure to understand the poem but a choice to make it other than a poem – in this case, a language for the moral economy of rural self-government.[1] In a different context but with a similar effect, Robert Crowley, printing the poem in the Protestant reign of Edward VI, declared the author a reformer who, like John Wyclif, "doeth moste christianlye enstruct the weake, and sharply rebuke the obstinate blynde."[2] The wry recent comment that "life would be much simpler if one could show that Wyclif...was the unknown author of *Piers Plowman*" shows that many still think of it as a tract for and symptom of its times.[3] Subtler readings, including some of the best in the criticism, assume that the poem's difficulties are not created *by* it for its intellectual or artistic ends, but *for* it by ideology's contradictions, theology's puzzles, or the brutalities of political domination; its difficulties, then, are taken as the honorable scars of violent encounter with something tougher or realer than art.

But while readers and scholars join in wanting to find something more exigent than poetry behind *Piers Plowman*'s manic energy, they chronically differ over what that was. The feeling that the poem has encountered something that overwhelmed its design arises not because one can see anything that obviously did so, but because the poem conveys the sensation that something has. That is, making the reader feel the presence of a history that has broken the poem's design is one of the most complex accomplishments of that design.

How is this a question of literary history? A contrast with Chaucer will clarify. That he marks a new generation in a cosmopolitan literary history, that he follows upon Dante and Petrarch – and with them upon Jean de Meun, and with them all upon Ovid and Virgil – are points he treats as givens. Courtship performed, in all relevant senses of the noun, governed (sometimes tyrannically, as *The Legend of Good Women*'s prologue attests) by convention, he treats – at least until writing the *Canterbury Tales* – as poetry's given matter; Chaucer's poems achieve their novelty through performance of derivation, citation, and allusion. This literary agenda is clearest when derivation and citation themselves become indirections, as when *Troilus and Criseyde* deliberately misidentifies its source (conjuring "Lollius" from Horace) and transparently mischaracterizes its process (translating "every word" [1.394–7]). Books, in a tradition self-aware and coherent, form the substance from which Chaucer's poems arise and to which they look to return: they originate from books (the *Metamorphoses* in *The Book of the Duchess*, the *Aeneid* in *The House of Fame*) and hope to join them (the classical "makyng" catalogued in the *Troilus*'s envoy [5.1789]).

Even the reader new to *Piers Plowman* can see that it works differently. It seems at once incompletely literary and oppressively textual. It is saturated with writing. The Latin words and phrases and lines, marked in manuscripts by script or rubrication and in modern editions by italics, are ubiquitous, scoring the surface of the text with their own. But *books*, as objects, do not appear.[4] *Texts* do, as units cut loose from context and intruding upon the poem rather than shaping it. They befall its action and thought in unanticipated and unanticipatable encounters. Texts are persons you meet (B.4.143), landmarks you pass (B.5.567), destinations you come to (C.18.4); things you might build on (B.1.86 and elsewhere) or pull from a bag and eat (B.14.47–50); instruments you can blow and the breath you blow them with (B.5.506–7); mute objects (C.2.39); warning signs (B.5.461).[5] They appear as bodies foreign to the poem, not discursive models it has internalized – things it meets with rather than things it thinks with.

Langland repeatedly sets up frameworks of literary affiliation and repeatedly knocks them down. We can study the logic of his procedure in the narrator's interview with Holy Church in passus 1. Such authoritative instruction of visionary narrator by a female, supernatural figure is a type-scene;

instances of it begin or feature prominently in Boethius' *Consolation of Philosophy* (524), *The Romance of the Rose* (c. 1230–80), and Deguileville's *Pilgrimage of Human Life* (c. 1330–55), all of which the poet knew. In each of these, the guide (Philosophy, Reason, and God's Grace respectively) is authoritative, knowing where fulfillment is and how the dreamer might reach it. In each, the narrator's response to this figure determines the literary and moral form the narrative takes (dialectical progress, rejection and debasement, lapse and return respectively) and creates its complexities. Langland's Holy Church is different. On the one hand, the rhetorical gestures signal that she has the same adequacy and authority these others do. Her lines about love ("whan it hadde of þis fold flessh and blood taken / Was neuere leef vpon lynde lighter þerafter, / And portatif and persaunt as þe point of a nedle," B.1.155–7) have a weight earned by their precision and intellectual beauty; the structure of moral explanation she assembles is nowhere refuted or outflanked, and remains pertinent through its final crisis. Unlike the *Rose*'s dreamer, Will does not reject her instruction: indeed, his request to "knowe þe fals" (B.2.4), which prompts her disappearance as Meed comes on stage, is meant to detain her. It is not even clear whether she disappears permanently, whether we are to identify with her the "Holy Church" that appears in the final passus (a barn, this time, not a woman), or even to recall her at that point. She does not prove inadequate to *Piers Plowman*; *Piers Plowman* portrays itself as inadequate to her.

By this technique, which takes several forms, Langland uses literary resources while seeming to escape literary status. He deploys his predecessors' conventions, but he works their failure, and creates in it the effect of art shipwrecked on reality – redefined, in effect, as ideology, as a simplifying and frangible device unequal to what it would frame. It is an effect of which Langland is a master, creating by literary means the impression that literary premeditation dashed disastrously against the real. In Holy Church's discourse and her anticlimactic evanescence, he both affirms the truth she teaches and reduces conventional poetic modes of presenting that truth as *mere* conventions, too stylized and brittle to survive real experience or real thought. And by that same device, he both acknowledges his literary predecessors and reduces them to *mere* literature. What seems to be his poem's failure, swallowing complexities that its literary form cannot metabolize, proves its most distinctive success, handing its readers the slightly harrowing literary sensation of encountering something real. When showing his mastery of poetic registers and styles, he makes them confess their subjection: his uncanny mimicries (like his "lethally exact" evocation of alliterative romance style describing Meed's "bower"[6]) have the effect of parody, as if poetry, just by being poetry, confesses its frivolity and inadequacy.

The best comprehensive accounts of the poem's form show how it manages a mobile and centripetal energy, designing a coherent work from what seem chance lines of inquiry, by repeatedly re-engineering the moment of beginning.[7] A sudden explosion of contentious energy derails one narrative or expository route, promotes the disruption itself to defining importance, and precipitates structure from the mess that results: this is its characteristic process. The Prologue disintegrates in street cries ("hote pies, hote!," B.Prol.226), the exposition of the pardon in the argument of Piers with the priest ("The preest and Perkyn apposeden eiþer ooþer, / And þoruȝ hir wordes I wook," B.7.144–5), the dialogue with Scripture in Trajan's intrusion ("Ye? baw for bokes!" B.11.140). The poem thus seems to unfold more by the fortune of unplanned encounters than by design. That its formal divisions are called "passūs," "steps," seems to promise progress toward a goal, as does the figure of pilgrimage that the poem fitfully adopts. But the narrator's actual steps ("er I hadde faren a furlong feyntise me hente / That I ne myȝte ferþer a foot for defaute of slepynge," B.5.5–6) suggest rather something erratic. The poem's processual form – its pretense that it has no ultimate form beyond its own undeliberated process – means that it represents its literary history as if it is simply history, as if what it takes from its literary models, the forms with which it tries to shape its material, proves to be just epiphenomenal choices dusted from its surface by dumb luck.

The poem represents its *internal* history as processual also. It incorporates into its narrative the signs of that revision-history that yields its multiple versions, in those episodes that recall the narrator's previous career of authorship, like Imaginative's reflections on his makings (B.12.16), and the narrator's own recollection of hostile reception (C.5.3–5). Some in its early audience knew of the revisions;[8] the references to them imply that *Piers Plowman* itself caused many of the poem's complexities, and thereby seem to push the relevance of its literary models still further to the background.

For this reason, although one way to "survey" literary history leading up to *Piers Plowman* would be to focus on immediate alliterative predecessors like the dream-vision debate poem *Wynnere and Wastour* (see Chapter 2), or the somewhat more widely copied, less fully "alliterative" satire *The Simonie*, a premise to the poet's likely use of those English poems and its other, more certain models in French and Latin would be that *Piers Plowman* starts from literary models and then pulls off its most characteristic effects by reproaching their inadequacy. The means of feigning exit from literary history was already suggested by some of those literary models, beginning with the very designation of the "passus." What suggested that term? In the remarkable first poem of Deguileville's "pilgrimage" trilogy, *The Pilgrimage of Human Life*, the narrator first encounters the Boethian figure of Grace-Dieu, who "receives" him (as Holy Church has received Will) in baptism; this scene is one clear source of Will's interview with Holy Church. Grace-Dieu brings him to baptism as to a great sea crossing; to his anxieties, she reassures him that this sacrament "is the first crossing [passage] of every good pilgrimage...This step is not against your interest," and follows it with a wordplay in which the play of *step* and *negation* in Langland's "passus," where the promise of progress is supplanted by the fact of digression, seems already implied: "Ne t'est *pas* ce *pas* contraire" (literally, "this is not a backwards step for you," 438, 445). Indeed this whole episode of Deguileville's *Pilgrimage* articulates, but does not perform, what Langland makes the very premise of his poem's structure as well as of its "passūs." Deguileville's narrator, flinching at the thought of baptism's "crossing," is rebuked by Grace-Dieu. The sacrament's grace brings you to the heavenly Jerusalem; nothing less than a great and adverse journey could earn such reward: "You want to go to Jerusalem, so you must pass the great sea; the 'sea' in question is this world here, which is full of many anxieties"; only by persevering through "tempests and torments, storms and winds" (425–30) can he reach such a goal. Crossing the ocean of this world proves no vaster or more uncharted than the act of baptism. In this anticlimax, the *Pilgrimage* makes a theological point about grace, but it also recalls and avows its chosen limitations, signals how much its structural device of a pilgrimage clearly mapped must leave out. The *Pilgrimage* will seriously portray sin and its sufferings, but not its worst and most baffling suffering: the failure of clarity and belief, the disorientation of a disobedient self that cannot keep its grip on truth. Though the narrator falls to temptation and for a time cannot reach Grace-Dieu and her partner Raison, he always knows where they are. The more frightening possibility of being really alone on the "ocean" of life, which the *Pilgrimage* knows but admits it does not portray, becomes the central conceit and structural principle in *Piers Plowman*: a soul experiencing itself as a country vast and unmapped.

I think Langland had these passages in mind as he began *Piers Plowman*, but they are not sources in the usual sense. They are instead sources of suggestion, challenges laid down by a predecessor work that brilliantly accomplished some aims while sharply imagining what doing so left out. Every work draws a line, marks a point of achievement toward which it has labored; and at the same time, the labor displays what its own logic points beyond, what other aims are left unachieved. To put it another way, every work implies narratives of literary filiation and influence of which it might be a part, and that narrative implies what might follow next, what new turns the story might take. This is how innovation is prompted within, and by the fact of, literary continuity. (Langland was as alert as anyone to the indignity of merely repeating what was there already: "þer are bokes ynowe / To telle men what dowel is, dobet and dobest boþe" [B.12.17–18] is a rebuke that cuts.) Deguileville signaled the recognition that any portrayal of moral inquiry that omits the experience of moral disorientation has at least partially falsified it. Guillaume de Lorris and Jean de Meun had pointed in a similar direction by making their narrator a fantasist immune to moral inquiry, whose story thus had all the unreality of fiction without its analytic power. That recognition of the falsifying tidiness of moral fiction implied an ambition still unfulfilled: to portray such inquiry untidily, uncushioned by figuration, convention, or evident design. It is a paradoxical ambition: a design that would seem undesigned, a structure for making structure seem broken by what it tries to order. Langland pursues this ambition; he articulates it. Deeper even than the desire to effect things is the desire to encounter them without concept; this the poem names as its desire: "Yet haue I no kynde knowyng," the narrator objects to Holy Church, "ye mote kenne me bettre" (B.1.138), as if there were some teaching that could do more than teaching can in fact do. Will wants to know in a way that is more than knowing. The poem itself works to cue a similar yearning in its audience, the yearning to touch history, to feel it in the making, to experience the poem as if what one had experienced was more than a poem. *Piers Plowman* will go on speculatively to resolve the relation of the fictive and the imaginative to the real;[9] yet it presumes an antithesis between them, which it never affirms as a serious proposition but upon which it builds the sense that it reaches past its own formal existence.

Piers Plowman and later literary history

The last paragraph recalled two familiar truths – that narratives create desires in their readers, and that literary works can create desires in their successors – that together suggest a third, less familiar one: that these two processes are really aspects of one process. The paradoxical achievement of *Piers Plowman*, visible to anyone who reflects, I have already named: the most artful aspect of its structure suggests that it is unequal to sustaining any structure. Once a poem that seems to distance itself from literary exemplars and from the very process of literary exemplarity becomes itself a literary exemplar, the most natural response is to select one of these premises, unstably yoked in paradox, as the stable point of reference. The most prominent fact about *Piers Plowman*'s literary aftermath – that is, the consistency with which two responses incongruous with each other continue to appear – derives (I will now suggest) from this paradox. Its direct effects on literary history have been fitful, visible most especially in its own time and just after, in the later sixteenth century, and after the middle of the nineteenth.

One strand in this literary tradition is woven from those readers and writers, beginning with the 1381 rebels and including Robert Crowley, who treat the poem as a document and a point of affiliation. Whether they believe the poem's fictions of artlessness, directness, and immediacy or affect to believe them (the former in Crowley's case and the latter in the rebels', I think), they treat the poem's figures and its rhetorical appeals as emerging from and returning to an encounter with its social and political world. Writing in response, they embrace the fiction that something unfictive has broken through the literary cortex, which may then be disregarded as supernumerary or adopted as a badge of allegiance. Those scholars most eager to discover in the poem a brush with medieval experience – the experience of rural or town labor, of reformist passion, of belief baffled by its own thought – follow a similar impulse. It is not hard to suspect (in oneself, first of all) that many have been drawn to the poem by the sheer feel of moral or intellectual or economic struggle had at first hand. Similarly, its pose of literariness compromised by history may have helped make its study a growth-industry for a generation of historicist criticism,[10] in which *Piers Plowman* often appeared as a phenomenon of what we might call a *local pastness*, stubbornly particular, resistant to formalization, unassimilable to grand narratives. These are not new impulses; they operate in J. J. Jusserand's use of the poem in painting his word-pictures of medieval England.[11] Such a positioning can, though it need not, underwrite a conservative or a progressive political agenda; at about the same time as Jusserand, the artist, writer, publisher, textile designer, and "libertarian socialist" William Morris diagnosed *Piers Plowman* as an epiphenomenon of its moment (a kind of "Lollard poetry" that was "no bad corrective to Chaucer") and for that very reason could use it to help conjure the utopian future of Morris's *News from Nowhere* (1890).

This affective or even impulsive mode of reading *Piers Plowman* is also perforce an anti-aesthetic or unaesthetic one, and it could sponsor kinds of identity, ways of occupying commitments that Langland's poem specifically avoids. *Pierce the Plowman's Crede*, written within a very few years, borrowed one aspect of Langland's manner and one portion of his imaginative lexicon for an attack on the orders of friars.[12] The narrator vainly seeks solid religious instructions from what prove to be the corrupt orders of friars, and finds instead in "Peres...the pore man, the plowe-man" (473), an interlocutor as authoritative as Langland's Holy Church and more durably effective. And that is precisely its difference from *Piers Plowman*, which raises expectations of religious knowledge it will not fulfill, roiling theological questions instead of sedating them. It is possible to think Langland's poem unserious because of such unsettledness; but if it is not, it is from that very unsettledness that its seriousness comes. The *Crede* is confident in the sort of self-evidence *Piers Plowman* has no hope of: its descriptions of the Dominicans' church (158–218) and of Piers's destitution (421–42), certainly its most memorable passages, both assume that to grasp what the poem portrays is to grasp its truth: that Christ is found with the poor plowman, not the rich friars. Whether the poet saw only this in *Piers Plowman* or chose only this from it we cannot be sure, but two things can be said. First, the tone of reformist urgency that he borrows is a true property of *Piers Plowman*. But second, the *Crede* leaves out what in *Piers Plowman* makes the urgency complex, that its imperatives recoil in an unclarity of means and ends; the *Crede* evicts the complexity in favor of efficacy. The *Crede*'s ablest modern defender does not deny this aspect of the poem, but presumes it.[13] Where *Piers Plowman* ramifies, proffering and withdrawing clarity, the *Crede* narrows.

The *Crede* also narrows *Piers Plowman*'s shuffling of identities into a single exemplary subject position, which the poem as well as its eventual protagonist occupy. It makes the marks of Piers's marginalization the marks of his authority and of its own; it is pleased to imagine itself the gad-fly outsider taking on institutions whose resources it could never match. This claim to a plain-speaking authority that comes from "outsider" status is a premise that writers in this strand of Langland's literary afterlife use with a sureness that becomes blandly routine by the sixteenth century.[14] The very title of the prose tract *I, Plain Piers, Which Can Not Flatter* (*c.* 1546) illustrates how artlessness has become its own justification. Langland's appeal as a supposedly countercultural and counterhegemonic figure seems still strong; the introduction to an anthology of marginalized British poetry at the end of the twentieth century was titled, in avowed reference to *Piers Plowman*, "A Fair Field Full of Folk."[15]

Langland's mighty line: alliterative craft and its afterlife

What Langland plaited together others unravel – that sense of reality revealed by the failure of virtuosity, and the virtuosity that so successfully performs such failure. There is, however, another rift in the "*Piers Plowman* tradition": his admirers rarely try to imitate his poetic line as a reproducible structure of acoustic artifice. The *Crede* tries harder than most, but its author exhausts his metrical resources just keeping isochrony at bay. In most, alliteration is chiefly a positioning, a way of assuming a stance: *I, Plain Piers*, the Protestant tract just mentioned, gestures vaguely at alliteration just long enough to claim its identity ("I Piers plowman fol-lowyng ploughe on felde, my beastes blowing for heate") before quitting an evidently unfruitful labor.[16] The phrase by which Chaucer's Parson dismisses Langland's initial rhyme – "rum ram ruf" – imagines it as pointless ornament, in itself vacuous. But that is because he regards verse itself as pointless ornament: "Ryme hold I but litel bettre," he goes on (*Parson's Prologue*, 43–4). Chaucer recognized the real rhythms of the alliterative line, and evokes its Langlandian form once, also in connection with the Parson. In his *General Prologue* portrait, what catches the unpremeditated vigor of his moralizing voice, and differentiates that voice in the narrator's indirect discourse, is just the premeditated art he later rejects: "shame it is, if a prest take keep, / A shiten shepherde and a clene sheep" (1.504–5). In a single effortless moment Chaucer has evoked this rough speaking voice by casting it as an alliterative line with three alliterating staves, one misplaced, and a functioning caesura ("A shíten shéperd | and a cléne shép"), which also scans obediently as a five-beat heroic line. The portrait, often carelessly called "Wycliffite" in its implications, approaches nearer to an understanding of parochial pastoral care that could be inferred from Langland's poem. (Chaucer's Parson, like the Wycliffites, has "Langlandian sympathies."[17])

By using the sound of *Piers Plowman* this way in passing, Chaucer shows that he not only recognized some of the power of the alliterative line as Langland made it, but that part of its power was connected with a particular idea of speech. To Anne Middleton's idea that the Ricardian poets promoted the idea of a "public voice" one might add distinctions; and one of them is that the narration of *Piers Plowman* is that of a private voice clearing itself to speak out *into* a public, a private self speaking of common things.

To make that brief moment in the *Canterbury Tales*, Chaucer pulls in momentarily a verse form distinct from his own: he does not thereby herald a rethinking of his metrical practice. Even this brief use, however, displays how the alliterative line could function as a counterpoint or rhythmic obbligato moving athwart the forward movement of the iambic line while still settling snugly into it. Spenser's calculated poetic debut, *The Shepheardes Calendar*, has the figure of "Piers," which is usually and rightly taken to draw on Langland's plowman and the curious association with Protestantism he had by then acquired;[18] but he does more interesting work than that. Developing a new medium for narrative poetry, the *Calendar* experiments with metrical and stylistic possibilities that could interrupt and vary a pentameter that had grown banal in its fluency. In the May eclogue (Piers and Palinode), a heavy though irregular alliteration and a four-beat, syllable-variant line combine to make something rougher and fresher than the iambic line planed smooth by previous generations. It does not sound like *Piers Plowman*, but it shows how a master of prosody might imagine fitting the cadence of its alliterative long line into the scale of the heroic line. It also does not sound like anything that might last, but by the time of *The Faerie Queene*, Spenser's strikingly frequent two- and three-term alliteration confidently signals, from its very first lines ("Lo, I the **m**an whose **m**use whilome did **m**aske, / As time her **t**aught"), a filiation from *Piers Plowman*, and a desire to reconcile its stylistic lineage with Chaucer's. The initial rhyme of internal alliteration works together with the final rhymes to strengthen the identity of the line, to keep it audible as a unit, a structural backdrop that leaves him free to vary more audaciously the length of syntactical units and the distribution of pauses, which is one of his contributions to the history of narrative poetics in English.

Langland's poetic line gave an impulse to the sound of Spenser's poetry at the end of the sixteenth century; its effect on the timing and structure of iambic verse was thus propagated through succeeding generations, through the model Spenser had composed. Such an impulse was felt again in the nineteenth century after the publications of Whitaker's and especially of Skeat's editions. Gerard Manley Hopkins had read *Piers Plowman* by the 1870s; he read it again in 1882, around the time he wrote the "preface" that named "the old English verse seen in 'Pierce Ploughman'" one of two historical exemplars of sprung rhythm.[19] This observation does not mean that Hopkins learned the rhythm from Langland – its proximate sources are probably classical – but his rereading in 1882 (when, truth to tell, he did not much like it) might have encouraged the medial caesura by which his later poetry pressed into order the crowding of stresses that were Milton's chief legacy to him. Nearly the opposite process displays itself two generations later with W. H. Auden, who named his major influences as "Dante, Langland, and Pope."[20] Where Hopkins profited from finding Langland's caesura, Auden gained by losing it. An unfinished and unpublished poem written when he was twenty-five is a dream-vision that begins with a calque on the first line of *Piers Plowman*: "In the year of my youth when yoyos came in."[21] The "feld ful of folk" appears as the crowd in St. Pancras. Although there are some stunning Langlandian lines, the effect is slogging and static. Fifteen years later, he tried again at alliterative epic and produced *The Age of Anxiety*. He in a sense repeated Spenser's development, subduing the medial break by dropping dips and enjambing lines. Like the earlier poem, it signals its debts to Langland: the verse begins with a musing speaker staring into a bar-room mirror as Will looks into the bourn. But the enjambments and the shorter line create a strangely private style of vagrant meditation, voices half in public echoing back into their own privacy. The emphatic caesurae of the younger poem reappear here chiefly in the hilarious bits overheard from the bar's radio ("*Definitely different. Has that democratic / Extra elegance. Easy to clean.*").[22]

The poets who used *Piers Plowman* to help remake verse were not much less partial than those who ignored its verse. They respond to and learn from its deliberate artfulness, the technical precision that creates its music. But just as other readers and writers reacted to Langland's fictive urgency as if it were not fictive, these responded as if it were not urgent. Spenser and Auden use it to tame the pentameter, if not to break it; Hopkins must be a rare instance of poetic intensity relaxed under Langland's influence: what he gained from *Piers Plowman* was not urgency but control. This divided response is unsurprising: it is hard at once to cite Langland's poem as a literary exemplar while repeating its apparent impatience with literary exemplarity.

Hard, but not impossible. Shortly after the turn of the fifteenth century, two poems accomplish a counter-literary urgency precisely as they affiliate themselves with *Piers Plowman*. The earlier, known as *Richard the Redeless*, begins in a plausibly Langlandian manner: "And as I passid in my preiere ther prestis were at messe, / In a blessid borugh that Bristow is named."[23] It continues with an alliterative style good enough to fool Skeat, who published the poem as Langland's. The "And" that begins the poem acts as if it continues the action of *Piers Plowman*'s final vision, which begins with Will going "to chirche / To here holly þe masse"; sleeping there, he has the spectacular vision of Piers "peynted al blody," "riȝt lik in alle lymes to oure lord Iesu" (B.19.2–8), which precipitates the final crisis. *Richard the Redeless*'s opening in effect diverts Langland's poem at just that point, offering an alternative vision and an alternative ending, concluding not with Sir Penetrans Domos but with Lancaster's putsch. The bravado impudence with which it hijacks *Piers Plowman* relies on the fiction of continuity to set off the spectacular discontinuity between the host poem and its parasite. The break in literary history represented by *Richard the Redeless* advertises itself in the poem's first line and invites its readers to assume, to feel as palpable, the presence of a history that explains it. It claims to be written just as Richard II and Henry of Lancaster, the king and the usurper, move toward confrontation in Bristol, to be uncertain of the event, and to offer timely counsel that might "meuve" Richard "of mysserewle" (32) and save his throne. The poet, conventionally enough, asks his reader to "amende that ys amysse" in the poem, but he reinvigorates that convention with a bizarre turn: "For yit it is secrette and so it shall lenger, / Tyll wyser wittis han waytid it ouere" (61–2). These lines imply that the reader has stumbled upon an unreleased draft of a document of public importance, an urgent reformist initiative composed, reviewed, and revised in samizdat circulation among an invisible college of intellectuals who (the reader might infer) secretly collaborated to prop a tottering regime, to save their realm and their liege. It speaks as if our reading is an accident it had not anticipated. The recognition dawns that one has discovered the past made in secret, that one is overhearing a conversation one had not been invited to join.

It is all a fiction, too good by half to be true. The poem was probably written some time later, certainly after Richard's deposition and likely after his death. The poem's urgency, its fears and secrecy, its pressing appeal for help, are all part of its game. *Richard the Redeless* works up the electric sensation of political crisis; and a second piece probably by the same poet constructed, ten years later, a fictive literary history on this same fictive pretext. *Mum and the Sothsegger*, as it is now called, complains that the king gives ear to Mum – one politically "mum" about hard public truths – while Sothsegger, the teller of those hard truths, finds himself "yputte into prison or ypyned to deeth / Or ybrent" for his candor. The speaker, finally resolved to tell dangerous truths, does so by pulling from a bag, cataloguing, and summarizing "many a pryue poyse" ("secret poem") already available to diagnose the realm and its ills, poems unknown hitherto because "Mum and his ferys / . . . bare a-weye the bagges" (1342). The truths have been spoken but have remained hidden – and "pryue poyse" suggests that in this bag is *Richard the Redeless* itself, which is itself "yitt . . . secrette" and which, according to this later fiction, remained secret because censorship had kept it so. *Mum and the Sothsegger* seems to imagine that the king's fall proves the fact and the viciousness of this censorship: could Richard have but read *Richard the Redeless*, he would still be king.

These poems are brilliant, but so densely topical that they now are almost unreadable; the effect of historical immediacy they confect depends on having knowledge enough to see the gaps and implications. The device of using such gaps to establish immediacy through tactical unspecificity is, it seems, derived from Chaucer, not Langland, and thus illustrates how what have been taken as a "Chaucer tradition" and a "*Piers Plowman* tradition" are part of something less settled than a tradition, but more undifferentiated.[24] Chaucer, it has become clear, knew *Piers Plowman* at least by some point in the composition of the *Canterbury Tales*,[25] and he derived from it a technique for prompting readers (as would the poets of *Richard the Redeless* and *Mum and the Sothsegger*) to draw inferences that would inflict the feeling of history as an immediate presence that breaks the work's premeditation, but does it in a way that (as had Langland) built those inferences and those experiences on the internal relations of its parts, relatively independent of historical reference.

Explaining this history-effect returns us to the Parson. His tale is a penitential manual, built around an exposition of the seven vices, of the sort ideally to be used in catechizing the faithful in making searching and efficacious confessions. Such an exposition of the vices structures the central didactic moment of Langland's second vision, in the vast and brilliant confession scene of B.5. In the *Tales*, the "confession" that follows upon the Parson's instruction in the most complete manuscripts is Chaucer's "retraction," which, thanking God for any profit his poetry conferred, "revoke[s]" whatever amounts to the translation or composition of mere "worldly vanitees." "Vanities" are literally empty things, things of no value; the sin here renounced is that of wasting time and talent on things of lesser value. It is the fault of which Imaginative accuses Will in the B text of *Piers Plowman* ("þow medlest þee wiþ makynges and myȝtest go seye þi sauter" [12.16]) and of which he, urged by Conscience in the C text, acknowledges himself guilty ("y haue ytynt tyme and tyme myspened" [5.93]). Anne Middleton has shown that Chaucer found in *Piers Plowman* an abrupt rebuke to his own poetic stance, a rebuke implying that he condemned himself to a perpetual adolescence, idled away in fawning spectatorship of courtly leisure. Langland, disastrously and by contrast, suggested that poetry is work for grownups.[26] Middleton focuses on Chaucer's Pardoner, but we can see in the *Tales'* final moments the deep effects of Langland's challenge on their large conception, and how Chaucer responds to *Piers Plowman*'s implication that a poetry willing to face real things will find itself deranged by them. Facing in the Retractions, at the very end of his poem, "the salvacioun of my soule" (10.1089) as a question of uncertain issue (as Langland begins his: "tel me þis ilke, / How I may saue my soule" [B.1.83–4]), he places not only his previous works but the components of the one just completed, under immediate judgment, revoking "the tales of Caunterbury, thilke that sownen into synne" (1086). Every reader who encounters this retraction faces one question: Is it to be construed within the fiction of the *Tales* or not? And the reader who encounters it at the end of a serial reading faces another: Which tales conduce to sin and so are revoked? At just the moment the *Canterbury Tales* concludes, those most basic questions of judgment and design that the fact of conclusion would suggest were by necessity already settled – what to include, what to omit, to what purpose, and on the grounds of what good? – are re-opened and left hanging: Chaucer signals that there has been an authorial re-evaluation but does not communicate its decisions. The reader trying to follow this passage's suggestions can do so only by memorially passing the work just read under the norms of review its author has just invoked. The *Tales* are placed under an enduring sign of re-evaluation and revision, informed by discriminations signaled but not communicated. By this concluding fillip, Chaucer has found a way for making a poem seem ambushed by experience – a device internal to the *Tales* that did not require the historical knowledge that *Richard the Redeless* and *Mum and the Sothsegger* did, and one accomplished in a single, retrospective gesture, without Langland's own balking and redirections. Just as Chaucer conferred a Chaucerian device on some of Langland's followers, he found a Langlandian device that gave the chronic, deliberate incompletion of the *Canterbury Tales* the significance of a final intention.

4

JILL MANN

Allegory and *Piers Plowman*

Piers Plowman is remarkable not only for the variety of allegorical modes that it employs, but also for the way that it freely – even wantonly – mixes the allegorical with features of the real world.[1] The landscape that the dreamer sees at the beginning of the poem sets the "field full of folk," which is thronged with realistic representatives of everyday fourteenth-century society, between the tower of Truth and the "dongeon" inhabited by Wrong. Lady Meed travels to Westminster and debates with Conscience before a king who seems to have fought Edward III's campaign in Normandy (3.189).[2] The series of major personifications that dominates the first half of the poem (Holy Church, Reason, the Seven Deadly Sins, Wit, Study, Clergy...) is joined in the latter part by individuals from history (Trajan) or biblical narrative (Abraham, Moses, the Good Samaritan). And, of course, a pivotal role is played by Piers Plowman himself, poised between allegory and realism, who organizes a society that includes not only knights, ladies, wastrels, and beggars, but also the personified figure of Hunger.

How can Langland manage to hold all these disparate elements together? In attempting to answer this question, I will begin by separating out some of the different strands of his allegory, and the literary traditions from which they spring, and analyzing how they function. These traditions embrace biblical typology, personification-allegory, and narrative allegories based on major metaphors, such as the battle, the journey, or the garden, and I shall suggest that what links these apparently disparate allegorical modes is that they all activate the latent potentialities in the ordinary structures of language.

Medieval writers were familiar with classical definitions of allegory as "other-speaking" (*alieniloquium*), that is, "saying one thing and meaning another," and also with the notion that this "other-saying" most often takes the form of a series of metaphors.[3] Like any metaphor, allegorical narrative brings together two apparently unrelated areas of discourse: plucking a rose and making love to a woman; fighting a battle and resisting temptation; going on a journey and searching for salvation. But the conjunction of the two areas of discourse is not, or should not be, random or arbitrary. As William Empson put it, "Part of the function of an allegory is to make you feel that two levels of being correspond to one another in detail, and indeed that there is some underlying reality, something in the nature of things, which makes this happen. Either level may illuminate the other."[4] That is, allegory works by what Empson calls "Mutual Comparison."[5] Whereas we normally expect to be able to distinguish the "tenor" of a metaphor from its "vehicle ("my love [tenor] is a rose [vehicle]"), and to privilege the former as the subject of the comparison, in allegory tenor and vehicle are on an equal footing, and indeed it is sometimes hard to say which is which, as is often the case in *Piers Plowman*.[6] The crucial element in Empson's description is the tertium quid, the "something in the nature of things" that is suggested by the metaphorical conjunction, and that seems to make it more than a piece of verbal wit. (One might contrast Donne's image of two lovers as a pair of compasses, which strikes us as the product of the poet's ingenuity rather than an existential truth.)

Figura

The tertium quid that links two different phenomena is perhaps clearest in the case of biblical typology, to which Erich Auerbach famously gave the name *figura*.[7] The popular conception of *figura* is that it is a simple matter of pairing off events in the Old Testament with events in the New. Jonah's three days and nights in the belly of the whale are paralleled by the three days and nights that Christ spent in Hell between the Crucifixion and the Resurrection (Matt. 12:39–40); Abraham's willingness to sacrifice his son Isaac is paralleled by God's willingness to sacrifice his son Jesus. This sort of parallelism, as A. C. Charity has said, easily becomes "somewhat wooden, a mechanical game of contrivance," which is "of purely aesthetic interest."[8] Both Auerbach and Charity emphasize that typology implies the constant generation of an open-ended *series* of events, stretching into the future as well as the past. That is, *figura* links two (real, historical) events in such a way that "the first signifies the second, the second fulfills the first," but at the same time both events "have something provisional and incomplete about them; they point to one another and both point to something in the future, something still to come, which will be the actual, real, and definitive event."[9] There is more: this series of recurring resemblances is grounded in an eternal reality, "at all times present, fulfilled in God's providence, which knows no difference of time."[10] Figural events are linked not only horizontally, across the plane of history, but also vertically, in connection with a divine order that "is always present in the eye of God and in the other world, which is to say that in transcendence the revealed and true reality is present at all times, or timelessly."[11]

Figural history is thus, as it were, an allegory written by God, an "allegory in deeds" (*allegoria in factis*), as distinct from an "allegory in words" (*allegoria in verbis*). Its climax is the life of Christ, the true fulfillment of the series of "sub-fulfillments" (to use Charity's term) that precede and follow it, which point not only to other events in this life but also to the eternal reality that they make manifest. Finally, to understand this historical allegory is not just an aesthetic but a moral act, as Charity argues: it acts as a *claim* on the Christian believer, a challenge to realize this eternal reality in the individual life (as the story of Abraham and Isaac makes a claim on the reader's own obedience to the divine will).

In figural allegory the tertium quid is thus the eternal reality that connects historical events in a meaningful way. Personification allegory may seem, in contrast, to have a merely human origin, to be a kind of game. Yet, as has often been noted, this type of allegory quasi-inevitably embodies a "Platonizing" tendency. That is, it assumes or implies that abstractions such as Truth, Justice, Love, Hate, Pride, Avarice and the like are not mere words, but reflections of Ideas that have a real, albeit supra-sensible, existence. (Indeed in the Platonic view they have a *more* real existence than the phenomena of the concrete world that reflect them.) Personification allegory treats the linguistic existence of these entities as evidence of their *actual* existence, and makes their operation in the sensible world visible by linking these abstract nouns with concrete verbs. So, for example, Langland's Seven Deadly Sins manifest themselves in a string of concrete instances of human behavior, through which Avarice or Envy or Sloth can be grasped as active principles at work in human life.

Prudentius

The first use of personifications as the basis of a full-scale narrative is found in Prudentius' *Psychomachia* (*c.* 400), a battle between personified vices and virtues.[12] For Prudentius and his readers, these personifications were not rhetorical fictions, but powerful forces at work in the real world. The misleading translation of the title as "the battle in the soul," rather than "the battle for the soul," has created the assumption that this battle takes place within an individual psyche. In psychological terms, the pairing of opposing vices and virtues looks overly simple and schematic. But, as Hans Robert Jauss has shown, this is also a universal battle, which takes place simultaneously on the plane of history.[13] Prudentius lived at a time when Christianity was under attack, both from without, by paganism, and from within, by heresy (Arius, Pelagius). So the battle begins, not with Pride versus Humility, but with Faith versus Worship of the Old Gods, and after the main battle is over, the triumphant Virtues are treacherously attacked by Discord, whose other name is Heresy (710); disguised as a friend, she strikes Concord with a dagger. The poem also makes reference to a string of biblical figures who bring a historical dimension to the battle: for example, it opens with a recapitulation of events in the life of Abraham, and goes on to invoke Judith's victory over Holofernes (58–71), Job's suffering (163–71), and David's victory over Goliath (291–304), as *figurae* of Chastity, Patience, and Humility. The battle, that is, takes place simultaneously on the plane of a timeless reality in which these abstract forces confront each other, and on the plane of salvation history (*Heilsgeschichte*). It is this dual perspective, linking sensible and supra-sensible realities, that takes the allegory beyond the individual psyche and makes it a vision of the world.

Medieval allegories

Medieval allegories developed the possibilities represented by Prudentius' poem in various directions. I will mention only those that are most relevant to Langland. One line of development is represented by the twelfth-century Latin allegories of Bernard Silvestris and Alan of Lille, which moved away from biblical typology and used personification in the service of a quasi-scientific exploration of the natural world. The goddess Natura is the central figure of Bernard's *Cosmographia* and Alan's *Complaint of Nature*: acting as God's "vicar," she generates and regulates animal, vegetable, and human life. In place of providential history, we have a quasi-autonomous and quasi-timeless world, subject to intrinsic natural laws. Although Langland's enterprise is a very different one, he quite probably shows the influence of these writers in the important role that he gives to natural forces alongside moral and intellectual personifications. Kynde (Nature) plays a key role at several moments, and is even, in one of the poem's most surprising moves, identified with God (9.26–9). Kynde Witte (Natural Intelligence) is also a recurring figure. The beast fable of "Belling of the Cat" that closes the Prologue predicates a naturally established balance between competing forces (cat versus rats and mice), and the personified Hunger is summoned by Piers to play a similarly regulatory role in the plowing of the half-acre (see Chapters 1 and 7).

Dante's *Divine Comedy* develops allegory in the opposite direction: renouncing personification, he extends the role of *figura* by using two

non-biblical persons, Virgil and Beatrice, and investing them with significance through their role in his fictional narrative in addition to their historical lives.[14] They resemble biblical *figurae* in that they are real historical
individuals whose significance transcends the individual. Virgil's role, as
many commentators have suggested, exemplifies the capacities of natural
human reason,[15] the highest achievement possible in pagan times. Both in
history and in Dante's poem, Virgil is a precursor. His *Aeneid* celebrates the
founding of the Roman Empire, which Dante saw as the necessary preparation for the coming of Christianity.[16] His account of Aeneas's visit to the
Underworld is a kind of fictional "sub-fulfillment" of Christ's Harrowing of
Hell. His Fourth Eclogue, with its prophecy of a Golden Age initiated by the
birth of a new race sent down from heaven, was in the Middle Ages seen as
a prophecy of the birth of Christ; the poet Statius, whom Dante and Virgil
meet in Purgatory, claims that this poem was the cause of his conversion to
Christianity (22.64–93). Yet Virgil himself remained a pagan, whose eternal resting-place is in Limbo. Bounded by his historical limitations, he can
guide Dante down through Hell and up the mountain of Purgatory, but no
further.[17] Virgil's place is taken by Beatrice, who arrives at the center of a
complex procession of figures representing biblical history. She is not only
herself, a woman whom Dante loved, she is also a *figura* of Christ.[18] First
saluted with Gabriel's greeting to Mary, "*Benedicta* tue ne le figlie d'Adamo"
("Blessed art thou among the daughters of Adam": 29.85; cf. Luke 1:28) and
the bridegroom's words in the Song of Songs, "*Veni, sponsa, de Libano*"
("Come, bride, from Lebanon": 30.11; cf. Cant. 4:8), she is then welcomed
with the cries that greeted Christ on Palm Sunday: "*Hosanna*" (30.51) and
"*Benedictus qui venis*" ("Blessed are you who come": 30.19; cf. Matt. 21:9).
The masculine ending on the Latin adjective ("Benedictus" not "Benedicta")
is significant: her advent re-enacts the advent of Christ, not only his birth
and his triumphal entry into Jerusalem, but also his Second Coming to
minister the Last Judgment.[19] As with biblical *figurae*, the repetition of a
pattern, even in a fiction, adumbrates the eternal realities that bring it into
being.

Virgil gives way to Beatrice, but his presence is movingly felt in Beatrice's
arrival. The angels cry not only "*Benedictus qui venis*," but also "*Manibus,
oh, date lilia plenis!*" ("Give lilies with full hands": 30.21), a line taken from
the lament for the death of the young Marcellus, nephew of the emperor
Augustus, at the climax of Book Six of the *Aeneid* (883), here turned into a
greeting for Beatrice, who also died young. And as Dante recognizes Beatrice,
he turns to Virgil and expresses his emotion in the words with which Dido
acknowledges her burgeoning love for Aeneas: "I know the signs of the
ancient flame"[20] – only to find that Virgil has vanished.

Ma Virgilio n'avea lasciata scemi
di sé, Virgilio dolcissimo patre,
Virgilio a cui per mia salute die'mi.
(30.49–51)

But Virgil had left us bereft of himself, Virgil sweetest father, Virgil to whom
I gave myself for my salvation.

As with Statius, Virgil has once again enabled another's salvation but not his own. The triple repetition of Virgil's name expresses the grief that plunges Dante into tears, even though he is in Eden and Beatrice has returned. The lament for the lost Marcellus functions both as a celebration of Beatrice's arrival and as an anticipation of the loss of its author Virgil. Joy at the one is rooted in grief for the other. What Dante realizes to the full in Virgil and Beatrice is the emotional potential in *figura*, the human warmth that personifications lack. Whatever historical and spiritual significance these figures have, it is mediated through the deep emotions that bind Dante to them.

The relevance of this to Langland can be judged from Pamela Gradon's suggestion that Piers Plowman is a special kind of *figura*.[21] Even though he lacks historical existence (see Chapter 11), the poem itself creates a quasi-history for him, as his various appearances accumulate and, what is more, endow him with a more-than-individual significance. Initially he seems to be a simple peasant, a type of the honest Christian layman, but as the poem progresses he takes on connotations of the priesthood, of the apostle Peter, of the pope as head of the Church, and of Christ himself. He embodies in himself "Christ's human nature but also man's nature as perfectible by grace."[22] And as Dante recreates in his readers his own emotional responses to Virgil and Beatrice through their appearances in his narrative, so Langland creates through the course of his narrative an increasing emotional attachment to Piers, to the extent that the dreamer swoons at the mention of his name (16.18–19), and at the poem's end he has himself become the object of the spiritual search (20.385–6).

Dante's quotation of the *Aeneid* at the arrival of Beatrice also reminds us that his relation with Virgil is a relation with a *book*: it is through Virgil's writing that Dante "knows" him. Alongside the Bible, the *Aeneid* functions in the *Comedy* as what Maureen Quilligan calls a "pretext" – that is, a text for whose words new meanings are generated by historical (or quasi-historical) events.[23] Langland does not attach the same importance to classical literature, and for him the Bible is the "pretext" par excellence. But he shares with Dante the notion of a personal encounter with the book, an encounter that gives new life to its words and incorporates them into the events of an individual life. The Latin quotations from the Bible that pervade *Piers Plowman* not only derive new meaning from each context but also serve as a constant source of the poetic imagery and metaphor that structure the poem.

Dante's *Comedy* also resembles *Piers Plowman* in that it is focused on the experiences of a first-person narrator. In this Dante had been anticipated by *The Romance of the Rose*, which grounds its entire allegory in the psychology of the first-person narrator. Salvation history here gives way to the account of an individual love-affair; the God of Israel is replaced by the God of Love, the past is pagan and classical (Saturn, Venus, Narcissus), and Nature is primarily important as the stimulator of sexual desire. All very unlike Langland. Yet *Piers Plowman* resembles the *Rose*, not only in its first-person orientation, but also in the use of long expository monologues delivered by the personifications or type figures who aim to instruct the dreamer or each other, whether in the art of love, as in the *Rose*, or in the winning of salvation, as in *Piers Plowman*. Deguileville's *Pilgrimage of the Life of Man*, which explicitly imitates the *Rose* but transforms it into a first-person account of the Christian's journey to the heavenly Jerusalem, is in terms of subject-matter closer to Langland. However, the visual riddles that are Deguileville's most distinctive allegorical mode (for example, Penance with a broom in her teeth, which turns out to represent the cleansing power of the tongue in confession) have only sporadic reflexes in *Piers Plowman* (Anima lacking tongue or teeth, perhaps).[24]

Allegory in *Piers Plowman*

Brief and schematic as this survey of the allegorical tradition is, it will provide a vantage-point from which to appreciate the richness and density of texture that Langland gave his allegory by drawing on these diverse models; it will also help us to understand his own original development of the tradition. A good place to start is the narrative sequence that runs from passus 16 to the end of passus 17, beginning with the Tree of Charity and continuing through the dreamer's encounters with Abraham, Moses, and the Good Samaritan. Throughout this sequence, allegorical personifications and metaphorical motifs are combined with typology in fluid and shifting configurations.

Passus 16: the Tree of Charity

The Tree of Charity begins its life as a figure of speech in Anima's reply to the dreamer's perplexity as to "what charite is to mene" (16.3). Anima explains that it is a tree, whose root is mercy; its trunk is "ruthe" (pity), its leaves are "lele wordes," its blossoms are "buxom [obedient] speche and benigne lokynge," and the whole tree is called Patience. On this tree grows the fruit Charity. So far, this account resembles any number of other medieval "trees of virtues" (or vices), where the tree image is simply a diagrammatic way of organizing relationships between concepts.[25] It is, in David Aers's terms, a "picture model" rather than a "disclosure model."[26] But as Langland explores the different connotations of the image, it gradually comes to life. It acquires a historical dimension when the dreamer expresses a wish to see the Tree and asks where it grows: Anima explains that it grows in a garden "that God made hymselve" (16.13) – that is, the human heart – and that the land is tended by Liberum Arbitrium, under the supervision of Piers Plowman. Though the garden is within the heart, the references to its being made by God himself and cultivated by free will create typological resonances with the Garden of Eden (here conceived as a latent dimension of the human soul). At the same time, the mention of Piers Plowman links the Tree with the surrounding narrative of the poem. Its cultivation ceases to be purely metaphorical, insofar as it recalls the real-life agricultural labor depicted in the plowing of Piers's half-acre. But it also anticipates the plowing of passus 19, where Piers sows the seeds of the four cardinal virtues in man's heart, using an ox-team drawn by the four evangelists. Reality and metaphor meet on the same narrative plane. Against this larger background, the Tree comes to represent not only Charity but also a principle of natural *growth* that manifests itself both for bad – as in Wrath's work grafting lies on to friars who bear "leves of lowe speche," culminating in the "fruit" of their quarrel with parish priests (5.135–46)[27] – and for good – as in Holy Church's description of the complex unfolding of love as "plante of pees" (1.152–8), or the notion that if the members of the religious orders lived like their founders, "Grace sholde growe and be grene thorugh hir goode lyvynge" (15.423).

Anima's mention of Piers Plowman's name at the point we have reached in passus 16 makes the dreamer swoon for joy (16.18–19); Piers's previous role in the narrative of the poem has created a warmth of feeling comparable to that linking Dante to Virgil. Impelled by this emotional impulse, the potential for growth in the tree-image begins to realize itself: when the dreamer awakes from his swoon, the Tree has ceased to be a static metaphor, and both it and Piers himself are present before him. The Tree now has three props that keep it from falling, and Piers explains that they are the three persons of the Trinity, who protect it against attacks from the World, the Flesh, and the Devil (16.25–52). In response to the dreamer's question as to where these three identical-seeming props come from, "In what wode thei woxen and where that thei growed" (16.56), Piers explains that they come from *another* tree, which is the Trinity:

> I shal telle thee as tid what this tree highte.
> The ground there it groweth, goodnesse it hatte;
> And I have told thee what highte the tree: the Trinite it meneth.
>
> (16.61–3)

Some critics have failed to notice that a second tree is introduced here; E. Talbot Donaldson, who did notice, judged this "pluralizing of the tree image" to be an artistic mistake.[28] On the contrary, it seems to me to establish the provisional and shifting nature of the allegorical configurations here, none of which becomes definitive. What we are left with is not a final significance, but a complex sense of a cluster of characteristics united in the image of the tree – what we might call "tree-ness" (see also Chapter 8).

So far the mode is still expository, but from this point on the Tree becomes the center of dramatic action. The dreamer's attention shifts to the fruit of the Tree, which, Piers explains, is of three kinds: Matrimony, Continence, Maidenhood. The dreamer asks Piers to pull down an apple so that he can see what it tastes like; Piers shakes down the apples, which cry out piteously as they fall to the ground, where the devil is waiting to pick them up and carry them off to Hell – "Adam and Abraham and Ysaye the prophete, / Sampson and Samuel, and Seint Johan the Baptist" (16.81–2). The biblical names open out the tree-image toward the plane of history as well as the plane of Langland's fiction. This dual perspective is maintained as Piers, "for pure tene" (anger), seizes the second prop from the Tree and chases after the devil to get back the fruit, "*Filius* by the Faderes wille and frenesse of *Spiritus Sancti*" (16.88). As he takes on the person of Christ, Piers enters salvation history; in the conclusion to the episode, the angel Gabriel tells a maid called Mary that "oon Jesus, a justice sone, moste jouke in hir chambre,"

> Til *plenitudo temporis* tyme comen were
> That Piers fruyt floured and felle to be rype.
> And thanne sholde Jesus juste therfore, and bi juggement of armes,
> Wheither sholde fonge the fruyt – the fend or hymselve. (16.92–6)

Underlying this passage is not only the notion that Jesus is the "fruit" of Mary's womb (Luke 1:42), but also the notion that time has its own growth towards "ripeness." The biblical phrase, "the fullness of time," is used by Paul to refer to the Incarnation (Gal. 4:4–5); it also looks forward to the apocalyptic harvest at the end of time (Apoc. 14:17–20).

The initial static description of the Tree of Charity had blossoms and fruit appearing together (16.7–9). Incorporated into this brief replay of salvation history, the tree-image symbolizes the temporal process, a process that will culminate with the bearing of fruit. The replay is initiated by the dreamer's desire to eat an apple, but although this desire inevitably recalls Adam's Fall, we are not invited to see it as sinful. Instead, it demonstrates his desire to incorporate himself into the events he is beholding, whose outcome is at this point uncertain. Piers's pursuit of the devil has all the angry spontaneity of a farmer chasing small boys stealing apples, "happe how it myghte" (16.87). This fictional re-creation of salvation history demonstrates the typological principle that history is both repetitive and unpredictable: Christ's entry into history is at once the fulfillment of past events and something radically new. A. C. Charity points out that the God of the Old Testament is characterized both by steadfastness and by newness: he is, as it were, the *same* God who will always surprise you. God's ability to create ever new possibilities out of nothing is the very demonstration of his sameness.[29] Langland's account of Piers's pursuit captures this unpredictability. It is a kind of fictional "sub-fulfillment" of salvation history, enabling us to grasp, first, that it has its roots in charity, and secondly, that the process of growth that eventually bears fruit in Mary's womb is routed through pain, death, and anger. Finally, and most interestingly, it suggests that there is meaning not only in the moral and spiritual implications of the Fall, but also in its historical specificities: it prompts us to focus on the question "why a tree?" The typological fulfillment of the tree of Eden in the tree of the Cross (18.359–60) is only one answer to this question; the aspects of "tree-ness" that the developing drama has highlighted suggest others, making *real* trees participatory in the divine mysteries.

Passus 17: Abraham and Moses

The dreamer's motion toward personal involvement in this episode is more fully realized in the dramatization of his personal encounter with salvation history that follows. As he frantically searches for Piers Plowman, the dreamer meets Abraham and Moses on the road. Both are given roles in the "chivalric drama" initiated by the mention of Jesus jousting to reclaim Piers's apples. Abraham is "an heraud of armes" who is seeking a "ful bold bacheler" (16.177–9), while Moses is a "spie" in search of a knight (17.1). Both are also firmly linked with their biblical histories: Abraham relates his personal encounter with the Trinity, in the shape of the three men who visited him "in a somer ... as I sat in my porche" (16.225), while Moses is carrying a "pece of an hard roche" on which are inscribed the commandments given him by the "knyghte" on Mount Sinai (17.1–11). But their biblical names emerge only belatedly or obliquely, and they identify

74

themselves as personifications, Faith (Abraham) and Spes or Hope (Moses). The historical figures of Abraham and Moses are identified with two of the theological virtues named by Paul: faith, hope, and charity (1 Cor. 13:13). Charity, in the form of the Tree, has initiated this narrative sequence, and in the form of the Good Samaritan of the parable, charity will also conclude it. New Testament virtues are thus adumbrated in Old Testament history: Abraham *acts as* Faith when he obeys God's command to kill his son Isaac, and Moses *acts as* Hope when he brings the commandments on which salvation is to be founded (17.16–17). Like Dante's Virgil, they are historical embodiments of a supra-sensible reality.

Yet the encounter with the Good Samaritan shows that the Old Testament virtues of Faith and Hope are insufficient without the New Testament virtue of Charity, of which the Good Samaritan is a fictional *figura* and Christ the real-life fulfillment. In the re-enactment of the parable (17.48–83), Faith and Hope play the roles of the priest and the Levite who are unwilling to offer assistance to the wounded traveler, but the Samaritan tells the dreamer they are to be excused, because the wounded man can be cured only by "the blood of a barn [child] born of a mayde" (17.94). The narrative fiction of traveling and searching, the "chivalric drama" that will culminate in the joust in Jerusalem, creates the sense that salvation history is pressing forward to its fulfillment. Abraham and Moses are not mere figures summoned up from the past; they are poised on the brink of a future development. Abraham is a "herald" because he proclaims the future coming of the "lord" who will deliver from Hell both him and the "patriarkes and prophetes" in his bosom (16.177, 269). Moses is searching for the owner of the "seal" that will give legal validity to the "writ" bearing the commandments (17.3–5), "And that is cros and Cristendom, and Crist theron to hange" (17.6). The Samaritan is encountered riding to the joust in Jerusalem – that is, the Crucifixion.

This episode is, however, more than a reimagined moment of the past. Rather, it is the dreamer's personal encounter with Abraham/Faith and Moses/Hope, an encounter that includes incomprehension and rejection. Why, he asks Hope, is a "newe lawe" necessary, when Abraham has told him that belief in the Trinity is all that is necessary to be saved (17.24–32)? The key phrase here is the dreamer's parenthetical "thus Abraham me taughte" (17.28). This simple phrase has a double reference: it suggests not only the dreamer's encounter with Abraham in the poem's fiction, but also the Christian's encounter with Abraham in the pages of the Bible. As with Dante's Virgil, Abraham "teaches" through his existence in a book. And the book presents the dreamer with a challenge: how to integrate the Old Law with the New.[30] This is a challenge that is not over and done with, part of history, but one that has to be repeatedly confronted and resolved in contemporary life.

The climactic response to this challenge in *Piers Plowman* comes, of course, in Langland's vision of the Harrowing of Hell in passus 18, where Christ invokes the Old Testament principle of "an eye for an eye" to justify his release of the imprisoned patriarchs and prophets (18.339–48). But the integration of the Old and New Testaments is already evident in the commandments inscribed on Moses's piece of rock (17.10–14a). Instead of the familiar Ten Commandments given to the biblical Moses (Exodus 20:1–17), there are only two: "*Dilige Deum et proximum tuum*" ("Love God and your neighbor"). These two injunctions can be found in the Old Testament (Deut. 6:5 and Lev. 19:18), and in passus 15 the double command is said to be "parfit Jewen lawe" (583), but the "glose" to this text, "gloriously writen with a gilt penne," "*In hiis duobus pendet tota lex et prophetia*" ("On these two hang all the law and the prophets"), makes it clear that Langland is quoting Christ's answer to the question "which is the greatest commandment?" (Matt. 22:37–40). On Moses's piece of rock, the new commandments replace the old ones, but as the "gloss" makes clear with its reference to "the law and the prophets," this is because they *subsume* the old ones. What the allegory is bringing to our attention is not just the web of relations underlying salvation history, but the mysterious properties of language. Two different verbal formulations converge on the same meaning, in such a way that one can be understood as mysteriously contained in the other.

Finally, we may note that when this passage of Matthew is repeated in Luke, the reference to the law and the prophets is omitted, but there is a new addition: the questioner asks "who is my neighbor?", to which Christ responds by telling the parable of the Good Samaritan (Luke 10:29–37). So we can see why Langland follows the double command on Moses's rock, "Love God and thy neighbor," with his own retelling of the parable; the links between different passages of the Bible shape his narrative. As one biblical text "glosses" another in a seemingly endless sequence, so Langland's text creates new contexts that elicit fresh meanings from the language of the Bible.

Passus 7: The pardon

The process of condensation that collapses Ten Commandments into two can help us to understand the notorious episode in which Piers Plowman tears the pardon sent by Truth. After nearly 100 lines specifying the various good works to be performed by the different classes of society if they wish to earn Truth's pardon, the document containing this pardon is unfolded, and proves to contain two lines only: "*Et qui bona egerunt ibunt in vitam eternam; Qui vero mala, in ignem eternum*" ("Those who have done well will enter into eternal life, but those who have done evil will enter eternal fire"). The priest who is reading the document alongside Piers declares that he "kan no pardon fynde" (7.111), whereupon Piers, "for pure tene," pulls the document in two and declares that he will abandon his agricultural labour and devote himself to "preieres and penance," weeping instead of sleeping.[31] There is no room here to discuss this problematic passage in full (see also Chapter 1), but my reading of it assumes that "weeping" is the role of the monastic life.[32] Without making the allegory crudely schematic, we can see Piers as passing from an active to a contemplative role, as he finds new meaning in Christ's injunction, "*Ne soliciti sitis*" ("Take no thought [for your life]" [7.127]; Matt. 6:25; Luke 12:22). As for the pardon itself, I agree with A. C. Spearing that the just dispensation of reward and punishment is *already* a pardon, since it represents a "second chance" of salvation, earned by Christ rather than humankind.[33] If its literal words proclaim justice, its "illocutionary force" is a pardon.[34] Or, to put it in Paul's words, the priest can see only the "letter that killeth," and not the "spirit that giveth life" (2 Cor. 3:6). In tearing the document, Piers is symbolically passing through the letter to the spirit that makes the declaration of justice into a simultaneous expression of mercy. St. Bernard provides an illuminating parallel: "when the veil of the letter that kills has been rent asunder by the death of the crucified Word, the Church, led by the spirit of liberty, penetrates to His secrets."[35] As with the Tree of Charity scene, anger marks the spontaneous irruption of the radically new. The typological overtones of Piers's gesture suggest Moses breaking the tablets of the law, Christ overturning the tables of the money-changers, and the rending of the temple veil at his death, signaling this as a moment of change and challenge. This much has been suggested before, but what has not been given proper attention is the oddity of the transition from the longer account of the pardon to the shorter. If Langland had begun with the two-line version and then extrapolated the fuller version as a "gloss" on it, we should not find the procedure strange. Reversing the order makes the relation between the two into a mystery. As with the fusion of the two sets of commandments on Moses's rock, the manoeuvre draws attention to the pregnancy of language, its strange capacity to generate new meanings that transcend the immediate literal sense, realizing its implications in a fuller form.

Far from rejecting the literal, Langland subjects it to intense scrutiny in the attempt to penetrate its latent potentialities. Moses's "patente" (a legal document applicable to all) clearly derives from Paul's reference to the metaphorical "charter of the law" ("chirographum decreti") that was cancelled, "nailed to the Cross," by the Crucifixion (Col. 2:14).[36] Langland gives this image a new twist by connecting it with the hidden metaphor in Matthew 22:40: "In his duobus mandatis universa lex *pendet*, et prophetae." The word "pendet" ("hangs") generates the notion that the seal sought by Moses is "cros and Cristendom and Crist theron to *honge*." The metaphorical seal hanging on the legal "patente" startlingly becomes the reality of Christ hanging on the Cross. Paul's image is dramatically and brilliantly inverted: the document is not cancelled but sealed by the Crucifixion. The submerged pun in the Latin text of the Bible reveals the event that will fulfil the Old Law ("universa lex") in an act of love.

This is just one example of many. For Langland, biblical metaphors are not accidental but a series of encoded messages that link the physical and spiritual worlds. And his poem imitates this aspect of the Bible: images and words accrue their own meanings through repetitions and linkages. This is what Robert Hollander calls "verbal figuralism."[37] The tree image is a good example. We have already seen that the Tree of Charity "grows," as it were, out of the tree of knowledge in the Garden of Eden, but elsewhere other biblical trees are brought into play. For example, in passus 9, Langland is expounding the principle "like father, like son." If you graft on to an elder-tree, he says, it would be surprising if you got sweet apples, citing Christ's words in the sermon on the Mount: "*Numquam colligitur de spinis uva nec de tribulis ficus*" ("Grapes are never gathered from thorns nor figs from thistles"; 9.147–52 and Matt. 7:16). In passus 2, Holy Church draws on the same biblical passage in explaining that Meed is false because she takes after her Father Fals, "right as kynde [nature] asketh": "*Qualis pater, talis filius. Bona arbor bonum fructum facit*" ("Like father, like son. A good tree brings forth good fruit"; 2.25–7 and Matt. 7:17). We have already seen the tree as an image of growth, of the passing of time, and the bearing of fruit. In these two passages it suggests in addition kinship – lineage and natural genetic inheritance. "Adam was as tre and we aren as his apples," as Langland puts it in the C-text version of the Tree of Charity passage (C.18.68). The tree image thus makes contact with the images of kinship that recur throughout the poem, not only in the personifications who, to a degree unusual in narrative allegories, are related to each other, but also, for example, in the idea that Christ is "brother" to humankind (18.377, 394–6).[38] As we have seen, the notion of the tree's cultivation links it with the poem's recurrent agricultural imagery, while the dreamer's desire to eat the apple links it with the pervasive images of eating and drinking.[39] Langland's images, that is, have a tendency to form connecting networks that eventually make up something like an alternative world. What this "virtual" world suggests is that the same principles – "tree-ness" in this instance – are at work in physical reality and in its intangible spiritual counterpart. In the first of the two passages cited above, Wit is talking about real human lineage, whereas in the second, Holy Church is talking about the "kinship" between different vices and the way they are propagated in the world. The insubstantial world of abstractions mirrors the physical world of nature.

So it is no accident that when Langland introduces the problematical relationship of justice and mercy, in the angel's speech to the king in the Prologue, it is expressed in terms of the agricultural imagery that takes on concrete form in the plowing of Piers's half-acre.

> Qualia vis metere, talia grana sere:
> Si ius nudatur, nudo de iure metatur,
> Si seritur pietas, de pietate metas.
> (Prol.136–8)

Sow such grains as you wish to reap. If justice is made naked, you will reap naked justice; if mercy is sown, you will reap mercy.

Once again, the metaphor takes its origin in the language of the Bible: "whatsoever a man soweth, that shall he also reap" (Gal. 6:7). Placed in the context of Langland's agricultural imagery, it suggests that justice and mercy are subject to the same laws of natural growth that are evident in the sowing and harvesting of Piers's half-acre. And as the parallels between metaphors and concrete realities proliferate in the poem, it becomes difficult at times to say which generates which – or even to distinguish the two. The earthly king of the Prologue and passūs 3–4 is clearly paralleled by Christ the king, but is this because Christ is metaphorically called a king, or because the earthly king is a shadowy reflection of a heavenly reality? Behind the two figures we can sense an abstraction that we might name "king-ness," which exists both in eternal and temporal forms.

Language as allegory

By these means Langland's "verbal figuralism" finds common ground with his personifications, which likewise face two ways, toward the concrete physical world and toward the world of supra-sensible reality. And this common ground is visible in the everyday usages of language. For Langland's personifications do not make up a fixed and limited dramatis personae: instead, they are constantly springing into life as a metaphorical verb briefly endows them with a quasi-human activity, and then sinking back into abstract nouns once more. As I have shown elsewhere, this creates constant difficulties for editors of *Piers Plowman*, who must decide when to bestow the capital letter that, according to modern conventions, marks out a personification, and when to withhold it.[40] The inconsistencies that inevitably result can be very illuminating. For example, Langland describes how gluttons "bedden hem esily,"

> Til Sleuthe and sleep sliken hise sydes;
> And thanne wanhope to awaken hym so with no wil to amende.
>
> (2.99–100)

It is not obvious why the editor should take Sloth to be personified while "sleep" and "wanhope" are not, especially since waking someone up is more easily imagined as a human action than stroking someone's sides. Perhaps it is because Sloth appears as a major personification in the confessions of the Seven Deadly Sins – but there "wanhope" is personified too, in Repentance's warning, "Ware thee fro Wanhope, wolde thee bitraye" (5.445).[41] Another illuminating example occurs in Holy Church's advice to the dreamer on the use of his money:

> For rightfully Reson sholde rule yow alle,
> And Kynde Wit be wardeyn youre welthe to kepe,
> And tutour of youre tresor, and take it yow at nede
> For housbondrie and he holden togidres.   (1.54–7)

The verb "rule" and the nouns "wardeyn" and "tutour" make it easy to see Reson and Kynde Wit as personifications (and they appear as such elsewhere in the poem) – but why not "housbondrie" as well? The close association between all three abstractions, and the personal pronoun "he," suggests that they are all three on the same footing. At the same time it is easy to see that the personifications here are merely vivified forms of the kind of metaphor that is frequent in common parlance. "You should be ruled by reason" is an everyday kind of expression that hardly seems to merit the name of personification.

One could cite many more examples of this sort, as any reader of the poem can easily verify by testing the effect of bestowing or withholding capital letters on abstract nouns. The point is not to criticize any editor's practice, but to show how Langland's personifications are constantly coming to be and passing away, arising out of ordinary language and subsiding into it. This is a feature of Langland's allegory that sets it off from other major narrative allegories, which work with a fixed list of personified figures. The function of the poet's practice is to make the reader constantly aware that abstract nouns represent real, if invisible, agents in the world, interacting with (or through) human beings and other corporal entities. The variety of allegorical modes that we encounter in *Piers Plowman* reflects the different modes of being of the agencies at work in human life. Justice and Mercy, for example, enter the poem in the angel's speech, as abstract nouns apparently opposed to each other. At the beginning of passus 18, this opposition is dramatically enacted: they appear as four fully fledged personifications, Truth and Righteousness, Mercy and Peace, who argue vigorously about the possibility of rescuing the damned souls from Hell. The debate is suspended as Langland recounts Christ's Passion and the Harrowing, and resolved in Christ's triumphant speech to Satan in which he explains that he may "do mercy thurw rightwisnesse" (18.390): the Old Law of "a tooth for a tooth" makes it just that a beguiler should be beguiled, and that Christ's death should balance the death of the damned. "*Non veni solvere legem sed adimplere*" (18.350). "Think not that I am come to destroy the law, or the prophets: I am not come to destroy but to fulfill" (Matt. 5:17). The Old Law metamorphoses into the New: Moses's "patente," sealed by the Cross, becomes the "patente" of Pees (18.185) by which salvation is guaranteed. Returning to Truth and Righteousness, Mercy and Peace, we find that their motion toward each other no longer expresses confrontation, but a meeting; they kiss each other and celebrate their reconciliation with a dance that weaves their opposing motions into a harmonious whole. Finally, Langland quotes the biblical text from which this scene has emerged: "*Misericordia et Veritas obviaverunt sibi, Iusticia et Pax osculate sunt*" (18.423a; Ps. 84:11). The Old Testament text finds its fulfillment in the New; the biblical metaphor is realized as an allegorical action. Setting the account of the Harrowing within the outer framework of the debate between the Four Daughters of God is Langland's way of making apparent the invisible forces that are engaged in this pivotal event. The verse of the Psalms, no longer a merely rhetorical expression, finds its moment in reality.

For Langland, then, language – whether in the Bible or in common speech – is the means by which we can grasp the different dimensions of reality, its complex structures and relationships. Language is the key to the "something in the nature of things" that makes allegory more than just a game. Maureen Quilligan argues that the true subject of allegory is language itself. The *allos* (Greek "other") in the word "allegory" names "the fact that language can signify many things at once . . . the often problematical process of meaning multiple things simultaneously with one word."[42] For modern readers, many of the parallels between the material and the immaterial worlds that Langland finds (or creates) in his exploration of metaphor and personification may seem to be the product of cultural history rather than a clue to eternal verities. But the question of what, exactly, language reflects – whether its structures derive from the nature of the world or from the nature of the human brain, and what this would mean in either case – is one with which we are still engaged.

PART II

Historical and intellectual contexts

5

ROBERT ADAMS

The Rokeles: an index for a "Langland" family history

Introduction

Virtually all modern scholarly readings of *Piers Plowman* have labored under a misconception about the author: that we must either take at face value, and be content with, the attenuated, stereotyped autobiography provided by the B and C versions of the poem, or that we must adopt an affected agnosticism about the author's real circumstances, beyond what is provided by a near-contemporary in the most direct surviving evidence identifying *Piers Plowman* with a William Langland: a single note written in an early fifteenth-century hand at the end of a manuscript copy of a C version of *Piers Plowman*, now kept in Trinity College, Dublin (MS 212, fol. 89v). The note, which was discovered in the 1830s by the editor and British Library curator Sir Frederic Madden, reads as follows:[1]

> Memorandum quod Stacy de Rokayle pater Willielmi de Langlond qui stacius fuit generosus et morabatur in Schipton' vnder Whicwode tenens domini le Spenser in comitatu Oxon' qui predictus Willielmus fecit librum qui vocatur Perys Ploughman.

> Note that Stacy de Rokele [was] the father of William Langland; this Stacy was of noble birth, and dwelled in Shipton-under-Wychwood, as a tenant of Lord Spenser in the county of Oxfordshire; which aforesaid William made the book that is called *Piers Plowman*.[2]

If one opts to rely on the poem alone, Langland can be seen as a clever but perpetually impoverished itinerant clerk in lower religious orders. This version of Langland may have worked a day-job as a chancery scribe in London, lived in a low-rent neighborhood and was trying to support a wife and daughter with occasional chantry jobs and spiritual directorates while disdaining physical labor as improper for a person of his educational attainments (see the "autobiographical" passage in C.5.53–65). By contrast, if one takes the agnostic view, one can ignore the poem's autobiographical references as rhetorical ploys and dismiss the entire topic of authorial biography with a brief generalization such as this: the poem's philosophical sophistication, combined with the information from the early fifteenth-century Trinity manuscript note, suggests a considerably less seedy author than the overt references in the fiction – a younger son of a country gentleman, someone who may, in fact, have been a member of one of the more conservative monastic orders.

Both of these approaches, however, although capturing fragments of a larger truth, are outdated on account of their timidity and exclusivity. Thanks to the recent work of Oxford geneticist Bryan Sykes,[3] we now know that, for the British Isles at least, any two modern men of Anglo ethnicity who share a surname are likely to be related as family, albeit distantly; moreover, the likelihood of a blood relationship becomes much greater if the surname in question is moderately uncommon. This likelihood increases geometrically as one moves backwards through time into a world much more thinly populated than our own, a world where few people even had surnames. As scholars from the nineteenth century on have recognized, at least the note in the Trinity manuscript provides reliable information about Stacy (Eustace) de Rokayle (or Rokele): there was a nobleman by this name living in the necessary period in Shipton-under-Wychwood as a tenant of the Despensers.[4] But if we do accept the reliability of the genealogy indicated in the Trinity manuscript's note, we are immediately confronted with a relatively uncommon surname, Rokayle (aka Rokele), and with an abundance of further surviving documentary evidence for the lives and social station of that family, a very prominent and widespread late medieval clan. If the author of *Piers Plowman* was in fact a Rokele, he would have been thoroughly exposed to an upper-class worldview and had access to assets quite different from those usually assumed for him.

Why would the poet take the name "Langland"? The possible answers to this are both more intriguing and less surprising than they might be in a later period, when surnames were more settled (and stage-names or *noms de plume* more defined conventions). It has long been suggested that the different name was evidence that William was a bastard son; and, even though the poem occasionally takes direct aim at bastards, this does not rule out the possibility of the author's own illegitimacy.[5] Perhaps the name was borrowed from his mother's patronym. "Langland" might have further significance for the poet's life-long involvement in his poem and its issues: a "long land" is a strip of land that a plowman plows (*OED*, s.v. "land," sb., 1.7). It is clear that the poet is identifying himself still more precisely and idiosyncratically when he says "I have lyued in londe...my

86

name is longe wille" (B.15.152), and the same nickname may lurk behind the mythical region mentioned in the poem as the Lond of Longing (B.11.7–9, 46–7; cf. C.11.169–73, 194–5).[6] The situation may be more complicated than his using a narrowly literary pseudonym, however; a legal record from July 1385 mentions "William, called Long Will" ("Willelmus vocatus Longwyll"), indicating – if this is our poet – that Langland may have used the nickname "Long Will" in life as well as literature, and moreover that he may have sometimes preferred this nickname to any surname at all.[7]

Notwithstanding these complexities of Langland's self-identification, we have a major clue to his background and family history in the link to the Rokeles convincingly provided by the memorandum in the Trinity College manuscript. From the twelfth through the fourteenth century, Rokeles were often prominent in their home counties (primarily Essex, Kent, Norfolk, Suffolk, Buckinghamshire, and Wiltshire) and sometimes were positioned at the very pinnacle of the landed gentry, just below the nobility proper. In fact, one of the few details revealed in *Piers Plowman* about Langland's own life story tends to confirm this elite status – the patronage he enjoyed while young:

> Whan y ʒut ʒong was, many ʒer hennes,
> My fader and my frendes foende me to scole
> Tyl y wyste witterly what holy writ menede
> And what is beste for the body, as the boek telleth,
> And sykerost for þe soule, by so y wol contenue.
> And foende y nere, in fayth, seth my frendes deyede
> Lyf þat me lykede but in these longe clothes.
> Yf y be labour sholde lyuen and lyflode deseruen,
> That laboure þat I lerned beste þerwith lyuen y sholde:
> *In eadem vocacione qua vocati est &c.* (C.5.35–43a)

The line that demands our attention especially is "My fader and my frendes foende me to scole" (36), for it is a clear indication that the patronage the poet enjoyed secured him an education he could parlay into a livelihood, about which he would go on to rationalize in the remainder of passus 5 of the C text. Langland does not appear in Emden's registers for the universities of Oxford or Cambridge – though an older relative of his, a Benedictine monk from Norfolk, took a doctorate in theology at Oxford in 1332–3 (see the index below) – but he certainly had a professional level of education in theology.[8] But if Langland was not a member of a traditional religious order (which he was not, unless the C-version "autobiography" is pure fiction), obtaining such an education in the fourteenth century would have been massively expensive.[9] This means that Langland probably had, at least for a period of years when he was a student, access to disposable wealth beyond the means of all but a very few people. That wealth almost certainly came, if not directly from his father (who died sometime after 1361), from his extended family, patrons, and friends ("my frendes").

David Aers touched on Langland's obvious "Tory" bias twenty-five years ago, when he noted that the stern attitude displayed toward the laborers of the half-acre, in passus 6 of the B version of *Piers Plowman*, is precisely that of the great landholders.[10] However, since then no one has ever addressed the massive evidence of a profound social distance that separated "William de la Rokele," at least in his own mind, from the pious author of *Patience* no less than from the City poets, Chaucer and Gower. Bits of the evidence for this social chasm are, as Aers noticed, implicit in *Piers Plowman* itself, but much of it is extrinsic. Illuminating that evidence is what I hope to do with the historical index below, by supplying some hitherto neglected references to Langland's extended family and their prominent public role in his own time as well as in the generations that preceded his birth.

In the interest of brevity, I have usually provided only one, or at most two, citations for each Rokele listed (though some of them have many more available and two of them have dozens). Moreover, the materials available in printed editions or online represent only a small proportion of the surviving medieval documents.[11] Yet although we lack "life records" for the poet of *Piers Plowman* other than the Trinity manuscript note and the intriguing self-portrayals in the poem, we can use this family network to outline and provide the tools to help excavate the family and the world from which he came.

Index to the Rokeles

Names of major figures are printed in small capitals. Since the first names often repeat, as is common in medieval families, individuals with the same first name are distinguished by century (e.g., XIII) and listed by number of those holding that name in that century (e.g., #3). Known or suspected relatives who bear a different surname are given entries as well, indented, following the Rokele to whom they were most closely related.

XI. *(The eleventh century)*

WILLIAM DE LA ROCHELLE (late 11th c.): royal messenger and documentary witness in the courts of William Rufus and Henry I

[*Regesta Regum Anglo-Normannorum*, 4 vols., ed. H. W. C. Davis, Charles Johnson, H. A. Cronne, and R. H. C. Davis (Oxford, Clarendon Press, 1913–69), 1:85, 110; 2:58]

XII. *(The twelfth century)*

Godefrid de la Rachele (early 12th c.): grandfather of Richard de la Rokele [XII, #1]; lived in reign of Henry I (1100–35)

[*Pedigrees from the Plea Rolls: collected from the pleadings in the various courts of law, A.D. 1200 to 1500*, ed. George Wrottesley (London [1905]), 261]

HUMPHREY DE ROKELE (mid 12th c.): served as a witness, *c.* 1135–40, at the founding of Walden Abbey (Essex) by Geoffrey de Mandeville, Earl of Essex; he may have been one of Geoffrey's household knights

[John Leland, *Antiquarii de rebus britannicis collectanea* (Oxford: Sheldonian Theatre, 1715), 1:32; Leland suggests 1136 as the date of the founding; but see *The Book of the Foundation of Walden Monastery*, ed. Diana Greenway and Leslie Watkiss (Oxford, Clarendon Press, 1999), 171; they suggest *c.* 1140]

1. Richard de la Rokele (mid 12th c.): father of William de la Rokele [XII, #1]; held land in Essex

[*Pedigrees from the Plea Rolls: collected from the pleadings in the various courts of law, A.D. 1200 to 1500*, ed. George Wrottesley (London [1905]), 261]

2. Richard de la Rokele (late 12th c.): earliest known Rokele tenant at Appleton, Norfolk; probably associated with Geoffrey Fitz Peter, Earl of Essex

[R. H. Mason, *The History of Norfolk, from Original Records and Other Authorities Preserved in Public and Private Collections, Part V* (London, Wertheimer, Lea & Co., 1885), 48]

WILLIAM DE LA ROKELE, aka "William Doo" (mid 12th c.): the grandfather of Richard de la Rokele [XIII, #3] and holder of South Ockendon, Essex

[*Victoria History of the County of Essex*, ed. W. R. Powell (Oxford University Press, 1978), 7:118]

> WILLIAM D'OU (mid 12th c.): probably the maternal uncle of William de la Rokele [XII, #1]; a tenant of the Mandeville earls of Essex
>
> [*The Red Book of the Exchequer*, ed. Hubert Hall (London, Her Majesty's Stationery Office, 1896), 1:345–47]

2. WILLIAM DE ROKELLA (mid 12th c.): listed in the 1160s as holding land at Boarstall and Brill (Buckinghamshire), both apparently as tenant in chief

[*The Great Roll of the Pipe for the Thirteenth Year of the Reign of King Henry the Second, A.D. 1166–67* (London: The Pipe Roll Society, 1889), 102; *The Great Roll of the Pipe for the Fifteenth Year of the Reign of King Henry the Second, A.D. 1168–69* (London, The Pipe Roll Society, 1890), 87]

XIII. *(The thirteenth century)*

EUSTACE DE LA ROKELE (late 13th c.): great-grandfather of William Langland; main tenancy at Wotton Underwood, Buckinghamshire

[Samuel Moore, "Studies in 'Piers the Plowman,'" *Modern Philology* 12 (1914), 46]

GREGORY DE ROKE(S)LE [also spelled "Ruxley"] (late 13th c.): merchant and goldsmith; twice elected mayor of London in the late thirteenth century (1275–82, 1284–6); perhaps not actual kin to the other major Rokele family in the eastern London suburbs, but he owned several properties in Kent (Ruxley, North Cray, and Lullingstone) near their key manor of Beckenham

[*DNB* (2004), under "Ruxley"]

Peter de la Rokele (late 13th c.): leader of a group sued for trespass by the Abbess of Lacock (Wiltshire) in 1278

[*Calendar of the Close Rolls* [Edward I], *A.D. 1272–1279* (London, Her Majesty's Stationery Office, 1900), 1:507]

PHILIP DE LA ROKELE (late 13th c.): eldest son of Richard de la Rokele [XIII, #3]; inheritor of his primary holdings in Essex and Kent; father of Maud de la Rokele [XIV]

[*Victoria History of the County of Essex*, ed. W. R. Powell (Oxford University Press, 1978), 7:118]

1. Richard de la Rokele (early 13th c.): granted a tenancy at Trowse (near Norwich) by William de Curzon, in a marriage settlement; probably a close relative of Richard de la Rokele [XII, #2]

[Francis Blomefield and Charles Parkin, *An Essay towards a Topographical History of the County of Norfolk* (London, 1806), 5:459]

2. Richard de la Rokele (mid 13th c.): holder of several Norfolk properties, e.g., Appleton and Watton; probably grandson of Richard de la Rokele [XII, #2] and relative of Richard de la Rokele [XIII, #3]

[Francis Blomefield and Charles Parkin, *An Essay towards a Topographical History of the County of Norfolk* (London, 1808), 8:329]

3. RICHARD DE LA ROKELE (mid 13th c.): Chief Justiciar of Ireland, 1261–5; grandson of Geoffrey Fitz Peter, Earl of Essex; close friend of Edward I; estates in several counties, mainly Essex

[E. B. Fryde and D. E. Greenway, *Handbook of British Chronology*, 3rd edn. (Cambridge University Press, 1986), 161]

> JOHN FITZ GEOFFREY (mid 13th c.): Chief Justiciar of Ireland, 1245–56; son of Geoffrey Fitz Peter, Earl of Essex; uncle to Richard de la Rokele [XIII, #3]
>
> [Robin Frame, "Historians, Aristocrats, and Plantagenet Ireland, 1200–1360," in *War, Government and Aristocracy in the British Isles c. 1150–1500: Essays in Honour of Michael Prestwich*, ed. Chris Given-Wilson *et al.* (Woodbridge, Boydell and Brewer, 2008), 141–3]

4. Richard de la Rokele (late 13th c.): a younger son of Richard de la Rokele [XIII, #3]; tenant, from eldest brother Philip [XIII], of several properties in Norfolk (Colkirk and Gateley)

[*Calendar of Inquisitions Post Mortem* [Edward I] (London, His Majesty's Stationery Office, 1912), 3:216–17]

5. RICHARD DE LA ROKELE (late 13th c.): a friend of William Beauchamp, Earl of Warwick; frequent legal witness for him; probably from Buckinghamshire

[Caroline Burt, "A 'Bastard Feudal' Affinity in the Making? The Followings of William and Guy Beauchamp, Earls of Warwick, 1268–1315," *Midland History* 34 (2009), 156–80; esp. see 167, table 2 and n. 51]

1. William de la Rokele (early 13th c.): the father of Richard de la Rokele [XIII, #3]; holder of South Ockendon, Essex

[*Victoria History of the County of Essex*, ed. W. R. Powell (Oxford University Press, 1978), 7:118]

2. William de la Rokele (mid 13th c.): a younger brother or cousin of Richard de la Rokele [XIII, #3]; he was sheriff of Waterford

[*Calendar of Patent Rolls* [Henry III], *1266–1272* (London, His Majesty's Stationery Office, 1913), 6:443]

3. William de la Rokele (mid 13th c.): a younger son of Richard de la Rokele [XIII, #3]; stayed behind in Dublin to manage family affairs when his father left on crusade (1270)

[*Calendar of Ormond Deeds*, ed. Edmund Curtis (Dublin, Stationery Office, 1932–43), 3:383–4]

xiv. *(The fourteenth century)*

Alys de la Rokele (mid 14th c.): member of the Rokele family at Trowse (Norfolk); she received a still extant personal letter, *c.* 1340, filled with current gossip about the French war; author of the letter was probably Richard de la Rokele [xiv, #3]

[For the text of the letter, see Helen Richardson, "The Affair of the Lepers," *Medium Aevum* 10 (1941), 20]

EUSTACE DE LA ROKELE (mid 14th c.): father of William Langland; held land in Oxfordshire and was active in public life through at least 1361

[Ralph Hanna, *William Langland* (Aldershot, Variorum, 1993), 26–7]

GODFREY DE LA ROKELE (mid 14th c.): steward of the Earl of Northampton, William de Bohun; royal steward of the honor of Reylegh and supervisor for repairs at Hadleigh Castle in the 1370s

[*Calendar of the Patent Rolls* [Edward III], *1367–1370* (London, His Majesty's Stationery Office, 1913), 14:432]

1. JOHN DE LA ROKELE (mid 14th c.): a prominent lawyer from Easthorpe, Essex; involved in land transactions with a relative named William de la Rokele [xiv, #7]

[*Court Rolls of the Borough of Colchester*, 2 vols., ed. and trans. Isaac Herbert Jeayes ([Colchester], Borough of Colchester, 1921–41), 1:xxix]

2. John de la Rokele (mid 14th c.): a Benedictine monk from Norfolk who took his doctorate in theology at Oxford in 1332–3

[Joan Greatrex, "Monk Students from Norwich Cathedral Priory at Oxford and Cambridge, *c.* 1300–1530," *English Historical Review*, 106 (1991), 581]

3. John de Roke(s)le (mid 14th c.): rector of the church of Chelsfield; grandson of Gregory de Roke(s)le [xiii]; tenant of Lullingstone, Kent; died in 1361

[Edward Hasted, *The History and Topographical Survey of the County of Kent* (Canterbury, W. Bristow, 1797), 2:541]

MAUD DE LA ROKELE (mid 14th c.): born in Ireland in 1286, granddaughter of Richard de la Rokele [xiii, #3]; wife of Maurice le Bruyn; last Rokele tenant at South Ockendon, Essex; died before 1355

[*Victoria History of the County of Essex*, ed. W. R. Powell (Oxford University Press, 1978), 7:118]

PETER DE LA ROKELE (early 14th c.): grandfather of William Langland; held land in several counties, primarily in Buckinghamshire; royal justice for Lincolnshire, 1324

[*Calendar of the Close Rolls* [Edward II], *1323–1327* (London, Her Majesty's Stationery Office, 1898), 4:101, 120]

1. Philip de la Rokele (early 14th c.): probable grandson of Sir Richard de la Rokele [XIII, #3]; apparently inherited his tenancy near Colchester

[R. H. Britnell, *Growth and Decline in Colchester, 1300–1525* (Cambridge University Press, 1986), 45]

2. Philip de la Rokele (mid 14th c.): probable great-grandson of Sir Richard de la Rokele [XIII, #3]; a lawyer in Colchester

[*Court Rolls of the Borough of Colchester*, 2 vols., ed. and trans. Isaac Herbert Jeayes ([Colchester], Borough of Colchester, 1921–41), 1:xxix]

1. Richard de la Rokele (early 14th c.): son of William [XIII, #2]; petitioned Edward II in 1318 for restoration of his father's Irish holdings

[*Calendar of the Close Rolls* [Edward II], *1313–1318* (London, Her Majesty's Stationery Office, 1893), 2:531]

2. Richard de la Rokele (early 14th c.): holder of several Norfolk properties, e.g., Appleton and Watton; father to William [#5]

[*Inquisitions and Assessments Relating to Feudal Aids...AD 1284–1431* (London, His Majesty's Stationery Office, 1904), 3:408, 450]

3. RICHARD DE LA ROKELE (mid 14th c.): a younger son of Richard [#2]; charged with supervision of the property of Dowager Queen Isabella at Castle Rising, Norfolk

[*A Descriptive Catalogue of Ancient Deeds in the Public Record Office* (London, Her Majesty's Stationery Office, 1894), 2:159]

4. Richard Rokayle (mid 14th c.): a close relative of William Langland, who sold family land near Shipton in 1355 to John de Churchill

[National Archives reference for this transaction is CP 25/1/190/21, number 5. A summary from the Feet of Fines, as well as an image of the document, is available at www.medievalgenealogy.org.uk/fines/abstracts/CP_25_1_190_21.shtml]

1. Robert de Rokele (early 14th c.): held the tenancy at Astwood (Bucks.) *c.* 1306–25

[*Victoria History of the County of Buckingham*, ed. William Page (London, Constable, 1927), 4:270–1]

2. Robert de la Rokele (mid 14th c.): held "Rockell's Farm" near Saffron Walden (Essex) from Humfrey de Bohun, Earl of Hereford and Essex in 1372

[Philip Morant, *The History and Antiquities of the County of Essex* (London, 1768), 2:590]

Roger Rokayle (late 14th c.): a close relative of William Langland, who sold family land near Shipton in 1391

[National Archives reference numbers for this transaction are E 326/3268 and E 326/3269]

Thomas de la Rokele (mid 14th c.): a Norwich merchant who seems to have had a limited partnership in the 1340s with another local merchant named William But

[*Calendar of the Close Rolls* [Edward III], *1339–1341* (London, Her Majesty's Stationery Office, 1901), 5:168, 428]

Walter de la Rokele (early 14th c.): a member (with his brother/cousin William) of the Knights Templar; forced to "recant" in 1309; probably from Oxfordshire or Berkshire

[*The Proceedings against the Templars in the British Isles*, ed. Helen J. Nicholson (Farnham, Ashgate, 2011), 1:107, 162, 177 (for the testimony of Walter)]

1. William de Rokele (early 14th c.): a member (with his brother/cousin Walter) of the Knights Templar; forced to "recant" in 1309; probably from Oxfordshire or Berkshire

[*The Proceedings against the Templars in the British Isles*, ed. Helen J. Nicholson (Farnham, Ashgate, 2011), 1:107, 162, 177 (for the testimony of Walter)]

2. WILLIAM DE LA ROKELE (early 14th c.): first cousin to the poet's father, Eustace, and father of William Langland's second cousin; frequently in trouble with the law when he was young

[*Calendar of the Patent Rolls* [Edward II], *1313–1317* (London, Her Majesty's Stationery Office, 1898), 2:425]

3. William de Rokele (early 14th c.): vicar of the parish church of St. Peter and St. Paul in Newport Pagnell, 1303–19

[George Lipscomb, *The History and Antiquities of the County of Buckingham* (London, J. & W. Robins, 1847), 4:286]

4. WILLIAM DE LA ROKELE (mid 14th c.): Langland's second cousin, in charge of four of Queen Philippa's estates in the 1350s and 1360s; son of William [#2]

   [*Calendar of the Close Rolls* [Edward III], *1369–1374* (London, Her Majesty's Stationery Office, 1911), 13:260]

5. William de la Rokele (mid 14th c.): holder of several Norfolk properties, e.g., Appleton and Watton

   [*Inquisitions and Assessments Relating to Feudal Aids...AD 1284–1431* (London, His Majesty's Stationery Office, 1904), 3:523]

6. William de Rokele (mid 14th c.): a young clerk in Colchester, active in local politics and real estate in the 1360s; presumably a son of the Colchester Rokeles

   [*Calendar of the Patent Rolls* [Edward III], *1358–1361* (London, His Majesty's Stationery Office, 1911), 11:57]

7. WILLIAM DE LA ROKELE (mid 14th c.): priest of Redgrave (Suffolk), *c.* 1356–62; a relative of the Easthorpe (Essex) lawyer, John de la Rokele [XIV, #1]; used by John in 1361 as a trustee for his properties

   [BL Harley Charter 55.E.4; see *Catalogue of Seals in the Department of Manuscripts in the British Museum*, ed. W[alter] de G[ray] Birch (London, British Museum, 1887–1900), 3:445]

8. William de la Rokele (mid 14th c.): priest of Easthorpe (Essex), *c.* 1352–6; presumably the same person as William de la Rokele [XIV, #7]; co-owned several properties with John de la Rokele [XIV, #1] near Colchester

   [*Calendar of Entries in the Papal Registers Relating to Great Britain and Ireland: Papal Letters, vol. 3*, ed. W. H. Bliss and C. Johnson (London, Her Majesty's Stationery Office, 1897), 487; also *Feet of Fines for Essex* (Colchester, Wiles & Son, 1949), 3:116, #1134]

9. WILLIAM ROKELE (mid 14th c.): traveling companion of Thomas Beauchamp II on trip to Brittany, 1368

   [*Calendar of the Patent Rolls* [Edward III], *1367–1370* (London, His Majesty's Stationery Office, 1913), 14:134]

10. WILLIAM ROKELE (mid 14th c.): took the first tonsure from the Bishop of Worcester, *c.* 1339

[*A Calendar of the Register of Wolstan de Bransford, Bishop of Worcester, 1339–49*, ed. R. M. Haines (London, Her Majesty's Stationery Office, 1966), 199]

xv. *(The fifteenth century)*

Margareta Rokyll (early 15th c.): friend and probable servant of the Countess of Hereford; listed as a witness in her 1425 will

[*Register of Henry Chichele, Archbishop of Canterbury, 1414–1443*, ed. E. F. Jacob (Oxford University Press, 1938–43), 2:322]

Robert Rokele (early 15th c.): filed his will at Saffron Walden (Essex) in 1422; probably a son or grandson of Robert de la Rokele [xiv, #1]

[National Archives: PROB 11/2B; for weblink, use www.nationalarchives. gov.uk/documentsonline/detailsresult.asp?queryType=1&resultcount= 1&Edoc_Id=1053869]

Rokell (early 15th c.): servant of the Duke of York; listed as a beneficiary in his 1415 will

[*Register of Henry Chichele, Archbishop of Canterbury, 1414–1443*, ed. E. F. Jacob (Oxford University Press, 1938–43), 2:65]

6

JAMES SIMPSON

Religious forms and institutions in *Piers Plowman*

Which comes first: institutions or selves? Liberal democracies operate as if selves preceded institutions, since electors choose their institutional representatives, who themselves vote to shape institutions. Liberal ideology, indeed, traces its genealogy back to heroic moments of the lonely, fully formed conscience standing up against the might of institutions; those heroes (Luther is the most obvious example) are lionized precisely because they are said to have established the grounds of choice: every individual will be able to choose, in freedom, his or her institutional affiliation for him or herself. The act of choice is, in such a worldview, the initiating act from which institutions follow. Institutions are secondary to selves, and especially to the initiating act of conscience.

The extreme, libertarian strand of that tradition regards all institutions with suspicion. Not only government, but schools and all government agencies, along with all churches not one's own, are not the solution, but the problem. This tradition champions what might be called a "liberty to" model of liberty, as distinct from what might be called a "liberty from" model. "Liberty to" proclaims this definition of liberty for the individual: "the condition of being able to act or function without hindrance or restraint; faculty or power to do as one likes" (*OED*, sense 2a). "Liberty from," by contrast, recognizes the priority of institutions that grant liberties to individuals or corporations.[1] In its extreme (though by no means uncommon) form, "liberty to" arrogates for itself what had been the sole prerogative of God, to act in absolute freedom.[2]

Such an ideology, in both its less and more extreme forms (i.e., its liberal and libertarian forms), will produce its characteristic forms of history and literary criticism. Its historians will write institutional histories as histories of dissent from institutions. This tradition locates dissent because it admires dissent, persuaded as it is that the fully formed conscience is capable of producing persuasive, ethically impressive alternatives to oppressive institutions.

The literary critics who subscribe to such an ideology will treat the individual as a self-contained unit, independent of, and prior to, the institutions within which the individual is situated. The individual in this tradition is, as the word implies, indivisible; the individual is, in Lee Patterson's words, "understood not as conditioned by social practices and institutions but as an autonomous being who creates the historical world through self-directed efforts."[3] The function of literary criticism will be to delineate "character," and to locate unmediated agency as a desired ideal, rather than to analyze the ways in which self and institutions are mutually dependent. For both historians and literary critics in the liberal tradition, the individual is separable from, and prior to, institutions.

The liberal tradition and its offshoot the libertarian tradition trace their genealogy principally to the Reformation of the sixteenth century. What is the news on this question from the pre-Reformation church? By and large, pre-Reformation culture places the institution before the self. The self, and particularly the conscience as the source of deepest ethical and spiritual counsel, is intimately shaped by the institution of the church. This shaping is both ethical and spiritual; by no means least, it ensures the soul's salvation, through administering the sacraments especially of baptism, penance, and the Eucharist. The conscience is not a lonely entity in such an institutional culture. It is, rather, the portable voice of accumulated, communal history and wisdom: it is, as the word itself suggests, a *con-scientia*, a "knowing with."[4] This tradition will admire and produce histories not of dissent but of institution-building and institutional commitment, such as church history and hagiography. It will regard the institution as prior to the individual; it will also represent selves experiencing individuality as an intensely painful problem.

The late fourteenth-century English poem *Piers Plowman* admires dissent; it recognizes the need for new institutional forms, and it trusts, up to a point, the capacity of conscience to generate those new institutional forms. Does this mean that Langland regards the self as prior to institutions? Does this mean that Langland's protagonist Will is a self-contained, indivisible "character," an abbreviation for "William," as the great nineteenth-century editor W. W. Skeat refers to him?[5] Does this mean that for Langland institutions are secondary to the prior entity of the self?

In this chapter we will see that, for Langland, the self is fundamentally dependent on institutions, and in particular the institution of the church. For Langland, ecclesiology – how the church is shaped as an institution – is not separable from ideal forms of selfhood. For him, ecclesiastical satire is inseparable from imagining the self's ideal form. For all that, Langland's is indeed a poem of dissent, in which the conscience does challenge the church. One hundred and forty years before Luther's courageous act of conscience-driven dissent in 1517, Langland imagines that same dissent. He is also, however, deeply skeptical of that dissenting act, since he knows that a damaged church produces a damaged conscience. This is one of the many reasons why Langland's is a great poem: *Piers Plowman* inherits a model of the church that had become untenable, and it knows it. The poem's extraordinary and disrupted range of formal choices is the form that knowledge takes.

Religious institutions

The pre-Reformation Western Church is a large and variegated entity. The purview of Langland's poem takes many of these institutions into account, but focuses with special energy on one ecclesiastical institution, that of the friars. This chapter begins by sketching the institutional shape of the church.[6] In the penultimate section, I show why Langland should focus so vigorously and so critically on the friars.

The principal division within the pre-Reformation church was between the secular clergy and the religious orders. The secular clergy (from Christian Latin *saecularis*, "of the world") was devoted to the care and instruction of the laity (from Greek *laius*, "people"), or people, especially through administering the sacraments. Secular clergy were located in parishes, and organized around a bishop, whose principal seat, or *cathedra* (meaning "seat" in Greek), was located in a cathedral, itself situated in a major urban center. In Langland's England, the Archbishop of Canterbury held primacy over that of York. And the archbishops were in turn ultimately subject to the jurisdiction of the pope in Rome.

The religious orders, by contrast, were those orders subject to a *regula*, or rule. For the most part, the religious lived in communities bound by their rule; in late medieval England there were upwards of 800 such communities, living under eight or so major types and sub-types of rule.[7] The main divisions among the religious orders were between monks (and nuns), canons, and friars. Monasteries (so called from Greek *monos*, meaning "single") were first founded in the West in the early sixth century by St. Benedict, in the wake of the fall of Rome (dateable for convenience from AD 410): after the earthly city collapsed, monks retreated to places far removed from cities. Of course monastic foundations were, as engines of learning, prayer, and social influence, necessarily tightly bound into larger systems of worldly power, but the monastery was in principle a self-enclosed heavenly city, imitating the heavenly Jerusalem wherein monks practiced a life of contemplation. Each monastery or convent (for women religious) was subject to a rule, the first of which is the Benedictine rule, under the direction of an abbot or abbess.

Benedictine monks trace their founding to the early sixth century; monasteries were the principal form of regular life in Western Europe until the rapid opening up of Europe from the late eleventh century, when new religious foundations sprang up in response to new social and spiritual needs. The most important and flourishing of these new foundations was that of the regular canons. Canons lived under a rule, the first of which was the Augustinian Rule. Like monks, Augustinian canons lived a communitarian life without private property, though unlike monks they lived in urban centers, and their function was not primarily contemplative; it was instead to serve in public ministry, such as the provision of schools and hospitals.

New, reformist monastic orders emerged in the later Middle Ages (e.g., Cistercians, founded 1098, contemporary with the proliferation of Augustinian canons), but the hugely significant development in the religious orders came in the early thirteenth century, with the emergence of the fraternal orders (so-called from Latin *frater*, meaning "brother"). Whereas monks had fled the fallen city, friars emerged in the newly resurgent urban culture first of Italy, and then, with remarkable rapidity, across all of Western Europe. As European trade and urban centers developed, so too did a corresponding spiritual culture, though in opposition to commercial culture. Thus St. Francis, the son of a rich merchant of Assisi in central Italy, stripped himself of his secular garb in the main square of Assisi, to the acute embarrassment of his merchant father. The first orders of friars were those of Francis and Dominic; by Langland's time there were two further orders of friars, those of the Carmelites and the Augustinians. All were so-called mendicant orders, from the Latin word *mendicare*, meaning "to beg." Friars had no independent, stable source of income; wedded as they were to poverty, they were instead dependent on the charity of their surrounding communities. Friars not only introduced an extraordinarily vital spiritual and artistic culture into Europe; in the thirteenth and fourteenth centuries they also dominated university culture at such important centers as Paris and Oxford.

The pre-Reformation church that Langland knew, then, was by no means a monolithic institution; it was instead highly variegated, and made up of many sub-institutions, themselves the product of different historical moments. The countryside and townscapes of England were, and remain, marked by these institutional developments: great cities had their cathedrals; significant cities and towns had their parish churches and houses of canons and friars; villages had their parish churches; and the countryside was punctuated by abbeys. Take, for example, the variegated ecclesiastical topography of medieval London, *c.* 1400. The map (Figure 1) shows the following institutions: St. Paul's Cathedral, which dominated the medieval landscape for centuries in its placement on the highest point in the city; then, just a stone's throw away from St. Paul's, there is the friary of the Dominicans, known as the Blackfriars Convent, which was constructed in the late thirteenth century (later the site on which the first Blackfriars Theater was situated, where Shakespeare's company performed); to the north of St. Paul's, the Convent of the Grey Friars, or Franciscans (formally founded in 1223, after the Black Friars in 1216); in addition to the priories of Benedictines and canons at the city's margins, stand dozens of parish churches, as indicated by the + symbols on the map. In fact, a quick survey of any area within and without the walls of medieval London conveys a helpful, even if historically distant, impression of the many facets of religious life Langland encountered in this city – reminding us, in turn, that any notion of the medieval "church," conceived in the singular, is intensely qualified by the very presence and shape of the inhabited environment.

How does Langland represent the church, then? At the poem's beginning and end he represents it as a single, ideal entity: in passus 1 the indisputably authoritative figure Holy Church instructs Will, and in passūs 19–20 we witness the construction of the Barn of Unity, a new, vernacular construction with, astonishingly, the plowman Piers Plowman as pope.[8] Leaving aside these ideal, single representations for the moment, let us turn instead to Langland's representation of particular, historically verifiable sub-institutions of the church he knew. As we observe these particular representations, we shall also see that Langland's church is, in his account, in serious disarray.

In the rapid snapshot effect of the poem's Prologue, we already witness glimpses of different institutional representatives. We start with figures on the very margins of the institutional church, anchorites and hermits who do not move from their cells and who devote themselves to "preieres and penaunce" in a life of abstinence (B.Prol.25–8). These are clearly monastic figures, turned resolutely away from the world, though monastic figures on the margins even of monastic society: these are truly solitary, virtuous figures living as if dead to the world.[9]

All the other ecclesiastical figures targeted in the Prologue are visibly failing. The first of these failures are the friars, whose spiritual functions have, by this account, been wholly subsumed by systems of material gain:

> I fond there freres, alle the foure ordres,
> Prechynge the peple for profit of the wombe
> Glosed the gospel as hem good liked;
> For coveitise of copes construwed it as thei wolde.
> (B.Prol.58–61)

The next ecclesiastical figure in the Prologue is a lowly member of the secular clergy empowered by a local bishop, a pardoner who preaches as if he were a priest, and absolves sinners for material profit that is then shared between pardoner and parish priest (B.Prol.68–82). Parish priests themselves, along with their bishops, abandon their parishioners and run to London for more lucrative royal or baronial appointments, "for silver is swete" (B.Prol.83–99). Above all, we catch a glimpse of the papal court itself, and the cardinals (the "courtiers," as it were, of the papal court, or curia) who have presumed to make their own pope (B.Prol.100–11). This is almost certainly a reference to the schism within the Western Church that occurred from September 1378 (shortly after which the B text of *Piers Plowman* was likely written), when French cardinals elected their own pope, thus creating two popes, a situation that obtained until 1415. Langland's church, the church across most of the period of writing and rewriting *Piers Plowman* (c. 1365–88) can be described as a double-header.

To be sure, Langland is writing a specific genre in the Prologue, that of estates satire, which is predisposed to moral attack.[10] But hardly a single gesture in the rest of the poem gives any brighter image of a specific institution within the church. Take for example the priests who welcome Meed, the personification of bribery, to Westminster in passus 3: one of them takes her "bi the myddel" (B.3.10) as she arrives. In her exceptionally adroit self-defense, Meed underlines the ways in which gift-giving is what makes the papal world go around: she declares that the pope and his cardinals both receive and distribute "presents" "to mayntene hir lawes" (B.3.215–16). Meed herself might call these gifts "presents"; her opponent Conscience calls them bribery, or reward beyond desert. Undeserved payment is not restricted to the highest levels of the church: meed declares that priests who preach also "asken mede" among various forms of payment (B.3.223–34).

In passus 5, in the confessions of the deadly sins, we hear that Wrath acts as a friar in convents so as deliberately to stir up enmity among the nuns (B.5.135–6). In passus 7, a priest disagrees with the non-ecclesiastical figure Piers Plowman about the "pardon" sent from St. Truth, when Piers is clearly more perceptive about the nature of works and pardon (B.7.105–38). Langland is here registering profound dissatisfaction with the sale of indulgences, the issue that will be the flashpoint for the break-up of the Western Church in the Reformation of the sixteenth century. In passus 8 Will accosts two friars, "maistres of the Menours" (i.e., Franciscans), who give him a self-serving answer in response to his question as to where he might find "Dowel," or right action in the world (B.8.6–19). Or in passus 13 Will aggressively witnesses the greedy, self-satisfied academic Doctor of

Divinity, "godes gloton," guzzling and overeating on the dais at a feast (B.13.78–111).

All these vignettes underline the corruption of separate institutions of the church, but none so damagingly as the friars. In passus 20, after the agricultural laborer Piers has built the Church as the Barn of Unity, and has been appointed effectively as pope of this new, apostolic church, the church is attacked by Antichrist. The first in the train of the attackers behind Antichrist are the friars: "Freres folwede that fend, for he gave hem copes, / And religiouse reverenced hym and rongen hir belles, / And al the convent cam to welcome a tyraunt" (B.20.58–60).

The church that Langland knew was a church whose broad history he knew. His sense of history, however, is consistently a sense of decline from pristine beginnings. In passus 15, the figure Anima critiques the contemporary institution of the church by broad comparisons with its historical beginnings. The ideal of charity is essentially located in the past, "fern ago." As examples of those who lived charitably in poverty, Anima cites the early hermits Antony (to whom the origins of monasticism are drawn), Egidius, and Paul (claimed as the founder of the Augustinian Friars) (B.15.269–89), as well as some great figures of the primitive church, Paul the Apostle, the disciples Peter and Andrew, and Mary Magdalene (B.15.290–306). He also says, in making the same point, that religious should not take alms from unjust rulers, but act "as Antony dide, Dominyk and Fraunceys, / Beneit and Bernard [bothe], whiche hem first taughte / To lyve by litel and in lowe houses by lele mennes fyndynge" (B.15.420–2). Each of these figures is associated with the idealistic founding of an order (apart from Antony, who has already been mentioned, the orders are as follows, respectively: Dominican friars [1216]; Franciscan friars [1223]; Benedictine monasticism [c. 530]; and Cistercian monasticism [1098]). Closer to home, but still in the historical frame of Christianity, Anima also refers admiringly to the conversion of England:

> Al was hethynesse [heatheness] som tyme Engelond and Walis,
> Til Gregory garte [made] clerkes to go here and preche.
> Austyn at Caunterbury cristnede the kyng there,
> And thorugh miracles, as men mow rede, al that marche [region] he
>   tornede [converted]
> To Crist and to Cristendom . . .   (B.15.442–6)

The past of all these institutional elements of the church is inspired and glorious; the present is neither. Langland shares a sense of the church's profound disarray with the vigorous movement coming into focus in the period of *Piers Plowman*, that of the Lollards.[11]

Religious institutions and the ideal self

We have so far seen snapshots, as it were, of Langland's view of the church's specific institutions; unless placed in a distant past, these snapshots are consistently, fiercely negative. I turn now to the way in which this negative representation of ecclesiastical institutions works in the dynamic movement of *Piers Plowman*.

Langland's poem is divided into two principal sections: a *visio*, or vision, of society as a whole (B text passūs 1–7), and a *vita*, or life (passūs 8–20). The *vita* is that of one person, Will, or, more properly, the ideal person to whom Will, as the human will, belongs. The second part of the poem is, then, a *Bildungsroman*, an education of the soul to its ideal form. The form of the poem matches the ideal form of the person: this part of the poem can, indeed, be called a "person-shaped" poem.[12] The poem, that is, takes its own form as it fills out the ideal form of the soul. The *vita* turns the questions of the *visio* inward; the poem becomes literally psychoanalytical, as Will questions different and deeper faculties, or powers, of the soul of which he is himself a part.

What parts, or powers, of the soul does Will question? The psychological traditions that Christendom inherited from classical sources divided the soul, or psyche, into a primary division of a willing, desiring, loving part of the soul on the one hand, and a reasoning, analytical part of the soul on the other. Whereas Will is the will, or desiring part of the soul, the figures questioned by Will are the reasoning parts of the soul. The poem's actants (they cannot properly be called "characters") are, then, powers of the soul, with names such as Wit and Imaginative. Will also questions the educational and ecclesiastical institutions that ideally train the soul to its ideal form.

The *vita* answers to the failings of the *visio*. The *visio* ends in crisis with the austere, apparently unattainable demands of Truth's pardon, to "do well," absolutely. Doing well might sound simple enough, but if there is one certainty that emerges from the *visio*, it's this: no one does well, and certainly not absolutely. Will, the desiring part of the soul, longs, then, to know the answer to this fearsome question. And so as he turns inward, he poses the same question, with increasing intensity, to each of the rational and/or education figures who should know the truth: "What is Dowel?," or what, Will asks, constitutes action in the world that will satisfy the sobering, apparently unbending standards of God's justice, or what Langland calls "Truth"?

As Will's soul moves through the crises of passūs 8–14, so too do the separate faculties of the soul coalesce. Whereas, that is, passūs 8–12 had been a psychoanalysis, the poem becomes, from passus 15 forward, a psychosynthesis, heralded by the appearance of Anima, the whole soul. And as the poem becomes a psychosynthesis, reaching into deeper psychological resources of charity, so too does it turn inevitably to ecclesiological, or institutional, questions: how should the church be grounded in order to produce the ideal, charitable form of the soul? The education of the soul, that is, necessarily entails the reformation of the church. Institutions, in sum, play a major part in the construction of the ideal self.

Passus 15, in fact, mirrors the institutional pattern of passus 1: whereas in passus 1 the church had berated the individual soul Will, in passus 15 the situation is reversed: having been educated through trial in a deep understanding of how humans might meet the standards of God's justice, Anima, the whole soul, can finally speak up. And when he does speak (Anima is, ungrammatically, male), he addresses two questions: charity on the one hand, and ecclesiology on the other.

Our training in the liberal tradition renders, perhaps, the connection of these two subjects surprising: for many modern readers, the question of the deepest sources of the self is entirely separate from any institutional question. These two subject matters might, that is, seem entirely disparate, the one (charity) being concerned with the most profound source of the self, while the other (the church) addresses the problem of an external institution. If it is reasonably the business of Anima to treat charity (one of his names, after all, is *Amor*), we might want to ask why Anima should treat the church. In the texture of Anima's speech as a whole, however, we can see that a treatment of charity is inseparable from a treatment of the church. The two subjects are intimately related, because, for Langland, selves are grounded in institutions. Another sub-name of Anima is "Conscience," "Goddes clerk and his notarie" (B.15.32). This involves the public functions of challenging or not challenging the world around him. In passus 15, then, the individual soul (in an ideal form) addresses the church, as a reforming conscience. The church as an institution is an inherent part of the story of the soul's education.

Can Langland's conscience reform the church?

The poem, then, enacts a psychosynthesis, at the end of which the individual soul is capable of understanding the deepest sources of charity on the one hand, and has the authority to reform the entire church on the other. Langland, it would seem, does recognize that institutions nourish the soul, and does recognize that the soul's fullest expression is inseparable from the establishment of a capacious, sacrament-dispensing church.

We began with a question: Which comes first, church or self? We seem to have arrived at a provisional answer: At least soul and Church, that is, exist for each other. Where precisely, however, does Langland locate the source of reform: in the church or in the soul? Which is more reliable? In this section I offer one example that suggests that Conscience, and only Conscience, is capable of a truly reforming impulse. My second, more powerful, example suggests the reverse: that a Conscience produced by a failing church is incapable of reforming that church. A failed church produces a failed Conscience. In this second example, we shall also see why the institutional failing of the friars is lethal for the health of the individual soul.[13]

My first example is that of Conscience's academic feast in passus B.13. In this vision (the fourth), Conscience invites Will and Clergy to a feast. The other specified guests are an academic Doctor, and Patience, a mendicant pilgrim. Will sits at a side table with Patience, while Conscience, on high table, politely conducts a searching examination of his guests: what, he asks for the last time in the poem, is Dowel?

Much literary criticism of *Piers Plowman* across of the twentieth century devoted itself to scoring off Will as the problem: the *vita* of the poem was about his moral progress; the institutions that trained Will were regarded as unproblematic; all Will had to do was follow their advice. In Conscience's feast of passus 13 we can see how limited that view is; to be sure, Will is intemperate in his attack on the Doctor of Divinity, but so too are the clerical figures at Conscience's feast strictly limited. Their limitations propel Will, and Conscience, into reformist positions, beyond the church.

At first Will himself poses the question about Dowel to the representative of the academic establishment in its complacent and well-heeled actuality, the academic Doctor introduced at the beginning of the passus. The academic friar is totally unaware of the pressure of Will's question;[14] he casually tosses it aside: "'Dowel?' quod this doctour – and drank after – / 'Do noon yvel to thyn evencristen – nought by thi power'" (B.13.103–4). This is the occasion for a satirical attack on the friar, and Will tries to capitalize on the moment as it is offered to him (B.13.105–10). Conscience, however, is the host, or overriding presence, at this meal, and he does not attack the Doctor, but rather defers courteously, if shrewdly, to the Doctor's theological learning:

> Sire doctour, and [if] it be youre wille,
> What is Dowel and Dobet? Ye dyvynours [theologians] knoweth.
> (B.13.114–15)

The Doctor's answer to this courteously posed question reveals the self-protecting, self-aggrandizing mentality of the educational institution: Dowel is defined as doing as "clerkes techeth"; Dobet as he who teaches; and Dobest as he who both teaches and acts according to his own teaching (B.13.115–17a). In these three steps the Doctor complacently assures himself of both his power and his honor: his power resides in the fact that he controls the unlearned in what they are to regard as "doing well," while his honor is affirmed in the preservation of the higher stages of moral life to teachers themselves. The inadequacy of this declaration is evident most immediately by the fact that the Doctor does not himself do as he teaches, as Will points out.

Conscience does not take issue with this reply. Instead, he shrewdly allows its inadequacy to speak for itself beside the discreet answer of Clergy, to whom Conscience now poses the same question. Whereas the Doctor represents the academic institution in its literal actuality, Clergy here seems to represent the academic institution in its ideal potentiality. Conscience certainly feels more at ease with Clergy: he addresses him familiarly in the singular, unlike his plural, polite address to the Doctor: "'Now thow, Clergy,' quod Conscience, 'carpest what is Dowel'" (B.13.118). Clergy's answer betrays none of the self-protecting assurance of the Doctor. He says that he is unwilling to answer the question, since Piers the Plowman, who appeals only to the "science" of love, knows better (B.13.120–30).

Remarkably, then, Clergy acknowledges the hesitation of the entire academic establishment in the presence of a plowman's knowledge. Piers, says Clergy, sets each "science" at nothing, except the "science" of love; to call love itself a "science" in this context is to insist that, paradoxically, the essential knowledge is not academic, but moral: the poem's narrative is being propelled beyond academic learning precisely by an academic figure, who expresses the proper humility of the learned before the biggest questions.

It is clear by now that Conscience is quietly conducting a polite but searching examination of his guests, which is what we would expect, after all, from the faculty of the conscience. The last figure to whom the question is put at the academic feast, and in the poem, is Patience. Patience is a totally non-academic, eremitic figure, who has been invited to this feast only as a mendicant pilgrim, and who sits at a side table with Will (B.13.29–36). Middle English "pacience" bears much more of the semantic force of its Latin root, *patientia* (meaning "suffering"), than the Modern English word "patience" (see *MED* sense 1(a)). Conscience trusts Patience's long-suffering experience above academic learning:

> Pacience hath be in many place, and paraunter [perhaps] knoweth
> That no clerk ne kan, as Crist bereth witnesse:
> *Pacientes vincunt &c.* [the suffering overcome]   (B.13.133–4a)

Likewise, Patience's exposition of the Dowel triad points to the importance but limitations of academic learning. For in this academic milieu, his answer suggests a cognitive development that embraces, but transcends, the academic culture represented in its potentiality by Clergy: to learn is to do well; to teach is to do better; and to love one's enemies is to do best (B.13.136–9). Here, too, then, is a figure who is taught, like Piers, by the "science" of love; but his attitude to academic learning is not hostile: he includes learning and teaching as part of his triad. Unlike the complacent Doctor, though, he does not construct the triad for the self-aggrandisement of the academic institution, but instead opens the dobest element up to a radically Christian concept of love: *dilige inimicos* ("love [your] enemies").

At this meal at the court of Conscience, the higher reaches of academic, theological learning are also seen to be impervious to the sense of Patience's paradox. The Doctor is quite untouched by the spiritual force of Patience's riddling speech, dismissing the idea of the paradoxical might of suffering as nonsense. He declares that "Al the wit of this world and wight [vigorous] mennes strengthe / Kan noght [par]formen a pees bitwene the Pope and hise enemys" (B.13.174–5). These words reveal the blinkered and uncomprehending view of the academic Doctor, since it is precisely what Patience has been saying, though with a different intent: it is not, indeed, "wit" or "strengthe" that can achieve the peace prophesied by Patience, but "will" and suffering.

At this point we see the full force of Conscience, who acts in an astonishingly disruptive manner. He signals where his sympathies lie by overturning the etiquette of his role as host in his own academic feast. He abandons his position as host and master, and announces that he is leaving to be "pilgrym with Patience til I have preved moore" (B.13.182). This is a radical choice from an educational point of view, since it involves abandoning educational and ecclesiastical institutions, and entrusting himself to the marginal figure Patience, on the road; Conscience wants to "preve" in the experiential sense, rather than the academic, rational sense. Educational institutions, ecclesiastical teachers, and rational procedures can no longer contain the poem's spiritual energies and perceptions. And it is, revealingly, Conscience who drives the poem into deeper spiritual and more powerfully reformist territory.

My second example, which runs counter to the first, occurs in passus 20. Will dreams that he sees the coming of Antichrist, who is followed by friars. Conscience counsels the "fools" of Christ to retreat into the Barn of Unity. After two attacks on the Barn, Conscience calls on Clergy to save him, in response to which the friars offer their services; at first Conscience rejects their offer, but ultimately courteously allows them to enter, on condition that they have suitable physical provision, that they leave the study of logic, and that they do not multiply uncontrollably (B.20.212–72). The friars, under the instructions of Envy, do precisely what they have been forbidden to do by Conscience, while the attack on Holy Church continues.

This act of courtesy toward potential enemies is made out of mercy, but in making it Conscience does, nevertheless, attempt to guard the church against the threat to which the friars expose it. For one of the first points Conscience makes is that the friars will have "breed and clothes / And othere necessaries ynowe" (B.20.248–9). So Conscience wishes to change the very foundation of the fraternal orders in respect of their mendicancy.

Conscience's act of mercy serves, however, to provoke, rather than stem, the threat to the newly constructed Church, the Barn of Unity. Whereas Conscience himself had gone on the road, in purifying poverty, with Patience in passus 13, in passus 20 Conscience recognizes that poverty can also corrupt, particularly if it is the basis of an institution. For the material need of the mendicant friars prompts them to sell the sacrament of penance short. If, in Langland's view, the church's principal reason for existence is to dispense the sacrament of penance, then the friars are destroying the church by transforming the sacrament of penance into a business. This last point is dramatically enacted in the final movement of the poem, which focuses on the question of beggary in relation to the sacrament of penance.

Conscience's initial act of courteous mercy in passus 20 is to all of Christendom under the pestilential attack of Kynde; his second is to the mendicant orders in particular, and his third is to a single friar, Friar Flatterer (B.20.356). The logic of these last two moments is to test the strength of the church against the power of sin represented by Antichrist. The strength of the church is tested by first defining the institutional danger of begging, and then by seeing how begging affects, and corrupts, the sacrament of penance. This sacrament is crucial, since it allows Christians to "capitalize" on the Atonement, by "paying back" their spiritual debts to Piers the Plowman. In this last moment, the entry of Friar Flatterer, not only is the church effectively rendered useless, but Conscience himself is weakened.

Conscience now calls for a spiritual "leche," or doctor, to heal those who are wounded by sin under the attack of Antichrist. The confessor appointed by Conscience is too demanding for the wounded, and Contrition asks Conscience to call instead Friar Flatterer, since, he says, many a man is wounded through hypocrisy (B.20.316). Contrition's suggestion is itself hypocritical, and Conscience at first resists it, saying that the secular clergy, or Piers Plowman, are perfectly adequate to act as "leche." Suddenly, however, Conscience himself changes his mind, and agrees that the friar be fetched.

This is a second astonishing moment involving Conscience, since the source of greatest spiritual strength, the individual conscience, is itself weakened. The implication of this scene must be that for Langland the individual conscience is sustained by the institution of the church, and that individuals are in a profound sense constituted by the church; as the church is threatened, so too is the individual conscience. Conscience accepts a hypocrite; the line between accepting a hypocrite and being a hypocrite is very thin.

These two examples, then, demonstrate Langland's divided position with regard to the force of Conscience: passus 13 champions that force, whereas passus 20 questions it. Whatever we make of that contradiction, we are in a position to answer two questions: why should Langland attack the friars with such force; and where, precisely, does Langland locate the source of reform, in the church, or in the soul?

Langland attacks the friars with such force precisely because he is profoundly drawn to a mendicant culture (see passus 13),[15] but also because he simultaneously recognizes that an institution without material grounding is going to become a corrupt institution (see passus 20). The friars do not have a material grounding; as a result, they corrupt the sacrament of penance and they therefore destroy the church.

Langland would seem to locate the source of reform in the individual conscience. That is certainly the conclusion to be drawn from passus 13. If that is true, we might want to place the poet in the vanguard of the Reformation and its new, confident account of the fully formed individual conscience as prior to any institution. The very fact that we might want to make that case is itself suggestive. The fact that the case cannot be made convincingly is more suggestive, of Langland's transitional status. This status is underlined by the poem's ending, as Conscience leaves the church, alone (B.20.381–7), crying after grace. However much this might seem at first blush triumphantly to herald the Reformation moment, the departure of Langland's Conscience is no triumph, but rather a tragedy. Like much great art, *Piers Plowman* is indeed prophetic. Langland does foresee the Reformation, but he recoils from what he foresees.

The function of institutional satire

From what has been argued so far, we can see that satire of institutions is by no means incidental to the fate of the soul for Langland. In *Piers Plowman*, institutional critique is just as much a part of a program of spiritual reform as is personal inspiration and, as we will see, it shapes the kind of satire Langland practices. If Conscience is the unerring arbiter of the truth, then we would expect Langland's ecclesiastical satire to be delivered without qualifications of any kind, except those imposed by due caution. We would expect his satire to have the confidence, that is, of divine judgment. Does it? In this final section I intend to show that Langland resists the aspiration to deliver absolute judgments. He refuses the absolute authority of conscience as if it could survey human action as from a position outside history. Instead, he remains committed to the reformist energies of history, energies that can be activated only from within the flow of history. He refuses to make absolute distinctions between the saved and the damned, and his satire refuses to make absolute judgments.

Revolutionary satire derives its legitimacy from eschatology: one can see confidently into the present, and isolate those who must be rejected, because one already knows the end of the story. Knowing the end legitimates confident understanding of the beginning, too: the revolutionary satirist moves confidently through history, discriminating the saved from the damned there also. A reformist satire, by contrast, is less ready to discriminate between saved and damned, because the reformist is located within history. The reformist defers eschatological judgment to God.

The frontispiece to Foxe's *Acts and Monuments* of 1563 (see Figure 2) exemplifies the polemical advantage of satire as eschatological judgment driven by a conscience in full possession of certainty. Its lower divisions represent a historical battle: on the middle left the persecuted evangelical saints burn, trumpets raised to hail the elect on Christ's right. On the bottom left the Word is preached, without a word added to or subtracted from the Tetragrammaton in Hebrew letters, illuminating the sermon. To the bottom right, by contrast, a Corpus Christi procession leads toward the celebration of the Eucharist in the middle right panel, in which the Host is offered up, as if to the devils, on Christ's left. The contrast between right and left is historically specific: it is satire of the present. The image as a whole, though, borrows iconography from another, ahistorical scheme. The image of Christ seated on the rainbow, drawn ultimately from Revelations 4:3, also derives from standard iconography of the Last Judgment. In this image, then, Christ does not judge sinners and saved at the end of time. Instead, he already discriminates between the saved and the damned in this life. Eschatology, or the end of time, is thus transferred to the flow of time and historical conflict. Absolute judgment is made from within the flow of history. Because the True Church is truly known across time, indifferently to historical sequence, non-scriptural practice can be damned with the confidence of divine approval.

What bearing do these remarks have on the practice of satire in *Piers Plowman*? I will answer this question with regard to Langland's treatment of the institutional church's most prominent representatives, the clergy.

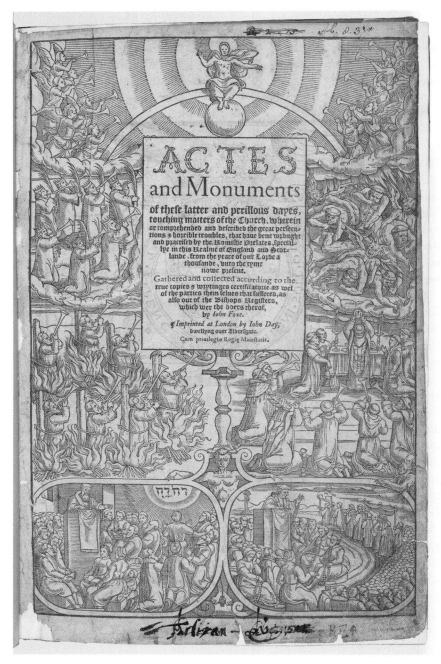

Figure 2 John Foxe, *Actes and Monuments of These Latter and Perillous Days, Touching Matters of the Church . . .*, London, John Day, 1563, frontispiece.

One of the most recurrent features of revolutionary moments is their targeting of intellectuals, or, to put it another way, targeting of those with specialized forms of knowledge. This is no less true of the cultural revolution of the sixteenth century than it was of the cultural and political revolutions of China and, say, Cambodia in the 1970s. In *Piers Plowman*, too, clerics come under severe attack. As we shall see, however, Langland resolutely resists the temptation to invest that satirical attack on intellectuals with eschatological force. Instead, he locates his vision profoundly within this world, and so accepts, and even underlines, the limits of that vision and that "sufferance." As a result, he calls on the past of his own poem.

As we have seen, Antichrist attacks at the end of *Piers Plowman*, apparently capping the poem's own movement from passus 16 forward through biblical time – through the Old Testament to Christ's birth and ministry, to the Crucifixion and Resurrection, and from there to Acts and, finally, to Revelation. In keeping with a powerful antifraternal tradition, the friars are intimately associated with Antichrist: "Freres folwede that fend, for he gaf hem copes" (B.20.58). Under the ferocious attack of Antichrist, Conscience twice calls for Clergy's help. At the first call, it is the friars, representing Clergy, who fail Conscience. Precisely by way of bolstering their position, indeed, the friars go to university: "Envye … heet freres go to scole / And lerne logyk and lawe" (B.20.273–4). This dark account of university learning, associated as it is with the onset of Antichrist at the end of time, would seem to align Langland with a well-established eschatological tradition of anticlerical satire.

Langland, however, refuses to draw on the maximal energies of that tradition to which he is clearly alluding. For he refuses to invest his satire with the eschatological force of absolute divine judgment. He certainly evokes the Last Judgment, in his account of Christ's life. After his act of Dobest, of giving power to Piers to absolve humans of sin duly repaid, Christ ascends to heaven, where "at domesday" (not now), he will judge "The goode to the Godhede and to greet joye, / And wikkede to wonye in wo withouten ende" (B.19.198–9). What replaces that future judgment in the here and now of worldly time is the Pentecostal descent of the Holy Spirit, who distributes weapons for the fight with Antichrist ahead. In the time of that struggle, Christ's "sufferance" allows space to all manner of men. That sufferance is grounded in Christ's mercy, and disallows the finality or the anger of judgment in this world. In the time of this world, "Piers the Plowman peyneth hym to tilye / As wel for a wastour and wenches of the stewes / As for hymself and hise servaunts" (B.19.438–40).

The fact that Conscience errs in allowing Friar Flatterer into the church is equally an acceptance of the limited vision, and the consequent check on anger, that Christ's own sufferance entails. That limited vision is a refusal of eschatological certainty and eschatological anger. What we find instead is a reaching back into the poem's own energies and narrative. For Conscience's final, and repeated, call for Clergy fulfills a prophecy from within the poem itself. Even after the friars have betrayed the church, Conscience, at the poem's end, continues to call for Clergy: "Conscience cryed eft and bad Clergie helpe hym" (B.20.376).

This repeated call fulfills the prophecy agreed on by both Clergy and Conscience much earlier, in passus 13, in what at face value looks like a permanent separation. Conscience, to Clergy's initial disgust, leaves the academic feast to convert the world with Patience. He would, he says, "have pacience parfitliche than half thi pak of bokes" (B.13.202). Clergy, however, accurately prophesies the time when Conscience will need Clergy: Conscience will see the time "Whan thou art wery forwalked, wilne me to counseille." Using a revealing pun, Conscience agrees: "If," he says, "Pacience be oure partyng felawe and pryvé with us bothe, / Ther nys wo in this world that we ne sholde amende" (B.13.207–8).

The pun embedded in the phrase "partyng felawe" expresses the point about Langland's recuperative satire: the phrase can mean both "fellow with whom we take our leave" (a sense surely activated at this moment of leave taking) and "our partner." The narrative history of Langland's poem accentuates the provisional partings of satire, before registering the recuperative restorations. It's true, of course, that we do not see this recuperation of Clergy by Conscience in action; we only hear patient Conscience passionately wish for it. The individual conscience needs the church as much as the church needs the individual conscience; the individual conscience's attacks on the failings of the institution are essential though in no way absolute.

7

MATTHEW GIANCARLO

Political forms and institutions in *Piers Plowman*

More than any other poem – indeed, perhaps more than any other work of art from its era – *Piers Plowman* is suffused with the language and sensibilities of contemporary institutions. This is one of the most challenging aspects of the work for a modern reader. *Piers Plowman* is not primarily a narrative of characters, nor one driven by plot, nor even a poem of particularly striking visual imagery or technical verbal artistry, although it certainly has moments of all these. Rather it is, as James Simpson has argued, a poem investigating the contours and dynamics of different institutional discourses and forms: the Church and schools; government and law and bureaucracy; local authorities and national politics; marriage, property, and family; and more.[1] Its first and apparently most vigorous audiences were individuals drawn from these same secular and ecclesial institutions, "public men" and "professional readers" (see Chapter 10) who found in *Piers Plowman* not just a reflection of the institutional conditions of their lives, but a vibrant expression of the urgent questions and crises attending them.[2] As we travel with the dreamer through the allegorical landscape we find it populated by recognizable institutional landmarks and settings, scenarios evoking a familiar experience with the social structures of law, right, and public power – all of which demand an ethically and critically inflected understanding of authority, fidelity, legality, and truthfulness.

It remains the case, however, that interpreting the political forms and institutions in *Piers Plowman* requires nuance and, above all, a sense that, as Emily Steiner has noted, the poem is "less concerned with reproducing political conflict than it is with modeling political structure."[3] That is, *Piers Plowman* has less investment in commenting on the current events of the day than it does in drawing our attention to the very structures that inform and shape what is possible in society, and hence, what counts as political (as opposed, say, to spiritual, or personal, or communal) in the first place. In this regard, *Piers Plowman* not only highlights and occasionally redraws familiar boundaries, asking readers to think hard about why the political world takes the shapes that it does. It also compels us to acknowledge the important differences between medieval and modern definitions of political forms and institutions. For example, in Langland's day as before, the distinction between ecclesial or "church" institutions and secular or "political" institutions – roughly, between "church" and "state" – was real yet porous, each distinct in authority but frequently overlapping in powers and personnel. Our separation of medieval "political" institutions from "religious" ones can seem at times highly artificial. Was kingship, whose representatives were from the eleventh century at least (if not from biblical precedents) treated with trappings and rituals that implied they were ordained by God, a wholly "secular" institution? Were members of the priestly caste, whose literacy allowed numbers of them to serve the accounting and other scribal needs of royal and other administrative offices, representatives of a "religious" institution? Even as that question is posed, the very meaning of "institution" trains our attention on its medieval specificity. Our modern concept of an *institution* emerges from this period, the late fourteenth and early fifteenth centuries, when the word is first attested in English as both a verb and a noun, an act (*institūten*) and a thing or concept (*institūciŏn*).[4] The medieval noun, unlike ours, refers to an *action*: the "founding of" a kingdom or a religious house, or the establishing of a more abstract social structure such as a code of law or procedure for political order. In other words, the modern technical and sociological understanding of discrete social institutions (e.g., hospitals, schools, banks, government agencies, court systems) is not so germane to the poem as the more conceptual and performative one.

Likewise, *Piers Plowman* investigates the institutions of government and coercive public authority in kingship and lordship (a particular anxiety of the author), as well as forms of communal governance; voices and documents of law, justice, and the courts; trade, guilds, business, and the fundamental arrangements of work and labor, both urban and rural; education and schooling; the family; and that most elusive but unavoidable product arising from the cross-current of institutions, the individual. The person/*persona* is defined both by them and against them, and personal autonomy, especially the autonomy of "Will" as faculty and character, is both established or instituted as well as restricted by the horizons that such forms offer. In these broad issues, the literary forms and generic innovations of the poem engage most productively with the politics of its day.

Institutional visions in the Prologue and passūs 1–7

As has been noted, political imagery stands out from the very start in the Prologue with the heavenly "tour on a toft" and the hellish "dongeon" in the dale (Prol.14–15).⁵ The second is not a dungeon in our modern sense of a subterranean prison but another tower, a donjon, the innermost keep of a castle and hence equally an architectural symbol of political dominion.⁶ Castles were, literally, structures of secular political power on the medieval landscape. Here at the front of the poem they symbolize, with the field of folk between them, the full scope and variety of society: sacred, profane, and mundane. The people of the field live between them, and the clergy as well as the laity share the mixed but distinct realms of churchly and worldly offices. An exemplary moment of institutional critique comes right at the start of the Prologue, where the narrator comments critically on the clergy's roles in secular government:

> Somme seruen þe kyng and his siluer tellen,
> In Cheker and in Chauncelrie chalangen his dettes
> Of wardes and of wardemotes, weyues and streyues.
> And somme seruen as seruantʒ lordes and ladies,
> And in stede of Stywardes sitten and demen.
> Hire messe & hire matyns and many of hire houres
> Arn doon vndeuoutliche; drede is at þe laste
> Lest Criste in Consistorie acorse ful manye.
>
> (Prol.92–9)

The "Checker" was the office of the Exchequer, the department responsible for royal revenue and revenue-related court cases. Interestingly it took its name from the "checkered" or checkerboard cloths upon which the royal accounting was performed. "Chauncelrie" was the office of the Chancellory, later called the Chancery, the court of royal grace under the office of the Chancellor that handled the "conscientious law" in matters of equity such as property, trusts, and guardianships. In both cases these secular legal and governmental offices were often held by church prelates, as they were in Langland's day. But even church courts, such as the "Consistorie"/Consistory courts of a church diocese – here raised to the level of allegory as the court of Christ's final judgment – or the "Chapter" courts of a religious house, could also display a similar mixing of secular and ecclesial functions. Langland is obviously exercised about the abuse of estate and station displayed by this mixing of secular and prelatical positions. But he also reveals, less polemically, the simple fact *of* it, that these church and secular offices of law and governance stand in a productive but uneasy interchange.⁷

Both the multifarious folk and the ambiguous "courte" are described before the establishment of kingship, which follows in the famous opening vignette of the founding of regnal authority. As with the tensions of courts and offices, the institutional estates of the realm – "King," "Commons," and "Knighthood" – are founded in a delicate balance:

> Thanne kam þer a kyng; knyȝthod hym ladde;
> Might of þe communes made hym to regne.
> And þanne cam kynde wit and clerkes he made
> For to counseillen þe kyng and þe commune saue.
> The kyng and knyȝthod and clergie boþe
> Casten þat þe commune sholde hire communes fynde.
> The commune contreued of kynde wit craftes,
> And for profit of al þe peple Plowmen ordeyned
> To tilie and to trauaille as trewe lif askeþ.
> The kynge and þe commune and kynde wit þe þridde
> Shopen lawe and leaute, ech lif to knowe his owene.
>
> (Prol.112–22)

Here the "commune(s)," a word repeated six times in eleven lines, appears to mean both the "common" population of the community, and the specifically institutional aspect of the "commons" *qua* estate as a foundational source of sovereignty: "Might of the communes made hym to regne." It was in this latter sense that the parliamentary estate of "the Commons" came to take its place securely in the governing order during the course of the fourteenth century. This institution of kingship in the Prologue shifts its details slightly over the A, B, and C versions without losing its fundamentally constitutional character. King, knighthood, commons; "kynde wit," clergy, crafts; law and *leaute*: all are set in relation to one another and also are put into play, like pieces positioned on a chessboard, as a ground-setting exercise that notably defers the clear presence of the institutional Church. The following declaration by the clerkly "lunatik" to the king, as well as the counsel from an Angel and a "Goliardeis," further expounds on the power and limitations of secular kingship. The Angel speaks admonitory verses in the Latin language of officialdom in particular because "lewed men ne koude / Iangle ne Iugge þat Iustifie hem sholde" (Prol.129–30). Similarly the Goliard gives learned Latin counsel, and "þe commune" – that is, the commons as community, presumably the "lewed" ones who could not understand the Angel's Latin – also replies "in vers of latyn . . . *Precepta regis sunt nobis vincula legis*" ["the king's commands are to us the chains of law"] (Prol.143–5). From here, in the B and C versions the focus then immediately shifts to the beast-fable allegory of the Parliament of Rats and the Belling of the Cat, offering yet another displaced image of secular governance and public (mis)rule, this time in parliamentary assembly. And as he did with his earlier comments on the court, the narrator declines to express his judgment with a coy demurral: "What þis metels bymeneþ, ye men þat be murye, / Deuyne ye, for I ne dar, bi deere god in heuene" (Prol.209–10). When we reach the concluding hotchpot of characters and crafts depicted at the Prologue's end, we have been taken through an allegorically capacious overview not just of the kinds of people who reside in that fair field, but also of the kinds of governance incumbent upon them – courtly, kingly, parliamentary – even as the narrator has declined to provide direct comment. *Piers Plowman* thus opens with a political and institutional primer, a veritable glossary of terms, a catalog of institutions (some more palpably identifiable than others), and a litany of examples of the necessarily coded practice of political criticism.

This preliminary establishment of the terms of governance thus sets up the two critical episodes that follow in the *visio* of passūs 1–7, the Marriage and Trial of Meed in 2–4 and the Pilgrimage and Plowing of the Half-Acre in 5–7. If the conceptual foundation of secular authority is depicted in the Prologue, then the Marriage of Meed episode is an attempt to investigate critically just how that system of authority and governance really works in the world. It is wholly reflective of contemporary institutional practices. After her sermon on love, Lady Holy Church turns to Meed as an example of "the fals" in the world, and Meed herself is to be wedded to "one fals fikel-tonge" in a ceremony witnessed by all "that longeth to þat lordeshipe, þe lasse and þe more" (2.41, 46). The ceremony will be public with the enfeoffment of properties and lordships to the couple (as approved by "Symonye and Cyuylle"), that is, until Theology objects to the wedding and the whole matter must be moved to the King's courts at Westminster for proper determination (2.63, 114ff.). Westminster, next to the city of London, was the legal heart of the realm and, by Langland's day, the mostly permanent home for the high courts of justice: the King's Bench and the Common Bench (the two most prominent courts dealing with royal legal matters and the "common" law, respectively); the Exchequer; and courts such as the Chancery that were direct offshoots of the King's council. It was also the quasi-permanent place of parliament, which retained its identity as a primary court of justice even as it grew into the main legislative and deliberative body of central government. There Meed is brought before the King's council, but not before her influence is felt as well by friars and confessors, "Maires and Maceres þat menes ben bitwene / The kyng and þe comune to kepe þe lawes," and many others who fall under her sway (3.76–7). The King tries to betroth Meed to Conscience but Conscience objects, and in turn Meed defends herself as necessary for the good health of the kingdom.

This argument before the King in passus 3 becomes a full-fledged parliamentary debate in passus 4 with the arrival of Reason at the court and with Peace's presentation of a parliamentary bill of complaint against the crimes perpetrated by Wrong (4.47–79). True to character, Meed labors to have these crimes excused with a simple fine. In a scene that was doubtless deeply resonant with the frequent parliamentary controversies and public debates about law and public order under Edward III in the 1370s, Reason holds out for an ideal of stern justice: "'And yet,' quod Reson, 'by þe Rode! I shal no ruþe haue / While Mede haþ þe maistrie to mote in þis moot halle'" (4.134–5). In the end the decision goes against Meed and Wrong, and the King declares that his justice will not be bought off. This oblique allegory proceeds through the different ascending spheres of secular justice as a local marriage ceremony is taken to the Westminster courts, then to the King's council, and finally to the high court of parliament attended by "peple in þe moot halle and manye of þe grete" (4.159). The narrative thus leads the reader through the worldly offices of institutional authority distinct from the church courts. At the same time Conscience presents a unified ideal of justice, one ruled by "Resoun," as the reconciliation of all courts:

> I, Conscience, knowe þis for kynde wit me tauȝte
> That Reson shal regne and Reaumes gouerne...
> Shal neiþer kyng ne knyght, Constable ne Meire
> Ouercarke þe commune ne to the Court sompne,
> Ne putte hem in panel to doon hem pliȝte here truþe;
> But after þe dede þat is doon oon dome shal rewarde
> Mercy or no mercy as Truthe may acorde.
> Kynges Court and commune Court, Consistorie and Chapitle,
> Al shal be but oon court, and oon burn be Iustice.
>
> (3.284–5, 315–21)

With this short catalog of courts – King's Bench and Common Pleas representing the secular, Consistory and Chapter/"Chapitle" courts for the ecclesial – Conscience metonymically appeals to all the institutional sources of contemporary justice, in a dream of "oon court." Conscience's idealism here reflects directly on the King's beleaguered efforts to reach a settlement, as even Peace, in turn, is willing to accept Meed's payments in place of strict justice. If Conscience and Reason are the voices of a rather unrealistic idealism, the King nonetheless tries to reconcile "truthe" with the pragmatic demands of money and status. He establishes (or renews) his royal advisory council at the end of passus 4 with the presence "of clerkes and of Erles" as well as Reason and Conscience (4.189). Abstract idealism is thus made to meet hopefully with aristocratic and bureaucratic realism. Nor is this necessarily just a sop to sentiment. The ancient expectation that a king would take *consilium et auxilium* ("advisement and aid") of his "proper" counselors was strong enough to provide at least partial justification for rebellion and dethronement when a king supposedly did not, as in the cases of both Edward II in 1327 and Richard II in 1399. Far from enacting royal absolutism, then, the Visio's King reacts to the crisis embodied by Meed – the first major pressure-point of the poem – by pragmatically trying to fulfill the desires for both licit legal authority and strong central governance, royal authority ruled by "reason" (that is, in the common medieval equivalency, law). The form of this deliberation imitates the course of secular court procedures and a season of court proceedings at Westminster. It is a legal and deliberative process allegorically reflecting the way things *should* work, even as the debate has been, at times, lively and uncertain.

This progress through the institutions of secular legal authority in passūs 2–4 – where Meed goes from periphery to center, from the localities to the Westminster courts, to the King's council, and finally to the high court of parliament – helps to clarify the order of events in passūs 5–7, which present a similar kind of spiritual progress. In the dreamer's second vision, Reason preaches to the folk and urges them to abide by the fundamental structures of familial, clerical, and political discipline (5.28–59). This sermon provokes the people, now personified as the Seven Sins, to seek Repentance. As with the opening controversy over Meed's marriage and subsequent progress to the source of (secular) law-giving authority, the folk's need for justification and reconciliation drives them to pursue "Seynt Truþe" (5.57), but they do not know where to go. At this point Piers Plowman appears, with the assurance that he knows the road to Truth "as kyndely as clerc doþ his bokes" (5.538), and he will direct them there for no pay. When the folk call for Piers to lead them personally, in passus 6 he first establishes proper social order on his half-acre for working toward a good harvest. The knight will guard and protect, women will spin and make cloth, and Piers and others will faithfully plow and provide food: "And alle kynne crafty men þat konne lyuen in truþe, / I shal fynden hem fode þat feiþfulliche libbeþ" (6.68–9). This supposedly preliminary ground-clearing exercise comes to take the place of the pilgrimage itself, indeed *is* the pilgrimage in Piers's arrangement. So we are at another foundational moment with society being both formed and re-formed by the people's penitential spiritual progress from sermon to repentance, to "pilgrimmage," to satisfaction, and finally to pardon. The process starts again with the institutional establishment of a proper estates' order, this time organized around productive modes of labor and a loosely trifunctional schema of those who work, those who fight, and those who pray.

And in another procession to controversy and conflict, "wastoures" or unproductive and unruly loafers are the disjunctive element – like unruly

Meed before – that the political order cannot easily reconcile to a virtuously functioning polity:

> Thanne Piers þe Plowman pleyned hym to þe knyȝte
> To kepen hym as couenaunt was fro cursede sherewes,
> "And fro þise wastours wolueskynnes þat makeþ þe worlde deere … "
> Curteisly þe knyȝt þanne, as his kynde wolde,
> Warnede wastoure and wissed hym bettre:
> "Or þow shalt abigge by þe lawe, by þe ordre þat I bere!" (6.159–66)

But Waster cares little for the law and even less for the ineffective knight, and he has only threats for Piers. Where secular force fails, only the power of Hunger drives Waster to do productive work, abject and pitiful as it is. In the end the laborer still holds grievances against the structures of secular authority that force him to toil in unfavorable conditions:

> He greueþ hym ageyn god and gruccheþ ageyn Reson,
> And þanne corseþ þe kyng and al þe counseil after
> Swiche lawes to loke laborers to chaste.
> Ac whiles hunger was hir maister þer wolde noon chide
> Ne stryuen ayeins þe statut, so sterneliche he loked.
>
> (6.316–20)

While the conflict may be allegorically personalized to one character, "Waster," against other personalized figures (the Knight and then Hunger), the struggle is also clearly political and institutional. Waster curses the King and his council (that is, the royal council) who, along with parliament, were the authors of the strict post-plague labor statutes of the mid fourteenth century ("swiche lawes" and "the statut") alluded to here.[8] These laws imposed severe legal restrictions and punishments on laborers who refused to work for low wages or who presumed to go mobile in search of better pay. As such this whole scenario, resonant as it is with contemporary law and institutional controls, puts the episode's foundation myth of secular institutional order in quite a different light. Less a product of divinely enlightened cooperation and "Reson," society here appears as little more than a dance of mutual antagonism, of obtuse lords, repressive laws, and angry laborers, all operating under the ever-threatening shadow of hunger and dearth. Even in the next passus when Treuthe sends the pardon to Piers for the benefit of all the different estates – for laborers like Piers, "Kynges and knyȝtes," "bysshopes yblessed" and expert "of boþe lawes" canon and civil, "Marchauntȝ" and others (7.13–23) – it seems that what can be had is not the stable promise of "Truth," only a "trewe" or truce, a temporary cessation of conflict and disorder (6.331). Indeed even this concord seems in doubt. The delivery and interpretation of the pardon itself in passus 7 also provokes debate and wrangling and, with its tearing in the B text, an example of violent rupture. The document ostensibly meant to deliver proof of reconciliation becomes yet another source of public discord and disagreement, as well as another pressure-point in the narrative's progress.

Thus from the socio-political foundations of the Prologue to an exploration of law, justice, and equity in passūs 1–4, to another societal re-foundation, penitential journey, and institutional-spiritual crisis in 5–7, the forms of secular political structure provide the framework that Langland exploits for organizing his inquiry. The driving and repeated question for all the institutional allegory is taken from the Psalter: *Domine, quis habitabit in tabernaculo tuo?* – "Lord, who will dwell in your temple/house?" (Ps. 14:1, repeated at 2.39, 3.234, 7.53, and later at 13.127). That is, who shall be saved, and what will ensure both personal and communal salvation for the folk of the field? Even in this ostensibly spiritual question earthly politics are never far away, as in Langland's repeated complaints against men of station and law:

> Pledours shulde peynen hem to plede for swiche [i.e., the poor] and helpe;
> Princes and prelates should paie for hire trauaille:
> *A Regibus & principibus erit merces eorum.*
> Ac many a Iustice and Iurore wolde for Iohan do moore
> Than *pro dei pietate* pleden at þe barre . . .
> *Domine, quis habitabit in tabernaculo tuo.*
> Ac to bugge water ne wynd ne wit ne fir þe ferþe,
> Thise foure þe fader of heuene made to þis foold in commune;
> Thise ben truþes tresores trewe folke to helpe,
> That neuere shul wexe ne wanye wiþouten god hymselue. (7.43–6, 53–6)

The very practical argument here about lawyers working *pro bono* and nobles paying what they owe shifts naturally to the broader question of who will receive God's eternal blessing for their good deeds. In turn it also evokes, perhaps unexpectedly, a traditional and classical definition of the foundational elements of civic earthly society. These are the things provided by God to be held in common *before* the establishment of markets and money, not to be denied to anyone: access to fresh water and air, the freedom to take fire from fire, and trustworthy counsel (here "wit"), that is, basic truthfulness and communal goodwill.[9] The question of who will live in God's house thus unavoidably touches on how we make our houses now, so to speak, in the present world, and with what basic assumptions. By the end of the *visio*, then, Langland's sustained critique of "ye maistres, Meires and Iugges" (7.190) sets up the following quest for Dowel in the *vita* as, among other things, a journey to understand more deeply the foundational elements of political order.

Spiritual and personal politics in passūs 8–18

The transition in passus 8, as the newly central narrator Will "romed aboute / Al a somer seson for to seke Dowel" (8.1–2), moves us forward and inward from these early institutional provisions. Of the several episodes and themes contained in the central passūs of *Piers Plowman*, many can be highlighted for their recognizable institutional forms: Dowel defined as "trewe wedded libbynge folk" (9.110), for example, and the many evocations of marriage and the family; or the cheerless lord's hall in passus 10; or the Master's school dinner with Clergy, Conscience, and Patience in passus 13. What unifies most of these institutional settings in some way, from both a secular and an ecclesial perspective, is the troubled question of *dominium*, of lordship and right rule, licit institutional wealth and authority in the world. This issue carries over from the *visio*'s concern with the proper establishment and execution of fundamental authority.

The contemporary challenge of the Wycliffites and later Lollards raised the issue of *dominium* in specifically institutional terms, turning the traditional language and categories of personal moral reform to the critique of church and government. While Langland's allegory obviously partakes in this critique, it also draws deeply from the vocabulary of secular authority for its positive moments as well, as in this definition of the relations among Dowel, Dobet, and Dobest by Thought:

> Dobest is aboue bothe [Dowel and Dobet] and bereþ a bisshopes crosse;
> Is hoked at þat oon ende to holde men in good lif . . .
> And as dowel and dobet [amonges hem ordeigned],[10]
> Thei han crowned a kyng to kepen hem alle,
> That if dowel and dobet did ayein dobest,
> And were vnbvxum at his biddyng, and bolde to don ille,
> Thanne sholde þe kyng come and casten hem in prison,
> And putten hem þer in penaunce wiþoute pite or grace,
> But dobest bede for hem abide þer for euere.
> Thus dowel and dobet and dobest þe þridde
> Crouned oon to be kyng, and by hir counseil werchen,
> And rule the Reme by rede of hem alle,
> And ooþer wise and ellis noȝt but as þei thre assente. (8.96–7, 100–10)

Many of the same terms from the *visio* are present here again (and in a scarcely concealed three-estates symbolism): a crowned king and council for the governance for the "realm," royal governance by informed assent, and even another penitential dungeon for the recalcitrant and unbuxom. The difference now is the degree of abstraction in the ethical reading of the allegory, not just the political. The "Reme"/realm here is the individual. The question of *dominium* therefore relates to the internal establishment of right rule in the self-as-community as much as in the community-as-self, the corporate life of the individual and vice versa. So, for example, when Clergy counsels Will to abide the "comune lyf" of faith, sufferance, and correction, he counsels the proper devotion to the tenets of personal reform even in the face of communal intransigence: "Thouȝ it auailled nouȝt þe commune, it myȝte auaille yowselue" (10.278). Politics has turned inward with its metaphors, as it does repeatedly throughout the *vita*.

This new orientation of governance, inward and Will-directed, leads to the thorniest and most allegorically complex stretches of the poem. But it also helps to flesh out the ethical valence of what has come before. Of the several ethical terms attendant to secular governance, none is more frequent and important but less amenable to translation than the simple word *leaute*. As we have seen, it makes an early and important appearance in the Prologue as a companion to the Law –

> The kynge and þe commune and kynde wit þe þridde
> Shopen lawe and leaute, ech lif to knowe his owene
> (Prol.121–2)

– and, a few lines later, as a kind of political affection evoked by good rule:

> "Crist kepe þee, sire kyng, and þi kyngryche,
> And lene þee lede þi lond so leaute þee louye...!"
> (Prol.126–7)

In passus 2 Lady Holy Church warns the dreamer not to judge hastily the "lordship" of Meed and False until *leaute* is properly observed:

> "Knowe hem þere if þow canst, and kepe þee from hem alle,
> And lakke hem noȝt but lat hem worþe til leaute be Iustice..."
> (2.47–8)

But later, at the trial of Meed, "Leaute" joins in the condemnation of Meed's crimes against the community:

> Loue leet of hire liȝt and leaute yet lasse,
> And seide it so loude þat soþnesse it herde.
> (4.161–2)

And it is the King who declares testily, "I wil haue leaute in lawe, and lete be al youre ianglyng" (4.180). Further examples emerge as *Piers Plowman* progresses.

Even more than "Reason" – which can be understood variously as "law," "justice," "sound judgment," "right principle", or even "proper control" – *leaute* has a semantic range both wide and often unfamiliar.[11] It is not exactly synonymous with "law" or "lawfulness," although it certainly retains that etymological aspect in all instances. Rather, it emerges as an affective and ethical relation *to* the institution of law, and to the necessity of lawfulness; hence its common alliterative collocation with "love." *Leaute* is both a societal and a personal quality, a communal and individual affective relation and thus a political emotion. Its force carries over from the communal world of passūs 1–7 to the psychological landscape of 8–18. During the inner dream of passus 11, when Will is angry at the friars for their mercenary treatment of church burials, he briefly meets the allegorical character Lewte:

> And lewte louȝ on me for I loured on þe frere;
> "Wherefore lourestow?" quod lewtee, and loked on me harde.
> "If I dorste," quod I, "amonges men þis metels auowe!"
> "ȝis, by Peter and by Poul!" quod he, and took hem boþe to witnesse:
> "*Non oderis fratres secrete in corde tuo set publice argue illos.*"
> "They wole aleggen also," quod I, "and by þe gospel preuen:
> *Nolite judicare quemquam.*"
> "And wherof serveþ lawe," quod lewtee, "if no lif vndertoke it? . . . "
>
> (11.84–91)

In some ways this is a strange thing for *leaute*/Lewte to say, in effect to call for the necessity of correction and criticism in the face of fraternal objection: "ech a lawe it graunteþ" (97), as he says. Again it is the proximity of ecclesial and secular law, and the spirit supposedly informing them, that draws the question of *leaute* to the fore here. The whole scene reinforces not only the importance of judgment but also the deeply ethical character of it for the individual, as a manifestation of an individual will's encounter with very public abuses of law and authority.[12]

This encounter provokes another point of crisis as Will falls into deep anxiety about the prospects of his own salvation, "wheiþer I were chosen or nouȝt chosen" (11.117). Will argues from an extended metaphor of the secular law's strict restrictions on charters and arrerages or unpaid debts (described as the force of "reson" [11.124, 131]) that he can be saved only through penitence and the mercy of God. At this point the thoroughly secular figure of the emperor Trajan bursts in, declaring the salvific force of love and *leaute*:

> "Ye? baw for bokes!" quod oon was broken out of helle.
> "I Troianus, a trewe kny3t, take witnesse at a pope
> How I was ded and dampned to dwellen in pyne
> For an vncristene creature; clerkes wite þe soþe
> That al þe clergie vnder crist ne my3te me cracche fro helle,
> But oonliche loue and leautee and my laweful domes."
>
> (11.140–5)

In one of the most striking juxtapositions of secular and ecclesial institutional claims, Trajan declares the spiritual efficacy of his pagan and secular lawfulness, which the narrator endorses as exemplary as well: "Lo! ye lordes, what leautee dide by an Emperour of Rome... / Wel ou3te ye lordes þat lawes kepe þis lesson haue in mynde / And on Troianus truþe to þenke, and do truþe to þe peple" (11.158–9). As he says, "Loue and lewtee is a leel science" (11.167).

Not just lawfulness or justice, then, but something deeper and more fundamental: what true piety is to faith, *leaute* is to the law, giving its secular face something of a sacred aspect.[13] That its best advocate should be a pagan Roman emperor – even one saved by the intervention of a pope – alerts us to the continued mixing of ecclesial and secular institutional categories, even in the deepest reaches of the poem's internal psychological investigation. The strongest representative of *leaute* is thus also the strongest image of idealized *dominium* and lordship, a just judge and king.

As well as the various legal and political images that populate the narrative, its many "translation moments" and interpretive impasses also reflect a passionate and deep concern for justice. Most famous is the moment when the priest translates the pardon in passus 7:

> "Piers," quod a preest þoo, "þi pardon moste I rede,
> For I shal construe ech clause and kenne it þee on englissh... "
>
> (7.107–8)

The translation of the pardon into understandable English (in the following lines) clarifies the terms of divine justice as delivered by the document. Most of the laity were untrained in the formal Latin of the church or the Anglo-French language of the law. So working with simple translations of a legal "writ" (that is, a formal written court document or royal command), or of some other official document, was also undoubtedly a familiar activity. As such it reflects another common aspect of institutional experience, the decipherment of documents, procedures, and ideas required for getting on with the law and government as well as with the church. Similar scenes recur repeatedly, in different contexts and tones: Meed's half-understanding of her Latin text that needs to be explained (3.331–53); Repentance's reading of Reason's demands "rolle[d] . . . in þe Registre of Heuene" that must be translated to English (5.271–9); Will's declaration (following Augustine) that the unlettered win salvation while the learned are damned (10.458–71); Patience's definition of poverty and its extended gloss (14.275ff.); the similar extended gloss on Anima's many names (15.22ff.); and several more. An authoritative Latin text is put into plain(er) English, but also at times the narrator directly states that a text or principle which *should* be put into plain English is hidden by its formal Latin or oracular obscurity. Will demurs to interpret the significance of his "metels" more than once; or he declines showily to translate a critical passage:

> Holi writ bit men be war – I will noȝt write it here
> In englissh on auenture it sholde be rehersed to ofte,
> And greue þerwiþ þat goode ben – ac gramariens shul rede:
> *Vnusquisque a fratre se custodiat quia vt dicitur periculum est in falsis fratribus.*
> Ac I wiste neuere freke þat as a frere yede bifore men on englissh
> Taken it for his teme and telle it wiþouten glosyng.   (13.71–5)

Here as elsewhere, the dreamer directly avers that "if lewed men it knewe" (11.108), the unglossed text would lead to trouble, especially when it comes to the contentious issue of clerical possessions and the control of wealth.

By passus 15 where the thickest cluster of these translation moments occurs, this textual decoding combines secular and ecclesial critique in the passionate condemnation of possessioners, clerics who held benefices and other secular wealth. If religious orders kept their institutional integrity, Anima says,

> þanne wolde lordes and ladies be looþ to agulte,
> And to taken of her tenauntȝ moore þan trouþe wolde,
> Founde þei þat freres wolde forsake her almesses
> And bidden hem bere it þere it yborwed was . . .
> *Numquid, dicit Iob, rugiet onager cum herbam habuerit aut mugiet bos*
> *cum ante plenum presepe steterit? . . .*
> If lewed men knewe þis latyn þei wolde loke whom they yeue,
> And auisen hem bifore a fyue dayes or sixe
> Er þei amortisede to monkes or monyales hir rentes.   (15.309–21)

Even as Langland critiques the obfuscatory language of Latin officialdom, he exploits a technical word such as "amortisede," an Anglo-French legal term referring to the largely illegal practice of granting property or rents to the church outside of the control and jurisdiction of the crown.[14] A supposedly spiritual practice provokes a secular legal rejoinder that the laity (or "lewed men") should think twice before granting, irrevocably, property (construed here as income or "rentes") to the church. In a way it seems we are right back at the beginning with the controversy surrounding Meed, debating again the role of money and payment in the order of society, how that money should change hands, who gives out payments and reward to whom for what reason. We can now appreciate the Langlandian mode in which the critique of individual sinners is also a critique of institutional power, and of the legal terms and political languages enabling such patterns of material exploitation. And so the narrator's constant exhortations to the rich and powerful to do law and justice – "Ac if ye riche have ruþe and rewarde wel the pore, / And lyuen as lawe techeth, doon leaute to hem alle" (14.145–6) – combine with his traditional eschatological concern for reward in heaven – "for3ifnesse of hir synnes, and heuen blisse after" (14.154) – to argue for the transcendental force of what earthly *leaute* can do.

This unique narrative combination – of institutional critique through the loaded translations of authoritative discourse, the conflation of secular and ecclesial institutional forms, and the politicization of the allegorical landscape of the soul – also clarifies the role of the other major secular figure of the *vita*, Haukyn the Active Man. He is a minstrel, a waferer and way-farer, a figure of the *activa vita* with a spotted coat and a spotted conscience, himself almost more an institution than individual: a married family man working in the world, thoroughly sinful yet seeking to do well and better, as best he can. Over the long course of Patience's preaching Haukyn is taught the meaning of those virtues he needs to cultivate for salvation. But it is the true meaning of poverty that stops him up short. He requests Patience to translate it into digestible terms: "ye moste kenne me þis on englissh" (14.277). Patience does so at length. So taught, Haukyn weeps tears of true repentance for his sins, but what he weeps for perhaps surprises us:

> "Allas," quod Haukyn þe Actif man þo, "þat after my cristendom
> I ne hadde be deed and doluen for dowelis sake!
> So harde it is," quod haukyn, "to lyue and to do synne.
> Synne seweþ vs euere," quod he and sori gan wexe…
> [He] swouned and sobbed and siked ful ofte
> That euere he hadde lond ouþer lordshipe lasse oþer moore,
> Or maistrie ouer any man mo þan of hymselue. (14.323–31)

Land, lordship, "maistrie": somewhat incongruously (given what we have been told about him), Haukyn's greatest spiritual regret is his abuse of *dominium*, his worldly power over others to whom, presumably, he has done neither law nor *leaute* as Patience has advised. In truth he has not really appeared to be one of "ye riche men" (14.144) whom Patience chided, nor is he aristocratic. But if we read Haukyn less as a character and more as a characterized institution – secular man under the law – his anxiety makes more sense. His sorrow and dread are, at least in part, for the very system that makes men like him oppress other men like him, a system which he now understands more rightly from the perspective of poverty.

From Trajan to Haukyn, emperor to pauper, we thus run the gamut of secular political *dominium* from high to low, virtuously salvific to villainous and damnable. The concluding apocalyptic vision at the end of passus 15 combines this comprehensive critique with a call for clerical dispossession that is almost an inverted foundation-moment:

> If knyghthod and kynde wit and þe commune and conscience
> Togidres loue leelly, leueþ it wel, ye bisshopes,
> The lordeship of londes lese ye shul for euere,
> And lyuen as *Levitici* as oure lord yow techeþ.   (15.553–6)

Knighthood, Commons, and Kynde Wit – three originals who processed with a "kyng" in the Prologue – are now joined by Conscience to take back secular *dominium* from where it has been ill-placed by the Donation of Constantine: "Takeþ hire landes, ye lordes, and leteþ hem lyue by dymes" (15.564). Haukyn's personal spiritual crisis thus gives way to another public vision of institutional reform.

Fittingly, then, at the start of passus 16 the narrator calls Patience's whole disquisition a "faire shewyng" (16.1), meaning not just an explanation but also, technically, a kind of bill of complaint, a list of urgent issues that must be addressed before the law. Bills were said to be "shown" in courts and in parliament, their contents read out in preparation for setting a policy.[15] This weighty process of display and deliberation, and its demands for reform both personal and public, prepare the reader for the inner-dream of passus 16 and for the remarkable vision of the Easter narrative of passūs 17 and 18. Throughout these passūs, the language of law is deployed in traditional metaphors for the atonement and the fulfillment of the ancient promise to Abraham/Faith, for "Londe and lordshipe and lif wiþouten ende" (16.240). It will also be the end of "Luciferis lordshipe" (17.8). Legal terms, royal justice, and the secular principles of equity are invoked to explain the dynamics of salvation, with Jesus as both jouster and justice, the Crucifixion figured as a style of judicial combat. The defeat of the devil and harrowing of hell is presented as a recovery of seisin and *frank tenement*, that is, as a rightful recovery or "seizing" of property, and as the "raunsone" of God's lieges from bondage (18.348–9). The power of divine grace is also explained by appeal to the tradition of "the king's look," that even a convicted felon could be freed just at the glance of the king (18.379–83). And it is a "trewes"/truce called by Truth that reconciles the disparate demands of Mercy and Truth, Peace and Justice, who all exchange the kiss of peace (18.416–24).

All of these quasi-secular metaphors underwrite the climax of the *vita* in passus 18, as Will finally reaches his spiritual goal. Here we see fulfilled, for a moment, all of the promise and reconciliation that the repeated journeys of the *visio* and *vita* sought but did not achieve. The victory is personal and spiritual. Nonetheless it is worth keeping in mind that throughout these passūs, the issues of lordship, power, and political authority have provided the institutional-allegorical framework for understanding that spiritual journey, as well as its emotional pressures, in a manner more than simply symbolic. While Will and his wife Kitt and his daughter Calotte are clearly the individual beneficiaries of all the struggle leading up to this point, the social order at large also has a legitimate claim to share in the narrative's dynamic of messianic reform.

Conclusion, passūs 19–20: *Domine, quis habitabit in tabernaculo tuo?*

Certainly *Piers Plowman* would have a very different overall impact if it ended here at passus 18, with Will and his family joyously reverencing the Cross. And it is possible that early versions of the B text did end here. While there are many differences between the B and C versions, the two concluding passūs 19 and 20 (21 and 22 in C) are largely unchanged. This textual situation has generally been attributed to Langland's decision not to alter the end of the poem, or to his untimely death before he was able to complete his C revisions. But as Lawrence Warner has argued from the evidence of the surviving manuscripts, it also appears possible that the final two passūs are identical in B and C not because C was not revised, but rather because a new conclusion was crafted for the C version which was later grafted on to the manuscript of the B version that served as the source for all later surviving copies of the B text. That is, the text as we have it in both B and C, and hence the large majority of the surviving complete copies of the poem, reflects Langland's desire to revisit his ending by adding two more passūs, and his copyists' desire to include that substantial change in the poem's complete versions.[16]

If this was in fact how *Piers Plowman* developed (and the matter remains uncertain), it underscores the importance of the narrative's return to the secular world in the last two passūs and its critical re-encounter with the institutions of governance. After a long explication of Christ and Piers Plowman by Conscience (19.26–198), Will sees Grace as the *spiritus paraclitus* descend "to Piers and to hise felawes" (19.201) and then go with Piers to "the comune":

> Thanne bigan grace to go wiþ Piers Plowman
> And counseillede hym and Conscience þe comune to sompne:
> "For I wol dele today and dyuyde grace
> To alle kynne creatures þat kan hi[r] fyue wittes,
> Tresour to lyue by to hir lyues ende . . . "   (19.213–17)

Society is re-founded once again – for the third time, at least – by "the division of graces" among the people (*divisiones graciarum sunt* [19.228a]). As with previous metaphors of Christ as "knyght, kyng, conquerour" (19.27), the images and institutional terms that follow are both metaphorical and something more. All estates and labors are once again established, with a "kyng" and administrative officers:

> "Thou3 some be clenner þan some, ye se wel," quod Grace,
> "That al crafte and konnyng come of my 3ifte.
> Lokeþ that noon lakke ooþer, but loueþ as breþeren;
> And who þat moost maistries kan be myldest of berynge.
> And crouneþ Conscience kyng and makeþ craft youre Stiward,
> And after craftes conseil cloþeþ yow and fede.
> For I make Piers þe Plowman my procuratour and my reue,
> And Registrer to receyue *redde quod debes*."   (19.252–9)

Like a kingdom or a city with different craft guilds, the community is both diversified and unified, with Craft as "steward" and the various offices (procurator, reeve, register, and later purveyor) ideally settled in the virtuous figure of Piers. As well the "Cardynales vertues" are sown as seed-grains (19.274). The most important is the *spiritus justiciae* which has even the power "to correcte þe kyng if þe kyng falle in gilt. / For counteþ he no kynges wraþe whan he in Court sitteþ" (19.303–4). This is all preliminary to Grace's command that Piers make a building for his harvest and his community:

> "Ayeins þi greynes," quod Grace, "bigynneþ for to ripe,
> Ordeigne þee an hous, Piers, to herberwe Inne þi cornes." . . .
> And þerewiþ Grace bigan to make a good foundement,
> And watlede it and walled it wiþ hise peynes and his passioun . . .
> And called þat hous vnitee, holy chirche on englissh.
>   (19.317–18, 325–6, 328)

Here another foundation moment (and, we might note, another small translation moment) brings us to a new old "house." Holy Church is now not an allegorical lady as in passus 1 but a structure, an institution. As well Unity is a barn and thus also the focus for productive labor and capital accumulation. When Pride attacks, it becomes a fortress to protect "alle cristene peple," and Kynde Witte instructs Conscience to dig a moat and fortify it "as it a Pyl [i.e., fort] were" (19.361, 363). One building embodies institutional church, agrarian economy, and feudal state.

More darkly and contentiously, the Barn of Unity also quickly becomes the site of discord. "Clennesse of þe comune and clerkes clene lyuynge" are the essential elements of society, asserts Conscience, and this necessarily demands the principle of *redde quod debes* ("pay what you owe") for everyone, to everyone (19.379, 390–5). Everyone must pay their debts, spiritual and fiscal. A brewer quickly voices his dissent: "'Ye? baw!' quod a Brewere, 'I wil noȝt be ruled, / By Iesu, for al youre Ianglynge, wiþ *Spiritus Iustitiae* / Ne after Conscience, by Criste!'" (19.396–8). Each of the estates dissents in turn. A "lewed vicory" (19.409) complains about the abuses of the ecclesial hierarchy and the king's court, and the abuses both decried and practiced by the commons. A lord laughs about how he exploits his dependents through his manor officers of reeve, auditor, and steward (19.459–64). And finally a king "wiþ croune þe comune to rule" states flatly that he will take what he wants, when he wants, "for I am heed of lawe" (19.466, 469).

This order of speaking voices was probably intended to evoke the arrangement of contemporary parliamentary assembly, proceeding as it does from bourgeois commons to the clergy, nobility, and finally the king. The debate centers on just who is liable for their wealth and taxation in the kingdom to pay what they owe. As with the debate over Meed in passūs 2–4, all estates of the realm emerge equally degraded. In passus 20 Will questions the force of need in the face of the law, which (like hunger) drives individuals beyond the power of any human law. The last vision begins with this cue, as Will sees False "sprynge and sprede and spede mennes nedes" (20.55) so that Guile flourishes, Truth is cut away, *leaute* is rebuked, and Antichrist reigns (20.51–64).

Conscience calls on the remaining virtuous "fooles" and "al þe comune" to retreat to Unity, where they will hold out (20.74, 78). The final scene is a psychomachia, a battle of vices and virtues set in the allegorical Barn of Unity and the houses of state and law:

> [Symonye] came to the kynges counseille as a kene baroun
> And knokked Conscience in Court afore hem alle;
> And garte good feiþ flee and fals to abide,

And boldeliche bar adoun wiþ many a bright Noble
Muche of þe wit and wisdom of westmynstre halle.
(20.129–33)

If False seemed to lose in court in passus 4, here he seems to win. Like other virtues Leautee is disparaged as a churl (20.146), and Unity becomes a riot of confusion. Especially after the arrival and entrance of the friars (20.243), the purity and integrity of the Barn of Unity is as degraded as the secular courts it mirrors, as people "fleen to þe freres, as fals folke to westmynstre" (20.285). Where at the start of the narrative Westminster was at least potentially the arena for justice, by the end it has become a plain metonym for institutional venality and corruption. The arrival of the wily friar "Sir Penetrans Domos" is the *coup de grâce*, the undoing of community by the very principles of openness and inclusion (29.340). As with the courts, the challenge to Holy Church is simply more than Conscience can handle. And so the narrative ends with Conscience's departure from his house and from his own kingship, seeking the aid of Piers the Plowman. Unity loses its king Conscience as society has apparently lost its *leaute*.[17]

This final scene is dense and intense, but again we can easily see how the institutional forms of the secular state have provided much of the fodder for Langland's revision. The diseases and pains that afflict the Commons at the beginning of passus 20 – fevers and fluxes, "Coughes and Cardiacles," cramps and toothaches, "Biles and bocches and brennynge Agues" and more (20.81–5) – are the pitiful degradations of the human body that find their counterpart in the disorders of the body politic. Will travels "heuy chered . . . and elenge in herte" (20.2), sad and physically sickened by his experiences even now. Nor are the continued railings against abuses of dominion and wealth strictly impersonal. Certainly the repeated complaints against the moneyed manipulators of Westminster, those "beltway insiders" of fourteenth-century England, are impassioned. In the end the fall of the Barn of Unity is as personal as it is communal, attacked by a Pride "wiþ a kene wille" (20.374). It is betrayed, perhaps unwittingly, by a Contrition that grows uncontrite, refuses to waken, and forgets itself in a dream: "he lyþ adrent and dremeþ" (20.269–370, 377).

These details in particular seem to suggest, at the conclusion, that the dreamer himself comes to be reflected not just in his character(istic) Will or in the dynamic of his stop-and-start pilgrimages, both internal and external. He is equally present, or even more so, in the landscape of his communal horizon, and in the unsatisfactory but unavoidable world that he so desperately wants to see reformed – and so soberly sees to be beyond his individual power to do so. Hence the receding horizon of narrative offers renewed pilgrimage, itself an institutionalized expression of an anti-institutional dissatisfaction and Willful-longing, as the only available response. The genre of the renewed quest emerges, in the end, as the most fundamental political expression of politics' insistent frustrations, a foundation that refuses to stay settled.

8

ANDREW COLE AND ANDREW GALLOWAY

Christian philosophy in
Piers Plowman

"Philosophye," the English word, appears just twice in *Piers Plowman*, the second time brimming with chilly suspicion when we are told that Envy, a follower of Antichrist, "freres to philosophye he fond hem to scole" (20.295).[1] Here, as throughout the poem and indeed generally in medieval culture, "philosophye" refers mostly to Hellenic and Roman (i.e., pagan) ideas, methods, and authorities not directly illuminated by Christian insight and principles. "Philosofres," even once modified as "philosofres wise," appear another four times, yet here again we find meanings familiar to the medieval Christian reception of the ancient disciplines. Popular penitential treatises like the *Somme le Roi* (c. 1280) state the problem very plainly: "Des. IIII. vertuz cardonnaus parlerent mout cil anciain phylosophe, mes li Sainz Esperiz les done mieuz et enseigne cent tans, si com dit Salemons ou liver de Sapience" – or as translated in the late fourteenth-century *Book of Vices and Virtues*, "of þe four cardinal vertues speken moche þe olde philosofres, but þe Holy Gost ȝeueþ hem moche bettre and techeþ hem an hundred so well, as Salamon seiþ in þe boke of Wisdom."[2]

Clearly, there is "philosophye," and its academic *magistri*, and there are sacred truths and their Christian expositors. At best, "philosophye" (and "philosofres") is seen to anticipate the true principles of Christianity; at worst – per the fellowships that Antichrist's factotum doles out to friars – it is a perversion from Christian teachings, exactly the kind of worldly thinking St. Paul condemns when he rails against "philosophy and vain deceit [*philosophiam et inanem fallaciam*], according to the tradition of man, according to the elements of the world [*elementa mundi*] and not according to Christ" (Col. 2:8). This is the same *sapientia huius mundi* (the wisdom of this world) (1 Cor. 1:20) that Langland's Imaginative reproves in his naming the traditions of "patriarkes and prophetes" as "but a folye" (12.137).

Yet Imaginative's comment and Antichrist's educational program should not be taken to represent Langland's sole view, or the standard late medieval sense of such philosophical traditions. Medieval thinkers and theologians from the twelfth and thirteenth centuries on, deeply dependent on Aristotle, Plotinus, Seneca, and other pagan thinkers, fully recognized (to a degree that few early medieval Church Fathers would admit) that pre-Christian thinkers were often admirable figures, so committed to their principles that they constituted a humbling example to more historically and geographically fortunate Christians. As the late thirteenth-century *Somme le Roi* asserts – again in the words of its late fourteenth-century translator:

> in þes foure vertues studied þe olde philosofres, þat dispiseden al þe world and forsoken, for to purchas vertue and wisdom, and þerfore were þei cleped philosofres. For philosofre as moche is to seye as loue of science [*French: ameeur de sapience*]. A, God, how we schulde be a-ferd, whan þei þat weren heþen and wiþ-out any lawe y-write, þat wisten no þing of þe verray grace of God ne of þe Holi Gost, and ȝit clombe þei vp to þe hil of parfiȝtnesse of lif by strengþe of here owne vertue, and deyned not to loke on þe world; & we þat ben cristene and hadde þe grace and þe bileue veraliche . . . and more we myȝt do profiȝt in on day þan þilke myȝten in an hole ȝere, we lyuen as swyn here byneþe in þis grottes of þis world![3]

It is in this more positive sense of "philosopher" that Imaginative rebukes Will, who has interrupted a vision of Middle Earth by asking a challenging question of Reason, "for þyn entremetynge here artow forsake: / *Philosophus esses si tacuisses*" ["you would have been a philosopher if you had stayed silent"], from Boethius, *Consolation of Philosophy* 2, pr. 7, 20 (11.416–16a). The same entirely positive and apparently universal – rather than specifically "heathen" – sense appears when Grace, at the end of the poem, founds the general vocation of "Philosophres wise" (19.244).

Langland evidently exhibits variations or instabilities of meaning around the term "philosophye," but these should be viewed not as rejections of thinking about thinking but as markers of the poem's unsettled relation to scholastic inquiry and the university – and its flat contempt for lucrative governmental professions that depend on college degrees (swept up in the Prologue's survey as "Bisshopes and Bachelers, boþe maistres and doctours" who "seruen þe kyng and his siluer tellen, / In Cheker [the Exchequer] and in Chauncelrie chalengen his dettes" [Prol.87–93]). The poem's attention to academic thinking and discursive style is obvious and pervasive, as is its author's love of difficult and even abstruse arguments. At the same time, citation of the typical texts and authorities of academic style and consistency in developing arguments of the sort found in scholastic contexts are notably absent from the poem, disrupted by effects and goals that pull attention and understanding in other directions. In this light, one wonders how truly learned the poet was in materials we consider either "theology" or "philosophy," including the regular syntheses of both that characterized late medieval academic learning[4] – or how much he really learned when, as he claims, he was the beneficiary of "my fader and my frendes" who – just as Antichrist's minion Envy did for the friars – "foende me to scole" (C.5.36; see Chapter 5). The mystery of Langland's own education is inextricable from the unresolved problems yet attractions that "learning" offers in the poem.

Learned Langland

Piers Plowman is undoubtedly a learned and intellectually searching poem. But these attributes make it all the odder that the poet maintains almost complete silence on the names of medieval thinkers and theologians. He cites Albertus Magnus ("Albert the Great") only in reference to the "Experimentȝ of Alkanemye of Albertes makyng" (B.10.217), and apparently alludes to friar William Jordan in 13.25–214, which depicts a fat fraternal Doctor of Divinity as "þis Iurdan" who had just days ago "Preched" "bifore þe deen of Poules" (St. Paul's Cathedral; 13.84, 65–6). (The allusion thus features Jordan's public disputes in 1377 with Uthred of Boldon, Benedictine monk and Oxford doctorate who had mounted a long campaign against the friars' claims for their version of poverty and the "disendowment" of the rest of the church's wealth; Uthred's own tract is keyed to a punning use of the biblical text, "Periculum in falsis fratribus" ["peril in false brothers/friars"; 2 Cor. 11:26].[5] Facing the Doctor of Divinity, Will spits out the same text, though – in an odd slip into the poet's own identity – he refuses to "write it here / In englissh on auenture it sholde be reherced to ofte" [13.70–2].) The several references to St. Francis, St. Benedict, and St. Dominic seem to point to only one of the poem's many religious and political concerns: the fraternal orders. Plato, Aristotle, "Cato" (to whom was attributed the moral Latin distichs that were so widely read in basic medieval schooling), Avianus (the fourth-century Roman poet whose short, moralized poetic fables were also staples of the medieval schoolroom), and perhaps Averroes are mentioned, though the poet invariably recognizes them as pagan poets and taletellers as much as philosophers (10.178–9; 12.268; 12.259; 13.91).[6]

Langland can be forgiven for dropping some venerable names, as Chaucer does, like Plato's or "Sortes" (i.e., Socrates, in the common Latin form) without dwelling on the actual works involved, for Plato's writings were mainly limited in the Latin west to Calcidius' partial translation of the *Timaeus*, whose cosmology – outlining the "elements of the world" – had an enormous influence. But Aristotle, even in the thought of more or less anti-Aristotelian contemporary academics like the "Oxford Realists," including

John Wyclif (died 1384),[7] was central to medieval academic culture, a mainstay of the "scole" that both Envy's friar-students and Will were "provided for" to attend. Only once, in Imaginative's speech, does Aristotle receive enough attention to suggest something more than distant name-recognition, a mention taken up below.

So how are we to sort Langland's overt references to the foundational Church Fathers or "patristic" authorities – Augustine, Gregory, Jerome, and Ambrose (19.269–70) – with whatever evidence there is that he actually read their works? He mentions Augustine the most (fourteen times, excluding repetitions from previous versions), with Gregory coming in for a close second (ten times, excluding repetitions). There is also a cameo by the Greek Father John Chrysostom (15.117–18), though this reference identifies a rather poetically intrusive prose Latin quotation from an apocryphal commentary on Matthew, the only work associated with Chrysostom's name that circulated in the Latin west; as such it indicates, yet again, the poet's unpredictable resources of memory and texts. There is, however, a basic reason why Langland refers to Augustine the most in his poem – a reason that may help us loosely understand the poet's philosophical context, his place within it, and his response to it.

In fourteenth-century England, Augustine remained at least as significant as Aristotle in the minds of those most notable clerics who spent their lives shuttling between London and Oxford. One of those, John Duns Scotus (died 1308), used Augustine to argue for God's infinite power yet God's commitment to reward with eternal life those who did their best. Another, William Ockham (died 1347), looked to Augustine (through Scotus) to make the human "will" yet more primary in the human soul and in God's agreed-upon granting of "merit," but denounced Scotus's inconsistencies and qualifications to this divine "pact," by which the relationship between merit and reward no less than the laws of the universe could continue in spite of God's ability to alter them at any moment. These thinkers' focus on the radically free individual "will" puts them very close to the emphases in *Piers Plowman*. Another reader of Augustine, however, was Thomas Bradwardine (died 1349), archbishop of Canterbury, who cited Augustine to argue, in his mammoth and widely influential *De causa Dei*, for a "divine coefficiency" between the human will and God's will, and who denounced those who placed the human will in any supreme position (a position of "Pelagianism" that Bradwardine saw as a creeping plague). And yet another was Wyclif, who turned to Augustine in his dozens of major works to bring to a logical but deeply anticlerical focus the idea (from *The City of God* and fully developed by Augustinian friars before Wyclif took hold of it) that only those in a state of grace had real rights over property and

persons – which, to Wyclif (though certainly not to Augustine or Bradwardine), meant that a corrupt clergy should not be allowed to keep
their church's vast wealth.[8] This view too has some echoes in *Piers Plowman*: "Takeþ her landes ye lordes, and leteþ hem lyue by dymes" (tithes)
(15.564). So much was this the great century of Augustinianism and "neo-
Augustinianism" that even Chaucer's Nun's Priest can coyly indicate some
awareness of the problem of "free will" versus "divine predestination," to
boot in distinctively academic terms:

> But I ne kan nat bulte it to the bren
> As kan the hooly doctour Augustyn,
> Or Boece, or the Bisshop Bradwardyn,
> Wheither that Godds worthy forwityng
> Streyneth me nedely [necessarily] for to doon a thyng.
>
> VII.3240–4

As this passage shows, a remark about the "hooly doctour" Augustine is
simultaneously a comment about one of England's greatest Augustinians,
"Bisshop Bradwardyn" – revealing to us just how the intellectual context
informs anodyne banter about heady topics.

So what of Langland? Given that many of the most significant issues of
medieval philosophy, including a great deal of Neoplatonic thought, are
framed and pursued by Augustine, a close reading of his works alone would
get the poet quite far and supply him a very basic plan by which to construct
the architecture of *Piers Plowman*, and edify the various levels of knowledge and experience detailed over the entire course of the poem. To take a
simple example, Augustine, in his widely read guide on Christian teachers
and preachers, *On Christine Doctrine* (begun AD 397, finished 426), begins
with an adapted Neoplatonic hierarchy of "signs" by which the invisible is
mediated visibly in increasingly direct ways – first, the natural world itself
by which God least directly "speaks"; next, human words (first spoken then
followed by written testimonies) by which God more directly speaks; finally,
the incarnate and then Risen Christ by whom God most directly and fully
communicates and communes. Augustine then ends *On Christian Doctrine*
with a parallel hierarchy of "teachers," beginning with those who lack fine
rhetorical training but live such that their way of life "becomes, in a sense,
an abundant source of eloquence"; then those who preach God's truth fully
and eloquently, even if they do not live piously; finally those who embody
or practice as well as preach God's truth, serving as the highest clerical leaders, an ideal epitomized by Christ, of whom such highest teachers present
an *imitatio*.[9] These rankings, with their clear connections to how divinely

created semiotics or allegory itself works, can in some ways be paralleled by Langland's shifting definitions of the three "lives" of Dowel, Dobet, and Dobest. In the words of the character called Thought, the poet explains that Dowel is "Trewe of his tunge and of his two handes . . . Trusty of his tailende [reckoning], takeþ but his owene"; Dobet has "ronne to Religion, and haþ rendred þe bible, and precheþ þe peple Seint Poules wordes"; and Dobest is "aboue boþe and bereþ a bisshopes crosse" that is "hoked at þat oon ende to holde men in good lif" (8.78–106). Piers Plowman, who embodies all these "lives," also is one of the most semiotically rich figures in the poem, and in fact in the end becomes nothing less than the physical vehicle for Augustine's final ideal teacher, Christ: "This Iesus of his gentries wol Iuste in Piers armes," as Faith tells Will as they witness the (or a new?) Crucifixion (18.22).

None of this is proof that Langland closely studied Augustine's *On Christian Doctrine*, nor did the poet write or think like his university-trained contemporaries, whose tracts and sermons are, among other things, exercises in the citation and name-checking of authorities. Yet one should not take that fact to support the conclusion that the poet was merely a distant and indirect inheritor of the philosophical authorities, offering what G. R. Owst called "nothing more nor less than the quintessence of English mediaeval preaching gathered up into a single metrical piece of unusual charm and vivacity."[10] Such disparagement of the poet's depth of knowledge does not hold water. Scholars may never be able to map fully the intellectual range and resources of the author of *Piers Plowman* or the poem itself, but that may be because we have trouble fully assessing the entrepôt of learning that later fourteenth-century London and its environs constituted – the region that, whatever Langland's misgivings about its legal and commercial corruption and however distant we may wish to argue this "Malvern" bard remained from it, the poet frequented for most of his life.[11]

One can be clear: the poet's range and intellectual vagrancy were surely fostered by the varieties of learnedness that could be tapped in late fourteenth-century London and environs, including Westminster (for which see passus 3, and 20.129–39). Though its official academic student community numbered perhaps only 400, the City has been compared to Oxford and Paris in its intellectual resources, given its many mendicant priories and the exceptional brilliance of secular scholars it drew.[12] Both the Austin Friars' and the Carmelites' schools in their London priories had the status of *studia generalia*; the London Dominican house, Blackfriars (see Figure 1), was designated a *studium particulare theologiae*; the Franciscan house, Greyfriars, had supported in the fourteenth century scholars such as Walter

Chatton and Ockham, most of whose logical works were produced or revised there. Add to this account the range of resources for that other rich vein of learning in *Piers Plowman*: the law.[13] London was the center of civic and canon law learning and lawcourts, from the Arches, the appeals court of the Archbishop of Canterbury and considered the most important ecclesiastical court in England, to the walled lawyers' "Inns," supplying a stream of learned staff on which the royal civil service centered at nearby Westminster depended. This concentration contributed to a range of wider public debate that made questions of a seemingly abstruse academic nature pressing, such as the arguments over church wealth, the sacraments (especially the Eucharist), and the realm's economic obligations to Rome, or the City's to the king. A career with the right connections might weave through many of these locales, as it might skirt Oxford and back, without leaving an obvious trail in the surviving records, allowing quantities of inquiry and reading, or simply the long-pondered accretion of innumerable pieces of texts that circulated through these milieux.

In reading *Piers Plowman*, then, we have to do more than fix on a particular philosophical problem – yesterday synderesis, today imagination, tomorrow motion – and then offer up the appropriate reading of Langland from the point of view of that single issue. Instead, it seems best first to appreciate the varieties of learnedness around him, practiced every day in a number of different institutions, religious and secular. In that light appears a poet who is more perceptive than any other contemporary philosopher on what constitutes the grounds of philosophy and thought, questioning those very bases. *Piers Plowman*, in other words, reflects the work of a poet who did some careful picking and choosing, reading and engaging the received authorities by testing and questioning their very premises, the grounds of their claims about the importance of belief and the supremacy of reason to help humans generate an ethical, social, salvific, and lyrical thought – simultaneously. Langland's work is exceptional because it is representative in a uniquely brilliant way – speaking to his intellectual context in a manner no one else could do, much less imagine so vividly and strikingly in the dialectical manner of thinking itself.

Believing, reasoning, testing

> For hadde neuere freke fyn wit þe feiþ to dispute,
> Ne man hadde no merite myȝte it ben ypreued:
> *Fides non habet meritum vbi humana racio prebet experimentum.*
> [Faith has no merit where human reason offers experience.]
>
> 10.255–6a

Intellectual historians have sometimes described the Middle Ages as developing gradually toward a synthesis of "faith" (or doctrine) and "reason" in the twelfth and thirteenth centuries, spanning, for instance, the thought of Anselm through that of Thomas Aquinas, then steadily splintering in the fourteenth century, when thinkers like Scotus worked on the presumption that no conclusion of reason (of which he produced a great many exceedingly subtle ones) could ever touch the nature of faith; mystical works for the laity like the late fourteenth-century *Cloud of Unknowing* marked this fissure explicitly. Such an account, while helpful for organizing some large trends, struggles to assist a close analysis of *Piers Plowman* – not because Langland fuses reason with faith in some triumphant if old-fashioned Thomistic unity (it is clear that he does not) but rather because intellection and its associated discursive arts figure so centrally in the poem, and "faith" so problematically.

Dame Study's comment above offers a small but elegant example of how unpredictably the relation between faith and reason is posed in this poem. The quotation she cites is from Gregory the Great's sixth-century *Homilies*, although this excerpt is available in Langland's period in the liturgy, in first lesson of matins on the Sunday after Easter, and elsewhere; thus the question again emerges of how studiously deep his reading is. The usual force of that quotation is an emphasis on faith's supreme transcendence of reason, since otherwise faith would not have its own value of belief in "the evidence of things that appear not" (Hebrews 11:1). As Augustine (though no stranger to elaborate philosophical inquiry) famously stated in his reference to the Old Latin version of Isaiah 7:9: "unless you believe, you will not understand."[14] Most late medieval thinkers would say so as well. Aquinas, for instance, declared that faith involved assent without evidence of truth, whereas knowledge required that evidence.[15] Some academics in Langland's time would go further in affirming the supreme cognitive importance of faith: Wyclif, for instance, argued that any cognition, anything given the status of knowledge of the truth, requires faith that it *is* the truth, by which God made all assent to knowledge as knowledge founded on an implicit act of faith. Wyclif quoted Gregory's phrase frequently to argue against any claims (as by the *moderni*) for the power of strictly human intuitive cognition – which might, therefore, argue against Will's pursuit of "kynde knowynge" in *Piers Plowman*, unless the hopelessness of that is seen to expose the limits of the purely humanly created faculty.[16] Langland's London contemporary, the sheriff's clerk Thomas Usk (executed in 1388 in the purge by the "Lords Appellant" of anyone seen as a close supporter of Richard II) used the Gregorian phrase similarly, though despairingly, in the treatise he wrote in prison seeking to exculpate himself, the *Testament of Love* (c. 1386):

> For, of God, maker of kynde, wytnesse I toke that for none envy ne yvel have I drawe this mater togyder, but only for goodnesse to maintayn and errours in falstees to distroy... yet to ful faithe in credence of deserte, fully mowe [these reasons] nat suffyse, sithen, "Faith hath no meryte of mede whan mannes reason sheweth experyence in doyng." For utterly, no reason, the parfyte blysse of love by no waye, maye make to be comprehended.[17]

Unlike Wyclif and Usk, Dame Study turns the point of Gregory's passage inside out. The claim is no longer that faith must exceed reason, which would considerably demote intellection and hair-splitting disputation of the kind she represents. Instead, reversing this sense in a way worthy of her own name, Dame Study takes Gregory's phrase to mean that intellection, "fyn wit," is an elegant and essential tool for testing and "proving" faith, and granting merit only to the "man" who can manage this.

This small but surprisingly complicated handling of the meaning of an authoritative Latin quotation accomplishes several things. Most directly, it announces a poetics that is far more thought-driven and intellectually confident than other Middle English writing in Langland's period – when, indeed, many new instances of sophisticated vernacular writing, preaching, and translating were appearing. Second, it adopts a position that is far less certain about the outcome than most theological or clerical disputation, showing a positive eagerness to face *experimentum*. Third, related to that spirit of welcoming new *experimenta*, it shows that a passage from an authority no matter how august – even one of Langland's most regular buttresses, Gregory the Great – can be twirled into a sense that is unexpected if not wholly novel, demonstrating as well as arguing for the value of improvisational debating skills. Study shows the rhetorical reward as well as the uncertain intellectual venture of meeting challenges to faith head-on and open-endedly.

The phrase "fyn wit" itself is striking in this context: whereas other Middle English poets are committed to the courtly skills of "luf talkynge" like the poet of *Sir Gawain and the Green Knight* or Chaucer, and may invoke and praise "the craft of fyn lovynge" – pointing to French *fin amour* – Study invokes a quite different but no less rhetorically and argumentatively inflected value. Unless you can adroitly defend your views, Dame Study says, you are without merit when your faith is challenged, and indeed, your merit depends on your faith *being* challenged. In her paraphrase of Gregory, Study translates "*prebet experimentum*" as "ben ypreued," suggesting an implicit Latin pun of taking *praebere* "to offer, present" as if it were *probare* "to put to the test." The rest of her lines need careful translation as well: "For if someone did not have the fine wit to dispute about the faith, he would have no merit if [the faith] were ever put to the test."

Like all the figures in the poem, Study should not be understood to speak directly for the poet on all points, but this moment indicates issues found throughout the poem's narrative and through its successive revisions. "Proving" and "testing" faith with "fyn wit" runs through not only the overtly epistemological portions of the poem that Study dominates, sometimes described as the "inward journey,"[18] but also from the poem's beginning and continuing right through to the end – and, in the sense of the revising author's and other readers' continuations of this process, beyond. The theme of intellectual and ethical *experimenta* is announced with the narrator's initial wandering and gazing, and the theme is explicitly articulated as early as the words of a clearly authoritative figure, whose likeness to Lady Philosophy from Boethius' *Consolation of Philosophy* is more than superficial: Holy Church. This figure frames her seemingly unwavering lesson on "treuthe" as an affirmation of an open-ended process of comprehensive trying or testing: "Whan alle tresors ben tried, treuþe is þe beste" (B.1.207; also 85).

Though her discourse has often been seen to offer a wooden progression through predictable doctrinal points, she indicates throughout the importance of that testing or *trying* all things, a biblical proof-text for which appears throughout the poem: *omnia probate... quod bonum est tenete*: "test all things – hold fast to the good" (1 Thess. 5:21; see, e.g., *Piers Plowman* 3.339, 343).[19] This text establishes an approach not far from Chaucer's Wife of Bath's emphasis on "experience" to measure "authority" – not to offer a banal or silencing conclusion about "treuthe" (whatever we conclude that is), but to explore and experience both what is posited as truth and faith and their opposites, and learn from the results.[20] Holy Church's basic instruction of Will (whom she reminds, "I vnderfeng þee first and þi feiþ þee tauʒte" [1.75]) provides a surprisingly sophisticated methodological as well as topical introduction to the conceptual path he must take. It is entirely logical that, having been told he must try all things to learn "the true," Will asks as soon as she is done speaking for her to show him "by som craft to knowe þe false." "Lo where he stondeþ," she obligingly declares, opening the curtain on the marriage of False and Lady Meed (2.4–5).

Not all experiments turn out as predicted, as the uncertain "progress" of the poem shows. Because ideas have enormous power within and around the poem's actions, whenever the grounds of certainty fail, as they do in debate after debate in the poem, "fyn wit" and poetry fall silent. Episodic rupturing is frequent and inevitable, since the very value of faith (as Study has said) depends on its being "disputed," whereby only whatever remains after testing may be the purified residue. "Experimentʒ of Alkanemye" indeed. For all of the poem's scornful dismissals of knowledge for the sake of knowledge, in its subtle probing and testing of faith it shows an indirect though strong tie not only to what would become (in gross simplification of the range of late medieval arguments) Protestantism, but also the roots of what we have come to think of as "applied" science, as that can be traced to thinkers like Roger Bacon in the mid thirteenth century, but which also has a more anonymous tradition in the works of later medieval clergy interested in the "darker" sciences of geomancy, prophecy, alchemy, and language puzzles.[21] Although Aristotelianism, that center-point and sometimes target of the late medieval scholastic world, is, like "philosophye," rarely visible in *Piers Plowman*, the poem's principles are nonetheless profoundly attuned to the spirit of the Stagirite himself. Aristotle opens the *Metaphysics*, "All men by nature desire to understand": no principle more fully defines Langland's narrator. This heuristic aspect of the poem was not lost on at least some of its earliest readers. As the apocryphal "final chapter" added to the short A text in some fifteenth-century copies declares, near the end of Will the poet's life (which this added "final chapter" describes), Scripture assigns the allegorical figure *Omnia probate* to be Will's permanent companion, entrusting this poor "clerioun" to lead Will toward "þe burgh *quod bonum est tenete*" (A.12.49–52).

It is this testing and "experimental" mode that makes the poem's thought so difficult to plumb and categorize neatly; and as a direct result, its form to some readers has always seemed "disorganized" and "formless," the work of "a poet not securely in control of his material."[22] Even its key personifications and characters continuously change and develop in subtle or dramatic ways (Piers Plowman being the most obvious), a process whose sequence should be sought across the versions as well as through each one.[23] These modal problems also make very difficult the task of assigning the poem a specific intellectual position. Is the poem primarily "neo-Augustinian," focused on the unpredictable salvation of some chosen elite? Is it Pelagian, or "semi-Pelagian," in acknowledging the efficacy of good works in the scheme of salvation?[24] Is the poem imbued with a "monastic world-view" of apocalypticism and the pursuit of a general (social) perfection?[25] What do we make of its relentlessly caustic and ultimately revolutionary critique of the temporal wealth and power of the church and its official orders? And how does that critique sort with Langland's careful exposition of "lollares" in the C text, written during the rise of the heretical Wycliffite movement, which advocated for the disendowment of the church?[26]

Many combinations of these positions and affiliations are possible, and a nuanced set of several has often (though not always) seemed to critics preferable to placing the poem narrowly within a given "thought-form" (to use Morton Bloomfield's formulation of the goals of intellectual history).

Yet in whatever context or "form" of thought one situates the poem, we can be sure that no "-ism" will ever work in describing its "belief," for the sole reason that Langland persistently and openly queries what is always taken for granted in the most straightforward, authorized kinds of creedal Christianity. For some, the results will always seem more often shapeless than controlled. Others, however, will see that within its interrogation of commonplace terms, Langland's and his poem's intellectual sophistication and depth are persistently apparent, a unique presence amid the landscapes of both academic philosophy and vernacular poetry, and a major challenge to the presumption that either blunt critique or elegant poetic craft are inconsistent with intellectual stature.

Concrete universals and abstract givens

To verify any given sense of the shape of Langland's thought, we might look to the poet's presentation of the Trinity, insofar as doctrine about the triune deity was for centuries grounded in the Nicene and Athanasian creeds, the latter of which the poet has already cited in the Pardon scene (7.113–14). Surely Langland can extract a straightforward formulation of Trinitarian doctrine from the Athanasian Creed? Think again. The Trinity is everywhere in *Piers Plowman*, and never seems to mean the same thing from character to character, or even within the same character's presentation. The purpose of meditating on the Trinity is also multifarious. Where one character (Dame Study) will harangue about scholastic inquiry into the nature of the Trinity (10.52–68), another (Clergy) regards, even if in meandering fashion, the Trinity as a point of belief ("articles of þe feiþ" [10.239]; see 238–48). For his part, Anima represents both positions or, rather, a conflicted attitude on the usefulness of teaching and talking about the Trinity. He complains that "Freres and fele oþere maistres... moeuen materes vnmesurable to tellen of þe Trinite," leaving the laity in great doubt about this point of belief, and prefers instead teaching on the "ten comaundementȝ, and ... þe seuene synnes" (15.70–1, 74). He also, however, wishes that "Euery bisshop" (15.570) should travel throughout his "prouince" (like a friar?) and preach "on þe Trinite to bileue" (572). Whether the Trinity is confused by friars and taught more appropriately by the seculars – though of course friars could be bishops too – is not settled by Anima, who only complicates matters on the advisability of teaching the Trinity to the laity when he states that such teaching is essential to convert non-Christian monotheists: "And siþ þat þise Sarȝenes, Scribes and Grekes / Han a lippe of oure bileue, þe lightlier me þynkeþ / Thei sholde turne, whoso travaile wolde to teche hem of þe Trinite" (15.501–3; see 15.605–12a; see also Chapter 9).

(Conversion, so the thinking goes, is as simple as addition: you already believe in two – a prophet and a God – so add another to yield a Trinity that suits any monotheist: a single triune deity according to the Athanasian Creed, which opens with relevant theme "*Quicumque vult salvus esse* [Whosoever shall be saved]." Clergy made the theistic point earlier on: "For al is but oon god and ech is god hymselue: / *Deus pater, deus filius, deus spiritus sanctus*" [10.246–6a].) And later on, we discover that Anima's Trinitarian message for non-Christians is realized by Abraham (called "Faith" [16.176]), who teaches the Trinity at great length (16.181–224), however much he is later shown to be an ineluctably pre-Christian figure in the parable of the Good Samaritan (17.60, 91).

It is hard to imagine how to accept these or other passages as Langland's evaluative comments on the long history of Trinitarian theology; further-more, no particular point here emerges as the vanquished error of a time long past (modalism, adoptionism, and so forth). Langland may find doctrinal debates and specific theological errors beneath mention in an alliterative poem of such magnitude and sweep. And so instead, in Dame Study's sharply witty mouth, he offers caricature:

> Ac if þei carpen of crist, þise clerkes and þise lewed [laity],
> At mete in hir murþe whan Mynstrals beþ stille,
> Than telleþ þei of þe Trinite how two slowe þe þridde,
> And bryngen forþ a balled reson, taken Bernard to witnesse,
> And putten forþ presumpcioun to preue þe soþe.   (10.52–6)

Seeing that the Trinity has divided faiths as much as unified them, Langland perhaps makes here a similar point on a smaller scale: academic discussion of the Trinity is bound to foment argument and error among clerks and the laity alike. But to linger over this strange passage, we can ask what Langland could possibly be describing. The answer tells us something, in the end, about how the poet handles abstractions, how he thinks and how he wishes Will to think.

The Good Samaritan in passus 17 helps us make some sense of this passage, as he emerges as the pre-eminent expert on the Trinity in this poem, insofar as he has the lion's share of discussion about it (17.140–298). Likening the Trinity to a hand (God as fist, Holy Ghost as palm, Christ as fingers: 147–9) as one way of talking concretely about the Trinity to "Eretikes wiþ argument3" (139), he says that if your palm is injured in any way, your hand will not work – the lesson being that no injury should be done to the Holy Spirit: "So whoso synneþ in þe Seint Spirit, it semeþ þat he greueþ / God" (204–5). It does not take much to imagine how this abstract point, here made a bit more concrete through similitude, might be rendered into a tale about internecine conflict among the Trinity in which one member is injured by the others, "how two slowe þe þridde." Everywhere in this long speech Langland exhibits the tendency to exemplify the abstract and particularize the universal, as if to practice in poetry precisely the sort of "kynde knowing" that Will seeks to acquire, time and again. Such "kynde knowing" is a *way*, rather than a *what*.

This much is certain, then: Langland is decidedly uninterested in openly talking favorably about the kind of speculative philosophy that would come to characterize the excesses of scholasticism: the modern cliché that scholasticism asks how many angels fit on the head of a pin finds its equivalent, in Langland's day, in asking about other possible worlds, golden mountains (Chatton contra Ockham[27]), and flying men deprived of senses (Ibn Sina [Avicenna][28]). This is not to exclude questions about whether God can create an object so heavy even he cannot lift it, or – notoriously – whether God can restore one's virginity, as Peter Damian asked.[29] Nor should we neglect to clarify that the cliché about angels on the head of a pin is at several removes from the real inquiry about the continuum, by Scotus among others: "Utrum angelus possit moveri de loco ad alium locum motu continuo [whether an angel can move from one place to another place through continuous motion]."[30] Langland frowns upon such high and strange matters, through the character of Dame Study. She is relentless, condemning anyone who "wilneþ to wite þe whyes of god almy3ty" – wishing "his ei3e were in his ers" (10.127–8); berating friars and posers who dream up fake topics for speculation for an affluent laity after the Black Death who desperately seek distraction and consolation – "Freres and faitours han founde vp swiche questions / To plese wiþ proude men syn þe pestilence tyme" (10.72–3); and denouncing the rich who imitate clerks asking abstruse questions: "hie3e men . . . / Carpen as þei clerkes were of crist and of his my3tes, / And leyden fautes vpon þe fader þat formed vs alle" (10.104–6).

Yet Langland has his own questions to ask, and they would seem outlandish only for the ways in which they estrange the simplest, most repeated terms of late medieval Christianity: "What is charite?," Will blithely asks (15.149; see 14.98 with 16.2–3). And an answer he gets in what can rightly be described as the *cognitive, synaesthetic apex* of the poem, the scene containing the Tree of Charity, which, according to Piers, "meneþ" "the Trinity" (16.63; see also Chapter 4). If that is what the tree means, scholars have not taken Piers entirely at his word, since numerous sources to the Tree of Charity have been proposed – all in the effort to explain if not literalize this enigmatic image. There is no consensus in the field of Langland studies as to which source or analogue best explains the origins of the Tree of Charity, or its particular features – its structure, its fruit, its props, its tripartite modes.[31] Perhaps the closest single analogue is the most widely popular one, the "garden of virtues" with the tree representing Jesus in the middle, depicted by the widely translated pastoral guide, the *Somme le Roi*, already mentioned. That Tree's roots are God's "outrageous charite" ("tres grant amour et l'outraigeuse charité"); its leaves are holy words, its flowers saintly thoughts, its fruit the twelve apostles, its branches virtues and glorious examples.[32] But Langland's image and scene build to an "outrageous" excess for which there is no basis in that fairly pedestrian source. And perhaps that is Langland's point. To draw from that great philosophical cliché, readers haven't seen the forest for the Tree, haven't acknowledged that the sensory overload presented here, and experienced by Will, is itself the point, typifying in one richly dense image Langland's capacity to complicate the commonplace, as if this image is truly the one answer to Will's question or any question at all. If, in other words, Aristotle was right in saying that "[w]ithout an image thinking is impossible," then the image Langland constructs here is decidedly the basis upon which no single thought can be had, much less a memory that can recount in every detail all that was seen in one glance.[33]

In that respect, there is one other tree, this from the medieval academic sources, that at least approximates the Tree of Charity in terms of densely layered effects and sheer multiplicity, supplementing or counterbalancing the tree in the popular *Somme le Roi* and its dull English translations. That is Porphyry's Tree, which, as Umberto Eco explains it, "blows up in a dust of differentiae, in a turmoil of infinite accidents, in a nonhierarchical network of *qualia*."[34] Eco means this point negatively – means to say that the widespread diagram known as Porphyry's Tree fails to clarify matters at all, despite the fact that Petrus Hispanus, among others such as Ramon Llull and William Sherwood, intends to communicate clearly with this figure in his *Arbor porphyriana*: "The Porphyrian Tree makes these matters plain to you."[35] Will's plain question yields a complicated, visual answer in the Tree of Charity, and in this way seems to be a riposte to scholastic, diagrammatic visuality, something like an anti-image to the common mode of diagramming modes of knowing within medieval logic. Whatever logic there is to the Tree of Charity, it is beyond comprehension, or at least cannot be grasped in one cognitive act. No wonder the Tree of Charity overburdens the system and shuts it down entirely: testing faith with this "fyn wit," the inner dream in which this wondrous image is figured ends suddenly, and things take a turn toward simple, biblical narrative – the exposition of Christ's life (16.90).

Thinking

If Langland is keen to expound upon the thought and practice of faith and belief – showing us that the thought of either expresses quickly their limits and thus reasserts the primacy of practice – then what of the thought of thought, which in one line of intellectual history from Descartes to Hegel to Heidegger represents the central task of philosophy? If the Tree of Charity scene does not demand a different kind of thinking, or spark even an idle thought about what can be both perceived and known, then it is hard to imagine what might. But that different kind of thinking, knowing, and perceiving is modeled by Piers Plowman, who has a deeper knowledge of charity – "Ac Piers þe Plowman parceyueþ moore depper" (15.199; see 16.103) – than do the "Clerkes [who] haue no knowyng...but by werkes and wordes." The point here is that the common trope in much Latin and vernacular writing condemning the ignorant laity and celebrating the intellectual class is reversed: now the *magistri* appear to have the cognitive capacities of the lewd, who are said to judge reality by observing spontaneously what is before them, words and works. It takes Piers Plowman to split the difference and perform something like metacriticism, seeing into things productively though paradoxically, both particularly and universally. No divine himself, he nonetheless has the divine ability to read minds and see thoughts: "Piers þe Plowman parceyueþ moore depper / What is þe wille and wherfore þat many wight suffreþ: / *Et vidit deus cogitaciones eorum* [And God saw their thoughts]" (15.199–200a; see 7.136–8 on "who lerned þee on boke?"). Simply put, Piers Plowman can do what no one in the discipline of theology can, insofar as Dame Study herself has already gone on record stating that theology gets "mistier" the "moore I muse þerInne" and "þe depper I deuyned" (10.186–7). Langland has offered us, in short, a complex epistemological justification of the more familiar point uttered by Scripture: that "kete [bold]" clerks who "konne manye bokes" are "none sonner saued, ne sadder of bileue / Than Plowmen and pastours and pouere commune laborers" (10.464–6; it is approximately here that the A text ends).

Yet there is more to say about these passages, for it appears that Langland knows exactly how these cognitive claims would resonate in the lecture rooms of medieval Oxford, or he wouldn't write these lines in such a status-conscious way that signals just what cultural capital is good for, and what it cannot buy. We do not mean the facile point that a smart Plowman would be an outrage for a clerk to behold, much less suffer. Rather, the poet understands what it means to speak of a thought that goes "depper," a perception that is "moore depper." And philosophers engaged in late medieval mathematics, limit-thinking, and contemporary forms of atomism – from Gerard of Odo in Paris to the successive Oxonians Henry Harclay, Walter Chatton, and William Crathorn – understood this thought, too.[36] For they formulate propositions about the very grounds of the created order by first speculating about the greatest cognitive capacities, asking how far down into the indivisibles, into the tiniest parts of the created order, can God see and think, how deep into the *minima naturalia* can he really go? Langland gives Piers Plowman an ability scholastics can only dream of or, per Dame Study, simply fail at doing. So it is with a special, epistemological interest that Langland concocts the seemingly innocent allegory that is the figure of Piers Plowman, neither God nor man, neither scholastic nor plowman, yet oddly all of these things at once, rendering "philosophye" truly transcendent but deeply immanent.

Anima's comments (above) on Piers Plowman's mind-reading thus go to the heart of what it means to philosophize for Langland, in the best sense of that vocation that sheds the academic taint of the term "philosophye." Indeed, the poet remakes the word into a new meaning by looking back to an old quotation, here cited by Imaginative in his discourse with Will:

> *Philosophus esses si tacuisses.*
> [A philosopher you would have been if you had remained silent.]
> Adam, wiles he spak no3t, hadde paradis at wille,
> Ac whan he mamelede about mete, and entermeted to knowe
> The wisedom and þe wit of god, he was put fram blisse.
>
> (11.416–18)

Because Piers Plowman simply perceives and knows, and forgoes blabbing about scholasticism, he makes up for what Adam himself lost in Paradise – his philosophical ways. In seeing godlike into our thoughts, Piers Plowman would be that philosopher, whose depth of perception, as Anima defines it, makes his rare speeches seem even more potently restrained or pithy, insofar as what he says is almost always reducible to the basics of pastoral instruction and religious devotion.

It begins to make sense why any character claiming to have cornered the market of thought, much less philosophy, theology, clergy, learning, and wit, will appear decidedly "unphilosophical," in this unusually general and ideal sense of that word Langland has hereby promoted. Enter Thought, who has nothing to say about thinking itself, which is odd not only by definition, but also given the large amount of late medieval philosophical opinion emanating outward from Scotus and Ockham, that – for whatever the great differences between these two philosophers – holds that thinking is linguistic, within the media of propositions. Why can't Thought even *talk* about thinking? To the extent that there is a "problem of language" in this poem, just as there is a "problem of knowing" and a problem of "belief,"[37] the poet refuses to construct the human mind out of materials offered by propositional logic or faculty psychology, precluding the possibility of extracting a *Denkform* from the poem that is abstracted from the disclosive, *narrative form* in which the poem itself "thinks."

As noted above, to think in Langlandian terms is to do so in the real time of his heuristic narrative, testing and probing. This is why Thought deals not with abstractions, and the abstractive, and instead offers instruction on the everyday habits of moderation, virtue, and Dowell, Dobet, Dobest (8.80–110). Will is at a loss when hearing Thought and implies that Thought has not offered food for thought, no morsels he can "savor": "Ac yet sauvoreþ me noȝt þi seying, so me god helpe! / More kynde knowynge I coueite to lerne" (8.112–13). Will says, in other words, that he cannot "ruminate" when in thought, or with Thought – here, that longstanding tradition of *ruminatio* as contemplative chewing and tasting or, as Bede says of Caedmon, who "stored up in his memory all that he learned . . . like one of the clean animals chewing the cud."[38] It's an idea Nicholas Love carries forward into the fifteenth century in his translation of the pseudo-Bonaventuran *Meditationes Vitae Christi*, which early on emphasizes the "swete taste" of "gostly chewyng" as a mode of scriptural understanding.[39]

That Will seeks to savor, to consume slowly rather than hastily, theological matter makes a great amount of sense in view of the problem, detailed later in the poem, of stuffing oneself too quickly with chewy theology. Of all people, Dame Study construes the sin of gluttony to involve, in part, the clerkly appetite for high theology: clerks "dryuele at hir deys þe deitee to knowe, / And gnawen god in þe gorge whanne hir guttes fullen" (10.57–8). "God," Dame Study says, "is muche in þe gorge of þise grete maistres" (10.67) – a sentiment that, incidentally, helps explain the meaning of Chaucer's own visceral reference to sacramental theology ("turnen substaunce into accident") in the Pardoner's Tale (lines 252–7), an abstract reference to God in the gut. The point is that Will cannot consume high theology, no matter how it is served up: he acquires no clear ideas after walking with Thought for three days, "Disputyng on dowel day after ooþer" (8.118). Frustrated, Will demands that Thought advance a theme to "preuen hise wittes" (125) in front of a new interlocutor, none other than Wit himself.

Wit, taking over from Thought, speaks for almost the entirety of passus 9. Because he opens with a discussion on the "Castel þat kynde made" (9.2) and transforms this Timaean image of the body-as-elements into a discussion of "inwit," marriage, reproduction, bastardy, and social order, in which the term "kynde" resonates (25–55, 86, 91, 112, 129, 131, 144, 160), it becomes clear that Wit here seeks to accomplish what Thought could not: to connect with Will's preferred mode of understanding, "More kynde knowynge I coueite to lerne" (8.112–13). The trouble is we never learn whether Wit's speech impresses or helps Will, because, at the beginning of passus 10, Wit's wife, Dame Study, silences Wit altogether, blaming him for casting pearls before swine (10.9–10). Will eventually gets a word in edgewise, beseeching her to "kenne me kyndely to knowe what is dowel" (10.151), and Dame Study offers a, at best, tangential reply that only prolongs Will's desire "to lerne" (8.113): "I shal kenne þee to my Cosyn þat Clergie is hoten [called]" (10.153). Will's request for such "kynde knowyng" is never granted, but his curiosity about "Dowel and dobet and dobest" motivates Clergy to change the conversation from the problems of belief – of course, not without first discussing the Trinity (244–56) – to those of the problems of doing, endorsing what amounts to a prescription for behavior modification therapy, a course in the three grades of doing: doing well, doing better, doing best.

It is here that Clergy imagines a world in which everyone is perfectly behaved, or punished for misbehaving: that world is the "cloistre" or "scole" (306), a "heuene...on þis erþe, and ese to any soule" (305). None of this is surprising, coming from Clergy, who (like the stereotypical image of the modern professor) construes the macrocosm only by looking out through a pinhole in the microcosm. That he never enters into a discussion of what exactly is *learned* in these institutions points to the idea that education is as much about schooling and scorning persons to be well-mannered literate subjects capable of applying their skills in the ecclesiastical bureaucracy as it is about making them intelligent, smart, or philosophical human beings. And what does Will learn from Clergy's example? He learns to dispute with Scripture and exclaim "*Contra!*," exactly like a clerk (349) – all along challenging, among other things, the relevance of learning to both good behavior and salvation. And in reply, all Scripture offers is more scorn (11.1).

On causes

But what about Imaginative, who near the end of passus 11 and the beginning of passus 12 assumes the role of instructing Will? What kind of thinking does Imaginative enable? No other character in *Piers Plowman* has received as much commentary by philosophically minded scholars as this one – though Conscience is a close second.[40] Yet few, if any, of these studies discuss why it is that Imaginative, like Thought, seems patently "unphilosophical" (in Langland's most radical sense) and more interested in retailing points of Christian instruction and lay moderation.[41] He also repeats many points. He defends both Reason and Clergy against Will's presumptuously petulant dialogue with those figures, and, as noted, breaks the news to Will that he would have been a philosopher ("*Philosophus esses si tacuisses*" [11.416a]) if he would have held his tongue and let Reason speak for a change. He accuses Will, furthermore, of wasting time writing poetry – "þow medlest þee with makynges [writing poetry]" – when he should instead "go seye þi sauter" (12.16). So far, Imaginative is not looking very imaginative at all, in the sense of exhibiting what is his precise philosophical or cognitive function: to present images given from the senses over to understanding and reason.

Imaginative's accusations, however, are revealing for what they tell us about both philosophy and books, underscoring precisely what Imaginative regards as valuable in the natural sciences and in book learning itself. His is a decidedly bookish presentation, with his citation of authorities and examples reading like a reading itself. He speaks of Lucifer, Samson, and Solomon as if they come right from the pages of a Fall of Princes text regarding those "that al wan, elengeliche ended" (12.44). He speaks of what the "poetes" say about "briddes and . . . beestes" (237, 236) as if he were reading from a medieval bestiary (238–76). Imaginative is now getting imaginative, even literary. He believes that when natural science is not rendered into allegory, as medieval bestiaries do best, then it amounts to knowledge for knowledge's sake, which is the error of the early history of philosophy, by "Dyuyneris toforn vs" who present a "kynde knowyng" that "com but of diuerse siȝtes" (130–5). Imaginative has two needles to thread here, then: (1) he must defend book learning and pre-Christian philosophy but admit that such learning within Christian philosophy has important limits; and (2) he must distinguish what Will is seeking – "kynde knowyng" of how to save his soul – from the observational, experimental knowledge also called "kynde knowyng" (12.125) and "Kynde Witte" (128).

In this, there may be the poem's most direct commentary on Aristotle's view – upheld in more sophisticated ways by late medieval Nominalists – on the founding role of sensory data in creating the basis of the universal substances that were generated by the mind only.[42] But this is all dismissed by Imaginative as irrelevant to salvation. Thus Imaginative concludes that soteriology is one that is fundamentally unknown to such "Dyuyneris toforn vs," finally named as Aristotle "þe grete clerk," who "likneþ in his logik þe leeste fowel oute," yet "wheiþer he be saaf or noȝt saaf, þe soþe woot no clergie, / Ne of Sortes ne of Salomon no scripture kan telle" (12.130, 268, 269–71). This point goes to the very basis of Aristotelian inquiry itself – that survey of the natural world and the investigation of causes. Addressing Will who "sekest after þe whyes" (12.217), Imaginative declares that:

þow studiest, as I leue,
How euere beest ouþer brid haþ so breme wittes.
Clergye ne kynde wit ne knewe neuere þe cause,
Ac kynde knoweþ þe cause hymself, no creature ellis.

(12.223–6)

The only "kynde wit" relevant here, in other words, is what Kynde (i.e., God) "knoweþ . . . hymself." So much for that classic Aristotelian method that proceeds from appearances, to essences, to causes, to the thought of First Causes. Apparently, one can think *deeper*, but not *higher*. Yet it remains perfectly legitimate to go the way of a *Christian* Aristotelian like Aquinas and know that the First Cause "is" without knowing the mysteries of *how* it causes all to be. Such a position lands the thinker right at the intersection of philosophy, doctrine, and science – terms that Aquinas intertwines in the *Summa theologiae* (I, Q.1, a.1). Indeed, Imaginative seems to heed the distinctions established by Aquinas in his most important and influential philosophical and theological work: the "philosophical sciences [disciplines]" (*philosophicas disciplinas*) are "built up by human reason" (in the "I Answer That"), whereas divine science or theology "surpasses the grasp of . . . reason," and involves "truths" that are "taught by a divine revelation."[43] Even here, in the notion that there is revelation, Imaginative stops short, failing to explain how such revelation works, even at the expense of reading the Pentecost – well known in traditional exegesis as a scene of illumination from the Holy Spirit (see, e.g., 19.227–51), as nothing more than a kind of baptism necessary for salvation (12.280–97). There are, simply, limits to what the imagination should imagine, and by that imposition Langland offers up a proto *Critique of Pure Reason*.[44]

But is the thought, or imagining, of causes a forlorn venture? Are we, in other words, to accept Imaginative's self-imposed limits on imaginative activity or, worse yet, are we to include ourselves in Anima's accusation that to ask pesky questions about causes, as Will does about the "cause of alle hire names" (15.45), is to make yourself "inparfit . . . and oon of prides knyȝtes" (15.50)? Possibly. For in the C text of *Piers Plowman*, Langland thinks on causes by other means – namely, in the so-called "grammatical analogy" that a revised Conscience returns to wield against Meed to emphasize how dubious is her version of "reward." In this elaborate expansion of the earlier debate, Langland reaches far afield to argue that "direct relation" or "relatif rect" (C.3.355) of proper reward is possible only through the existence of that "graciouse antecedent" who is God (354) with whom all subsequents must agree, grammatically, so as to exist in unity and concord: "That is vnite, acordaunce in case, in gendre and in noumbre, / . . . þat alle maner

men, wymmen and childrene / Sholde confourme hem to o kynde on holy
kyrke to bileue" (395–8). Failing to conform to such a unity, persons fall
out of "relacioun rect" (361) and into indirect relation and bad grammar.
Langland spells out the significance of these kinds of relations, and how
they foster corruption and stoke the desire for money and social privilege
(374–406a).[45]

Perhaps the poet elaborated this section so baroquely because the challenges to "faith" in it were so central, and were left unsettled by the tools
of analysis and "fyne wit" available to the poet in A and B. In C, the turn
to Christian allegory, the Trinity (405–5a), and political analysis signals, it
seems, a move to the scholastic science of metaphysics, brought to bear on
centrally practical and secular issues of the social economy. Thus, *finally*, in
this important addition to the C text, Langland introduces topics found in
the most recondite of philosophical disciplines – that of speculative grammar, as D. Vance Smith shows[46] – to render in its most difficult terms the
project of conceptualizing genealogies and lineages, such as Meed's, and
therefore causes and, in turn, economies in general. The sense of a literary
as well as intellectual experiment in these arguments is palpable: "knowen
y wolde . . . for englisch was it neuere!," the King exclaims (343). Langland
neither here nor elsewhere expounds on causes like Aristotle or Aquinas,
via the widely known "four causes" (efficient, material, formal, final) that
informed many Latin and, soon enough, English prologues;[47] but, eccen-
trically if not uniquely, he does not hesitate to render in poetic form the
speculative grammatical topics dear to Thomas of Erfurt and Scotus. It
seems obvious that this is not a youthful education finally expressing itself,
but a product of long-sustained reading and thinking, testing a stunning
range of philosophical resources against a material and social problem that
looms larger with each expansion of Conscience's discourse to address it.

A greater understanding of the poet's curiosity about this area of philosophy can perhaps be gleaned by his overly intense investment in grammar
itself, evinced everywhere in the poem. Langland is eager to indicate that bad
grammar guarantees the failure of both philosophy and physics (by which he
likely meant the full understanding of *De physica*, where Aristotle's famous
theory of "four causes" is laid out [book 2, ch. 3]):

> Grammer, þe ground of al, bigileþ now children,
> For is noon of þise newe clerkes, whose nymeþ hede,
> That kan versifie faire ne formaliche enditen,
> Ne nauȝt oon among an hundred þat an Auctour kan construwe,
> Ne rede a lettre in any langage but in latyn or englissh . . .
> Doctours of decres and of diuinite maistres,

That sholde konne and knowe alle kynnes clergie,
And answere to Argument3 and assoile a *Quodlibet* –
I dar no3t siggen it for shame – if swiche were apposed
Thei sholde faillen of hir Philosofie and in Phisik boþe.

(B.15.372–6, 380–4)

Reckon with such a claim – "Grammer, þe ground of al" (15.372) – and it becomes clear that for Langland grammar means something more philosophically significant than writing and speaking well: it is the ground from which philosophy, physics, and even astronomy proceeds.[48] It is the structure of all. It is what comprises the "book of the world" – that great figure for God's inscription of signs in all of creation. That motif was a commonplace among the late medieval scholastics like Hugh of St. Victor, John of Salisbury, St. Bonaventure, and Roger Bacon. As the mid thirteenth-century pioneer in the widespread academic interest in grammar's philosophical rather than simply rhetorical and persuasive uses, Bacon (1214/20–92) probed the degree to which all signs, in order to be signs, depend on the intention – the "will" – of the sign's conceiver. He considers, for instance, the hard case of spontaneous "interjections," which he regards as having a different degree of intentionality than the other seven medieval "parts of speech."[49] Langland is no Bacon, but he does appreciate the structuring principle of grammar itself, as shown in this passage – which is why if one fails in grammar, then a host of other errors follow, including bad astronomical calculation (15.370–1), faulty psychological understanding, and a failure "to deuyne and diuide, figures to kenne . . . / As Astronomyens þoru3 Astronomye, and Philosophers wise" (19.240, 244).

That Langland emulates and extends in often unique ways some of the most pressing topics of late medieval "language" theory and ideas of relations, as well as Augustinian or Anselmian theology and philosophy, certainly indicates that we should give him the benefit of the doubt about the depth of his philosophical knowledge, and certainly not assume that it is driven by simple pieties easily confirmed by thumbing hastily through this or that help text. It is constructed to test faith by testing faith in all things – including the tools of poetry and thought he has used to do this. Even his reflections on astronomy as a kind of divine mathematics point to his likely awareness of the so-called "Oxford Calculators" associated with Merton College – Bradwardine, William Heytesbury, John Dumbleton, Walter Burley, and Richard Swineshead – all masters of the natural sciences and the arts of logical disputation.[50] So too his sense of the human "will," which is continually tied to a philosophy of the episode and "event": a sense in which infinite possible futures open up at every moment, and the contingency of them all makes the human will, however pitiably underequipped, the center of a universal drama.[51]

Whether Langland learned much from university is less relevant than how he elaborates some of the fundamental ideas that developed vigorously in the late medieval university and beyond, in sermons, treatises, *florilegia*, and innumerable clerical contexts, and, increasingly, in late medieval London among lay intellectuals and clergy, including those commissioned to serve and administer the burgeoning civic and secular state whom Langland so knowledgeably chastises.[52] What finally affirms the ideal of a "philosopher wise," in the broader meaning of "ameeur de sapience" that the poem implicitly and sometimes explicitly advances, is the sheer fact of the poem itself – that a work like *Piers Plowman* exists in the first place, that it was conceived and executed or, to use the philosophical idiom, thought into being out of a literary and social history that cannot fully explain its inception or the long trajectory of writing and revision that comprises its versions, its distinctive and unending experiments.

9

SUZANNE CONKLIN AKBARI

The non-Christians of
Piers Plowman

Three kinds of non-Christians appear in *Piers Plowman*: Jews, Muslims (or "Saracens"), and what we might call generic non-Christians – that is, those who have not become Christians simply because they had no opportunity to hear the word of Christ, having been born too early or too far away to have been exposed to Christian doctrine. The representation of Muslim non-Christians in medieval western texts has been addressed recently by several historians and literary scholars, including in John Tolan's *Saracens* (2002) and in my own *Idols in the East* (2009), as well as in the older but still useful studies of Norman Daniel, Dorothee Metlitzki, and Richard Southern. These studies have shown that the representation of non-Christians has a complex but intertwined genealogy, with the portrayal of one subset of non-Christians often involving conventions used to depict another. For example, the term that most commonly denotes "idol" in medieval vernacular texts is "mahom" or "mahon" (French; English "mahoun" or "mahound"), drawn from the name of the prophet of Islam.

Conventions drawn from anti-Judaic discourse, as we will see below, were applied to Islam, as well as to other forms of pre-Christian idolatry. Accusations of heresy, too, were intertwined with anti-Muslim and anti-Jewish invective. This tradition of depicting non-Christians, moreover, was complicated by the actual historical circumstances of medieval Muslims, Christians, and Jews, who at different times and in different places lived in close proximity. Their cohabitation was often marked by violent conflict and discord, but on occasion by mutual understanding and exchange.

The depiction of non-Christians in medieval literature must therefore be understood not only in terms of the actual history of relations between different faith communities (which were also separated, in most cases, by ethnic affiliation), but also in terms of the ideologies that underlay the construction of religious identity. Yet approaching this topic in *Piers Plowman* presents a special challenge: while medieval literary works such as the *Song of Roland*, Chaucer's Man of Law's Tale, or Dante's *Inferno* each present a relatively self-contained, internally consistent view of the non-Christian "other," Langland offers no such certainty to his reader. Instead, his poem presents a range of possible perspectives, leaving the reader to sift through the various theological positions on non-Christians that might be adopted by a believer. This chapter therefore begins with a short account of how the text of *Piers Plowman* obliges the reader to weigh certain specifically defined alternative positions against one another. It then turns to the depictions of non-Christians at some key moments in the poem. The ambiguities of these depictions of non-Christians vary, moreover, between the B and C versions of the text, though this is further complicated by the variations to be found within the poem's manuscript tradition.

This chapter addresses all three kinds of non-Christians found in *Piers Plowman* – Jews, Muslims, and generic non-Christians – beginning with an examination of the ways in which the poem constructs Christian identity based on the imagined identity of the pre-Incarnational Jew, going on to explore how the ambiguity in Jewish identity (as seen from the Christian point of view) inflects the Christian view of non-Christian others, especially Muslims. These latter were seen as both participating in a retrogressive return to the so-called "Old Law" of Moses and embarking upon a novel Christian heresy. The chapter will then consider what I have called the generic non-Christian, especially the figure of the so-called "virtuous pagan" that is the focus of Langland's exploration of whether God could choose to grant salvation outside of the sacrificial covenant of Christ. This part of the chapter places the poem's presentation of non-Christians in the context of Langland's vision of salvation history, in which the temporal succession of Judaism, Christianity, and Islam – as well as the typological prefiguration of Christ's rule provided by the imperial rulers of ancient Rome – provides the framework for Langland's apocalyptic expectations. The discussion of Langland's account of the "virtuous pagan" is briefly compared to similar explorations of the theology of salvation found in Dante's *Divine Comedy* (1308–21) and the Middle English alliterative poem *Saint Erkenwald* (*c.* 1390), and is placed in the context of Walter Hilton's more dogmatic view of the possibilities of salvation for non-Christians as presented in his *Scale of Perfection* (also *c.* 1390).

The time of salvation

In *Piers Plowman*, the poet offers a wide range of perspectives, leaving it to the reader to come to a conclusion that approximates – that is, comes as close as it is possible to come, in a post-lapsarian world, to – truth. To some extent, the placement of such an interpretive obligation on the reader is a typical feature of allegory in general.[1] Yet this impulse is at its most acute in *Piers Plowman*, as a brief comparison with another fourteenth-century devotional allegory, Dante's *Divine Comedy*, makes clear. In the earlier poem, Dante continually corrects his reader both through direct address (e.g., *Inferno*, 9.62–3; *Purgatorio*, 8.19–21) and through the narrator's painstaking process of seeking to know and repeatedly undergoing reproof when he errs, whether by Virgil in Hell or Beatrice in Paradise. In *Piers Plowman*, by contrast, the reader is instead offered a series of possible alternatives. Beyond the interpretive obligation placed on the reader by the genre of allegory, and beyond the heightened expectations that Langland places on his own reader, the effort to interpret the poem's theological positions is further heightened by the often substantial differences that separate the poem's various redactions, especially the B and C texts; finally, the complicated textual tradition of the fifty-odd surviving manuscripts, none of which seems to descend directly from any of the others, adds a further level of hermeneutic uncertainty.

The reader is placed in a difficult position, not only as a result of the generic expectations characteristic of allegory, heightened in Langland's treatment of the genre, but also by the existence of multiple redactions of the poem. Some critics deal with this latter complication by simply assuming that the revisions of the C version supersede the text of the B version. With regard to the question of salvation, for example, David Aers asserts that the more narrow, Augustinian theological position expressed in the C version is unequivocally to be taken as Langland's final (and orthodox) word on the subject.[2] This view of the final authority of the C text makes sense only if we read the work first of all as theology and only secondly as poetry, and moreover if we assume that Langland made the alterations that appear in C out of theological conviction, not out of circumspection in response to increased policing of orthodoxy. We cannot know with certainty what factors motivated the revisions that generated the C text, with its greater dogmatism and theological precision. We can, however, as Elizabeth Kirk suggests, choose "to face the fact that these poems are poems and not treatises, without ceasing to learn from medieval theology, philosophy, and pulpit oratory."[3] That is, we must recognize the extent to which, as visionary poetry, *Piers Plowman* requires a certain degree of ambiguity in order to ensure that the poem dynamically produces a spiritually reformed reader, through a rigorous process of education, rather than simply producing a directly and simply informed reader in the way that a non-poetic, theological treatise might do.

It is crucial to have some sense of Langland's method of spiritual forma-
tion of his reader in order to take stock of the depiction of non-Christians
found in *Piers Plowman*. Especially in the B text, the poem does not offer a
single clear statement of orthodox theological positions on Jews, Muslims,
or other non-Christians. (It does not even offer clearly defined positions
that are less than orthodox, as we find in Dante.) Instead, Langland offers
what David Benson calls a "dialectic," requiring the reader to sift through
the multiple theological options as part of the quest for truth and personal
reform of the spirit.[4] Like Prudentius' *Psychomachia* and the anonymous
medieval play *Everyman*, *Piers Plowman* stages a range of voices, some of
which are clearly to be dismissed, but many of which are to be taken very
seriously. Yet while in the *Psychomachia* and *Everyman* the vices and virtues
are personified with highly essentialized qualities and in conceptually pure
terms, something very different happens in *Piers Plowman*. The personifications, especially the newly coined personifications, represent different
possible subject positions, some of which espouse points of view that the
reader is apparently supposed to support (or, better, learn to support), while
others espouse points of view that the reader is supposed to find lacking.
As Nicholas Watson puts it, Langland "maintain[s] an extraordinarily flexible relationship between poet, poem, and world in which the intellectual
quest of the poet, the spiritual journey of the narrator, and the historical
development and decline of Christian society are presented in ever-changing
balance."[5] Now, it does not follow that the reader who, at least temporarily, comes to hold a position that the poem later disavows or shows to be
lacking is to be seen as a defective, "fallen" reader; on the contrary, it may
be that such failures are simply part of the process that the reader (or the
soul) must endure in order to move forward on the road of faith. It is clear,
however, that the reader is meant at least to try to judge these different subject positions and to test them out against what he or she knows of religious
doctrine and rightly guided belief.

This dynamic, so central to the aims of *Piers Plowman*, casts the poem's
depiction of non-Christians in a peculiar light. While other kinds of medieval
literature present Jews, Muslims, and other non-Christians in terms of larger
discourses of religious alterity and bodily diversity, they do so in a consistent way; in other words, we can arrive at a coherent assessment of how we
are to understand "pagans" in the *Song of Roland*, or Jews in the Croxton
Play of the Sacrament.[6] In *Piers Plowman*, however, the dynamism of the
reader's engagement with the various subject positions creates a more complex web of interpretation. The depiction of non-Christians in the poem is
not internally consistent precisely because the reader is expected actively to
engage in interpretation, producing a reader who is not simply informed of

SUZANNE CONKLIN AKBARI

how she should understand the place of the non-Christian in salvation history, but who instead gradually comes to a fuller understanding of salvation
concurrently with her own spiritual reformation.

In considering the ways in which the three kinds of non-Christians
described above are presented in *Piers Plowman*, it is helpful to keep in
mind the temporal schema of salvation history, and the place of each of
these non-Christian identities within that time frame. The role of the Jewish
people in Christian salvation history is twofold: on the one hand, Jewish
history before the Incarnation of Christ was understood to be a prefiguration of Christian history, and within this schema important figures in Jewish
history were interpreted as types or foreshadowings of Christ or other sacred
figures. Moses's delivery of the enslaved children of Israel from bondage in
Egypt, for example, was understood as a foreshadowing of Christ's spiritual
delivery of Christian souls from the bondage of sin, and therefore Moses was
a type or prefiguration of Christ. In contrast to this fundamentally positive
view of Jewish history, centered on Jews who lived prior to the temporal
hinge of the Incarnation, we also find a much more explicitly negative view
of Jewish history applied to the period after the birth of Christ. In this
view, any Jew who was virtuous would recognize the divinity of Christ and
become a Christian. There could, therefore, be no such thing as a "good"
Jew after the time of the advent of Christ. The destruction of Jerusalem in
70 AD was understood as a dramatic confirmation of the displacement not
only of the physical site of the Temple, but of the religious community it
had represented.

Yet the simple binarism of this view – good Jews before the Incarnation,
bad Jews after the Incarnation – was, at a deeper level, more complex.
While the view that Jewish history before the Incarnation prefigured events
in Christian history necessarily presented prominent figures in that history
(such as Moses, Abraham, or David) in a positive light, Jewish identity was
seen as positive only in the sense that it was replaced or superseded by its
fulfillment within Christian salvation history. To put it another way, even
pre-Incarnation Jews were valued not as Jews, but only as foreshadowings or
prefigurations of Christians, or even of Christ himself. The "real" children
of Israel, from the point of view of medieval Christians, were constituted
in the body of Christ (that is, the Church). Moreover, the simple view that
post-Incarnation Jews were simply bad was complicated by the theological
position, influentially argued by Augustine, that the continued presence of
Jews in Christendom was not only to be tolerated, but was theologically
necessary. Jews would be a witness to the inexorable unfolding of salvation
history, and their conversion, in the fullness of time, would be a sure sign of
the approach of the Apocalypse.[7]

The place of Muslims within this vision of salvation history was similarly complex. On the one hand, Muslims (or "Saracens") were simply yet another manifestation of paganism, characterized by their devotion to idolatry as well as a tendency toward violent and lascivious behavior. This view of Islam as pagan idolatry is ubiquitous in the medieval literary tradition, in *chansons de geste*, romances, and mystery plays, and therefore texts that depart from this grotesque caricature – such as Langland's *Piers Plowman* or *The Book of John Mandeville* (with which Langland's work was repeatedly copied) – stand out for how they actually engage with Islam as a theology. In these texts, Saracens are seen not merely in terms of a specific religious orientation (rather than generic pagan idol-worship) but also in relationship to both Christianity and Judaism. For the Mandeville author, Muslims can be compared to Jews in their common failure to accept Christ; yet he differentiates sharply between their respective possibilities for salvation. "Because they come so near to our faith," he writes, "they can easily be converted to the Christian law" ["Et pur ceo q'ils vont si près de nostre foy sont ils de legier converty a christienne loy"].[8] Jews, by contrast, are presented in *The Book of John Mandeville* as an almost demonic threat to Christian unity: they continue to speak Hebrew, the Mandeville author asserts, simply in order to maintain the ability to communicate with and assist the enclosed tribes of Gog and Magog (conflated with the lost tribes of Israel) when they burst forth and attempt to massacre Christians during the End Times. While Langland does not demonize Jews in the way the Mandeville author does, he also indicates an openness to religious conversion on the part of Muslims: "For Sarʒens han somewhat semynge to oure bileue, / For þei loue and bileue in o Lede almyʒty, / And we lered and lewed, bileueþ in oon God" (B.15.392–4).[9]

By identifying the prophet Muhammad as a "Cristene man" (B.15.398) who deceived his followers with a mockery of the Holy Spirit in the form of a dove (B.15.400–8), Langland highlights the resemblance of Islam to Christianity, with a defective human figure inhabiting the place that can rightfully only be inhabited by Christ. In temporal terms, Islam comes after Christianity in the historical sequence of religions; paradoxically, however, in its inability to recognize (Christian) spiritual truths, Islam is a retrogressive return to the limitations of the so-called "Old Law" of the Jews. To put it another way, medieval Christian views of the temporal sequence of religions could be seen in two ways: in terms of the historical sequence Judaism – Christianity – Islam, or in terms of the ontological sequence Old Law – New Law – Old Law, in the sense that Muhammad's false "law" was simply a return to the Old Law of Moses rather than an innovation built atop the New Law offered by Christ.[10] While it might occur at a later point in historical time, Islam was not seen as an innovation or a reformation within Christianity, but rather as a leap backwards into a period of spiritual blindness. In view of this complex time schema with regard to spiritual salvation, it is unsurprising that the temporal position of the so-called "virtuous pagan" was similarly complex. Born before the Incarnation, or otherwise unable to have access to the redemption offered by Christian doctrine, the virtuous pagan was able to reach salvation only through an evasion of the normal laws of time.

Like medieval polemical biographies of Muhammad, such as the eleventh-century *Vita Mahumeti* or the thirteenth-century *Roman de Mahomet*,[11] the description of the prophet in *Piers Plowman* emphasizes the linkage of religious deviance and excessive materialism, whether expressed in the form of greed or lasciviousness. Langland associates Muhammad with the accumulation of material wealth, blaming the spiritual degeneration that precedes the apocalypse on the twin evils of "Makometh and Mede" (B.3.329). Like the author of the *Roman de Mahomet*, Langland attributes false miracles to Muhammad, describing how through fakery he deceived his gullible people, and stresses Muhammad's claim to be the messiah (C.17.159). Yet Langland differs from the earlier polemical accounts in his strong emphasis on the role of Islam as a Christian heresy, grouping "Saraens and scismatikes" (B.11.120) and stressing the similarity of Christianity and Islam (B.15.392–5, 606–12; cf. C.17.132–5). In this he resembles another medieval poet who sought to bring about reform of the church, Dante, who places Muhammad (along with Ali, founder of Shi'a Islam) in the circle of Christian schismatics in hell.

By comparing Christianity and Islam, Langland invites the reader to compare Christ and Muhammad. The comparison is particularly evident in an episode that Langland adapted from the *Golden Legend* of James of Voragine (or perhaps from James's own likely source, the *Speculum historiale*, or *Historical Mirror*, of Vincent of Beauvais).[12] Langland reports that Muhammad trained a white dove to come peck grains of corn that he had concealed in his ear; when his people saw the dove on the prophet's shoulder, he told them that the bird had come from heaven as a messenger from God (B.15.406–7). This kind of false miracle also appears in the *Roman de Mahomet*, where Muhammad is said to have hidden pots of milk and honey to make them seem to appear miraculously; like the author of the *Roman de Mahomet*, Langland presents the false miracle as evidence of Muhammad's subtlety ("hise sotile wittes," B.15.399). In addition, however, this episode serves to underline Muhammad's imitation of Christ. The dove, a "messager to Makometh," is clearly a parody of the Holy Spirit, characteristically represented as a white dove both in scenes of the Annunciation and in scenes depicting Christ's baptism. The dove is a false "messager," not a true mediator of divine power as the Holy Spirit is. Correspondingly then, Muhammad is also a false messenger, not a true mediary like Christ. This is why Langland states of the Muslims, "in a feiþ lyueþ þat folk, and in a fals mene" (B.15.506).

Because Langland draws this comparison between Muhammad and Christ, and because he characterizes Muhammad using conventions found in polemics like the *Vita Mahumeti* and the *Roman de Mahomet* which explicitly identify Muhammad as a manifestation of Antichrist, we might expect Langland to return to the figure of Muhammad in his own account of the last days and the coming of Antichrist, found in the final passūs of *Piers Plowman*. Instead, Langland distinguishes clearly between Muhammad and Antichrist: while he repeatedly calls Muhammad a "man" (B.15.396, 398), he implies that Antichrist is to be identified with Satan himself, "a fals fende" (B.20.64) that appears "in mannes forme" (B.20.52). Langland's association of Muhammad and Antichrist is much more limited than that found in other texts on the prophet. This is because Langland uses Muhammad not as a type of Antichrist, but as an example to establish the central role of the "mene" or mediary. For Langland, Muhammad differs fundamentally from Christ in being a "fals mene"; only Christ, as both God and man, is a perfect mediator between heaven and earth. As a "fals mene," Muhammad serves as an example of those who should be imitators of Christ, mediaries between the faithful and God: Langland concludes his account of Muhammad by stating that "Englisshe clerkes a coluere fede þat Coueitise hiȝte, / And ben mannered after Makometh, þat no man vseþ trouþe" (B.15.414–15). It can be dangerous and difficult to call for reform of one's own community; doing so through a comparison to some group or person wholly alien to the community makes it easier. Moreover, by avoiding the simple demonization of the prophet through a comparison to Antichrist, as was conventional in the polemical tradition, Langland instead requires his readers to consider the similarities between Muhammad and "Englisshe clerkes" of their own day, evaluating their level of faithfulness to "treuth." Muhammad serves not so much as a representative of a rival religious law as a measure against which to evaluate the faithfulness of Christian clerics to their own law, especially priests who are themselves a "mene" as they participate in the sacrifice of the Mass. This use of Islam as a spiritual foil – a spur to internal reform – is also found in *The Book of John Mandeville*, where the narrator has a private audience with the Sultan of Babylon. The Sultan tells his visitor that he and all Saracens know that a Christian victory in the Holy Land is sure to take place just as soon as "they serve their God more devoutly" ["ils serviront lour Dieu plus devotement"].[13]

Supersession and retrogression

The presentation of Saracens in general and the figure of Muhammad in particular is slightly altered in the C version of *Piers Plowman*, both in terms of content and in terms of context, since the descriptions of Muhammad discussed above are spoken by Anima in the B text, but by Liberum Arbitrium (Free Will) in the C text. Before turning to these passages, it is helpful to examine, if only briefly, the broader context for the comparison of the two versions, particularly the shifting depiction of Jews and Judaism which has been so well analyzed by Elisa Narin van Court.[14] Judaism functions in *Piers Plowman* as a template for Christianity, within the logic of supersessionism described earlier, in which significant figures and events in Jewish history before the Incarnation serve as prefigurations or foreshadowings of figures and events in Christian history. As Narin van Court has shown, Langland's depiction of Jews and Judaism differs significantly between the B and C versions of *Piers Plowman*. She suggests that this shift can be described in terms of a move from one conception of supersession to another: that is, from a focus on fulfillment to a focus on replacement, where Jewish identity is effaced as it is superseded by Christianity. Narin van Court's analysis of the representation of the Jews in the B and C texts is useful not only in itself but also because the representation of Jews serves as the foundation of the depiction of non-Christians more generally, in two ways. First, "Saracens" are often depicted in medieval texts as being akin to Jews, with the so-called "law of Muhammad" being understood as a retrogressive return to the "law of Moses" (as we saw in the *Roman de Mahomet*, discussed above). Second, within the logic of supersession, Jews and Judaism serve as a prefiguration of Christians and Christianity, and therefore normative religious identity (and, by extension, heretical departures from it) is based upon or derives from Judaism. In other words, the depiction of Jews in *Piers Plowman* sheds light on the depiction of Muslims both directly, through the association of Islam with the retrogressive "Old Law," and indirectly, through the template that Judaism was thought to provide for the conceptualization of Christian identity, as well as for heterodox departures from it.

In her account of the revisions found in the C text, Narin van Court emphasizes "the extent to which the dialectical tension that is so marked in the B text collapses in the C revision."[15] She argues that although many critics find Langland to be magnanimous in his account of non-Christian religions, much of that quality has been revised out of the C text: "the generosity that Langland demonstrates toward the Jews in B is radically transformed in C," with revisions that include "an increased divisiveness with regard to living (or idealized) Jewish communities, and a figure of the converted Jew to fulfill the poem's prophetic anticipations of Jewish conversion."[16] We might expect to find a comparable distinction in the treatment of Muslims in the C version, with a heightened emphasis on orthodox positions regarding the availability of salvation to non-Christians, and a more stringent articulation of the separation between Christianity and non-Christian religions. As we noted above, Langland resembles the author of *The Book of John Mande-ville* in the way he refers explicitly to the possibility of religious conversion on the part of Muslims: "For Sarʒens han somewhat semynge to oure bileue, / For þei loue and bileue in o Lede almyʒty, / And we lered and lewed bileueþ in oon God" (B.15.392–4). The lines in the C text that most closely correspond to this passage in the B text seem at first glance to be similarly generous, in theological terms: "For Sarrasynes may be saued so yf they so bileued– / In þe letynge of here lyf to leue on Holy Churche" (C.17.123–4). The repetition of this sentiment a few lines later seems, if anything, more inclusive, so that "Iewes and gentel Sarresines" are said to "lelyche... byleue.../ And o God þat al bygan with gode herte they honoureth / And ayther loueth and byleueth in o Lord almyhty" (C.17.132–5). Both Jews and Muslims are included here among those who worship the "one God who created all," "one God almighty," and still later in the same passus this apparently inclusive vision is enlarged to include also "scribes" (perhaps Pharisees): "For sethe þat this Sarrasines, scribz and this Iewes / Haen a lyppe of oure bileue, the lihtlokour, me thynketh, / They sholde turne" (C.17.252–4).

Yet such a reading overlooks the careful restrictions that are placed on the possibilities of salvation within the theological framework of the C version. The acknowledgment of the correspondence of Muslim and Christian belief found in B, where "þei" (that is, Saracens) "loue and bileue in o Lede almyʒty, / And we lered and lewed bileueþ in oon God" (B.15.392–4), is transformed in the C text, becoming at once more expansive (including Jews and "scribes") and more restrictive: "Sarrasynes may be saued so *yf* they so bileued– / In þe letynge of here lyf to leue on Holy Churche" (C.17.123–4; emphasis mine). In other words, Saracens might be saved "if" they were to become Christians, entering into the sacramental order of the church. Similarly, the assertion found in C that Muslims, Jews, and "scribes" all share "a lyppe of oure bileue" (C.17.253) does not imply that such folk are saved. Rather, it suggests that they might more readily be converted (literally, "turned") to Christianity: "the lihtlokour me thynketh / They sholde turne, hoso trauayle wolde and of þe Trinite teche hem" (C.17.253–4). Here, the burden of responsibility for the salvation of these excluded non-Christians lies upon those lazy Christians who have yet to take up the task of converting these ripe fruits ready for harvest by Christ. This narrower view of what might be required for salvation can best be understood in the context of the Trajan episode that appears earlier in the text (B.11.141ff.; C.12.73ff.), and which seems to suggest that there exist possibilities for salvation outside of the sacraments of the Church. (The Trajan episode is considered in more detail below.) The crucial feature to note in this context is the limitation placed on the inclusive vision of non-Christian salvation: it is open to them only "if" they believe in "Holy Church," and the significance of their shared "belief" in a single God is simply that they may be more readily converted to Christianity.

One further aspect of the C-text revisions regarding non-Christians deserves mention: that is, the short biography of Muhammad. While this account appears in both the B and C texts, the latter version goes beyond the former in its identification of Muhammad as a would-be "Messie" or Messiah (C.17.159), a deceptive counterpart to the true "Messie" (C.17.298, 303), Jesus. While the Jews fail to recognize Christ as Messiah, instead labeling him a "*pseudo-propheta*" (C.17.309), the Muslims wrongly identify Muhammad as Messiah. In other words, the Jews fail to recognize the Messiah when they see him, while the Muslims do recognize a Messiah – but the wrong one, Muhammad instead of Christ. In both cases, however, the error is one of partial or limited knowledge: as Langland puts it, both "Sarresynes and also þe Jewes / Conne þe furste clause of oure bileue, *Credo in deum patrem*" (C.17.315–16). They know in part, and are simply waiting to be taught the rest.

Such deficient, partial knowledge on the part of "Sarresynes" is also evident in a passage which is sometimes put forward as evidence of an inclusive attitude toward Muslims to be found in the C text,[17] in which the account of how Muhammad deceived his followers into believing that he was inspired by the Holy Spirit by training a tame dove or "coluer" to sit on his shoulder is immediately followed by a comparison with contemporary Christian clergy:

> In such manere [i.e., just as Muhammad called the dove],
>   me thynketh, moste the Pope,
> Prelates and prestis preye and biseche
> Deuouteliche day and nyhte and withdrawe hem fro synne
> And crie to Crist a wolde his coluer sende,
> The whiche is þe hy Holy Gost þat out of heuene descendet...
>   (C.17.243–6)

Such a view is put forward, for example, by Dorothee Metlitzki, who argues that in these lines "the Muslim Prophet in *Piers Plowman* is held up as an example to the Christian Pope," so that "Muhammad the evil enchanter has become Muhammad the political sage and has been accepted on an equal footing."[18] In other words, in this reading of the passage, the Christian clerics are urged to imitate Muhammad, calling upon the dove of the Holy Spirit just as Muhammad called upon the literal dove that perched upon his shoulder. Such a reading, however, completely inverts the temporal relationship of Christianity and Islam as understood in medieval texts, in which Muhammad's training of the dove is posterior to – a crafty imitation of – the true dove of the Holy Spirit, familiar in Christian iconography of the baptism of Jesus, as well as in depictions of Pentecost and the Annunciation. Christian clerics could never imitate Muhammad's calling upon his dove because his act was itself already secondary, a parodic imitation of the originary dove of the Holy Spirit.

Throughout the C version, we find a heightened focus on the need for internal reform on the part of the Christian community, beginning with the reform of the individual Christian soul. The account of non-Christians, whether Jews or Muslims, is geared toward that aim, with both of these religious laws serving each in their own way as a foil or defective counterpart to Christian orthodoxy. Yet the careful treatment of the possibility of salvation available to non-Christians found in the C text, where Muslims and Jews can be saved only if they "turn" or convert to Christianity and formally embrace the sacraments of the Church, is complicated by the account of Trajan found earlier in the text. On the one hand, we might read the restrictive account of salvation found in passus 17 of the C text, discussed above, as a corrective against the potentially destabilizing story of the salvation of Trajan. On the other hand, we might see the Trajan episode as a challenge to the orthodox position put forth in passus 17, inviting the reader to weigh in the balance the Augustinian view that salvation is possible only within the sacraments of the Church against the view that God's omnipotence is not circumscribed by any bounds, and that He can save whomever He will.

Opening the door to salvation: the case of Trajan

The Trajan episode in *Piers Plowman* has been thoroughly studied, most recently by Frank Grady in his account of the so-called "virtuous pagan" in Middle English literature, as well as within the larger context of medieval retellings of the story of Trajan's salvation, which appeared in a wide range of texts, including saints' lives and universal histories as well as literary works including Dante's *Divine Comedy* and the Middle English *Saint Erkenwald*.[19] The most widely diffused version of the story, and Langland's likely source, appears in the *Golden Legend* of James of Voragine, within his

life of Pope Gregory the Great. Among the saint's miraculous accomplishments is the astonishing salvation of the Roman emperor Trajan, who lived
before the time of Christ and should, therefore, have been excluded from
spiritual redemption. Moved by the memory of the emperor's compassion,
Gregory prays for Trajan's soul, and is answered: James of Voragine writes,
"The voice of God responded from above, 'I have granted your petition
and spared Trajan eternal punishment.'"[20] Already within the *Golden Legend* account, there is immense uncertainty regarding the status of Trajan's
redeemed soul, and the means of its salvation: James declares that "some
have said that Trajan was restored to life, and in this life obtained grace and
merited pardon," but that "others have said that Trajan's soul was not simply freed from being sentenced to eternal punishment, but that his sentence
was suspended for a time," while still others offer different explanations.[21]
This range of possible causes of salvation lies behind the multiple versions
of the Trajan legend to be found in the later Middle Ages, where the narrative provided a kind of test case or experimental model for thinking through
such questions as: What was required from the individual soul for salvation?
Are the sacraments of the Church necessary to salvation? Is God's omnipotence sufficient to transgress the limitations He voluntarily set for himself
in ordinarily requiring the sacraments of the Church for salvation to take
place?

Piers Plowman offers no such explicit philosophical or theological conclusion as to what might be the correct answer to these questions, nor does
it even suggest that such a conclusion might be possible. Instead, the story
of Trajan serves as a kind of eruption of grace into the poem, marked by
the voice of the redeemed emperor who cries out, "Ye, baw for bokes!"
(B.11.140; C.12.73). The urgency and sense of rupture provided by these
first words is emphasized in the opening lines of the passage, where the
speaker is first identified not by name but as "oon was broken oute of helle"
(B.11.140). The speaker goes on to name himself as "Troianus" (Trajan), "a
trewe knyȝt" who, although "ded and dampned to dwellen in pyne / For an
uncristene creature" (B.11.141–3), was subsequently saved. The question is:
How? Trajan himself refers to a number of possible factors, stating that

> Gregorie . . . wilned to my soule
> Sauacion for þe sooþnesse þat he seiȝin my weerkes.
> And after þat he wepte and wilned me were graunted grace,
> Wiþouten any bede biddyng his boone was vnderfongen,
> And I saued, as ye may see, wiþouten syngynge of masses,
> By loue and by lernyng of my lyuynge in truþe,
> Brouȝte me fro bitter peyne þer no biddyng myȝte.

> (B.11.146–52)

On one level, Trajan's salvation appears to be caused by Gregory's own exercise of will (he "wilned to my soule / Savacioun"); on another level, Trajan's salvation appears to be achieved through Gregory's compassion, expressed not only in prayer but also in his own tears ("he wepte"), which in turn incite divine compassion; on a third level, Trajan's salvation appears to be due to his own merit, a result of his having lived his life "in treuthe."[22] The multiple explanations of the nature of Trajan's salvation as given in the *Golden Legend* are here refracted, in Langland's provocative account, through Trajan's own explanations of how his salvation was effected.

Much scholarly debate has centered on the validity of Trajan's argument, the implications of his claims, and the philosophical and theological contexts within which these must be interpreted.[23] For our purposes here, considering the case of Trajan within the larger framework of Langland's presentation of non-Christians in general, it is most pertinent to note the ways in which Langland invites us to juxtapose the case of Trajan with the presentation of non-Christians elsewhere in the poem. This juxtaposition includes his reference to Trajan not only as a "paynym" (B.11.162) but as a "Sarsyn" (B.11.164), even though this term is normally used to refer to Arab Muslims, designating both religious and ethnic difference.[24] Some exceptions to this practice appear in Middle English romance, such as (for example), the pagan Danes who are identified as "Saracens" in *King Horn*.[25] Langland's reference to Trajan as a "Sarasene," however, may be more than an accident arising from a vague use of the term: we might instead see this as a deliberate invitation to the reader to juxtapose the Trajan story with the discussion of Saracen religious difference elsewhere in the poem. Moreover, the reader is also invited to compare the Trajan episode more specifically with the short biography of Muhammad that appears in the poem: the emblematic figure of the dove, trained by the deceitful prophet to trick his followers into believing that he was inspired by the Holy Spirit, appears widely in the iconography of Gregory the Great. The saint is depicted writing his great work, the *Moralia in Job*, under the influence of the Holy Spirit in the form of a dove whispering in his ear,[26] and the several versions of the saint's *vita* allude to the presence of the Holy Spirit in the form of a dove inspiring Gregory as he wrote.

This implicit comparison of Muhammad and Gregory, both associated with the iconic figure of the Holy Spirit as a dove, reinforces the ways in which the poem addresses the clergy, reminding them of their responsibility to mount renewed efforts to convert Saracens and Jews, and underlines the pivotal role of the Holy Spirit – whether represented parodically, as in the biography of Muhammad, or directly, in the "coluer . . . whiche is þe hy Holy Gost" (C.17.246–7). Langland's account of Muhammad, like the story of Trajan, serves as a kind of challenge to the reader, requiring an interpretive effort that does not merely consist of determining what might be an orthodox theological position on the matter (whether the salvation of Saracens or of pre-Incarnational pagans) but rather requires that the reader engage dynamically with the arguments as they are offered. In the case of Trajan, taking that redeemed soul at his word means embracing a radical position that the sacraments of the Church are not necessary to salvation; at the same time, however, it is impossible to deny the fact of Trajan's salvation, in all its awe-inspiring paradox. The solution may lie, as David Aers suggests, in simultaneously acknowledging the fact of Trajan's salvation while also recognizing the very limited nature of Trajan's own understanding of how his salvation was achieved. As Aers puts it, "Trajan may be freed from hell, but he has certainly not yet begun to reflect on the Christian gospel."[27] While Trajan's own "jaunty confidence in the needlessness of the revealed word of God in scripture"[28] is not to be imitated by the reader, the fact of Trajan's salvation is nonetheless a visible sign of the working of God's grace in the world.

Seen in this light, the temporal dimension of the Trajan episode becomes intelligible: living and dying before the Incarnation, Trajan lives in the wrong time to enjoy the salvation offered by the redemption of the Crucifixion. But God plucks him out of time, through the mediation of Gregory and his compassionate tears, and saves him – because he can. Trajan is identified first of all not as an emperor of Rome but as "oon was broken out of helle" (B.11.140), the rupture of hell's grasp mirrored in the abrupt emergence of the speaking voice. The same language of rupture reappears later in the passage, when love and truth are said to have broken the "gates of hell":

> Ac þus leel loue and lyuyng in truþe
> Pulte out of peyne a paynym of Rome.
> Yblissed be truþe þat so brak helle yates
> And saued þe Sarsyn from Sathanas and his power.
>
> (B.11.162–5)

Whose "love" and "truth" have the power to "pull" out the soul, to "break" these bonds? Surely not the individual soul, except insofar as that soul is moved by grace. This eruption of grace is a manifestation of divine power, and its acknowledgment of the unconstrained nature of that power – or, better, the limitations of any human intellect that attempts to comprehend that power – is what separates the poetry of Langland from the sober dogmatism of a theological treatise, such as the roughly contemporary *Scale of Perfection* by Walter Hilton (1380–96).

In Hilton's *Scale of Perfection*, the situation is unequivocal: "Jewes and paynemes" (that is, Saracens or Muslims) are both excluded from salvation, Jews because they believe the Incarnation to be nothing but "sclaundre and blasfemye," Muslims because they believe it to be "fantom and folie." Hilton notes that some people say that

> Jewis and Sarcenys and paynemes, bi kepynge of hire owen lawe, mown be maad saaf, though thei trowen not in Jhesu Crist as Holi Chirche troweth and as Cristen men doon, in as mykil as thei wene that her owen trouth is good and siker and sufficient to here savacion, and in that trouthe thei doon, as hit semeth, many good deedes of rightwisenesse.

But, Hilton states flatly, that "trouthe" is not enough: "Nai, it is not ynowgh so." The "trouthe" of the Jews and the Saracens is only "un unschapli trouthe," not to be confused with the perfectly formed truth of the Christian believer, and therefore they are "not reformed to the liknes of God, but goon to peynes of helle eendelesli."[29] Hilton's emphasis on the need for spiritual "reform," a term he uses repeatedly throughout this chapter, is in many ways very similar to the urgent call to reform found in Langland's *Piers Plowman*. The two works are diametrically opposed, however, in how they call for this reform: Hilton dogmatically instructs his reader what to believe, imposing reform from without, while Langland engages his reader in a dialectical process that produces reform from within. The non-Christians of *Piers Plowman* are not so much Jews, Muslims, and pre-Incarnational pagans as they are tools that the poet offers to his reader, inviting her to use them to shape her soul into a more perfect form of Christ.

PART III

Readers and responses

10

SIMON HOROBIN

Manuscripts and readers of
Piers Plowman

There has been a significant amount of interest in defining the readers of *Piers Plowman*, identifying their private and public affiliations, and determining their responses to the poem. John Burrow argued that Langland's poem had two distinct audiences: an older clerical readership and a more recent one composed of literate laymen.[1] Anne Middleton questioned this basic dichotomy, arguing that the clerical and lay readers formed a single audience involved in "counsel, policy, education, administration, pastoral care – those tasks and offices where spiritual and temporal government meet."[2] More recent work, especially that by Kathryn Kerby-Fulton and Steven Justice, has focused on Langland's London coterie readership, comprising civil servants, parliamentarians, and secular clerks.[3] In this chapter we will consider the question of Langland's audience from an examination of the poem's surviving manuscripts, using these sources as evidence for the way the poem was copied, circulated, and read throughout the fifteenth and into the sixteenth centuries.

Owners

The obvious place to begin a search for the poem's original readers is with the manuscripts' earliest owners. Unfortunately, it is not always easy to determine who was responsible for commissioning the production of a manuscript. The clearest category of evidence for a manuscript's patron is a coat of arms, from which it is generally possible to identify the individual for whom the manuscript was produced. However, only the most prominent and wealthy members of medieval society had coats of arms; such people were more concerned with commissioning lavish Latin liturgical manuscripts than copies of vernacular literary texts. Only a handful of manuscripts of *Piers Plowman* contain coats of arms, a fact that in itself tells us something about the status of its readers, and the degree of financial commitment that patrons were willing to invest in copies of the poem.

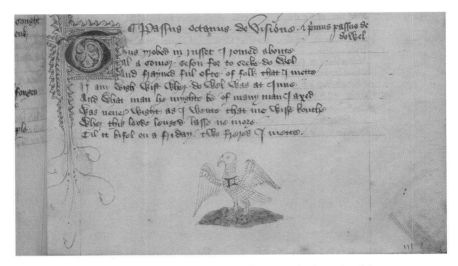

Figure 3 *Piers Plowman*, Newnham College, Cambridge MS 4, fol. 35r.

University of London Library, MS Sterling S.L. V.17 is part of a larger codex that originally comprised two other substantial manuscripts.[4] This manuscript contains the coats of arms of Sir William Clopton (d. 1419) of Quinton, Warwickshire, and his wife Joan Besford.[5] Since both coats of arms are included, it seems reasonable to assume that the manuscript was commissioned at some point during their marriage. The Clopton manuscript demonstrates a paradox inherent in the use of coats of arms as evidence of readership. The larger and more deluxe the manuscript, the more likely it is to contain a coat of arms. Yet such capacious miscellaneous collections tell us less about a particular patron's specific interest in *Piers Plowman*; when complete, the Clopton manuscript comprised 248 folios and contained six works in Middle English, including *Handlyng Synne, Mandeville's Travels, Estoire del Evangelie*, and the *Assumption of Our Lady*. The text of the Clopton copy of *Piers Plowman* is closely affiliated to another important manuscript of the C text, now Trinity College, Dublin MS 212, which contains a fifteenth-century inscription attributing the poem's authorship to William Langland, son of Stacy de Rokayle or Rokele, a tenant of lands owned by the Despenser family in Oxfordshire (see Chapter 5). There were close family links between the Clopton family and the household of Richard Beauchamp, Earl of Warwick, and his wife Isabel le Despenser, which suggest that these two manuscripts may derive from a shared copy passed between the two families.[6] There are further familiar links between the Despensers and another copy of the poem that contains a coat of arms identifying its earliest patrons. This manuscript, British Library, MS Harley 6041, includes the arms of the Hoo family of Bedfordshire, who intermarried with the Despensers. Despite their use in identifying original owners and tracing connections between families, not all coats of arms are readily identifiable. Newnham College, Cambridge MS 4, a copy of the B text, has an owner's badge depicting an eagle with a capital "L" on its chest, which has yet to be identified (see Figure 3). Without a firm identification, all this badge can tell us is that the owner was sufficiently prominent to have had a coat of arms.

Scribes

A second type of direct evidence for the poem's earliest readers is the presence of a scribal signature, by which the person responsible for copying the poem can be identified. There are six scribal signatures in manuscripts of *Piers Plowman*, although not all of these can be associated with an identifiable individual. The most straightforward identification is found in Bodleian Library, MS Digby 145, copied in 1532 and signed by its scribe Adrian Fortescue. Fortescue's great-uncle was the famous lawyer Sir John Fortescue, whose *Governance of England* is also included in the Digby manuscript. Like a number of scribes who copied the A text, Fortescue supplemented the short version with the longer C text, although he went further in including additional C passages in his copy of A, and even as far as inserting lines of his own composition. Fortescue's wife Anne also read the poem, marking lines that interested her with a pointing hand, making her one of the earliest known female readers of the poem.[7] Despite his sympathy for the poem's reformist agenda and his life-long support for Henry VIII, Fortescue was executed for "diverse and sundrie detestable and abhomynable treasons" in 1539. He was subsequently celebrated as a Catholic martyr and in 1895 was beatified by the Pope.

Another scribal signature appears in a colophon added at the end of Bodleian Library, Rawlinson Poetry MS 137, a copy of the A version with the only complete copy of passus 12. By comparison with the Adrian Fortescue signature, this one is considerably less promising for the purposes of identification: "Nomen scriptoris tilot plenus amoris." However, the clue to identifying this scribe lies in another manuscript in his hand: a copy of the *Prick of Conscience*, University College, Oxford MS 142.[8] In this manuscript the colophon provides us with the scribe's given name – "Nomen scriptoris thomas plenus amoris" – as well as the name of a colleague or associate, Ricardus Rauf. Now that we know the scribe's complete name, it is possible to identify him among fifteenth-century ecclesiastical records:

both Thomas Tilot and Richard Rauf are listed among the Vicars Choral in Chichester Cathedral in 1415.

The examples of Adrian Fortescue and Thomas Tilot show how useful the evidence of scribal signatures can be in enabling us to identify and trace the poem's earliest readers. Unfortunately, not all scribal signatures are so helpful. The scribe of British Library, MS Harley 3954 finished his conjoined B/A copy of the poem with the signature "Quod Herun." This manuscript was probably copied in Norfolk, but as yet no scribe of Norfolk origin has been proposed as the Harley copyist.[9] A more promising, yet equally untraced, signature appears at the end of Huntington Library, MS HM 137, a copy of the C text, where the scribe signed off: "Explicit peeres plouheman scriptum per Thomam Dankastre." Because professional scribes carrying out a commission for a patron generally remained anonymous, the addition of a scribal signature suggests that a manuscript was being copied for the scribe's own use. This is demonstrably the case with those manuscripts copied by Adrian Fortescue and Thomas Tilot, neither of whom was a professional scribe, and so may well also apply to Herun and Thomas Dankastre. Examples of manuscripts copied by scribes for their own use are particularly interesting evidence for the poem's reception, in that their scribes were unlikely to have been guided by the external demands of a bespoke booktrade, so that their copies of *Piers Plowman* reflect their personal responses to the poem more closely.

Even in cases where no scribal signature appears, scholars have been able to identify the copyist responsible through comparison of his handwriting with other manuscripts by known scribes. An important instance of such an identification concerns the copyist responsible for Trinity College, Cambridge MS B.15.17, the manuscript adopted by modern editors of the poem as their base text for editions of the B text (see Figure 4). The scribe of this manuscript has been linked with a prolific copyist of the works of Chaucer, responsible for copying the two earliest and most important manuscripts of the *Canterbury Tales*, subsequently identified as the professional London scrivener Adam Pinkhurst.[10] In addition to copying the Trinity manuscript, Pinkhurst has also been credited with carrying out a comprehensive series of corrections to the text and spelling of another copy of the B text: British Library, MS Additional 35287.[11] The extensive program of corrections made to the text of Additional 35287, with numerous erasures and crossings out on each folio, was carried out without concern for the manuscript's overall appearance. The result is a manuscript that was unlikely to have been fit for sale, and was perhaps intended to function as an exemplar for subsequent copying by further scribes. The identification of Adam Pinkhurst as the scribe responsible for copying the Trinity MS and

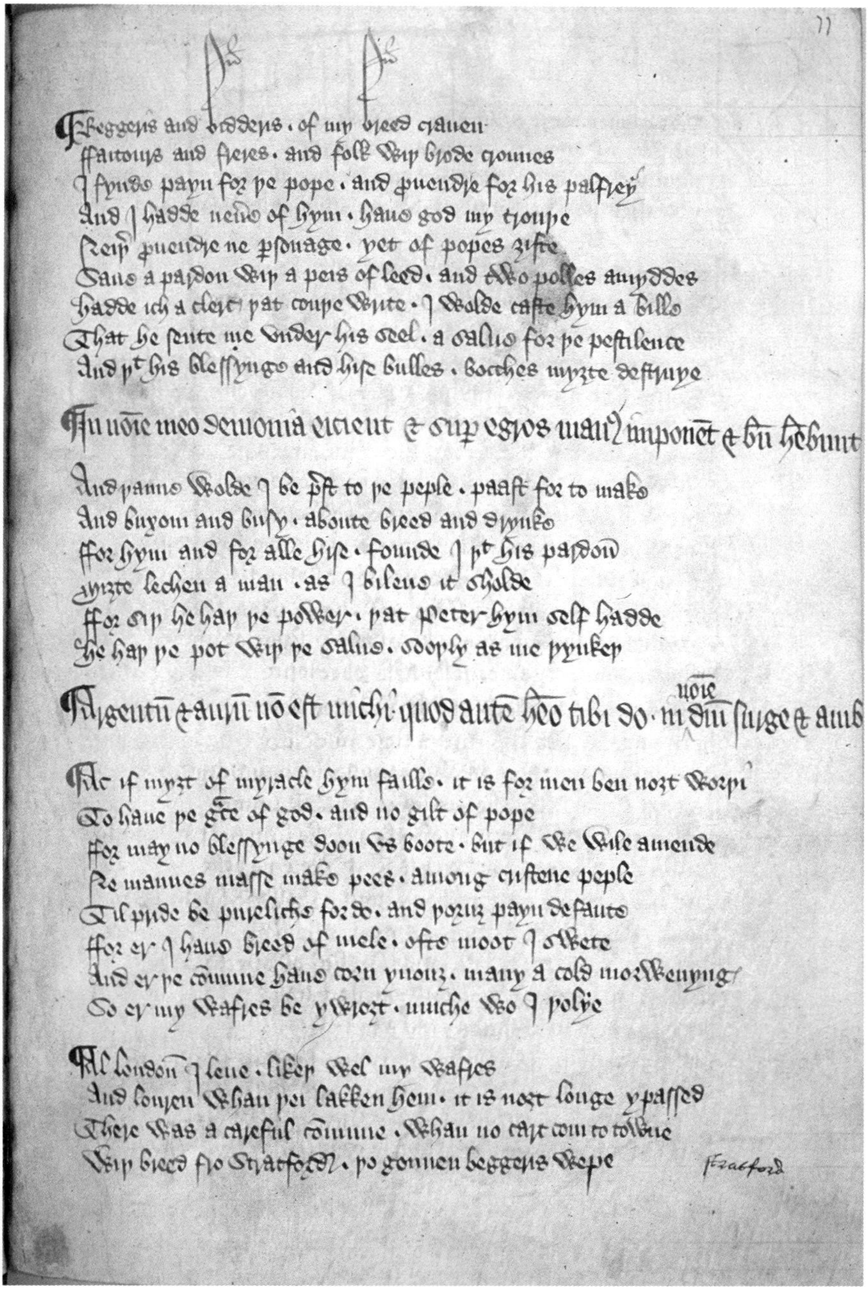
77

Beggers and bidders of my breed crauen
Faitours and freres and folk wiþ brode crounes
I fynde payn for þe pope and prouendre for his palfrey
And I hadde neuere of hym haue god my trouþe
Neiþer prouendre ne personage yet of popes ȝifte
Saue a pardon wiþ a peis of leed and two polles amyddes
Hadde ich a clerc þat couþe write I wolde caste hym a bille
That he sente me vnder his seel a salue for þe pestilence
And þat his blessynge and hise bulles bocches myȝte destruye

In nomine meo demonia eicient & super egros manus imponent & bene habebunt

And þanne wolde I be prest to þe peple paast for to make
And buxom and busy aboute breed and drynke
For hym and for alle hise founde I þat his pardon
Myȝte lechen a man as I bileue it sholde
For siþ he haþ þe power þat Peter hym self hadde
He haþ þe pot wiþ þe salue soþly as me þynkeþ

Argentum & aurum non est michi quod autem habeo tibi do in nomine domini surge & amb

Ac if myȝt of myracle hym faille it is for men ben noȝt worþi
To haue þe grace of god and no gilt of pope
For may no blessynge doon vs boote but if we wile amende
Ne mannes masse make pees among cristene peple
Til pride be pureliche fordo and þoruȝ payn defaute
For er I haue breed of mele ofte moot I swete
And er þe commune haue corn ynouȝ many a cold morwenyng
So er my wafres be ywroȝt muche wo I þolye

Al london I leue likeþ wel my wafres
And louren whan þei lakken hem it is noȝt longe ypassed
There was a careful commune whan no cart com to towne
Wiþ breed fro Stratford þo gonnen beggers wepe — Stratford

Figure 4 *Piers Plowman*, Trinity College, Cambridge MS B.15.17, fol. 77r.

preparing Additional 35287 as an exemplar to enable further copying suggests that he was a pivotal figure in the organization and supplying of the metropolitan scribal networks across which Langland's text was transmitted and copied.

As well as copying literary manuscripts like *Piers Plowman* and the *Canterbury Tales*, Adam Pinkhurst's hand has been identified in a petition written in 1387/8 for the Mercers' Guild, and adding entries to the guild's account books. Another *Piers Plowman* scribe can be associated with one of the London guilds through his copying activities. This is the scribe responsible for Bodleian Library, MS Digby 102, an early and accurate copy of the C text, whose scribe has been shown to have been employed by the Brewers' Guild to copy entries in their account book.[12] There is a clear contrast between the scribes who sign their manuscripts, who appear to be amateurs copying the text for their own interest, and the scribes of Trinity B.15.17 and Digby 102, who were professional scribes responding to the commission of a third party. This distinction is apparent in the format and appearance of the manuscripts themselves. The copies written by amateur scribes are considerably smaller in size, written in less formal scripts, using poor-quality materials, and with little or no decoration. By contrast, Trinity B.15.17 was produced on a more lavish scale: the leaves are bigger and the text is laid out with generous amounts of white space in the margins and even in the text column. Considerable time and effort has been invested in appearance, with proper names, Latin headings, and quotations boxed in red ink, and with elaborately decorated initials at the beginnings of passūs (see Figure 4). The layout adopted for this professional metropolitan manuscript is reproduced in several other copies of the B text, including Bodleian Library, MS Laud Misc. 581, Newnham College, Cambridge MS 4, and Bodleian Library Rawlinson Poetry MS 38, suggesting that it began to be established as a "standard" format, at least for copies of the B text. These manuscripts all present the text in a similar style of script, known as "Anglicana Formata" – leave blank lines between verse paragraphs, box the Latin quotations in red, and employ an identical form of explicit, referring to the text as a "dialogus": "Explicit hic dialogus petri plowman." Although they do not share all of these features, a group of early C manuscripts employs similar formats and layouts, suggesting that they too were copied in London workshops by professional scribes.

One of these C-text manuscripts was copied by a prolific copyist of vernacular manuscripts containing the works of Chaucer, John Gower, and John Trevisa. That this scribe was working in London, in the same circles as Adam Pinkhurst, is apparent from his contribution to a manuscript of Gower's *Confessio Amantis*. The copying of this manuscript was parcelled out to five separate scribes to expedite the production process; the scribe of the "Ilchester" manuscript, now University of London Library, MS s.l. v.88, was the fourth of these contributors (hence his appellation "Scribe D"). Another of the scribes who contributed to the Trinity Gower manuscript we have met already, namely Adam Pinkhurst ("Scribe B"), while Scribe E can be identified as the poet and professional Privy Seal copyist Thomas Hoccleve. Thus we find that a group of important and early witnesses of the B and C texts were copied using similar scripts and formats by a small circle of scribes, working in London in the early fifteenth century.[13] It is important, however, not to take the evidence for a "standard" format of *Piers Plowman* too far; we must remember that all manuscripts are individuals and very often have their own idiosyncrasies. A useful contrast to the evidence for the "standard" London *Piers Plowman* manuscript is Digby 102, whose scribe is known to have been a professional London clerk, working in close proximity to Adam Pinkhurst, but who presents the text rather differently from this "standard" London product. Where these copies all include the poem on its own, Digby 102 also contains a sequence of political and religious verse, Richard of Maidstone's metrical paraphrase of the Seven Penitential Psalms, and *The Debate between the Body and the Soul*. The scribe employs a version of Anglicana Formata, but on a much smaller scale, with individual lines squashed together as if space were at a premium. The need to conserve space may well explain the manuscript's most strikingly unusual feature: its setting out verse lines as prose, rather than using separate lines. This format has been adopted for all the manuscript's constituent texts, demonstrating that it must have been a deliberate scribal policy to introduce it. The scribe was clearly aware that the texts he was copying were in verse, as he is careful to employ punctuation marks to indicate line divisions, using distinct marks to distinguish ends of lines and half-lines.

Another scribe who signed a manuscript in which he copied *Piers Plowman* is John Cok, who included a brief extract from the poem, C.16.182–201a, in Gonville and Caius College, Cambridge MS 669*/646 (see Figure 5). John Cok (*c.* 1393–*c.* 1468) was apprenticed to a goldsmith but later became professed as an Augustinian canon and brother of St Bartholomew's Hospital, London, where he was responsible for compiling the hospital's Cartulary and several other manuscripts. Cok was closely associated with John Shirley, scribe and compiler of several important manuscript anthologies of Chaucer and Lydgate, who rented four shops from the hospital and who named Cok as an executor of his will.[14] The Gonville and Caius manuscript was later owned by Shirley, and there are many instances of his marginal annotation, "nota per Shirley," noting points of interest; it may be that Cok copied the volume as a gift for Shirley. The manuscript is an anthology of

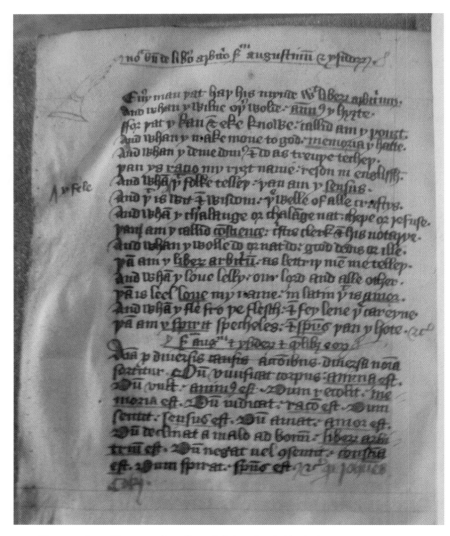

Figure 5 *Piers Plowman*, Gonville and Caius, Cambridge MS 669*/646, page 210.

devotional material, containing vernacular translations of the *Meditationes Vitae Christi*, and Richard Rolle's *Emendatio Vitae* and his *Form of Living*. The extract from *Piers Plowman* is written in a less formal hand and given the title: "nota bene de libero arbitrio secundum augustinum & ysidorum." The status of this extract is puzzling. No mention is made of *Piers Plowman* or its author, while the number of textual variants might suggest that it was reproduced from memory rather than copied from a written version of the poem. However, these variants testify to a close relationship with another surviving copy, Cambridge University Library, MS Ff.v.35, suggesting that Cok's extract was copied from this manuscript, or another closely related to it. The presence of an overlooked additional passage from *Piers Plowman* in the Gonville and Caius manuscript, C.16.116, further strengthens the likelihood that Cok had access to a complete copy of the poem, from which he excerpted discussions of freewill and poverty for himself and his fellow brethren.[15]

Dialect

It will be apparent from the discussion above that manuscripts of *Piers Plowman* circulated in different parts of the country; so far I have referred to copies written in London, Sussex, and Norfolk, but in fact the poem circulated very widely throughout the country. In this section we will examine the nature of the evidence for the geographical transmission of the poem, and consider its significance for our understanding of Langland's regional readership. We saw above that it was comparatively unusual for scribes to add a signature to a manuscript; details concerning the place of copying are even rarer. Given that, you might be wondering how we can determine where individual manuscripts were copied. The evidence for this is the dialect in which the text has been copied. Because there was no standard written form of Middle English, scribes were trained to use a local form of written language; many continued to employ dialect features throughout their careers. When copying a Middle English text written in a different dialect, a scribe might "translate" it into his own regional spelling system, or copy it exactly as he found it, known as "literatim" copying, thereby preserving the dialect of his exemplar. The diversity of scribal dialects witnessed in the surviving manuscripts of the poem demonstrates that the poem was frequently copied by regional scribes who translated their exemplars into their own local dialects. Using the data collected by the Middle English dialect survey, published as the *Linguistic Atlas of Late Mediaeval English*,[16] M. L. Samuels was able to suggest a localization for many of the surviving manuscripts of the A and C texts of the poem. The map showing the dialect localizations of copies of A and C suggested certain patterns concerning the regional dissemination of these two versions. Using his map, Samuels noted that manuscripts of the A text were written exclusively in regional dialects, with copies localized to Norfolk, Durham, Warwickshire, Lincolnshire, Sussex, and Shropshire. This evidence suggested that the A text circulated exclusively in the provinces, and was unknown to the professional book-trade in London. According to Samuels's dialect analysis, the C text was similarly unavailable in the metropolis; its copies were found to have circulated predominantly in the southwest Midlands. The B-text manuscripts presented greater difficulties for dialect analysis because many of their scribes appear to have mixed their own dialect forms with those of their exemplar, producing a complex mixture of forms (known as a "mischsprache"). Copying behavior of this kind is particularly associated with London, and it seems likely that many of these copies with mixed dialects were produced by scribes working in London. The London focus of the dissemination of the B text is supported by the dialects of the few localizable copies, most of which can be traced to the Greater London area and nearby Essex, Hertfordshire, and Cambridgeshire.

These dialect localizations have proved very influential in subsequent studies of the poem's audience and distribution. For instance, Kathryn Kerby-Fulton and Denise Despres drew upon the Hiberno-English localization of Bodleian Library, MS Douce 104 to argue that its scribe, who also provided a unique cycle of marginal illustrations to accompany the text, was a clerk at the Dublin Exchequer who repackaged the poem to make it relevant to the community of Anglo-Irish clericist readers.[17] Scholars have drawn on the lack of evidence for London copying of the A text to argue that this was not a distinct authorial version, but rather a work-in-progress that was leaked and circulated exclusively among provincial regions.[18] The clustering of C-text manuscripts in the southwest Midlands, and particularly the Malvern area with which Langland himself is thought to have had connections, has led some scholars to conclude that the revisions found in C, in which the more controversial aspects of the poem have been toned down, were carried out specifically with this regional, more conservative, audience in mind. This strong regional focus has even led scholars to claim that Langland himself had returned to Malvern to carry out these revisions and to oversee the copying and distribution of this final version of his poem.[19] Since Samuels's dialect study, some of these conclusions have been challenged and modified. While the surviving manuscripts of the A text show a remarkable range of regional dialects and demonstrate that this version circulated widely among those who were or had come from outside London, this does not mean that this version was unknown in London. The A text was probably composed in the 1360s, but our surviving manuscripts mostly date from the 1400s onwards, and so tell us little about the earliest copies. The complex textual affiliations that the surviving copies display provide clear evidence for numerous earlier witnesses that have since been lost, which may well have circulated in London.[20] Samuels himself noted that one of the earliest surviving copies of the A text, the "Vernon" manuscript, shows signs of having been copied from an exemplar written in the London dialect. Just because no surviving copy of the A text is written in a London dialect does not mean that this version was unknown in London.

Another of Samuels's conclusions that has been challenged concerns the exclusively southwest Midland distribution of the C-text manuscripts. As we saw above, some of these manuscripts were written by scribes who have since been shown to have been working in London, such as "Scribe D" of the Ilchester manuscript and the scribe of Digby 102, while others employ scripts and layouts that recall the "standard" format of the B-text manuscripts produced in the capital. More detailed analysis of the dialect of these copies of the C text has revealed a distribution of forms that shows that the south-western dialect features were carried over from their exemplar, rather than introduced by the scribes themselves.[21] This means that the scribes were copying "literatim," retaining dialect forms that derive from Langland's own southwestern dialect, while introducing some of their own forms, just like the London copies of the B text discussed above. Even with these modifications, Samuels's mapping of the regional distribution remains an invaluable starting point for a discussion of how the poem was distributed, copied, and read, both in London and "opelond."

Later owners

So far in this discussion we have focused on the evidence for the earliest stage of ownership of *Piers Plowman* manuscripts, as witnessed by the patrons who commissioned the manuscripts, and the scribes who copied them. Now it is time to turn to the evidence for secondary owners: those readers who acquired second-hand copies of the poem.

Evidence for secondary readership points to a continued interest in the poem in religious institutions. By 1500, Rawlinson Poetry 137, copied by Thomas Tilot of Chichester Cathedral, was owned by the Franciscan Convent in Canterbury, and Trinity College Dublin MS 213, a copy of the A text accompanied by the *Wars of Alexander*, can be associated with Durham Cathedral Priory. Harley 6041, commissioned by the Hoo family of Bedfordshire, was later owned by William Holyngborne, a monk of St. Augustine's Canterbury who witnessed the surrender of 1539. Bodleian Library, MS Bodley 851, the sole extant witness to the Z text, also an important anthology of Latin works, was owned by John Wells, Benedictine monk of Ramsey Abbey, Huntingdonshire, and student and later prior of Gloucester College, Oxford. Known as "Malleus hereticorum," the hammer of heretics, Wells was a prominent opponent of John Wyclif, and was the first to address the Blackfriars Council (1382) at which Wyclif's views were condemned as heretical. Another manuscript that may have been owned by a member of the regular clergy in the fifteenth century is Huntington Library HM 143, which contains the signature "Dom John Redbery." The use of the title "Dom," an abbreviation of the Latin "Dominus," is generally associated with members of the regular clergy in the fifteenth century.

Identifiable fifteenth-century signatures also witness to the poem's expanding secular audience. The name Thomas Jakes, entered in Cambridge University Library, MS Ff.v.35, has been identified as a member of Lincoln's Inn in 1465. Lincoln's Inn MS Hale 150, containing a copy of the A text of *Piers Plowman* alongside four Middle English romances, *Lybeaus Desconus*, *Merlyn*, *Kyng Alisaunder*, and *Seege of Troye*, copied in the first quarter of the fifteenth century by a scribe using a Shropshire dialect, was owned in the early sixteenth century by Anthony Foster of Wimbold's Trafford (a few miles northeast of Chester), a member of the household of the powerful Shropshire family the Fitzalans of Clun.[22]

A further category of evidence for reconstructing the poem's early readership is found in medieval wills and inventories, in which manuscript copies of the poem were listed and bequeathed to others. While this evidence is useful in providing the names of people who can be shown to have owned a copy of the poem, we must remember that the person receiving the manuscript did not necessarily have any particular interest in its contents. Because books were not considered especially valuable commodities in fifteenth-century England, especially vernacular literary books, there are few instances of wills in which copies of *Piers Plowman* are mentioned. The earliest recorded instance is found in the will of Walter Brugge, whose highly successful career as financial officer of the vast lands of the Mortimer family led to many lucrative, non-residentiary, ecclesiastical positions, including prebends at the cathedrals of St. Patrick's, Dublin, St. David's in Wales, York and Hereford.[23] The second instance of a bequest of a copy of the poem appears in a will of 1400, in which William Palmere, rector of St. Alphage's church, Cripplegate, left a copy of the poem to Agnes Eggesfeld.[24] This bequest provides a tantalizing suggestion of an early female readership for Langland's poem, but as nothing is known of Eggesfeld or her reaction to the gift, it remains impossible to gauge its significance. Other Londoners who passed on copies of the poem in the fifteenth century tend to reinforce the location of Langland's readership among members of parliament, guild companies, and the Inns of Court. In 1434, Thomas Roos, a mercer who rose to become Warden of the Mercers' Company, left his copy to his son Guy. An inventory of books owned by Thomas Stotevyle, of Dalham and Denham, Suffolk, a member of Lincoln's Inn, drawn up in 1459, lists "Petrus Plowman" alongside a number of literary works, including the *Canterbury Tales*. The booklist of Sir Thomas Charleton, speaker of the House of Commons, drawn up in 1465, includes "perse plowman" alongside copies of Chaucer's *Troilus and Criseyde* and *Canterbury Tales*. While the majority of bequests of the poem are found in the wills of Londoners, the poem's regional readership is further attested by the will of John Wyndhill, rector of Arncliffe in Craven, in the North Yorks dales, who left a copy to John Kendale, vicar of Grimston, in 1431. The inventory of the library of Sir Richard Brereton (who died *c.* 1559) of Lea Hall, Cheshire, sometime Lord Justice in Ireland, includes not one but two copies of the poem, although the value attached to the books suggests they may have been printed rather than manuscript copies.[25]

Reception

So far we have focused on identifying the actual individuals who commissioned, copied, and owned manuscripts of *Piers Plowman* in the fifteenth century. While such information is evidently important in allowing insights into the kinds of people who read the poem, and their personal and professional affiliations, it tells us little about how they read and responded to it. In this section we will examine the kinds of evidence available for study of the poem's reception.

One clue to the way the poem was read is provided by the other works that appear alongside it in its manuscripts. Given its length, it is unsurprising to find that many manuscripts contain only *Piers Plowman*. There are, however, instances of larger anthologies where the poem is found in the company of other works.[26] The work most commonly found alongside *Piers Plowman* in such anthologies is *Mandeville's Travels*; these two texts appear together in no fewer than five copies. There are three manuscripts that place *Piers Plowman* alongside *The Pistill of Susan*, two that contain the alliterative poem *Siege of Jerusalem*, and a further two with the pious romance *Ypotis*. These conjunctions suggest a readership who viewed the poem as a historical, pious romance. Other textual associations emphasize the poem's concern with religious and devotional instruction. There are three manuscripts that contain both *Piers Plowman* and the didactic religious poem, *The Prick of Conscience*,[27] and single manuscripts that include *The Lay Folk's Mass Book* and Robert Mannyng's *Handlyng Synne*.[28] Although *Prick of Conscience* survives in more manuscripts than any other medieval English poem (some 115 copies are known), the overlap in readership implied by these three manuscripts is further supported by the four further instances of *Piers Plowman* scribes who copied *The Prick of Conscience* in other manuscripts.[29] The heavily didactic content of *The Prick of Conscience* suggests an audience comprising members of the parish clergy tasked with preaching and the administration of pastoral care, copies of which were often made by local scribes for edificatory use in their parishes. The "holster book" format, a long and thick book designed to be portable, adopted for four manuscripts of *Piers Plowman*, might be further indication of use by itinerant parish clerks among their parishioners.[30]

For responses directly relevant to the text of *Piers Plowman*, we need to consider the various comments and annotations found in the margins of surviving manuscripts. Marginal annotations come in various kinds.[31] Some are limited to highlighting of certain words or phrases, using underlining, pointing hands, or the "nota" abbreviation. Other kinds of straightforward annotation function as subheadings, identifying various key moments in the text or drawing attention to particular characters. Common instances include the identification of the seven deadly sins alongside the beginnings of their respective confessions. Others include the naming of historical and biblical figures – Trajan, David, Aristotle, Gregory – or particularly dramatic moments in the poem's development, such as the tearing of the pardon. Because *Piers Plowman* remained popular in the sixteenth century, especially within reformist and antiquarian circles, much sixteenth-century annotation relates to those particular concerns. Thus we often find notes in sixteenth-century hands drawing attention to aspects of Catholic doctrine that were opposed by reformers, including indulgences, purgatory, and confession. Langland's anticlerical, especially antifraternal satire, is often a focus of reformist approval, with readers registering their distaste for flattering friars and their corrupt practices.

In addition to these responses, certain manuscripts preserve more idiosyncratic annotations, reflecting the more individual responses of particular readers. Cambridge University Library, MS Gg.iv.31, copied in the early sixteenth century, shows a particular interest in the poem's prophecies, titling the poem "The Prophecies of Piers Plowman," and highlighting such material using marginal glosses, cross-references, and a table of contents.[32] In Cambridge University Library, MS Ll.iv.14, a sixteenth-century reader who introduced a series of subheadings, "A Tower on a tofte," "A Dongion in a Dale," and so on throughout the text, also supplied a short glossary as an aid to readers struggling with Langland's more archaic and dialectal diction. This glossary includes entries like "carpe: talk," "lake: playe," "courbe: knele downe," "crokke: pott." Although the list of words is comparatively brief, occupying just two leaves at the end of the manuscript, it is a valuable index of the words that were considered unfamiliar to a sixteenth-century audience. It has been proposed that the author of this glossary was Robert Crowley, the poem's first printer, who may have used it as a guide for his reading of the poem, although he did not include such a glossary in his edition.[33]

An interesting sixteenth-century reader of *Piers Plowman* who was both reformer and antiquarian is Stephan Batman (*c.* 1542–84), the author of a number of works including *A Christall Glasse of Christian Reformation* (1569), *The Travayled Pylgrime* (1569), and a version of Bartholomaeus Anglicus' *De proprietatibus rerum: Batman uppon Bartholome* (1582), which served as a standard encyclopaedia in Elizabethan England. In addition to his literary pursuits, Batman was an important collector of medieval manuscripts. As part of his duties as domestic chaplain to the Archbishop of Canterbury, Matthew Parker, Batman became closely involved with other members of Parker's circle in identifying and salvaging the contents of monastic libraries following the Dissolution.[34] Batman boasted of having collected some 6,700 volumes for Parker, comprising a range of subjects: "of Diuinitie, Astronomie, Historie, Phisicke, and others of sundrye Artes and Sciences."[35] In addition to volumes that he collected on behalf of Parker, Batman assembled a substantial collection of manuscripts for his own use. More than twenty extant manuscripts have been linked with Batman's ownership, a collection which witnesses to a particular concern with Middle English devotional literature, and with *Piers Plowman*.[36] Two extant manuscripts of *Piers Plowman* were once owned by Batman, and contain annotations, and even an illustration, in his hand.[37] Batman's annotations include corrections and additions to the text that show that he must have had access to a further copy of the poem, the third edition printed by Crowley, or Rogers's 1561 reprint of that text. Batman's insistence on the value of reading medieval works like *Piers Plowman* in a post-Reformation era is expressed most overtly in his comments on the title page to one of his copies, now Bodleian Library, MS Digby 171, where he writes:

> This Booke is clepped: Sayewell, Doowell. Doo Better & Doo Best. Souche a booke, az diserveth the Reeding. Bookes of Antiquiti are wel bestowed one those whose Sober staied mindes can abyde the redyng, but commonly Frantik braines, suche az are more readye to be prattlers than parformers, seing this book to be olde, Rather take it for papisticall then else. & so many bookes com to confusion.

In his other copy, a conjoint A and C text, now Trinity College, Cambridge MS R.3.14, Batman has added lines from the B text, not found in either A or C (see Figure 6):

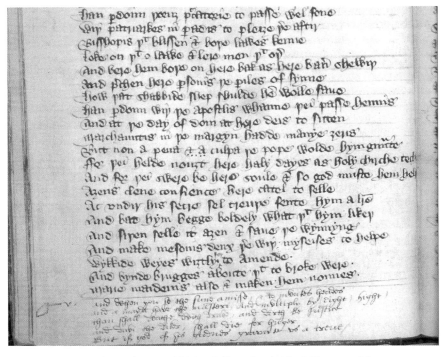

Figure 6 *Piers Plowman*, Trinity College, Cambridge MS R.3.14, fol. 42.

And when you se the sune amisse & to mvnkes heades
And a mayde have the masteri, and mvltiply by hight
than shall deathe withdrawe, and derth be Iustice
And davi the diker, shall die for hunger
But if god of his goodnes gravnte vs a treue

(B.6.327–31)

The inclusion of these lines at this exact point in the text demonstrates Batman's familiarity with the poem in its various versions. The choice of passage is also striking, given that it is found in two further sixteenth-century manuscripts, suggesting that it was particularly well known among sixteenth-century readers of *Piers Plowman* (see Chapter 11).[38] The first of these excerpts appears in a large manuscript miscellany, known as the Winchester Anthology, now British Library, MS Additional 60577, where it has been signed "Quod piers plowman," as if quoting Piers Plowman himself. The Winchester Anthology, a collection of lyrics, songs, sermons, and religious treatises, was copied in the late fifteenth century; the *Piers Plowman* extract was added in the early sixteenth century, perhaps by John Brynstan, a monk of St. Swithun's, Winchester, who subsequently became an Augustinian friar. The second instance of this extract occurs in an anthology of the sixteenth century, where another textually idiosyncratic version has been incorporated within a diverse collection of prophecies, now British Library, MS Sloane 2578. In each instance the passage contains a number of unique textual readings, suggesting that it was copied from memory rather than directly from a copy of the poem. The Sloane copy of the text makes no reference to either *Piers Plowman* or William Langland; in both cases we are presented with a similar problem to that concerning the extract copied by John Cok, discussed above. Did the scribes of these extracts know that they were quoting *Piers Plowman*, or did this fragment circulate entirely separately from the poem, enjoyed by readers largely unaware of its original context?

But while those interested in the poem's prophecies may have had little interest in the poem as a whole, or William Langland, other sixteenth-century readers scoured the manuscripts for evidence of the poem's author. A key figure in this group of antiquarians was John Bale, whose autograph compilation of notes concerning British writers records that the poem *Piers Plowman* was authored by one Robert Langland, born in Cleobury Mortimer, Shropshire, and quotes the poem's opening line. Bale's information is inaccurate in a number of ways – Langland's name was William not Robert, his family was based in Oxfordshire not Shropshire – but it does open a window on the activities of a group of antiquarians interested in the poet and his life. Bale's notebook contains four entries concerning *Piers Plowman*, in which he attributes his information to three people with whom he discussed the poem and studied its manuscripts. One of these, Nicholas Brigham, is known to have been a collector of manuscripts, and his collections likely supplied Bale with manuscripts with which he carried out his researches. Bale's quotation of the opening line of the poem in his notebook, "In a somer season whan set was the sunne," attests a variant reading, "set" for "softe," which is found in just one surviving manuscript of the poem. The possibility that this manuscript, now Huntington Library, MS HM 128, was one of the copies consulted by Bale is made certain by the presence of a note in Bale's hand on the front pastedown, in which he repeats the information recorded in his notebook. Above this note by Bale, a second hand of the early sixteenth century has added the ascription: "Robert or William langland made pers ploughman." The hand responsible for this ascription is that of another antiquarian, Ralph Coppinger, who served as Customs Collector in the port of London and died in 1551.[39] Coppinger inserted a similar authorship inscription in Laud Misc. 581, as well as the following record of a loan: "M*emorandum* þat I haue lent to Nicholas brigham the pers plough-man which I borowed of Mr. Le of Addyngton." The reference to Nicholas Brigham provides a link back to John Bale, suggesting that Bale may well have consulted the Laud manuscript as well as HM 128. One further member of this tightly knit circle of antiquarians was Robert Crowley, the poem's first printer. In the preface to his edition of the poem, Crowley described how his desire to know the name of the author led him to gather together "suche aunciente copies as I could come by" and to consult "such me*n* as I knew to be more exercised in the studie of antiquities, then I myselfe haue ben." It is clear that this search led him to John Bale, resulting in Crowley's attribution of the work to Robert Langland of Cleobury Mortimer.[40]

One further sixteenth-century antiquarian and collector of manuscripts can be shown to have handled at least two manuscripts of *Piers Plowman*. John Stow is well known as a collector of medieval manuscripts, although his literary interests focused principally on the works of Chaucer and John Lydgate. Stow is not known as a reader of alliterative verse, although his famously "spidery" hand can be found in two surviving copies of *Piers Plowman*, Trinity B.15.17 and Rawlinson Poetry 38. But his annotations tend to confirm his apparent lack of interest in the poem: in both manuscripts Stow has simply added the word "Stratford" in the margin alongside Langland's description of the practice of bringing bread into London by cart from Stratford (Figure 4). Stow's interests in *Piers Plowman* were evidently historical rather than literary; Stow treated the poem as a source for a social practice that he quoted verbatim in his *Survey of London*, transforming its alliterative long lines into prose:

> Moreouer in the 44. of *Edward* the third *Iohn Chichester* being Maior of London, I read in the visions of *Pierce Plowman*, a booke so called, as fol-loweth. "*There was a careful commune, when no Cart came to towne with baked bread from Stratford: tho gan beggers weepe, and workemen were agast, a little this will be thought long in the date of our Dirte, in a drie Auerell a thousand and three hundred, twise thirtie and ten, &c.*[41]

Stow, as the reception history of *Piers Plowman* reveals, was neither the first nor the last to reckon with, and then flatten, Langland's alliterative line (Chapter 3), or for that matter the only reader who construed the poem to be a social document rather than a poem (Introduction).

Conclusion

As we have seen, the manuscripts of *Piers Plowman* preserve a wealth of evidence concerning the poem's audience, the variety of ways in which the text was read, and the responses it elicited. But much research remains to be done in this area: new identifications of scribal hands, ownership inscriptions, and badges, and comprehensive studies of marginalia and annotation, will all help to fill out the picture that I have sketched of the way the poem was copied, circulated, and read.

I I

LAWRENCE WARNER

Plowman traditions in late medieval and early modern writing

Piers the Plowman is one of the most powerful and mysterious figures of the English literary tradition. His first appearance in Langland's poem occurs at the moment that the penitent sinners need a guide for their pilgrimage to St. Truth: "'Peter,' quod a plowe man, and put forth hys heade: / 'I knowe hym as kyndly, as clerke doeth hys bokes'" (sig. H.i^r = B.5.537–8).[1] Here he seems to be a simple laborer, but by the end of the episode he has organized a communal act of plowing, debated a priest, torn a pardon in pure anger, and indicated that his true calling is the penitential Christian life: "'I shal cease of my sowinge' quod pierce, '& swinke not so hard / Ne about my bealy joy, so busy be no more / Of praiers & of penaunce, my plowe shal be hereafter'" (sig. K.ii^r = B.7.122–4). Piers shows up sporadically throughout the rest of the poem with varying meanings attached to him. A few allegorical personifications mention him in the exchanges in the episode of the Doctor of Divinity's feast and its aftermath (passus 13); Anima equates him with Christ in his description of Charity (passus 15); the dreamer swoons at the mention of his name and then gets Piers to explain the Tree of Charity (passus 16); Jesus wears Piers's armor in his joust with the devil (passus 18); Piers serves as Grace's reeve, plowing with the four Church Fathers as oxen and planting the seeds of the cardinal virtues (passus 19); and in the final lines of the poem Conscience abandons the fallen Holy Church Unity, saying he will "walken as wyde as the world lasteth / To seke Pierce the plowman, that pride may destroy" (sig. Gg.i^v = B.20.381–2).

This brief summary indicates the richness of Langland's portrayal of Piers the Plowman. Yet this figure's influence on subsequent authors was almost entirely confined to his first appearance, the plowing episode, which served as a guarantee of Piers's honesty and simplicity, as opposed to the venality of friars, priests, bishops, and the rest of the ecclesiastical structure. Thus Chaucer's portrait of the Plowman in the General Prologue to the *Canterbury Tales*, which many readers have assumed to be inspired by Langland's figure: "He wolde thresshe, and therto dyke and delve, / For Cristes sake, for every povre wight, / Withouten hire, if it lay in his myght" (lines 536–8). No pardoner or friar is he. Chaucer's plowman is quiet and does not even tell a tale, but most subsequent instances of the plowman tradition give him plenty to say. For 200 years after the appearance of Langland's poem, the figure of the righteous plowman protesting the abuses of the age was a mainstay of satirical writings.

Folk figure or Langlandian invention? Piers the Plowman in the Rising of 1381

Most considerations of these plowman traditions take for granted that Langland was their progenitor, on the grounds that before *Piers Plowman* the figure of the shepherd was valorized, whereas that of the plowman was indelibly associated with Cain. Langland, in this reading, re-created and redeemed the metaphor. But this approach fails to account adequately for the powerful biblical and patristic tradition whereby preachers employed "the plowshare of the tongue." The assumption that the figure of the plowman became site of the holy and righteous only at Langland's hands also falters on the existence of a work about a Christ-like plowman, "De Duello Militis et Aratoris" ("On the Duel of the Soldier and the Plowman"), which was a standard item on the syllabus for students of Latin throughout the later Middle Ages.[2] Finally, if Langland did indeed create the figure of Piers the Plowman, he seemed to want his readers to identify him with such longstanding alliterative types as Tom Tinker, Robert the Robber (whom Langland mentions), or Miles Miller. It seems at least as likely that Piers the Plowman was a folk figure as that Langland invented him from scratch.

If this is a reasonable conclusion, an important early reference to Piers the Plowman may not witness to Langland's influence as has nearly always been assumed. John Ball famously called upon Piers the Plowman in his letters inciting the Rising of 1381, as exemplified in that to the commons of Essex:

> Johon Schep . . . biddeþ Peres Plouȝman go to his werk, and chastise wel
>   Hobbe þe Robbere, and taketh wiþ ȝow Johan Trewman, and alle hiis
>   felawes, and no mo, and loke schappe ȝou to on heved, and no mo.
> Johan þe Mullere haþ ygrounde smal, smal, smal;
> Þe Kynges sone of hevene schal paye for al.
> Be war or ȝe be wo;
> Knoweth ȝour freende fro ȝour foo;
> Haveth ynow, & seith "Hoo";
> And do wel and bettre, and fleth synne,
> And sekeþ pees, and hold ȝou þerinne;
> and so biddeth Johan Trewaman and alle his felawes.[3]

Here, as in *Piers Plowman*, we find Piers the Plowman, Hob the Robber (that is, Robert the Robber), and the injunction to "do well and better." It is possible that by 1381 Ball had read the A version of Langland's poem, which could have provided the source of these references. But Robert the Robber, at least, is a folk figure, and the notion of doing well and better, too, is commonplace (e.g., 1 Cor. 7:38), so it seems much more likely that both Ball and Langland are invoking standard scriptural texts than that the rebel preacher suddenly called on an obscure and new poem as source of such basic injunctions as "do well and better." (For an account that takes the letters to be referring to Langland's poem, see Chapter 3.) The origins of the plowman traditions, then, are murkier than we might have suspected, and their developments even after *Piers Plowman* became widely known continue to resist simple interpretations based on the notion of direct Langlandian influence. The plowman traditions that became so vibrant in the fifteenth and sixteenth centuries generated their own sets of confusion with regard to authorship, provenance, and even the basics of meaning.

Piers the Plowman *c.* 1400: *Pierce the Ploughman's Crede, The Plowman's Tale,* and the question of authorship

The most prominent appearance of Piers the Plowman after Langland's poem itself is *Pierce the Ploughman's Crede* (*c.* 1393–1400), of which one fifteenth-century manuscript excerpt, two complete sixteenth-century manuscripts, and two printed editions, of 1553 and 1561 (the latter together with *Piers Plowman*), survive. This poem's indebtedness to Langland is apparent in its employment of the alliterative long line, which it shares with the other members of the "*Piers Plowman* tradition," and a feature unique to it among this group: the appearance of Pierce the Plowman as figure of authority. The *Crede*'s narrator wishes to learn the Creed, and seeks out instruction from members of each of the four orders of friars in turn, who leave him muttering to himself on their falsehoods and faithlessness. On his travels he spies a simple poor man at the plow, who confirms that the friars are wolves in sheep's clothing and introduces himself as Piers. The reader is then subjected to a lengthy harangue by this plowman, directed primarily against the friars. While Langland often inveighs against the fraternal abuse of the sacrament of penance, he never does so in Piers's voice, as does the *Crede*:

> The power of the Apostells thei pasen in speche,
> For to sellen the synnes for silver other mede,
> And purlyche *a pena* the puple assoileth,

> And *a culpa* also that they may kachen
> Money other money-worthe and mede to fonge;
> And bene at lone and at bode as burgeses usithe.[4]

The language, as well as the sentiment, is heavily indebted to the episodes of Meed and the tearing of the pardon in *Piers Plowman*, but the *Crede* foregrounds, and thus renders somewhat less mysterious, Piers's own role in the proceedings.

Just after the appearance of *Pierce the Ploughman's Crede* a Wycliffite poet composed a diatribe against the ecclesiastical hierarchy, in the guise of a debate between a pelican and a griffin, as overheard by a traveler. Amidst the standard anticlerical materials here is a direct reference to the *Crede*:

> Chanons / canons / and suche disgysed
> Ben goddess enemyes and traytours
> His trewe relygioun han foule dispysed
> Of Freres I have tolde before
> In a makynge of a Crede
> And yet I coude tell worse and more
> (1062–7)[5]

At first glance this reference to the narrator's "making of a *Creed*" appears to be a claim that the author of this poem, now called *The Plowman's Tale*, also wrote the *Crede*, but critics now agree that it is simply a sign of the later poet's indebtedness to the earlier one in his approach to the clerisy. Yet this connection with *Pierce the Ploughman's Crede* would take on a new force around 1533, when the only surviving copies of the poem were produced. For in this version, found in a single manuscript and a single copy of a printing by the reformist printer Thomas Godfray, someone has added a prologue, in which a plowman, urged by the host to tell the gathering "some holy thyng," reports, "I herde ones teche / A preest in pulpyt a good prechyng" (46, 48): that is, the tale of the griffin and the pelican, now called *The Plowman's Tale*, which was incorporated into the *Canterbury Tales* in William Thynne's second edition of Chaucer's *Works* of 1542, where it remained in all editions until the eighteenth century.

It was becoming difficult to keep all these plowmen straight. John Leland's catalogue of the works of Chaucer, in his sixteenth-century *De viris illustribus*, begins:

Fabulae Cantianae viginti quattor, quarum dua soluta oratione scriptae
    Sed Petri Aratoris fabula, quae communi doctorum consensus Chaucero, tanquam vero parenti, attribuitur, in utraque editione, quia malos sacerdotum mores vehementer increpavit, suppressa est.

[Twenty-four *Canterbury Tales*, of which two are written in prose
   The Tale of Piers Plowman, however, which is attributed by the common consent of scholars to Chaucer's authorship, has been suppressed in both editions because it vigorously attacked the bad morals of the clergy.][6]

This item is universally taken to be a confused reference to *The Plowman's Tale*. While that is not impossible, it is more difficult than has been realized, because it is now apparent that Leland wrote this *c.* 1535–7, well before Thynne's inclusion of that tale in his *Works* of Chaucer in 1542.[7] Now, whatever poem he was referring to, he had not read it carefully: *The Plowman's Tale* has no Piers; *Piers Plowman* is no *fabula*, a "Canterbury tale." On that criterion the two cancel each other out. But every other indication, it seems, would favor *Piers Plowman* alone. As we have seen, only two copies of *The Plowman's Tale* produced before 1542 survive. No evidence indicates Leland's knowledge of this obscure poem, which had minuscule circulation. The phrase "Petri Aratoris," by contrast, proves his knowledge of *Piers Plowman*'s existence, which was extant in numerous manuscripts, three of which, plus one excerpt, were produced around the 1530s.

After 1550 it would have been difficult to make such a mistake, for in that year Robert Crowley issued three successive editions of *The Vision of Pierce Plowman*. Crowley depicted "Robert Langland" (as he, following John Bale, called the author) as a visionary, if not a prophet, in the address to the reader: in Edward III's time, "it pleased God to open the eyes of many to se hys truth, geving them boldenes of herte, to open their mouthes and crye oute agaynste the worckes of darckenes, as did John Wicklefe" (sig. *2[r]). There were now three major (and perhaps a number of minor) "plowman" poems, two of which were about Piers the Plowman, all of which had strong reformist characteristics. The appearance in 1561 of Owen Rogers's edition of both *The Vision of Pierce Plowman* (reprinted from Crowley's third edition) and *Pierce the Ploughman's Crede* (reprinted from Wolfe's 1553 edition) only cemented the prominence of this conjunction. While it is tempting to rush straight into analysis of the era's religious and artistic inclinations, we should not overlook the importance of these works to those antiquarians who followed Crowley in seeing the relevance of fourteenth- and fifteenth-century English literature to the latter sixteenth century.

On August 22, 1577, for instance, a learned commentator, perhaps Stephan Batman, a member of Archbishop Parker's circle, inscribed his copy of Rogers's production with a treatment of the problem, which had become only more confusing since Leland's day. The inscription opens with John Bale's Latin attribution of the "Visionem petri Aratoris" to Robert

Langland and description of the poet as a disciple of Wyclif (item 1 in a list) together with additional thoughts on authorship:

> 2. Mention is made of Peerce Plowghman's Creede, in Chawcers tale off the Plowman.
>
> 3. I deeme Chawcer to be the author. I thinke hit not to be on and the same þat made both: for that the reader shall fynde diverse maner of Englishinge on sentence; as namelie, Quid consyderas festucam in oculo fratris tui, trabem autem in oculo tuo etc.
>
> 4. And speciallie, for þat I fynde Water Brute named in this Creede: who was manye yeeres after þe author off þat Vision.[8]

The Plowman's Tale is here unquestionably Chaucer's, as is the *Crede*, of which this annotator "deems Chaucer to be the author" because of its reference to the earlier poem. But the author of "þat Vision" is not "on and the same" as Chaucer, a claim made on the grounds of dating and, it seems, the prominence of Latin therein but not in the *Crede*. The issue seems somewhat remote from our interests today, but it would remain central to many experiences of the plowman tradition, and even of the poetry of Geoffrey Chaucer, to whom a handful of readers, including such prominent ones as Humphrey Wanley, cataloguer of the Harley manuscripts in the 1720s, attributed *Piers Plowman* itself.

Piers Protestant

The most prominent manifestation of these plowman traditions was in the series of sixteenth-century pamphlets with titles like *I playne Piers, Pyers Plowmans exhortation,* and so forth. In the absence of many facts regarding their publication histories, it is hard to know whether these tracts created the market for Crowley's editions or vice versa. Either way, the mode of influence was much more on the level of general sentiment and even sound than that of language or theme. Piers the Plowman was not so much the protean figure sought by Will and Conscience in Langland's dream vision as a paradoxical figure whose very ancientness guaranteed the truth of his attacks on ancient, "Romish" beliefs. Typical of these pamphlets' approach is the opening to *A godly dyalogue & dysputacyon betwene Pyers plowman, and a popysh preest concernyng the supper of the lorde*: "It chaunced that this simple Pyers Plowman com to a certeyne house where as was a daner, prepared for the neyghbours dwelling ther aboute," where the conversation amongst the priests concerns the sacrament of the altar. By the end of this brief account, Piers has led the priests to the conclusion that the host at the Eucharist "is not the same body that our lady bare mynystred at the Aulter but onelye a remembrance of the same as it appereth."⁹ This "Piers the Plowman," like the teller of "Chaucer's" *Plowman's Tale,* has nothing obvious to do with Langland's poem, or with plowing for that matter, aside from his status as simple but wise outsider with substantial name recognition.

Yet whatever its benefits, the choice of the plowman as voice of authority put these authors in a paradoxical situation. On the one hand, according to the Protestant agenda here promulgated, salvation was by faith alone: the spiritual economy of good works, penance, and satisfaction via such acts as pilgrimage was prime evidence of Catholicism's bankruptcy. On the other hand, that exact spiritual economy infused Langland's portrait of Piers the Plowman's engagement with the sinners: they seek a guide for their pilgrimage, which in Langland's allegory becomes wholly fused with the necessity of "doing well," that is, winning and working rather than wasting. By invoking this figure, and the general symbol of the plowman who speaks out against clerical abuses, reformists were implicitly endorsing the legitimacy of penance and good works in the scheme of the Christian's life. Hence the emphasis on the need for amendment in a fascinating instance of one of these tracts, *I playne Piers*:

> Piers can tel you mykel more whiche he kepeth yet in store, to se yf you wyll amende, eles must here suche maner of gere, even to the worldes ende. Stones sayde the lorde shall beare recorde, yf other wytnes fayle, you kyll the wytnes trewe, God sendethe ever newe, lytle to your aduayle.¹⁰

Even in the heartland of the "Protestant Piers," then, the medieval hero of Ball's and Langland's works still retains elements of the medieval "darkness" out of which, or so claimed Crowley and others, Langland led his proto-Protestant readers.

Non-Protestant Piers

Yet we need not read against the grain of the early modern "plowman traditions" to recognize as much. For the narrative according to which *Piers Plowman*'s revival in the mid sixteenth century was a wholly Protestant phenomenon takes as its sole evidence the printed editions and pamphlets of that era. In doing so it inevitably ends up with a collection of Protestant plowmen. A comprehensive look at the materials that made up the plowman traditions of the sixteenth century, though, reveals a more varied landscape, indeed one in which Crowley and his compères were anxiously uncomfortable, and sought to reclaim a figure who had drifted beyond all control. In this light, the situation in the decades following Henry VIII's break from Rome is akin to that of around 1380, when it is unclear just where Piers the Plowman really belongs.

Take, for instance, this excerpt from *Piers Plowman*, found in British Library, MS Additional 60577 ("The Winchester Anthology"), fol. 212ʳ:

> Whene you se the sonne a mysse & two monkes heades
> And a mayed bere rule & reigne & multiply by eyght
> Then shall fruyt of þe erth fayll by fludes & foule wether
> And davy the dykar shall dye for hungar
> Except god of his marcy gyve & graunt a Treue
>   Quod piers plowman

At first glance this passage appears unexceptionable: excerpts of the poem show up all over the place. But both the attribution of this prophecy to Piers the Plowman, and the item's contexts, both material and spiritual, reveal a much different narrative. This collection was produced in Winchester Cathedral's Benedictine priory, St. Swithun's, and in the cathedral community itself after the monastery's dissolution, a provenance that imbues all its contents, including the *Piers Plowman* excerpt, with a full-blooded Catholicism (or recusancy).

The crucial phrase for our purposes is the one that justifies, or demands, its inclusion in any treatment of early modern Plowman traditions: "Quod piers plowman." Many readers have interpreted Crowley's publication of *Piers Plowman* as evidence that he and others saw it as prophesying the Reformation. Yet here, Piers the Plowman utters a prophecy in a context that is anything but reformist. The explanation of this paradox suggests that the figure of "Protestant Piers" was not the default one, but was instead a reaction against the powerful conjunction of Langland's figure – or, at least, the figure Langland had appropriated – and an oral, non-reformist mode of prophecy. In the case of the Winchester excerpt we have fascinating and particular evidence for this alternative chapter in the history of the Plowman traditions.

On the end pastedown of this collection, one John Buriton, monk of St. Swithun's, records that he purchased the book from John Brynstan, adding, in a lighter ink, the word "Erytike" under "brynstane," continuing, "otherwyse callyd whythere postata. I pray God he may repent and recant." We are fortunate to have a few records of Brynstan's life that put this startling accusation into context. He had been ordained deacon on December 22, 1520, and priest on March 21, 1522, but by the time he is recorded as having preached a sermon in Glastonbury Abbey church, some fourteen years later, he was an Austin friar. In this sermon, according to one witness,

Brynstan "said that 'he would be one of them that should convert the new fanggylles and new men, other else he would die in the quarrel,'" while others added "also that he said that 'all those that doth occupy the new books be lecherous and ready to devour men's wives and servants, and that he would be one of them that would bring down the new books, other else he would die in the cause.'" This looks like straightforward Catholic apologetics, but what he said next does not:

> They all say that the friar expounded the King's title as Supreme Head of the Church to the King's great honor, and the utter fordoing of the bishop of Rome's authority, – quoting Scripture in support of it. The friar answers that he said, "You with your new books, other ye be adulterers, filthy lechers, devourers of men's wives, daughters, or servants, other full of envy, malice, and strife, and ready to oppress and wrong your neighbours, and that I trusted to convert a great many of such erroneous persons, other to die in the quarrel."[11]

Brynstan's expounding of the King's title looks perverse if taken to be an endorsement of Henry's policies by a staunch Catholic. But it seems much likelier that Brynstan understood himself to be engaging in an ancient anti-clerical tradition rather than a partisan debate of his own day. He probably had in mind a model like this:

> And ther shall come a king & confesse you religious
> And beat you as þe byble telleth for breking of your rule
> And amend monials monkes and chanons
> And put hem to her penaunce. *Ad prestinum statum ire.*

which goes on to predict the disendowment of the Abbot of Abingdon; or, from that King's own perspective, this:

> For ye be but membres and I above all.
> And syth I am your allerhede, I am your allerhele,
> And holy church chiefe helpe & chefest am of þe comon.
> And what I take of you two I take it of þe teaching
> Of *Spiritus justicie*, for I judge you all.

Brynstan's sermon makes sense, that is, if it sounded to his listeners like *Piers Plowman* itself (sigs. N.ii[r] = B.10.322–5 and Ee.iii[r] = 19.470–4), whose status as an ancient collection of prophecies associated with the holy figure of Piers the Plowman guarantees, from this perspective, his inability to be assimilated into the Protestant paradigm, whether or not traces of the medieval symbolic meaning of labor persist in their own attempts to corral Piers to the cause.

Brynstan's contribution to the tradition of Piers Plowman writings of the sixteenth century figures so prominently here because it has received so much less attention than have those whose efforts were printed and thus archived in places like the Early English Books Online database. It exemplifies a major trend that helps to explain those items, especially Robert Crowley's 1550 productions of *The Vision of Pierce Plowman*. Crowley famously cites the lines Brynstan had inscribed in the Winchester Anthology as evidence precisely that Langland was not prophetic:

> As for that is written in the .xxxvi. leafe of thys boke concernynge a dearth then to come: is spoken by the knowledge of astronomie as may wel be gathered bi that he saith, Saturne sente him to tell. And that whiche foloweth and geveth it the face of a prophecye: is lyke to be a thinge added of some other man than the fyrste autour. For diverse copies have it diverslye. For where the copie that I folowe hath thus.
>
> > And when you se the sunne amisse, & two monkes heades
> > And a mayde have the maistrye, and multiplie by eyght.
> > > Some other have,
> > Thre shyppes and a shefe, wyth an eight folowynge
> > Shall brynge bale and battell, on both halfe the mone.
> >
> > (sig. *ii^v)

The standard explanation of Crowley's disattribution of the "monks' heads" passage from Langland is that he is distancing *Piers Plowman* from the Merlinesque, wild sort of prophecy that was so popular in the sixteenth century. But only ten or so of the poem's 7,000-plus lines might court such a response: so why is Crowley so worried? And why does he continue immediately with a denial of any prophetic status to the non-Merlinesque "there shall come a king" lines?

> Nowe for that whiche is written in the .l. leafe, concerning the suppression of Abbaies: the scripture there alledged, declareth it to be gathered of the juste judgment of God, whoe wyll not suffer abomination to raigne unpunished. Loke not upon this boke therfore, to talke of wonders paste or to come, but to amende thyne owne misse, which thou shalt fynd here moste charitably rebuked.
>
> (sig. *ii^v)

Crowley, I would suggest, is responding to a tradition rather than instigating one. The poem *Davy Dycars Dreame* (*c.* 1547), too, cites these Davy Dykar and Abbot of Abingdon passages in tandem, as does an odd entry in a collection of political prophecies collected by a rabid Protestant during Mary's reign (British Library, MS Sloane 2578). One instance that has never been publicized appears in a twelve-line poem telling what will happen in 1554, extant in at least four manuscripts, including Sloane 2578 itself, where it is cross-referenced with the *Piers Plowman* entry, and Oxford, Bodleian Library, MS Arch. Selden B.8, whose version I quote here (fol. 268^r):

And davy the dykar shal banne the daye
And peter shal wepe for denyeng of Chryste
And the Abbott of Abbyngton upon the sande
Shall buylde up hys house thatt a kynge threw downe

This item features rhyme and straightforward ballad meter. It could easily have been a song. So too are the looseness of the Winchester item, and its tag "quod Piers Plowman," suggestive of an oral mode rather than the vicissitudes of scribal transmission. It seems probable that these sorts of prophecies were associated with the folk figure of Piers the Plowman quite apart from his status as Langland's hero, perhaps even before that stage. It could well be that Brynstan knew nothing of Langland's poem and that he witnesses to an oral tradition wholly independent of it.

Not only did Piers the Plowman do his work on behalf of non-reformists: he also defended Catholic beliefs, on much the same grounds as he elsewhere lambasted them, that is, in his guise as voice of the true religion against the abuses of modern prelates. In *The Banckett of Johan the Reve unto Peirs ploughman, Laurens laborer, Thomlyn tailyer and Hobb of the hille with other*, in British Library, MS Harley 207, which a later hand in the manuscript dates to 1532 (which "may be too early for credibility," says Anne Hudson), Piers joins others in defending transubstantiation against the spokesmen of the Protestant faith: "Here Piers is entirely orthodox and conventional; perhaps more significantly, he is not the most important spokesman even of that viewpoint, as the main spokesman for the defence of the old religion is John the reve."[12] This is one of many pieces of evidence for Hudson's famous claim that "*Piers Plowman* in the two and a half centuries after its composition was more honoured in the name than in the reading."[13] Yet this remark assumes that all appearances of Piers come from Langland's poem in the first place. What appears to be subordination of the famous Piers to minor figures might be the remnants of an earlier tradition that John Ball and Langland himself invoked, in which "Piers the Plowman" finds company with, rather than leads out of the darkness, Lawrence the Laborer and his ilk.

Later in the century, Piers becomes, alone, a vociferous defender of the old faith, again with no indication that Langland figures at all. *Peers plowghman hys answer to the doctors Interrogatoryes & skrybes of the lawe* is a tract in defense of Catholic martyrs who died at Tyburn in 1582, now Yale, Beinecke Osborn MS a.18. Since the defendants know that silence will not save them, they beseech the interrogators "yet to pardon poore peers for his playnes" (fol. 2ᵛ). The tract goes on to present Catholicism as the older brother to the younger brother Protestantism, who has cut himself off from the ancient traditions of Europe. It is the voice of *I playne Piers*, setting up the simplicity of the old faith against the new-fangledness of the new, put to the opposite side of the debate with little difficulty.

Piers the Plowman in the age of Elizabeth

The reign of Elizabeth constituted the last era in which authors called on Piers the Plowman freely. *Peers plowghman hys answer* is only one instance: a few years earlier, in 1579, readers found a bizarre manifestation of Piers in two publications. In *Newes from the North* he shows up at a Yorkshire inn having spent all his money in London, now without "so much as to buy my seed Wheat, wherwith to sowe my land this season." He seeks a loan of five pounds from the host, offering as surety the books he has brought with him: "they were Billes, Answers, Replications, Rejoinders Copies of Depositions, and such like." The host asks what he would want with such trash: "'Trash, neighbour?' quoth Pierce: 'they stand me in above fiftie pound!'"[14] At least he is still a plowman, but this sounds more like an episode of situation comedy than another entry into the tradition represented by *Pierce the Ploughman's Crede* and its ilk.

His other appearance in 1579, in Edmund Spenser's *Shepheardes Calender*, does not achieve quite that effect, but its invocation of the tradition is no more faithful to the paradigm of the hardworking plowman who shows up the ecclesiastics. Piers appears in the May and October eclogues, which takes lines straight from *The Plowman's Tale* as well. Spenser, unlike some of the earlier poets we have considered, takes a considerable interest in the concept of labor that is at the heart of so much of the Plowman traditions. But that concept turns into a figure for his own labor as a poet, rather than that of the plowman or penitent. Hence Hobbinol's famous remark in the April eclogue:

> Soone as my younglings cryen for the dam,
> To her will I offer a milkwhite Lamb:
> Shee is my goddesse plaine,
> And I her shepherds swayne,
> Albee forswonck and forswatt I am.
> (fol. 13ʳ)[15]

This final line repeats the description of the speaker in *The Plowman's Tale*: "He was forswonke and all forswat" (line 14). But where the Plowman's tiredness and sweat are the products of plowing, Hobbinol's are the products of writing. In the ensuing May eclogue Piers himself shows up, likewise dissociated from his usual referent: "In this firste Æglogue, under the persons of two shepheards Piers & Palinode, be represented two formes of pastoures or Ministers, or the protestant and the Catholique" (fol. 16ʳ).

The Piers of *The Shepheardes Calender* neither plows nor, crucially, represents the lay outsider who calls the church to reform. He is now an insider, a pastor. "Spenser's poetry thus registers an important rupture in the language of labor," as Katherine Little observes: "once rural labor begins to be detached from its medieval, Christian significance (embodied by Piers) and refigured in terms of the pastoral mode, it no longer carries with it the same reformist possibilities that were so central to *Piers Plowman* and its tradition."[16] Piers by now represents unmatched poetic authority rather than social protest, a sense cemented in the closing envoy of the *Calendar*: "Dare not to match thy pype with Tityrus hys style, / Nor with the Pilgrim that the Ploughman playde awhyle" (fol. 52ʳ). Tityrus is definitely Chaucer, which would seem to render the second referent Langland rather than the author of *The Plowman's Tale* (since Chaucer, so the thinking went, wrote that too). And did the pilgrim play the plowman, or vice versa? However we are to decide such matters, there is no question that the Plowman tradition has found its most authoritative, mainstream poetic champion, even as its driving purpose over the previous two centuries was fading from view.

Piers made a few other shadowy and fascinating appearances at the end of the sixteenth century. "Martin Marprelate" included a reprint of *I playne Piers* as part of his series of Puritan mockeries of the Anglican episcopate. And in the 1592 play *A Knack to Know a Knave* Piers shows up to complain to the king that an unknown farmer keeps buying up all the land, leaving him and his family "driven to want" for the first time. The king is sympathetic: his father used to say

> That Piers Plowman was one of the best members in a common
> For his table was never emptie of bread, beefe, and beere,
> As a help to all distressed traveilers.[17]

This Piers is once again a figure of upstanding morals and leadership, of a sort; but unlike his predecessors he speaks only against economic, rather than religious, transgressions, is only a minor figure in the play, and is entirely beholden to other powers rather than being the paragon of righteousness over and above those powers precisely because of his status as an outsider.

The twentieth century

Piers the Plowman had now done the bulk of his work. In the seventeenth and eighteenth centuries, the plowman traditions that had been so vibrant for the previous two centuries gave way to an antiquarian interest, vibrant in its own way, in the questions of the identity of the poet, the question of how many editions Crowley published, the relations among *Piers Plowman*, the *Crede*, and the *Plowman's Tale* (as exemplified by Stephan Batman's discussion above), and so forth. The poem and its central figure became parts of the past rather than living forces. Yet his disappearance from literary history has turned out to enact his disappearance from Holy Church (or "Unity") at the end of the poem as Crowley printed it. For the shadowy version of Piers, in which he is the missing object of desire or pilgrimage rather than spokesman for righteousness, re-emerged in the middle of the twentieth century in fascinating ways.

In 1952 the New Zealand poet James K. Baxter wrote a sestina called "Letter to Piers Plowman." The crisis that prompts the letter, while immediate and urgent, is not the one dramatized in those letters, the *Crede*, *I playne Piers*, or *A Knack to Know a Knave*. The crisis is instead the subjugation of the spirit to the forces of post-war capitalism and conformity. The opening stanza invokes Piers as an almost divine figure:

> We have need of you, Piers, in this blind century
> To plough in the souls of men your naked furrow.
> In America, Ukraine, China, or this cold island
> Many have forgotten the language of the heart
> And in monotonous labour, the prisoners of pay,
> Die daily, broken on the wheel of custom.[18]

The enemy is not a spiritual charlatan, as is the flattering friar in passus 20 of the *Vision* that Crowley printed, but Hob the Robber, whose "most loathed enemy is the living heart." So far as I am aware, this addition to the "*Piers Plowman* tradition" is unique in alluding exclusively to the Piers of Ball's letter and ignoring Langland and *Piers Plowman*: the rebel leader "Woke John Trueman, John Nameless, and you at your furrow." But the spiritual authority accorded Piers in this "Letter" is more that found in the later visions of Langland's poem, and in the traditions we have been surveying, than that in Ball's letters alone.

One final work worth considering in light of these traditions will be known, at least by title, to all readers, but so far as I know never as a contributor to the literature of Piers Plowman. This is Thomas Pynchon's 1965 novel *The Crying of Lot 49*, whose affinities with Langland's poem are remarkable and pervasive, even if accidental. It takes the form of an allegorical quest for meaning by a seeker, Oedipa Maas, which ends without any clear-cut resolution. And this is all due to Oedipa's discovery in the novel's opening sentence that she "had been named executor, or she supposed executrix, of the estate of one Pierce Inverarity" (9).[19] Among the near-puns embedded in Pierce's surname might be "in + veracity," "into Truth," calling forth the circumstances of Piers's introduction to Langland's readers as guide to St. Truth. Images of plowing and furrowing recur throughout the novel, especially in the episode in which Oedipa encounters a sailor in a rooming house: "Cammed each night out of that safe furrow the bulk of this city's waking each sunrise again set virtuously to plowing, what rich soils had he turned, what concentric planets uncovered?" (125–6). Her discovery that this sailor suffers DTs prompts further reflection on the image: "Behind the initials was a metaphor, a delirium tremens, a trembling unfurrowing of the mind's plowshare" (128); a minute later, the metaphor applies to Oedipa herself: "Trembling, unfurrowed, she slipped sidewise, screeching back across grooves of years" (129).

Pynchon's contribution to a Plowman tradition is as distinctive to his moment in history as are those of the Lollard, early Reformation, or Elizabethan moments. Pierce never materializes to pronounce on modern-day scandals, indeed can hardly be unproblematically identified with righteousness. Pynchon is interested in plowing as both a sign of regeneration and an act of violence. Oedipa encounters a former SS officer, named Hilarius, who had fantasized that "At Auschwitz the ovens would be converted over to petit fours and wedding cakes" (138), a forlorn wish for the fulfillment of Isaiah 2:4 ("they shall beat their swords into plowshares"); Pynchon's 1990 novel *Vineland* even has a character named Isaiah 2:4. And his 1997 *Mason & Dixon* dramatizes the effects of a metaphorical furrow – the line dividing North from South – on the psyche of a nation that will be riven by racism and war in large part as the result of that action.

The plural in this chapter's title – "Traditions" – is necessary as a reflection of the multiple uses to which Piers the Plowman has been put over the centuries. The question of how much these traditions tell us about Langland's influence, or even whether they do at all, is interesting. There is little evidence in any of these items of the sort of sustained engagement with his allegory that is the hallmark of modern criticism – hence Hudson's quip about the poem being "more honoured in the name than in the reading." But narrow influence cannot be the only goal, especially if Piers the Plowman had had a robust existence as a folk figure before and apart from Langland's work. In the end, the more pertinent contexts for understanding and periodizing the transmission of this figure are what might be considered major economic and spiritual ruptures at various points throughout western history. The pressing question is not so much whether it is Langland who generates Piers's many appearances, as what local events and mindsets bring about the desire to invoke the figure. Gnomic prophets, tillers of the soil, objects of pilgrimage: such figures belong to something much larger than histories of poetic influence, and they will speak, or labor, or stand just beyond reach whenever the powerful of society turn against their fellow pilgrims to St. Truth.

12

NICOLETTE ZEEMAN

Piers Plowman in theory

The conversation between *Piers Plowman* and the more self-reflexive forms of modern critical practice – "theory" – is a two-way one, because the poem is itself profoundly self-reflexive and self-theorized. In recent years, the poem has been read via formalism, material and cultural history, a range of semiotic, hermeneutic, or deconstructive theories, psychoanalysis, and "body" and gender studies. However, its self-theorization is not merely a result of the fact that such bodies of thought, albeit in very different articulations, overlap with several medieval disciplines;[1] the poem's capacity to speak back to much modern and post-modern thought comes from its sustained exploration of the structures that inform, cut across, or even undermine social life and spiritual experience. In this respect, *Piers Plowman* speaks to twentieth- and twenty-first-century theory, concerned as this has often been with the deceptions and disingenuities of political, intellectual, and psychic life. And, insofar as the poem is exactingly critical of the modes by which we know, it shares the linguistic and hermeneutic orientation of much recent philosophy.

Yet in contrast to the works of Chaucer, there has been rather little overtly theorized reading of *Piers Plowman*. This disparity must be partly connected to the immediate local difficulties of comprehending Langland's text – difficulties that stand out all the more for being mingled with many passages of exhilaratingly immediate and vivid writing. Modern readers still have a patchy knowledge of the poem's conceptual frameworks on account of the fact that *Piers Plowman* engages with a huge range of textual traditions, several of which remain relatively unfamiliar to contemporary scholarship. As a result, much criticism of the poem continues to involve the identification of allusions, the solving of referential puzzles ("crux-busting"), and the pursuit of contexts and analogies for the poem's larger discursive concerns and narrative trajectories.[2] Insofar as modern and post-modern theory focuses on the identification of less immediately apparent types of structure, a process that inevitably problematizes common-sensical or "surface" readings, the lack of a consensus about those sur-face readings may have made the need for such theoretical work seem less pressing. Indeed, even apparently provocative theoretical propositions have often led Langland scholars directly back to the archive: Andrew Cole has recently pointed out that Morton Bloomfield's famous observa-tion that reading the poem is "like reading a commentary on an unknown text" has a rich theoretical and philosophical background, and derives from Friedrich Nietzsche's notions about the working of the intellect; yet the claim has usually been used as a justification for further pursuit of Langland's sources.[3]

However, the much-acknowledged "difficulty" of *Piers Plowman* is not just an accident of historical reception. It is almost certainly connected to the distinctively formal mechanics by which the poem performs much of its self-theorization, the way that it draws attention to its conceptual work through the imaginative structures of its textuality. The poem's difficulty is also connected to its larger critical project: a searching investigation of received epistemologies, whether authoritative, merely banal, or outright complacent; a sustained attack on institutionalized formulations and reifi-cations; an inquiry into the seemingly coherent "imaginary" of social and religious experience. As I have said, much of the time this critique is not expressed in analytical terms, but is embedded within the text's narrative ecphrasis and action; it is also found in its repeated destabilization and problematization of its own formulations, descriptions, narratives and, by implication, their referents, whether in the world, in texts, or in minds. D. Vance Smith describes this formal effect as a "resistance that runs deep in the poem."[4] The same could be said for the way in which *Piers Plowman* ostentatiously refuses to offer itself up to any readerly illusions of hermeneu-tic control. Not only does its constant questioning of its own terms mean that the grounds for interpretation shift from line to line, but its simul-taneous reflection on its own maneuvers means that it "talks back" from positions that are already conceptually self-aware. What is more, because within the poem Langland subjects those who claim to "know things" to intense scrutiny, he throws into question the position from which interpre-tation, and its claims to intellectual control, can be exercised from outside the text. This questioning is, as we shall see, by no means the only aspect of *Piers Plowman*'s self-theorization, but it is a crucial one, to which I shall return at the end of this chapter (see also Chapter 8). Meanwhile, let us look at the enormously varied range of critical theory that has been brought into dialogue with the poem.

Two Langlandians

There are two scholars whose theoretical work has dominated and shaped subsequent readings of *Piers Plowman* perhaps more than any others; it is no coincidence that both of them have made a point of reading Langland as a serious political and theological thinker in his own right. One is Anne Middleton, whose rigorous and incrementally developing readings of the poem bear more than a passing resemblance to the poet's own life-time work. The formalist underpinnings of Middleton's project are apparent in her sustained preoccupation with the impact of "literary" structure and the internal tensions that characterize Langland's text. However, her writings are also marked by an intensifying historical and political concern. This developing interplay between the literary and the historical can be seen in the mutation of her interest from what she describes in an early essay as Langland's pursuit of a simultaneously authoritative and immediate voice, a "middle way" of "experientially based didactic poetry,"[5] into a later preoccupation with the various ways that the historical poet inserts himself into the poem, even as she continues to reflect on the conceptual work performed by such self-insertion. In the essay "Kynde Name," for instance, she studies the social and juridical implications of Langland's mutating "system" of allusive and anagrammatic self-namings. In "Acts of Vagrancy," she claims that he uses the coercive 1388 Statute of Laborers to pose the question of his own poetic and cultural standing, staging "an incipient prosecution" of himself, "on grounds of idleness," as a "worker without papers," arguing that Langland's claim to writerly legitimacy derives not from any sense of the poem as finished "text," but from the poem seen as the documentation of an ongoing historical "life and . . . work."[6]

The cogency of Middleton's readings derives from her sense of the theoretical implications of poetic form. She describes the poet, for example, in terms that sound simultaneously formalist and political, as enacting an "oscillation between ambition and shame," between lay immediacy and clerical authority, between pugnacious self-assertion and poetic anxiety. Citing Edward Said on the poem's "exemplary uncertainty," she claims that Langland draws attention to "the ways in which, in life as in art, making sense of one's world is a matter of publishing a powerful fiction . . . of aligning oneself in relation to the distributive narratives of authority."[7] In her most influential essay to date, "Narration and the Invention of Experience," Middleton draws on the psychoanalytically inflected work of the French Marxist Pierre Macherey in order to identify what she describes as the poet's "involuntary authorial signature," a version of what Machery describes as the "unconscious of the work (not that of the author)."[8] For Middleton this signature is marked by Langland's repeated use of a narrative "episode," in which, despite its many forms, two protagonists, one "a figure who embodies inchoate desire and an indeterminate quality of 'natural knowledge,'" and the other "a representative of a traditionally authoritative institution," engage in a verbal combat that ends in "discord and irresolution."[9] In these episodes Middleton sees Langland playing out an agonistic (and therefore both dialectical and inconclusive) sense of what a political intervention might be. What can be seen particularly clearly here, however, is Middleton's sense of how narrative structure – and in particular repeated narrative structure – is for Langland a primary tool for theoretical self-reflection. Repetition is not just a sign of what Middleton elsewhere calls the "recursiveness" that is "the condition of the subject in temporal life" (though it may also be this); it is repetition that draws the reader's attention to the episode and the social and epistemological relations that it reveals. Elsewhere, Middleton makes a similar claim for the "chiastic" interplay of the two C-text autobiographical conversations with Reason and Need.[10] Whatever the degree of involuntariness or intentionality at work here (later Middleton seems to shift her ground, commenting on Langland's propensity to elevate "a seemingly fortuitous or peripheral preoccupation into a conscious principle of form"), what she identifies here are the specifically figural and narrative forms of Langland's self-theorization.[11]

The other scholar who has had the most impact on the study of *Piers Plowman* is David Aers, whose work is characterized by a constantly innovative and pugnacious use of political and theological theory. His first book, *Piers Plowman and Christian Allegory*, was formulated in opposition to what Lee Patterson called the "exegetical" school of medieval criticism. Its initiator, D. W. Robertson, Jr., claimed that, given the hegemony of the Church in the Middle Ages, literary texts could only be read using the techniques that Robertson extracted from the biblical commentaries of Augustine and other Church Fathers.[12] The claim – as Robertson and a few other scholars of the period applied it – not only homogenized the complex history of medieval scriptural exegesis, but also assumed that later medieval poets must be speaking with the same, single voice. Aers's critical debut showed that the allegorical narratives of *Piers Plowman* were not only politicized, but also structurally dynamic and mutatory – they simply did not conform to Robertson's schematic version of four-level biblical exegesis.

In the following decades, Aers produced an evolving sequence of essays on poverty, labor, Franciscanism, and the church in *Piers Plowman*.[13] Aers's sense of the poem is from the start "dialogic" (Bakhtinian) and dialectical (both Marxist and Hegelian).[14] In his early essays, he describes the poem as enacting an unresolved series of debates between "traditional ideologies" and what he describes as Langland's "imaginative" recognition of the forces of emergent capitalism and secular self-interestedness, forces that radically compromise the church's traditional spiritual solutions. Aers repeatedly insists on how theological "ideal abstractions" are "moulded by the material interests of particular groups and individuals in the culture." In these essays, Aers is also already alert to what he sees as the excessively easy solution to this problem offered by theories of voluntary poverty (which he associates with the Franciscans).[15] By 2002, in *Sanctifying Signs*, his reading of *Piers Plowman* has become not only dialectically resolved, but also explicitly Christian, reflecting a sustained engagement with the writings of Augustine, Thomas Aquinas, and Karl Barth. Aers now no longer describes the poem as oscillating between opposed positions, each of which has a different kind of valence, but as moving confidently toward the acknowledgment and "supersession" of earlier positions: "the dialectical process in which the [Franciscan] sign of poverty is constituted and . . . superseded – superseded but never forgotten, a constitutive part of the process which generates it." Aers insists that Langland repudiates the "Pelagian" idea that perfection can be achieved on earth through spiritual poverty, claiming instead that the poem's provisional synthesis is to be found in the recognition of devastating human fallenness and the redemptive work of the Good Samaritan/Christ.[16]

In Chapter 2 of *Sanctifying Signs*, on the sacrament of the mass, Aers's long-emerging reformist and proto-Protestant reading of Langland's view of the church as a material and social community comes to the fore. Although Langland does not often explicitly refer to the Eucharist, Aers argues that the poet everywhere implies it and anticipates its presence, along with the embodied, communal participation that it connotes, in "a complex dialectic of absence and presence"; the poem reveals that "individual spiritual life will flourish only in a community that fosters it, that salvation entails corporation into the body of Christ, the community that is the Church."[17] Aers's most recent work is explicitly theological (he has for a number of years held a joint professorial appointment in English and Divinity); but his work remains no less materially historical and politicized in its theorization of the poem and its ecclesiology.[18]

Theory, history, and politics

The historical and political focus in the work of Middleton and Aers sets the terms for much interpretation of *Piers Plowman*. Although some of this historical and political interpretation is minimally self-reflexive, much of it is highly alert to the ways that non-literary discourses and material events structure the Langlandian poetic imaginary.[19] Other writers have analyzed Langland's reflections on the ideological rifts of his culture. Britton J. Harwood, for example, has argued that the Plowing of the Half-Acre reveals a tension within feudalism between the primacy attributed to the sovereign and the dispersal of power among his subjects; he claims that Piers sides with landlords in resisting mobile laborers under the guise of the *wastours*, but is himself a peasant employer and, like those very same laborers, opposes the labor statutes enacted by the landed class.[20] Cole, likewise, has described the Plowing of the Half-Acre and the Tree of Charity scene in terms of the tension between feudal and proto-capitalist models of agriculture.[21] In his book on the Rising of 1381, Steven Justice claims that *Piers Plowman* represents that unusual phenomenon, a literary text that actually had an impact on contemporary historical event (see Chapters 3 and 11).[22] One of the most distinctive and widely read political readers of the poem, however, is James Simpson.

Simpson's early publications on *Piers Plowman* are studies of discursive form in the poem, which draw on later twentieth-century research into scholastic theories of biblical textual form. In *Piers Plowman: An Introduction*, however, he starts from a position similar to that of David Aers, that the poem, while "deeply anchored in a conservative literary, ecclesiastical and social culture," moves "towards positions of doubt and dissent" and an "active re-imagination of social and religious institutions." His original move is to argue that the poem's multi-genericism can be read politically, due to the fact that Langland associates particular modes of textuality with social institutions – "ecclesiastical and political attachments are written into [the poem's] formal choices." At the same time as the poet explores and critiques institutions, then, he invokes and dissects the textual forms that relate to them: as he investigates the institutions of pastoral care, he also investigates the languages of "sermon, confession, pilgrimage and pardon"; as he analyzes the institutions of education, he also analyzes the languages of satire and scholastic debate. Over the poem, Simpson claims, cognitive and intellectual languages are gradually replaced by the affective, riddling, and "poetical" language of spiritual desire. Langland's sense of the ideological implications of literary form is shown to be restless and vivacious.[23] In subsequent essays, Simpson locates a more utopian communal vision in the poem; claiming that "Langland insistently reimagines . . . the place of labour in the economy of salvation," for instance, Simpson argues that the good working society described in B.19 is based on the egalitarian and collaborative model of a religious fraternity.[24] A study of "will" in the poem "traces the movement whereby a distempered authorial will is absorbed into a larger order," gradually becoming identified with the will of the community, the "common will." This transformation is exemplified for Simpson by Conscience, who, when he penitentially leaves the Feast of Patience, simultaneously invokes "þe wil of þe wye and þe wil of folk here" (B.13.191); by B.19, "a whole society is imagined acting, within a renewed church, with one will, at which point "Will/will" becomes invisible, as it must."[25]

Other historically oriented studies have concerned themselves with the poem's subject and narrator, and the possibility that he is in some sense an authorial self-representation. In a similar vein to Middleton, Ralph Hanna claims that the narrator's description of himself as "an heremite, unholy of werkes" associates him with medieval anxiety about the regulation of hermits and the "ambivalence" of hermit status. Hanna proposes that the B-text narrator's defense of his "meddling with makings" is formulated as an "interstitial" version of the traditionally "mixed" life of the hermit, who protects himself from empty or fantastical thought by alternating devotional prayer with manual labor – though the fact that hermit life allows no place for poetic activity such as that of Langland means that his particular "labor" can only ever be dubiously "vicissitudinal" and "episodic."[26] Kathryn Kerby-Fulton draws on early modern studies of how the material circumstances of patronage, coterie groups, censorship, and reader-reception shape authorial self-presentation; acknowledging that the poem's "I" has both generic and historically specific features, she reads even its apparently generic features as bearing on the historical Langland. Observing the development of "the minstrel/scribe of A" into "the poet who meddles with makings in B" and "the defensively confessional but obliquely authoritative spokesman in C," she insists that we are throughout seeing imaginative versions of the historical Langland's relationship with his readers.[27]

Theory, language, and being

In 1987 David Lawton addressed "The Subject of *Piers Plowman*," not by engaging in speculations about the historical Langland, but by invoking a much more eclectic mix of twentieth-century theory to speak instead of the "subject" or "subjectivity" of the poem. His influential essay opens by repudiating the New Critical pursuit of "unity and integrity" (we might recall that early on Middleton described the poem's "I" as "a center of 'sense-making' for the poem").[28] Lawton then uses an array of linguistic, psychoanalytic, sociological, and Marxist theory in order to locate the poem's "I" at the point where the poem's multiple discourses and "systems" intersect, insisting we must abandon altogether any "presumption of continuity" in this subject, who is merely the "sum of the poem's concerns." For Lawton, *Piers Plowman* has a Bakhtinian dialogism, even heteroglossia, that allows the poet to "try on" many different subjectivities – and, finally, to "refuse" them all.[29] However, he also identifies a number of positions from which the poem's subject is able to critique the "monologia" of institutional discourse (exemplified for Lawton by the language of the penitential); indeed, as the essay proceeds, Lawton attributes "straightforwardly authorial...monologic moment[s]" to the "I" voice, responds to "the force and justice" of things said by Langland's subject, and sees "Langland" as "implicated, however equivocally" in the rejection of penitential discourse. Lawton too, then, attributes more poetic and political status to some discourses in the poem than others.[30]

Lawton's interest in discourse theory connects his essay to other readers who have invoked hermeneutic, semiotic, and post-structuralist concerns, and language-oriented philosophers, such as Heidegger, de Man, Derrida, and Wittgenstein, in relation to *Piers Plowman*. A brilliant and influential early intervention in this area is Mary Carruthers's *The Search for St. Truth*, which uses medieval hermeneutic and rhetorical theory to investigate the poem's concern with the "analysis of words as ambiguous tools of thought, capable not only of revealing a true cognition, but also of generating a corruption of understanding."[31] More recently, William Elford Rogers has used the semiotics of Charles Sanders Peirce to claim that *Piers Plowman* "is about" interpretation itself. Whereas Carruthers claims that Langland resolves some of his epistemological challenges in the language of typology, Rogers insists that for Langland "the rules for connecting signs never get fixed." According to Rogers, the poet's characteristic gesture is like that of Fibonacci's sequence (formed by adding the two previous numbers) to treat his own earlier formulations "as texts to be [re]interpreted."[32] Larry Scanlon, in contrast, draws on Paul de Man's theories of rhetoric and allegory in a recent study of personification, understood as a trope that foregrounds the tension between the allegorical and the mimetic that characterizes all allegorical narrative: with de Man, Scanlon argues that no text escapes the "register of the allegorical," and insists that even the most "utilitarian" allegory is still ultimately unstable and "dispersive."[33]

D. Vance Smith's *The Book of the Incipit* ingeniously focuses this problem on Langland's "beginnings" (a focus that is in many respects the logical consequence of Middleton's work on the narrative "episode"). Smith works with Heidegger, Husserl, Deleuze, Freud, Lacan, Foucault, and Said, but his overridingly Derridean claim is that for Langland the myth of origin and the moment of inception are fundamentally problematic. In a(n unnumbered) sequence of studies, he analyzes the way that Langland's beginnings are determined by a range of cultural, textual, and linguistic prehistories – "the necessary past that precedes every beginning" – as well as by their imagined teleologies and final causes. Not only can texts and subjects merely register the traces of their own origins, but the narrative representations of such originary moments are also compromised by new starts, subsequent contingencies, and the difficulty of sustaining textual – never mind ontological – "continuation." Smith meshes twentieth-century theory with medieval logical, grammatical, theological, and ethical theory and fourteenth-century history. *The Book of the Incipit* oscillates between claiming that the beginning is a special preoccupation of *Piers Plowman* – "the unusual medieval poem that begins again – not once but many times" – and recognizing in it "the originary structure of repetition." Although Smith proposes that *Piers Plowman* mirrors a preoccupation with beginnings that is characteristic of Langland's politically insecure historical moment, there is also an ahistorical aspect to the project: the poem becomes one avatar in the long history of philosophy's engagements with the problem of inception.[34]

An ambitious recent essay, "Negative Langland," develops this line of thought. Here Smith reads *Piers Plowman* through Hegelian and Heideggerian theories of negation and "the negation of negation." Unlike the self-cancelling double negatives of modern English grammar, the multiple negatives of post-Hegelian thought do not cancel each other, but preserve the cumulative and dynamic work of negation; "negation has a kind of presence." Whereas Aers, in a Hegelian mode, reads *Piers Plowman* as dialectical and ultimately synthesizing, Smith argues that the poem's protagonists and words are always multiply compromised or denied – the poem's dialectic is always the negation of a negation. For Smith, each definition of *dowel* or *will* negates the previous one; he observes the negation implicit in the passive virtue that underlies the authority figure Patience, and proposes that the poem ends up problematizing action itself. Exploring how the poem negates itself into ever more infinitely tangentialized positions, he insists finally that Langland's "complicated critique of the phenomenal world and the language we use in and for it" must owe something to the work of "negative theology."[35]

Starting from a very different philosophical tradition, Sarah Tolmie nevertheless ends up making some not dissimilar claims about *Piers Plowman*. She claims that Langland shares Wittgenstein's belief, articulated in the *Tractatus logico-philosophicus*, that language and the world have "homologous" logical form; this means that the tropes of Langland's allegory (words, personifications, etc.) provide meaningful ways of "picturing" or "showing" the infinite logical relations of elements in the world. However, this is only half the story: Langland's equally Wittgensteinian sense of the many perspectives from which these relations can be regarded also means that there are infinite ways of constituting them; "we are . . . reading a different poem each time," along with all the accompanying "differences of genre and teleology" that this implies.[36] In a subsequent essay, Tolmie develops this claim via the later Wittgenstein's theories about the "language game," his recognition that language can only function within particular rule-bound practices and family resemblances.[37] Tolmie also claims that for Langland, as for Wittgenstein, the "I" cannot be known except insofar as it is encoded as a third person or "object." Echoing (from a very different theoretical standpoint) Simpson's "Power of Impropriety," she suggests that the attachment of the will to the world means that finally "Will is... the wrong tool... to lever the self out of the world"; this, she says, is why Will is finally displaced by Conscience, a figure who "grants the necessity of his own interpenetration with the world." In this poem, Tolmie insists, "any project of personal reform" involves "a cascading series of shifts in the entire surrounding world."[38]

The psychoanalytic turn

A politicized version of Lacanian psychoanalysis shapes Aranye Fradenburg's "Needful Things." In this important (and under-cited) essay, Fradenburg focuses on the legal and ethical notion of "need": if the poor are supposedly entitled to their basic requirements, then the rich are supposed to give from what they have in excess. However, a Lacanian perspective means that this distinction is fundamentally unstable, because desire is metamorphic and voracious, and the "law structures and is structured by desire." Fradenburg, however, is less interested in the insatiable desires of the poor than in the pleasures of submitting to the law of charity for those who do actually possess goods; the threat of the poor thus takes the form of the duplicitous poor – the "sturdy beggar" who undermines the pleasures of charitable giving. Fradenburg has remarkably little to say about *Piers Plowman* itself; however, her meditations on the resentment of the "other" (and this includes the other within us) who undermines the complacencies of charity have much to tell us about why the poem "worr[ies] endlessly... over what should be given and how and under what circumstances." For Fradenburg "the problem of 'need' names something central to the economy of the subject's relation to the other" – and, therefore, to itself; commenting on the personification of Need in the poem's last passus, she intimates that it is no surprise that such anxieties might attain "apocalyptic proportions."[39]

In my own book, *Piers Plowman and the Medieval Discourse of Desire*, I have framed the poem's psychological and spiritual concerns in psychoanalytic terms, though I too am interested in the theoretical work performed by textual form. My starting point is Middleton's episode, but, unlike her, I read it as a repeated narrative in which a protagonist – not always intentionally – makes some kind of spiritual mistake; the mistake is followed by a rebuke and some form of deprivation, but, out of such cyclical crises, the poem generates new desire and the energy to propel itself forward. The episode represents the process by which Christian history and ideology recuperate human failure for sublimatory ends. Freudian and Lacanian psychoanalysis reveals the logic of this process, whereby guilt and its repression provide foundations for the sacred as well as mechanisms by which it can be accessed. Psychoanalytic paradigms thus allow us to read these Langlandian episodes as closed-circuit economies, leading inexorably to the divine; however, because psychoanalysis also models desire as metamorphically mobile and insatiable, it also allows us to read them as riskily open-ended.[40]

Middleton first showed how a particular repeated structure in *Piers Plowman* might function as a form of self-theorization. In the book just described, I also propose that Langland uses other narrative structures (and the contrasts between them) to reflect on the underlying structures of phenomenological experience. Langland distinguishes knowledge and desire, for instance, by using the contrasting tropes of personification (the personified word) and the seemingly holistic "person." He represents different kinds of spiritual understanding by using contrasting figures of hearing and seeing, teaching and vision, trust and experience, even having and "not having" (this last being a variant of more familiar Langlandian oppositions: acting and receiving, working and giving up work, *mercede* and *mede*, *dowel* and grace, justice and mercy). Once again, we find Langland's self-theorizations articulated through narrative and imaginative structure.[41]

Gender and the body

All of the theoretical approaches to *Piers Plowman* considered so far have served to point up the poet's own theoretical self-reflexivity. Because Langland tends to express this self-reflexivity by formal means, I have been arguing that it can only be recognized accumulatively, as Langland's characteristic moves return to draw attention to themselves. This is the case for his reiterative narrative episodes, dialectical structures, and beginnings, as it is for his sustained critique of terms and figures, and his constant problematization of voice and perspective. However, in the last area of modern theory I shall look at, gender and the body, fewer such recurring strategies are visible, suggesting less theoretical self-reflexivity, and therefore perhaps less self-awareness, on the poet's part.

Aers and Clare Lees wrote early Marxist-inflected place markers in this area, insisting that Lady Meed is not a transparent or transcendent allegorical "figure," but a gendered body that both shapes and limits Langland's discussion of the use of money. According to Aers, Langland's misogynistic description of Lady Meed as a prostitute describes the world of reward and commerce in terms of carnality; but this focus also enables Langland to avoid examining the detailed mechanics and local agencies of that world. According to Lees, the poet uses Lady Meed to portray the transactional world through "the institutions of the patrilinear family and patriarchal marriage," which allows him to concentrate on the commodification of women but, problematically, enables him to "obscure" women's participation in the modes of production.[42] In an issue of *YLS* with a special section devoted to gender studies, Stephanie Trigg follows up this point with an essay emphasizing exactly this kind of participation, exemplified in the life of Alice Perrers. Elsewhere, Elizabeth Fowler and Kathleen E. Kennedy too have recognized that, by making Meed a woman, Langland centralizes the issue of agency – whether in marriage law or in the politics of maintenance.[43]

Broadening the focus on gender, readers have noted *Piers Plowman*'s small number of female personifications, in comparison with other medieval allegories; such studies repeatedly return to questions about the gender and body of the narrator/poet figure. Helen Cooper starts from a traditional view that the female personification of abstract nouns reflects the feminine grammatical gender of these nouns in many European languages; she suggests that Langland was liberated by the disappearance of grammatical gender in Middle English, with the result that his personifications tend to be masculine because they are "parts," metonymies, of the narrator. She also notes Langland's fluidly masculinist attitudes – his tendency both to present as male figures who are traditionally female, and to mix genders even within a single personification.[44] Elizabeth Robertson and Masha Raskolnikov contrast the feminine personification of Anima in B.9 with the ambiguous personification of Anima in B.15, referred to as *hym* and *he*, but also strangely described as "oon wiþouten tonge and teeþ" (B.15.13–15). For Robertson, this development, affirmed in the multiple names of the B.15 Anima (in the C text renamed as Liberum Arbitrium), reveals that the soul is not some kind of a feminine object, but an "embodied agent" encompassing both sexes.[45] For Raskolnikov, such embodiment is part of the process whereby Langland, who begins conventionally enough with the feminine personifications Holy Church and Meed, gradually "disinvites" the feminine over the poem. Drawing on the work of James Paxson (discussed below), she finds this process to generate queer possibilities: for example, Anima's "challengingly open" body can be read as a "phantasmagoric vagina" but also as an anus; reminding us that the same personification is in the C text described as "a wille with a resoun" (C.16.175), she argues that Anima is one of the many masculine counterparts with whom "Will" seeks "homosocial, non-sodomitical" communion.[46]

A few years earlier, Paxson himself had turned the queering gesture directly on "Will" in two bold psychoanalytic essays on the tropology of personification. According to Paxson, just as rhetoric, imagined as a trans-forming or deforming body, is gendered feminine, so personification, "the figure of the figure," is also feminized. Pointing out "the link between the un-straightness of the queer and the un-straightness of *tropos*, 'a turning,'" he argues that "troping amounts to a kind of sodomy."[47] For Paxson, these themes are focused on the sexuality of "Will," as discovered in the passage where the narrator's wife and the personification Elde "beat" the narrator's penis until it is dysfunctional (B.20.195–8); here the "syntactical consolidat-ing of Elde, Will and Kit makes them into a trio of sodomists," and Paxson closes the second essay by finding a new, sexualized authorial "signature" in the appellation "Will." Paxson's rhetorico-psychoanalytic proposition is that "the semiotic conflation of imagined bodily copulation . . . with the textual generation of rhetorical effects . . . draws its vitality from the deep structure of tropes . . . at erotic and unconscious levels."[48]

The sense that there is something sexually unstable and self-flaunting about Langland's self-representation, but now shamefully so, is found in two essays apparently developed in dialogue with each other in the 1990s. In "School and Scorn: Gender in *Piers Plowman*," Ralph Hanna argues that *Piers Plowman* is shaped not only by an exclusionary masculine ethos, but also by an aggressive dynamic between the abject masculine subject and the female personifications who dominate him. Focusing on the C-text "autobiography," where Conscience asks Will if he is "broke . . . in body or in membre / Or ymaymed thorw som myshap," Hanna reads Will's answer, that he labors with the *lomes* of his paternoster, primer and psalter, as an admission that Will has exchanged a sexual "limb" for a clerical tool (C.5.33–4, 45–7). According to Hanna, Langland locates the castratory discipline of learning in the "scorn" of Study, and the poem's other "maladroit" or "contemptuous" female interlocutors; behind them is the historically documented commonplace of the school master's whip (to which Hanna attributes sexual overtones as a result of Latin *virga* mean-ing both "rod" and "penis"). Hanna implies that it is Langland's (typical medieval) schoolroom experience of violence at the hands of other men that lies behind his peculiarly insecure clerical masculinity, expressed in terms of misogyny.[49]

Middleton cites Hanna in support of a different and arresting case: that Chaucer's Pardoner is a response to the spectacle of the author presented by Langland's obsessive and unfinishable poetic project. Middleton first of all documents the pervasively masculine ethos of the poem. In an argument mediated by influential studies of the Pardoner, with his death's-head rhetoric and homosexuality, Middleton argues that the real erotic pleasures of the "lean" and insatiable but self-obsessed subject of *Piers Plowman* are disciplinary, penitential, intellectual, clerical, and poetical; periodic allusion to his sexual inadequacy signals not only his abjection, but also the redirection of sexual desire into an endless intellectual and poetic enterprise. The evolving trajectory of Middleton's long engagement with this subject, whose simultaneous shame and egotism she now describes as "self-loathing and a grotesque preening," can be seen in her claim that "Langland exposes, and Chaucer represents in the Pardoner, the corrosive and self-deceptive motive of self-glorification that dwells even at the heart of confession, self-humiliation, and penitential discipline." "Fiction-making" is discovered, she says, to be "a kind of verbal masturbation."[50] Here, of course, it is Chaucer, not Langland, who is commenting on a now "unacknowledged" text; and, while Langland has perhaps involuntarily "exposed" something about himself, it is Chaucer who has theorized it.

Theory's feast

These theoretically inflected readings have transformed our understanding of *Piers Plowman*. It is notable that many of them are sensitized not just to the overt articulations of Langland's theory, but also to the complex formal maneuvers by which he articulates it. Middleton comments that the episode is in the narrative "surface" of the text, available in what Raskolnikov describes as "literalizing" readings;[51] but insofar as readers might be tempted to pass it over in favor of content-oriented, local readings, it could also be described in terms closer to those used by Smith, as a "deep structure," accessible only when the reader pauses to notice its repeating structure and hidden iterative principle. Our difficulty in determining what is systematic about *Piers Plowman* arises not merely from the fact that Langland's is an imaginative and figural text (insofar as it is allegorical, after all, it contains many kinds of discourse); rather, it is because Langland is rarely explicit about his theoretical reflections:[52] they tend to remain immanent in the poem's textual "matter." On the one hand, their presence is signaled by effects of repetition, pattern, contrast, opposition, and negation; on the other hand, much of their unsettling power and analytical force derives from the uncertain business of sighting them in the words and things of the text. It is this embedded quality, after all, that simulates the difficult, and political, business of identifying such determining structures in the phenomenological world at large.

This effect is reinforced by the multiple forms of Langland's self-theorization. Depending on what the reader is looking for, different structures come into, and go out of, focus. Nor is this just facile eclecticism on Langland's part, for, in this respect too, the poem mimics the complexity of reading the world and the mind, and the way that one reading, one shaping of the text, inevitably superimposes on, overlays or masks, the traces of another. It is not surprising that some of Langland's most crucial structures have been found to be dialectical ones, seen most obviously in the poem's dialogues and debates, but also in its myriad local "negations," as well as in the large oppositional and critical moves by which the poem progresses (whether understood as synthesized or not). Nor is it surprising that these dialectics and deferrals often have such a combative and political animus: the poem's oppositions are grounded in social identities, whether institutionally "authorized" or lay and marginal, whether determined by "traditional ideologies" or speaking in terms determined by the material and embodied world, whether clerical and Latin, or lay and vernacular. The poem does not lose sight of the risks of material and cultural ossification: "authority, Langland would have his readers learn, is always in the making, always subject to processes it cannot grasp, but always tempted to reify itself, always tempted to posit a false transcendence for itself."[53]

We might recall, in conclusion, the Feast of Patience. Here a dazzling array of recognizable tropes appears, the familiar signals of Langland's self-theorization; the scene is open to several very different and nevertheless "Langlandian" readings. We are in an academic refectory dinner, and the indulgent *maister* sits at the high table, while Patience and the poem's "I" sit at a side table, "where students would have sat."[54] At the most obvious level, the abuse of material and social good is exemplified by the *maister*, who stuffs his face at the top table; the poet/narrator's outrage at having been given immaterial, biblical, and spiritual "food" is an utterly comprehensible pragmatic and institutionally politicized response. But Langland's obsession with the unstable relation between understanding and embodied life is yet again discovered in the tension between the gross conduct of the *maister* and his orthodox doctrine, or between the plausibility of the poet/narrator's outrage and his subsequent indifference to spiritual "food." And how does the politics of bodies and institutions relate to that of the spirit? Is this episode an instance of the shamed and rebellious animus that drives the poem (Middleton), or is it a comic instance of the strangely inevitable failures that are repeatedly charted across the poem (Zeeman)? Are the riddles that are part of Patience's "solution" to this scene evasions of real social and material problems (Aers), or are they an affective and spiritual escalation of the poem's value system (Simpson)? Is this scene, with its complexly deferred and enigmatic answers, an example of the epistemological uncertainty that grounds the poem (Smith, Tolmie), or is it just one stage to be superseded within a larger poetic and theological synthesis (Aers)? Or does it simply reveal its author to be the guilty and obsessive participant of a masculine and clerical coterie, unable or unwilling to arrive at praxis, settle differences, finish texts (Paxson, Middleton)?

Langland is only too aware of the risks of self-indulgence or solipsism inherent in the abstractive, analytical, and academic enterprise. We can see this in his portrait of his own academic, the *maister*, but also in the personification Clergy, a source of much excellent teaching and advice, who nevertheless suddenly at the Feast of Patience shrivels into a fetishizer of the ultimately trivial activity of crux-busting: "I shal brynge yow a Bible . . . And lere yow, if yow like, þe leeste point to knowe" (B.13.186–7). Throughout the poem, Langland reveals his obsession with the tendency of those in intellectual or "theorized" life to lose sight of the projects in whose service they operate, to get enmeshed in learning's local mechanics and pleasures; and he is equally suspicious of any claims that they might make about being above such things. Not only is his poem therefore often one step ahead of the would-be theorist, it also places the modern academic reader, like the medieval one, under the spotlight – explaining why Langland often theorizes neither in the language of the schools, nor even in a language recognizable as analytic or preceptive. The most trenchant theoretical reflections are, he intimates, experienced and reflected on from within the narrative work and embodied action of the poetic text.

NOTES

INTRODUCTION

1 *Alford, *Companion to Piers Plowman.*
2 Pages cited from these three volumes are presented henceforth in the text.
3 M. Bloomfield, *Piers Plowman as a Fourteenth-Century Apocalypse,* New Brunswick, Rutgers University Press, [1962].
4 *Hanna, *William Langland,* 2–3, 26–7.
5 M. Bennett, "William called Long Will," *YLS,* 26 (2012), 1–25.
6 *Hanna, *William Langland,* 8–10.
7 *Warner, *Lost History.*
8 *Vaughan, *The A Version.*
9 *Barney, "Langland's Prosody"; *Duggan, "Notes on the Metre of *Piers Plowman*"; see also Schmidt 2:248–60.
10 *Horobin, "'In London and opelond'" and *Hanna, *London,* 26–32, both arguing against M. L. Samuels's influential chapter in *Alford's *Companion.*

2 THE VERSIONS AND REVISIONS OF *PIERS PLOWMAN*

In addition to suggestions from the editors, I am grateful for many helpful interventions into a draft version from Anne Middleton, Thorlac Turville-Petre, and Sarah Wood.

1 *Brewer, *Editing Piers Plowman.*
2 *Doyle and Parkes, "Production of Copies of the *Canterbury Tales* and the *Confessio Amantis.*"
3 From *Manly, "*Piers Plowman* and its Sequence," to *Donaldson, *The C-Text and its Poet*; and see *Kane, *The Evidence for Authorship.*
4 But cf. *Mann, "Power of the Alphabet," and *Lawler's response, "A Reply to Jill Mann."
5 For discussion of one unresolved enigma, however, see *Adams, "The R/F MSS of *Piers Plowman.*"
6 See K-D, 35–7, 40–2; and *Davis, "Rationale for a Copy of a Text."
7 *Horobin, "Harley 3954 and the Audience of *Piers Plowman.*"
8 *Weldon, "*Ordinatio*"; for A materials, see *Adams, "Editing *Piers Plowman* B"; for importation of C at a point where F's source lacked eight leaves, see *Warner, "The Ending and End of *Piers Plowman* B."

9 *Turville-Petre, "Putting It Right."
10 See *Vaughan, *The A Version.*
11 *Wood, *Conscience and the Composition of Piers Plowman.*

3 LITERARY HISTORY AND *PIERS PLOWMAN*

1 S. Justice, *Writing and Rebellion: England in 1381*, Berkeley, University of California Press, 1994, ch. 2.
2 *The Vision of Pierce Plowman* (1550), ii^r.
3 M. Wilks, "Wyclif and the Great Persecution," *Studies in Church History*, subsidia 10 (1994), 29–63.
4 G. Shuffleton, "*Piers Plowman* and the Case of the Missing Book," YLS, 18 (2004), 55–72.
5 Citations are from the Athlone editions.
6 A. Galloway, *The Penn Commentary on Piers Plowman Volume 1: C Prologue-Passus 4; B Prologue-Passus 4; A Prologue-Passus 4*, Philadelphia, University of Pennsylvania Press, 2006, 290.
7 *Middleton, "Narration and the Invention of Experience"; *Smith, *Book of the Incipit.*
8 Such as the scribes of Huntington Library, MS HM 114 (R. Hanna, "The Scribe of Huntington HM 114," *Studies in Bibliography*, 42 [1989], 120–33) and of British Library, MS Harley 3954 (S. Horobin, "Harley 3954 and the Audience of *Piers Plowman*," in *Medieval Texts in Context*, ed. D. Renevey and G. Caie, New York, Routledge, 2008, 68–84).
9 M. Karnes, *Imagination, Meditation, and Cognition in the Middle Ages*, University of Chicago Press, 2011.
10 S. Lerer, "The Endurance of Formalism in Middle English Studies," *Literature Compass*, 1 (2004), 13 n. 35.
11 J. J. Jusserand, *English Wayfaring Life in the Middle Ages (XIVth Century)*, trans. L. Toulmin Smith, London, T. F. Unwin, 1890.
12 Cited from J. Dean (ed.), *Six Ecclesiastical Satires*, Kalamazoo, Western Michigan University Press, 1995.
13 B. Holsinger, "Lollard Ekphrasis: Situated Aesthetics and Literary History," *Journal of Medieval and Early Modern Studies*, 35, no. 1 (2005), 67–90.
14 *Kelen, *Langland's Early Modern Identities*, 48.
15 *Other: British and Irish Poetry since 1970*, ed. R. Caddel and P. Quartermain, Hanover and London, Wesleyan University Press, 1999.
16 *I Playne Piers Which Can Not Flatter a Plowe Man Men Me Call My Speche Is Fowlle, Yet Marke the Matter Howe Thynges May Hap to Fall* (n.d.), A.2^r.
17 D. Lawton, "Lollardy and the *Piers Plowman* Tradition," *Modern Language Review*, 76 (1981), 780–93.
18 D. Norbrook, *Poetry and Politics in the English Renaissance*, Oxford University Press, 2002, 53.
19 Gerard Manley Hopkins, *The Journals and Papers*, ed. H. House and G. Storey, Oxford University Press, 1959, 277, 284.
20 W. H. Auden, "Criticism in a Mass Society," in *The Intent of the Critic*, ed. D. Stauffer *et al.*, Princeton University Press, 1941, 132.

21 L. McDiarmid, "W. H. Auden's 'In the Year of My Youth...'," *Review of English Studies*, ns 29 (1978), 267–312.

22 W. H. Auden, *Collected Longer Poems*, London, Faber and Faber, 1968, 270.

23 Quotations from these poems are from H. Barr (ed.), *The Piers Plowman Tradition*, London, J. M. Dent, 1993.

24 S. Justice, "Chaucer's History-Effect," in *Answerable Style: The Idea of the Literary in Medieval England*, ed. F. Grady and A. Galloway, Columbus, Ohio State University Press, 2013, 169–94.

25 F. Grady, "Chaucer Reading Langland: The House of Fame," *SAC*, 18 (1996), 3–23; R. Hanna, *London Literature, 1300–1380*, Cambridge University Press, 2005, 242–57, and n.

26 A. Middleton, "Commentary on an Unacknowledged Text: Chaucer's Debt to Langland," *YLS*, 24 (2010), 113–37.

4 ALLEGORY AND *PIERS PLOWMAN*

1 *Paxson, *Poetics of Personification*, 77–8, sees this mixing as true of medieval allegory in general, but it does not usually come up to the level attained in *Piers Plowman*.

2 References to and quotations of *Piers Plowman* use Schmidt B.

3 Cicero, *Orator* 27.94, and *De oratore* 3.41.166; Isidore, *Etymologiae* 1.37.22, 26. See J. Whitman, *Allegory: The Dynamics of an Ancient and Medieval Technique*, Cambridge, MA, Harvard University Press, 1987, Appendix 1 (pp. 263–8), for a concise history of the term "allegory."

4 W. Empson, *The Structure of Complex Words*, 3rd edn., Totowa, NJ, Rowman and Littlefield, 1979, 346.

5 *Ibid.*, 345.

6 See *Mann, *Langland and Allegory*, 27–9.

7 *Auerbach, "Figura."

8 *Charity, *Events and their Afterlife*, 58.

9 *Auerbach, "Figura," 58.

10 *Ibid.*, 59.

11 *Ibid.*, 72.

12 *Prudentius*, ed. and trans. H. J. Thomson, Cambridge, MA, Harvard University Press, 1962, 1:274–343.

13 *Jauss, "Form und Auffassung der Allegorie in der Tradition der *Psychomachia*," 188–9.

14 *The Divine Comedy*, ed. and trans. C. S. Singleton, 6 vols., Princeton University Press, 1970–5; corr. edn. 1977.

15 *Auerbach, "Figura," 67–8; *Singleton, *Journey to Beatrice*, 257.

16 *Ibid.*, 89–92.

17 *Ibid.*, 66.

18 *Ibid.*, 72–3, 79–81. *Hollander, *Allegory in Dante's Commedia*, 159.

19 *Singleton, *Dante's Commedia*, 52–3.

20 *Purgatorio* 30.48: "conosco i segni de l'antica fiamma"; cf. *Aeneid* 4.23: "agnosco ueteris uestigia flammae."

21 *Gradon, *Form and Style*, 74, 101–13. See also *Salter, "Medieval Poetry," 87.

22 *Gradon, *Form and Style*, 76.

23 *Quilligan, *Language of Allegory*, 97–121.
24 Guillaume de Deguileville, *Le pèlerinage de vie humaine*, ed. J. J. Stürzinger, London, Nichols and Sons [1895]; trans. E. Clasby as *The Pilgrimage of Human Life*, New York, Garland, 1992. For a discussion of Deguileville's "visual riddles," with copious illustrations, see *Tuve, *Allegorical Imagery*, 145–218.
25 Katzenellenbogen, *Allegories*, 63–8.
26 *Aers, *Piers Plowman and Christian Allegory*, 13–14, 89.
27 See also the "braunches that burjoneth" out of the seven sins "and bryngen men to helle" (15.74–5), or the blight that spreads upwards from the rotten root of the clergy and deprives the people of flower and fruit (15.94–102).
28 E. T. Donaldson, *Piers Plowman: The C-Text and its Poet*, New Haven, CT, Yale University Press, 1949, 188.
29 *Charity, *Events and their Afterlife*, 21–34.
30 On this subject, see R. M. Ames, *The Fulfillment of the Scriptures: Abraham, Moses, and Piers*, Evanston, IL, Northwestern University Press, 1970.
31 For a conspectus of critical interpretations of this passage, see Derek Pearsall, *An Annotated Critical Bibliography of Langland*, Ann Arbor, MI, University of Michigan Press, 1990, 200–6, and in addition, *Steiner, *Documentary Culture*, 121–42.
32 St. Jerome's saying, "Monachus autem non doctoris habet, sed plangentis officium, qui vel se vel mundum lugeat" ("The duty of the monk is not teaching but weeping, to mourn for himself or the world": *Contra Vigilantium*, PL 23, col. 351C), was very widely quoted by medieval writers (sometimes with "lugentis" or "dolentis" in place of "plangentis"). A computer search in *Patrologia Latina* turns up over a dozen entries, including such well-known figures as Abelard and St. Bernard.
33 *Spearing, *"Piers Plowman,"* 234.
34 J. L. Austin, *How to Do Things with Words*, Oxford University Press, 1962, 98–100. For example, when the plain statement "there is a bull in that field" functions as a warning "do not enter the field," the warning is its "illocutionary force."
35 "At vero Ecclesia, scisso verbo occidentis litterae in morte Verbi crucifixi, audacter ad eius penetralia praeeunte spiritu libertatis irrumpit"; *Sermones super Cantica Canticorum* XIV.4, *Sancti Bernardi Opera*, vol. I, ed. J. Leclercq, C. H. Talbot, and H. M. Rochais, Rome, Editiones Cistercienses, 1957, 78.
36 *Steiner, *Documentary Culture*.
37 *Hollander, *Allegory in Dante's Commedia*, 105, 122, 131.
38 See M. T. Tavormina, *Kindly Similitude: Marriage and Family in Piers Plowman*, Cambridge, D. S. Brewer, 1995, ch. 3.
39 *Mann, "Eating and Drinking in *Piers Plowman*."
40 See *Mann, *Langland and Allegory*, for fuller discussion of personification allegory and the points summarized here.
41 "Wanhope" has a capital letter both in Schmidt B and in the text in vol. I of his *Parallel-Text Edition of the A, B, C and Z Versions*; however, in the list of corrections in vol. II of this edition (945) this is changed to "wanhope." The vacillation is a significant indication of the inherent ambiguity in Langland's usage.
42 *Quilligan, *Language of Allegory*, 26.

5 THE ROKELES

1 As noted and first transcribed by Thomas Wright, ed., *The Vision and the Creed of Piers Ploughman*, London, William Pickering, 1842, x–xi, note 3.
2 From *Hanna, *William Langland*, 2; transl. mine. A facsimile of the original leaf is in *Kane, *Piers Plowman* (plate 1).
3 E.g., *Adam's Curse: A Future without Men*, New York, W. W. Norton, 2004.
4 *Hanna (*William Langland*, 2–3, 26–7) prints a selection of the known documents mentioning Eustace de Rokele, chiefly as a juror in the local manorial court.
5 *Hanna, *William Langland*, 4.
6 Citations are to the Athlone editions. The author's "signatures" in his poem are collected and discussed in *Middleton, "William Langland's 'Kynde Name,'" 42–52.
7 *Bennett, "William called Long Will."
8 See Chapter 8 below.
9 The omission of Langland's name from Emden's registers proves nothing. It was perfectly normal, in the fourteenth century, for someone to finish an entire course of study for an advanced degree at Oxford or Paris and then leave without graduating. As J. A. Brundage notes, "it would not be in the least surprising that he [Langland] left without taking any degree; that's what the great majority of students apparently did, even if they stayed at the university for the number of years required for degrees. The expenses involved in taking any degree, but the doctorate in particular, were monstrously high. So much so that at the beginning of the fourteenth century Pope Clement V issued a decretal, *Cum sit nimis absurdum*...that attempted to limit doctoral degree charges to 3,000 *livres Tournois* – which was even so an awful lot of money. And his attempt failed" (personal email, February 2, 2008).
10 *Community, Gender, and Individual Identity: English Writing 1360–1430* (London, Routledge, 1988), 35–53.
11 A full discussion of the evidence for the entire Rokele clan may be found in *Adams, *Langland and the Rokele Family*. But much remains hidden in unpublished charters.

6 RELIGIOUS FORMS AND INSTITUTIONS IN *PIERS PLOWMAN*

1 *OED*, sense 2c: "Each of those social and political freedoms which are considered to be the entitlement of all members of a community; a civil liberty."
2 Isaiah Berlin, "Two Concepts of Liberty," in his *Four Essays on Liberty*, Oxford University Press, 1969, 118–72 (at 138). The essay was first published in 1958.
3 L. Patterson, "Historical Criticism and the Development of Chaucer Studies," in his *Negotiating the Past: The Historical Understanding of Medieval Literature*, Madison, University of Wisconsin Press, 1987, 3–39 (at 19).
4 P. Strohm, "Conscience," in *Cultural Reformations: Medieval and Renaissance in Literary History*, ed. B. Cummings and J. Simpson, Twenty-First Century Approaches 2, Oxford University Press, 2010, 206–23.

5 W. W. Skeat, ed., *The Vision of William Concerning Piers the Plowman ... by William Langland*, 2 vols., Oxford University Press, 1886, 2:xxvii–xxxii.

6 For a rich account, see *Southern, *Western Society and the Church*.

7 *Southern, *Western Society and the Church*, 214–15.

8 All references to *Piers Plowman* are from Schmidt B.

9 R. Hanna, "Will's Work," in *Written Work: Langland, Labor, and Authorship*, ed. S. Justice and K. Kerby-Fulton, Philadelphia, University of Pennsylvania Press, 1997, 23–66.

10 J. Mann, *Chaucer and Medieval Estates Satire: The Literature of Social Classes and the "General Prologue" to the "Canterbury Tales"*, Cambridge University Press, 1973.

11 A. Hudson, *The Premature Reformation: Wycliffite Texts and Lollard History*, Oxford, Clarendon Press, 1988.

12 J. Simpson, "From Reason to Affective Knowledge: Modes of Thought and Poetic Form in *Piers Plowman*," *Medium Ævum*, 55 (1986), 1–23.

13 Discussion of these two examples is drawn and abridged from *Simpson, *Piers Plowman: An Introduction to the B-Text*, 126–34, and 206–14 respectively.

14 The doctor is cautiously though definitely specified as a friar by Will at B.13.70–7.

15 For the initially surprising but, at a deeper level, entirely plausible account that Langland admires the friars, see L. Clopper, *"Songes of Rechelesnesse": Langland and the Franciscans*, Ann Arbor, University of Michigan Press, 1997.

7 POLITICAL FORMS AND INSTITUTIONS IN *PIERS PLOWMAN*

1 J. Simpson, *Piers Plowman: An Introduction to the B-Text*, 2nd edn. rev., Exeter University Press, 2007. See also Chapter 6 above.

2 K. Kerby-Fulton and S. Justice, "Langlandian Reading Circles and the Civil Service in London and Dublin, 1380–1427," *New Medieval Literatures*, 1 (1997), 59–83; A. Middleton, "The Audience and Public of *Piers Plowman*," in *Middle English Alliterative Poetry and its Literary Background*, ed. D. Lawton, Woodbridge, D. S. Brewer, 1982, 101–54; "The Idea of Public Poetry in the Reign of Richard II," *Speculum*, 53 (1978), 94–114; J. A. Burrow, "The Audience of *Piers Plowman*," in *Essays on Piers Plowman*, Oxford, Clarendon, 1984, 102–16.

3 E. Steiner, "Commonalty and Literary Form in the 1370s and 1380s," *New Medieval Literatures*, 6 (2003), 213.

4 See *MED* s.vv. *institū(t)en, institūciŏn*.

5 All text citations are from K-D.

6 Noted by J. Alford, "The Design of the Poem," in *A Companion to Piers Plowman*, ed. Alford, Berkeley, University of California Press, 1988, 32.

7 For a very useful guide to the extensive legal and institutional vocabulary of the poem see *Alford, *Glossary of Legal Diction*. A comprehensive overview of the specifically legal and governmental institutions of the period is provided by Bryce Lyon, *A Constitutional and Legal History of Medieval England*, 2nd edn., New York, W. W. Norton, 1980. See also more recently W. M. Ormrod, *Political Life in Medieval England, 1300–1450*, New York: St. Martin's Press, 1995, and Anthony Musson and W. M. Ormrod, *The Evolution of English Justice: Law,*

Politics, and Society in the Fourteenth Century, New York: St. Martin's Press, 1999.

8 On the context of contemporary labor legislation see especially A. Middleton, "Acts of Vagrancy: The C Version 'Autobiography' and the Statute of 1388," in *Written Work: Langland, Labor, and Authorship*, ed. S. Justice and K. Kerby-Fulton, Philadelphia, University of Pennsylvania Press, 1997, 208–317.

9 One classical source of this triad (expanded into four by Langland) of fundamental obligations is Cicero's *De officiis* ("On Duties"), book 1 chapter 16, drawing from the poetry of Ennius.

10 For this line I adopt the reading of MS L (Oxford Bodleian Library Laud 581) against K-D's emendations.

11 On *leaute* see the entries s.v. *leautē* (n.) in the *MED* and s.v. *lewty/lawty* in the *OED*. It derives from medieval Latin *legalitat-em* and is related to but distinct from both "loyalty" and "lealty."

12 On this crucial scene see especially E. Craun, *Ethics and Power in Medieval English Reformist Writing*, Cambridge University Press, 2010, 69–84.

13 On the meaning of *leaute* see also P. M. Kean, "Love, Law, and *Lewte* in *Piers Plowman*," *Review of English Studies*, 59 (1964), 241–61; and Simpson, *Piers Plowman*, 106–13.

14 See *Alford, *Glossary of Legal Diction*, s.v. "Amortisen."

15 See s.vv. *sheu(e)* (n.) and *sheuen* (v.) in *MED*, and especially s.v. *show* in *OED*, def. v.23.c.

16 L. Warner, *The Lost History of Piers Plowman: The Earliest Transmission of Langland's Work*, Philadelphia, University of Pennsylvania Press, 2011.

17 On the complexity of Conscience, which resonates here with Conscience's institutional and legal ramifications over the course of the poem, see Sarah Wood, *Conscience and the Composition of Piers Plowman*, Oxford University Press, 2012.

8 CHRISTIAN PHILOSOPHY IN *PIERS PLOWMAN*

1 Citations are to the Athlone editions, and to the B text except where otherwise specified.

2 *La Somme le Roi par Frère Laurent*, ed. E. Brayer and A. Leurquin-Labie, Société des anciens textes français, Paris, Paillart, 2008, ch. 52, 137, 235; *The Book of Vices and Virtues*, ed. W. Francis, EETS, os 217, London, Humphrey Milford, 1942, 124.

3 *Somme le Roi*, chap. 52, 139–43, 235–6; *Book of Vices and Virtues*, 124.

4 *Bowers, *Crisis of Will in Piers Plowman*; *Alford, "Langland's Learning"; *Galloway, "*Piers Plowman* and the Schools"; *Mann, "'He Knew Nat Catoun'"; C. Cannon, "Langland's *Ars Grammatica*," YLS, 22 (2008), 1–25.

5 See M. E. Marcett, *Uhtred de Boldon, Friar William Jordan, and Piers Plowman*, New York, Published by the author, 1938.

6 See *Hanna, "Literacy, Schooling, Universities." For the argument that "Seint Auereys" refers mockingly to the Arabic Aristotelian philosopher Averroes, see A. Middleton, "The Passion of Seint Averoys [B.13.91]: 'Deuynyng' and Divinity in the Banquet Scene," YLS 1 (1987), 31–40. Langland's canonization of the latter

is, by this reading, a "satiric fantasy" (and an informed one) meant to criticize the Doctor of Divinity for his overly naturalistic philosophy.

7 See A. Conti, "Wyclif's Logic and Metaphysics," in *A Companion to John Wyclif: Late Medieval Theologian*, ed. I. Levy, Leiden, Brill, 2011, 67–125.

8 See *Courtney, *Schools and Scholars*, 210–18, 307–24; also *Bowers, *Crisis of Will*, 41–60.

9 Augustine, *De doctrina Christiana*, ed. and trans. R. P. H. Green, Oxford University Press, 1997, 4.xxix.62–xxx.63, 280–3. For Augustine's adaptation here of Neoplatonism see M. Carmago, "'Non solum sibi sed aliis etiam': Neoplatonism and Rhetoric in Saint Augustine's *De doctrina Christiana*," *Rhetorica*, 16 (1998), 393–408, rept. in his *Essays on Medieval Rhetoric*, Farnham, Ashgate, 2012.

10 G. R. Owst, *Preaching in Medieval England: An Introduction to Sermon Manuscripts of the Period c. 1350–1450*, Cambridge University Press, 1926, 295.

11 On the claim that *Piers Plowman* turns away from the City, see D. Pearsall, "Langland's London," in *Written Work: Langland, Labor, and Authorship*, ed. S. Justice and K. Kerby-Fulton, Philadelphia, University of Pennsylvania Press, 1997, 185–207; the ties to London, however, are increasingly visible, as for instance in manuscript production: see Chapter 10 below. See also A. Galloway, "Non-literary Commentary and its Literary Profits: The Road to Accounting-ville," *YLS*, 25 (2011), 9–23.

12 Courtney, *Schools and Scholars*, 91–106.

13 See *Alford, *Glossary of Legal Diction*. Canon law in *Piers Plowman* has been less deeply investigated, but its importance is evident: see T. Arvind, "The Subject of Canon Law: Confessing Covetise in *Piers Plowman* B and C and the *Memoriale presbiterorum*," *YLS*, 24 (2010), 139–68.

14 The phrase appears frequently in works by Augustine: see, e.g., *De libero arbitrio*, 1.4, 2.6; *De magistro*, 37; *De doctrina Christiana*, 2.17.

15 See J. Owens, "Faith, Ideas, Illumination, and Experience," in *The Cambridge History of Later Medieval Philosophy*, 440–59 (454).

16 S. Lahey, "Wyclif's Trinitarian and Christological Theology," in *A Companion to John Wyclif*, 127–98 (144); e.g., John Wyclif, *Sermones*, ed. J. Loserth, London, Trübner, 1887, 1:172.

17 Thomas Usk, *Testament of Love*, ed. G. Shawver, based on the edn. of J. Leyerle, University of Toronto Press, 2002, book 2, ch. 1, 82.

18 *Wittig, "Elements in the Design of the Inward Journey."

19 See A. Galloway, *The Penn Commentary on Piers Plowman Volume 1: C Prologue-Passus 4; B Prologue-Passus 4; A Prologue-Passus 4*, Philadelphia, University of Pennsylvania Press, 2006, pp. 180–5.

20 See R. E. Kaske, "Holy Church's Speech and the Structure of *Piers Plowman*," in *Chaucer and Middle English Studies in Honour of Rossell Hope Robbins*, ed. B. Rowland, London, George Allen and Unwin, 1974, 320–7.

21 See *Galloway, "Rhetoric of Riddling."

22 For these views, see J. Norton-Smith, *William Langland*, Leiden, Brill, 1983, 102; M. Quilligan, *The Language of Allegory: Defining the Genre*, Ithaca, NY, Cornell University Press, 1992, 61; H. White, *Nature and Salvation in Piers Plowman*, Cambridge, D. S. Brewer, 1988, 2.

23 See S. Wood, *Conscience and the Composition of Piers Plowman*, Oxford University Press, 2012, 134–66.

24 R. Adams, "Piers's Pardon and Langland's Semi-Pelagianism," *Traditio*, 39 (1983), 367–418; R. Frank, *Piers Plowman and the Scheme of Salvation: An Interpretation of Dowel, Dobet, and Dobest*, New Haven, Yale University Press, 1957; *Aers, *Sanctifying Signs*.

25 M. Bloomfield, *Piers Plowman as a Fourteenth-Century Apocalypse*, New Brunswick, Rutgers University Press [1962].

26 See A. Cole, *Literature and Heresy in the Age of Chaucer*, Cambridge University Press, 2008, chs. 2 and 3.

27 M. Adams, "Universals in the Early Fourteenth Century," in *The Cambridge History of Later Medieval Philosophy*, 411–39 (438).

28 *Avicenna Latinus: Liber de anima seu sextus De naturalibus*, ed. S. van Riet, vol. 1, Leiden, E. J. Brill, 1972, I, 1; 36–7.

29 See I. M. Resnick, "Peter Damian and the Restoration of Virginity: A Problem for Medieval Theology," *Journal of Religious History*, 39 (1988), 125–34.

30 John Duns Scotus, *Ordinatio*, Liber secundus, Distinctiones 1–3, ed. C. Balic, Vatican, Typis Pollyglottis Vaticanis, 1973, 296 (d.2, q.5).

31 D. Aers, *Piers Plowman and Christian Allegory*, New York, St. Martin's Press, 1975; A. Cole, "Trifunctionality and the Tree of Charity: Literary and Social Practice in *Piers Plowman*," *ELH*, 62 (1995), 1–27.

32 *Somme le Roi*, ch. 50, 30, 203; *Book of Vices and Virtues*, 94. See R. Hanna, "*Speculum Vitae* and the Form of *Piers Plowman*," in *Answerable Style: The Idea of the Literary in Medieval England*, ed. F. Grady and A. Galloway, Columbus, Ohio State University Press, 2013, 121–40 (esp. 122–5).

33 "On Memory," in *The Complete Works of Aristotle: The Revised Oxford Translation*, ed. J. Barnes, 2 vols., Princeton University Press, 1984, 450a [1.714].

34 U. Eco, *Semiotics and the Philosophy of Language*, Bloomington, Indiana University Press, 1984, 68.

35 N. Kretzmann, trans., *William of Sherwood's Introduction to Logic*, Minneapolis, University of Minnesota Press, 1966, 54n13; Ramon Llull, *Arbor scientiae: Romae in festo sancti Michaelis archangeli anno MCCXCV incepta, in ipsa urbe Kalendis Aprilibus anno MCCXCVI ad finem perducta*, 3 vols., ed. P. Varneda, Turnhout, Brepols, 2000.

36 On these figures, see *Atomism in Late Medieval Philosophy and Theology*, ed. C. Grellard and A. Robert, Leiden, Brill, 2009.

37 See, respectively, *Smith, *Book of the Incipit*; G. Rudd, *Managing Language in Piers Plowman*, Cambridge, D. S. Brewer, 1994; S. Tolmie, "Langland, Wittgenstein and the Language Game," *YLS*, 22 (2008), 103–29; N. Zeeman, *Piers Plowman and the Medieval Discourse of Desire*, Cambridge University Press, 2006; *Harwood, *Piers Plowman and the Problem of Belief*.

38 Bede, *A History of the English Church and People*, trans. L. Sherley-Price; rev. R. E. Latham, Harmondsworth, Penguin, 1968, 252. See J. Mann, "Eating and Drinking in *Piers Plowman*," *Essays and Studies*, 32 (1979), 26–43.

39 *The Mirror of the Blessed Life of Jesus Christ*, ed. M. G. Sargent, Exeter University Press, 2005, 11.

40 B. Harwood, "Imaginative in *Piers Plowman*," *Medium Ævum*, 44 (1975), 249–63; A. J. Minnis, "Langland's Ymaginatif and Late-Medieval Theories of

Imagination," *Comparative Criticism: A Year Book*, 3 (1981), 71–103; *Karnes, *Imagination, Meditation, and Cognition in the Middle Ages*. Studies on Conscience range from Thomas Patrick Dunning, *Piers Plowman: An Interpretation of the A-text*, London, Longmans, Green, and Co., 1937, to Wood, *Conscience and the Composition of Piers Plowman* (who is the more flexible considering the diverse and shifting registers focused in this figure).

41 R. Hanna sees Imaginative as distinct from that version in the scholastic traditions; "Langland's Ymaginatif: Images and the Limits of Poetry," in *Images, Idolatry, and Iconoclasm in Late Medieval England: Textuality and the Visual Image*, ed. J. Dimmick, J. Simpson, and N. Zeeman, Oxford University Press, 2002, 81–94.

42 See Owens, "Faith, Ideas, Illumination, and Experience," 444.

43 Thomas Aquinas, *Summa theologiae*, 60 vols., trans. T. Gilby *et al.*, London, Eyre and Spottiswoode, 1964–73, 1.6 and 7.

44 See Minnis, "Langland's Ymaginatif."

45 See Galloway, *Penn Commentary*, 332–60.

46 Smith, *Book of the Incipit*, 157–70, 257–8n87.

47 See J. Wogan-Browne, Nicholas Watson, Andrew Taylor, and Ruth Evans, eds., *The Idea of the Vernacular: An Anthology of Middle English Literary Theory, 1280–1520*, University Park, The Pennsylvania State University Press, 1999, 70–1, 328–9.

48 See J. Alford, "The Grammatical Metaphor: A Survey of its Use in the Middle Ages," *Speculum*, 57 (1982), 728–60.

49 K. M. Fredborg, L. Nielsen, and J. Pinborg, "An Unedited Part of Roger Bacon's 'Opus Maius': 'De Signis,'" *Traditio*, 34 (1978), 75–136.

50 E. Sylla, "The Oxford Calculators," in *The Cambridge History of Later Medieval Philosophy*, 540–64.

51 On medieval ideas of "the event," and radical contingency as a theme in other late fourteenth-century Middle English literature, see J. Mitchell, *Ethics and Eventfulness in Middle English Literature*, New York, Palgrave, 2009.

52 On this audience see A. Middleton, "The Audience and Public of *Piers Plowman*," in *Middle English Alliterative Poetry and its Literary Background: Seven Essays*, ed. D. Lawton, Cambridge, D. S. Brewer, 1982, 101–23.

9 THE NON-CHRISTIANS OF *PIERS PLOWMAN*

1 *Akbari, *Seeing through the Veil*, 11–17; R. Copeland, *Rhetoric, Hermeneutics, and Translation in the Middle Ages: Academic Traditions and Vernacular Texts*, Cambridge University Press, 1991, 63–5, 81. See Chapter 4 above.

2 D. Aers, *Sanctifying Signs: Making Christian Tradition in Late Medieval England*, University of Notre Dame Press, 2004.

3 E. D. Kirk, *The Dream Thought of Piers Plowman*, New Haven, Yale University Press, 1972, 13.

4 C. D. Benson, "What Then Does Langland Mean? Authorial and Textual Voices in *Piers Plowman*," YLS, 15 (2001), 3–13.

5 N. Watson, "Langland and Chaucer," in *The Oxford Handbook of English Literature and Theology*, ed. E. Jay, D. Jasper, and A. Hass, Oxford University Press, 2009, 367.

6 On the *Song of Roland*, see *Kinoshita, *Medieval Boundaries*, 15–45; on the Croxton *Play of the Sacrament*, see L. Lampert-Weissig, "The Once and Future Jew: The Croxton *Play of the Sacrament*, Little Robert of Bury and Historical Memory," *Jewish History*, 15 (2001), 235–55.

7 On the Augustinian view, see J. Cohen, *Living Letters of the Law: Ideas of the Jew in Medieval Christianity*, Berkeley, University of California Press, 1999.

8 *Jean de Mandeville: Le Livre des merveilles du monde*, ed. Christiane Deluz, Sources d'histoire médiévale 31, Paris, CNRS, 2000, 277 (ch. 15).

9 Citations are from Schmidt. For further discussion of this passage see below.

10 *Akbari, *Idols in the East*, 223–8, 257–62.

11 On polemical biographies of the prophet, see *Tolan, *Saracens*, 135–69 (ch. 6, "Muhammad, Heresiarch"); on the *Roman de Mahomet*, see R. Hyatte, *The Prophet of Islam in Old French: The Romance of Muhammad (1258) and the Book of Muhammad's Ladder (1264)*, Leiden, Brill, 1997, 1–18.

12 On the sources and circulation of the account of Muhammad found in the chapter on Pelagius in the *Golden Legend*, see S. Mula, "Muhammad and the Saints: The History of the Prophet in the *Golden Legend*," *Modern Philology*, 101 (2003), 175–88.

13 Mandeville, ed. Deluz, 279 (ch. 15); for discussion, see *Akbari, *Idols in the East*, 55–7.

14 E. Narin van Court, "Hermeneutics of Supersession: The Revision of the Jews from the B to the C text of *Piers Plowman*," YLS, 10 (1996), 43–87.

15 Narin van Court, "Hermeneutics of Supersession," 47.

16 *Ibid.*, 47, 50.

17 On the concept of "universal salvation" in the B text versus the C text, see D. Pearsall, "The Idea of Universal Salvation in *Piers Plowman* B and C," *Journal of Medieval and Early Modern Studies*, 39 (2009), 257–81.

18 *Metlitzki, *The Matter of Araby in Medieval England*, 202.

19 See *Grady, *Representing Righteous Heathens*, 1–44; on the Trajan narrative, see G. Whatley, "The Uses of Hagiography: The Legend of Pope Gregory and the Emperor Trajan in the Middle Ages," *Viator*, 15 (1984), 25–63; *Vitto, *Virtuous Pagan*.

20 Jacobus de Voragine [James of Voragine], *The Golden Legend*, trans. William Granger Ryan, 2 vols., Princeton University Press, 1995, 1.178–9; Latin text in Theodor Graesse, ed., *Legenda aurea vulgo historia lombardica dicta*, Leipzig, Librariae Arnoldianae, 1850, 196–7.

21 *Golden Legend*, trans. Ryan, 1.179.

22 On the role of "treuthe" in Trajan's redemption, see E. Doxsee, "'Trew Treuthe' and Canon Law: The Orthodoxy of Trajan's Salvation in *Piers Plowman* C-Text," *Neuphilologische Mitteilungen*, 89 (1988), 295–311; A. Galloway, "Making History Legal," in *William Langland's Piers Plowman: A Book of Essays*, ed. K. M. Hewett-Smith, New York, Routledge, 2001, 7–39, esp. 16–19, 30.

23 For a survey of these, see *Grady, *Representing Righteous Heathens*, 20–2; for overview of the terms of the debate, see *Aers, *Salvation and Sin*, 84–8.

24 See *Tolan, *Saracens* 10–12 (on early etymologies of the term), 126–8 (on the use of the term to refer to non-Muslim "pagans"); *Akbari, *Idols in the East*, 113–15.

25 See D. Speed, "The Saracens of *King Horn*," *Speculum*, 65 (1990), 564–95.

26 See, for example, the author portrait in an eleventh-century manuscript of the *Moralia in Job*, Bamberg, Staatsbibliothek, MS Msc. Bibl. 84 (fol. 1r, author portrait); also the twelfth-century author portrait in Cleveland Museum of Art, J. H. Wade Fund ms 1955.74 (Engelberg, 1143–78), fol. 1.

27 *Aers, *Salvation and Sin*, 124.

28 *Ibid.*, 125.

29 Walter Hilton, *Scale of Perfection*, book 2, ch. 3 (ed. Bestul, TEAMS), lines 96–150.

10 MANUSCRIPTS AND READERS OF *PIERS PLOWMAN*

1 J. A. Burrow, "The Audience of *Piers Plowman*," *Anglia*, 75 (1957), 373–84, reprinted with a postscript in his *Essays on Medieval Literature*, Oxford, Clarendon Press, 1984, 102–16.

2 *Middleton, "The Audience and Public of *Piers Plowman*."

3 K. Kerby-Fulton and S. Justice, "Langlandian Reading Circles and the Civil Service in London and Dublin," *New Medieval Literatures*, 1 (1998), 59–83.

4 Washington, DC, Folger Library, MS v.b.236; Princeton University Library, Taylor MS 10.

5 T. Turville-Petre, "The Relationship of the Vernon and Clopton Manuscripts," in *Studies in the Vernon Manuscript*, ed. D. Pearsall, Cambridge, D. S. Brewer, 1990, 29–44.

6 R. Perry, "The Clopton Manuscript and the Beauchamp Affinity: Patronage and Reception Issues in a West Midlands Reading Community," in *Essays in Manuscript Geography: Vernacular Manuscripts of the English West Midlands from the Conquest to the Sixteenth Century*, ed. W. Scase, Turnhout, Brepols, 2007, 131–60.

7 K. Kerby-Fulton, "The Women Readers in Langland's Earliest Audience: Some Codicological Evidence," in *Learning and Literacy in Medieval England and Abroad*, ed. S. R. Jones, Turnhout, Brepols, 2003, 121–34.

8 S. Horobin, "The Scribe of Rawlinson Poetry 137 and the Copying and Circulation of *Piers Plowman*," *YLS*, 19 (2005), 3–26.

9 S. Horobin, "Harley 3954 and the Audience of *Piers Plowman*," in *Medieval Texts in Context*, ed. G. D. Caie and D. Renevey, London, Routledge, 2008, 68–84.

10 A. I. Doyle and M. B. Parkes, "The Production of Copies of the *Canterbury Tales* and the *Confessio Amantis* in the Early Fifteenth Century," in *Mediaeval Scribes, Manuscripts and Libraries: Essays Presented to N. R. Ker*, ed. M. B. Parkes and A. G. Watson, Aldershot, Scolar Press, 1978, 163–203; L. R. Mooney, "Chaucer's Scribe," *Speculum*, 81 (2006), 97–138; S. Horobin and L. R. Mooney, "A *Piers Plowman* Manuscript by the Hengwrt/Ellesmere Scribe and its Implications for London Standard English," *SAC*, 26 (2004), 65–112.

11 T. Turville-Petre, "Putting it Right: The Corrections of Huntington Library MS. HM 128 and BL Additional MS 35287," *YLS*, 16 (2002), 41–65; S. Horobin,

"Adam Pinkhurst and the Copying of British Library MS Additional 35287 of the B Version of *Piers Plowman*," *YLS*, 23 (2009), 61–83.

12 S. Horobin, "The Scribe of Bodleian Library MS Digby 102 and the Circulation of the C Text of *Piers Plowman*," *YLS*, 24 (2010), 89–112.

13 Other C-text manuscripts probably written in London during this period are Huntington Library, MS HM 143, British Library, MS Additional 35157, and the "Holloway" Fragment. For the latter see R. Hanna III, "Studies in the Manuscripts of *Piers Plowman*," *YLS*, 7 (1993), 1–25.

14 M. Connolly, *John Shirley: Book Production and the Noble Household in Fifteenth-Century England*, Aldershot, Ashgate, 1998, 165.

15 S. Horobin, "John Cok and His Copy of *Piers Plowman*," *YLS*, 27 (2013), forthcoming.

16 A. McIntosh, M. Samuels, and M. Benskin (eds.), *A Linguistic Atlas of Late Mediaeval English*, Aberdeen, Aberdeen University Press, 1986.

17 *Kerby-Fulton and Despres, *Iconography and the Professional Reader*.

18 See, for instance, R. Hanna, "On the Versions of *Piers Plowman*," in his *Pursuing History: Middle English Manuscripts and their Texts*, Stanford University Press, 1996, 203–43.

19 See, for instance, S. S. Hussey, "Langland the Outsider," in *Middle English Poetry: Texts and Traditions. Essays In Honour of Derek Pearsall*, ed. A. J. Minnis, York Medieval Texs, 2001, 129–37.

20 See further L. Warner, *The Lost History of Piers Plowman: The Earliest Transmission of Langland's Work*, Philadelphia, University of Pennsylvania Press, 2011, 2–4.

21 S. Horobin, "'In London and opelond': The Dialect and Circulation of the C Version of *Piers Plowman*," *Medium Ævum*, 74 (2005), 248–69.

22 On this manuscript see S. Horobin and A. Wiggins, "Reconsidering Lincoln's Inn 150," *Medium Ævum*, 77 (2008), 30–53.

23 R. Davies, "The Life, Travels, and Library of an Early Reader of *Piers Plowman*," *YLS*, 13 (1999), 49–64.

24 R. A. Wood, "A Fourteenth-Century London Owner of *Piers Plowman*," *Medium Ævum*, 53 (1984), 83–90.

25 R. Hanna, "Two New (?) Lost *Piers* Manuscripts (?)," *YLS*, 16 (2002), 169–77.

26 More detailed discussion can be found in *Middleton, "The Audience and Public of *Piers Plowman*."

27 These manuscripts are Bodleian Library, MS Eng. Poetry a.1, the "Vernon" manuscript, San Marino, Huntington Library, MS HM 128, and London, Society of Antiquaries, MS 687.

28 The *Lay Folks' Mass Book* is copied alongside the B text in Newnham College, Cambridge MS 4. *Handlyng Synne* is found in the Clopton manuscript discussed above.

29 British Library, MS Additional 34779 and Manchester, John Rylands Library, MS English 90; Corpus Christi College, Oxford MS 201 and Durham, Ushaw College MS 50; Rawlinson Poetry 137 and University College, Oxford MS 142.

30 The holster book format is used in British Library, MS Harley 3954, Rawlinson Poetry MS 137, Corpus Christi College, Oxford MS 201, and Lincoln's Inn, MS Hale 150.

31 C. Grindley offers a classification system for such marginalia in "Reading *Piers Plowman* C-Text Annotations: Notes toward the Classification of Printed and Written Marginalia in Texts from the British Isles 1300–1641," in *The Medieval Professional Reader at Work: Evidence from Manuscripts of Chaucer, Langland, Kempe, and Gower*, ed. K. Kerby-Fulton and M. Hilmo, Victoria, BC, University of Victoria Press, 2001, 73–141.

32 B. Davis, "The Prophecies of *Piers Plowman* in Cambridge University Library, MS Gg.4.31," *Journal of the Early Book Society*, 5 (2002), 15–36.

33 J. R. Thorne and M.-C. Uhart, "Robert Crowley's *Piers Plowman*," *Medium Ævum*, 55 (1986), 248–54.

34 For an account of Stephan Batman's life see R. Zim, "Batman, Stephan (*c*.1542–1584)," in *Oxford Dictionary of National Biography*, Oxford University Press, September 2004; online edition, January 2008, www.oxforddnb.com/view/article/1704, accessed 13 Nov 2009.

35 Quoted from C. E. Wright, "The Dispersal of the Monastic Libraries and the Beginnings of Anglo-Saxon Studies. Matthew Parker and his Circle: A Preliminary Study," *Transactions of the Cambridge Bibliographical Society*, 3 (1951), 208–37 (220).

36 For a list of manuscripts owned by Batman see M. B. Parkes, "Stephan Batman's Manuscripts," in *Medieval Heritage: Essays in Honour of Tadahiro Ikegami*, ed. M. Kanno *et al.*, Tokyo, Yushodo Press, 1997, 125–56.

37 S. Horobin, "Stephan Batman's Manuscripts of *Piers Plowman*," *Review of English Studies*, 62 (2010), 358–72.

38 L. Warner, "An Overlooked *Piers Plowman* Excerpt and the Oral Circulation of Non-Reformist Prophecy, c. 1520–55," *YLS*, 21 (2007), 119–42; S. L. Jansen, "Politics, Protest, and a New *Piers Plowman* Fragment: The Voice of the Past in Tudor England," *Review of English Studies*, 40 (1989), 93–9.

39 H. N. Duggan and R. Hanna (eds.), *The Piers Plowman Electronic Archive 4: Oxford, Bodleian Library, MS Laud Misc. 581*, Woodbridge, Boydell and Brewer, 2005.

40 For further discussion of these sixteenth-century readers see *Kelen, *Langland's Early Modern Identities*.

41 C. L. Kingsford, *A Survey of London, by John Stow: Reprinted from the Text of 1603*, Oxford, Clarendon Press, 1908.

11 PLOWMAN TRADITIONS IN LATE MEDIEVAL AND EARLY MODERN WRITING

1 *The Vision of Pierce Plowman, now fyrste imprynted by Roberte Crowley, dwellyng in Ely rentes in Holburne* (1550), from Lehigh University Library 821.1 L265p 1550, online at http://digital.lib.lehigh.edu/cdm4/eb_viewer. php?ptr=1027; I have added punctuation for ease of reading. This is Short Title Catalogue 19906, sigil cr¹ in K-D, whose passus and line numbers I provide. In quoting early materials I employ the modern uses of *i/j* and *u/v*, use thorn for *y* in the term *ye* (=*he*), and silently expand abbreviations.

2 *Wheatley, "Selfless Ploughman."

3 London, British Library, MS Royal 13 E IX, fol. 287ʳ, quoted in R. F. Green, "John Ball's Letters: Literary History and Historical Literature," in *Chaucer's*

England: Literature in Historical Context, ed. Barbara Hanawalt, Minneapolis, University of Minnesota Press, 1992, 195.

4 *Pierce the Ploughman's Crede*, lines 711–16, in *The Piers Plowman Tradition*, ed. Barr.

5 *The Plowman's Tale: The c. 1532 and 1606 Editions of a Spurious Canterbury Tale*, ed. McCarl.

6 John Leland, *De uiris illustribus: On Famous Men*, ed. J. P. Carley, Toronto, Pontifical Institute of Mediaeval Studies, 2010, 708–9.

7 *Ibid.*, Appendix 4, 844.

8 Silverstone, "*The Vision of Pierce Plowman*," *Notes and Queries*, 2nd ser., 6.142 (1858), 229–30; I have corrected some mistranscriptions.

9 *A Godly dyalogue & dysputacyon betwene Pyers Plowman, and a popysh preest concernyng the supper of the Lorde no lesse frutefull then necessarye to be noted of al Christen men specyally considering the great controuerses & varyaunces had therin now in your tyme*, W. Copland, c. 1550, no signatures. This is STC 19903, accessed via the Early English Books Online database (EEBO).

10 *I playne Piers which can not flatter*, London, 1550?, sig. E.ii^r. This is STC 19903a, accessed via the EEBO database.

11 *Wilson, The Winchester Anthology, 10–11.

12 *Hudson, "The Legacy of *Piers Plowman*," 260.

13 *Ibid.*, 263.

14 *Newes from the north. Otherwise called The conference betvveen Simon Certain, and Pierce Plowman*, London, 1579, sig. B.iii^r, STC 24062, accessed on EEBO; punctuation added.

15 Quotations are from *The Shepheardes Calender by Edmund Spenser: The Original Edition of 1579 in Photographic Facsimile with an Introduction by H. Oskar Sommer*, London, John C. Nimmo, 1890.

16 *Little, "The 'Other' Past of Pastoral: Langland's *Piers Plowman* and Spenser's *Shepheardes Calender*," 173.

17 *A Knack to Know a Knave*, London, 1594, sig. E.3^r, cited from *The Tudor Facsimile Texts*, ed. J. S. Farmer, n.p., 1911.

18 Quotations are from James K. Baxter, "Letter to Piers Plowman," in *Collected Poems*, ed. J. E. Weir, Wellington, Oxford University Press, 1995, 125–6.

19 Citations are by page number to Thomas Pynchon, *The Crying of Lot 49*, 1965; rpt. New York, Perennial Library, 1986.

12 *PIERS PLOWMAN* IN THEORY

Special thanks to Rita Copeland and Christopher Cannon for conversations about this essay.

1 Although the brief of this chapter does not include medieval "theory," Langland is in dialogue with medieval political, legal, grammatical, philosophical, theological, and psychological thought (see above, Chapters 5, 6, 7, and 8).

2 See A. Cole, "Commentaries on Unknown Texts: On Morton Bloomfield and Friedrich Nietzsche," *YLS*, 26 (2011), 25–35; on "crux-busting," see S. Justice reviewing J. Simpson (see below, note 23) in *YLS*, 6 (1992), 153–5 (153).

3 M. W. Bloomfield, *Piers Plowman as a Fourteenth-Century Apocalypse*, New Brunswick, NJ, Rutgers University Press, [1962], 32; see Cole, "Commentaries."

Compare the similar use made of John Alford's proposal that *Piers Plowman* is a text composed around the exegetical networks of its biblical and Latin quotations (J. A. Alford, "The Role of the Quotations in *Piers Plowman*," *Speculum*, 52 [1977], 80–99); and see how G. Kane and E. T. Donaldson's commitment to Langland's "vigorous, nervous, flexible and relatively compressed" poetry also has served to authorize the pursuit of the "difficult reading" in the manuscript archive (K-D, 130; see also L. Patterson, *Negotiating the Past: The Historical Understanding of Medieval Literature*, Madison, University of Wisconsin Press, 1987, ch. 3).

4 D. V. Smith, "Negative Langland," *YLS*, 23 (2009), 33–59 (39).
5 "The Idea of Public Poetry in the Reign of Richard II," *Speculum*, 53 (1978), 94–114 (105, 95).
6 A. Middleton, "William Langland's 'Kynde Name': Authorial Signature and Social Identity in Late-Fourteenth-Century England," in *Literary Practice and Social Change in Britain, 1380–1530*, ed. L. Patterson, Berkeley, University of California Press, 1990, 15–82; "Acts of Vagrancy: The C Version 'Autobiography' and the Statute of 1388," in *Written Work: Langland, Labor and Authorship*, ed. S. Justice and K. Kerby-Fulton, Philadelphia, University of Pennsylvania Press, 1997, 208–317 (245, 293, 288–9).
7 "Kynde Name," 45, 17, 77; also "Acts of Vagrancy," 209–11.
8 "Narration and the Invention of Experience: Episodic Form in *Piers Plowman*," in *The Wisdom of Poetry: Essays in Honor of Morton Bloomfield*, ed. L. Benson and S. Wenzel, Kalamazoo, MI, Medieval Institute Publications, 1982, 91–122 (93–4, 101); for other brushes with the psychoanalytic repressed, see Middleton, "Kynde Name," 22; "Commentary on an Unacknowledged Text: Chaucer's Debt to Langland," *YLS*, 24 (2010), 113–37 (114).
9 "Invention of Experience," 106, 98.
10 "Kynde Name," 47; "Acts of Vagrancy," 270–7.
11 "Acts of Vagrancy," 247; but see also 267, 269; and "Invention of Experience," 94.
12 D. Aers, *Piers Plowman and Christian Allegory*, London, Edward Arnold, 1975; on *Piers Plowman*, see D. W. Robertson and B. F. Huppé, *Piers Plowman and Scriptural Tradition*, Princeton University Press, 1951; Patterson, *Negotiating the Past*, ch. 1.
13 Aers, *Chaucer, Langland and the Creative Imagination*, London, Routledge and Kegan Paul, 1980, chs. 1–3; *Community, Gender and Individual Identity: English Writing 1360–1430*, London, Routledge, 1988, ch. 1; *Sanctifying Signs: Making Christian Tradition in Late Medieval England*, University of Notre Dame Press, 2004, ch. 5.
14 See *Chaucer, Langland*, 1, 42; *Community, Gender*, 3–4.
15 See *Chaucer, Langland*, chs. 1 and 2 (1, 34); *Community, Gender*, ch. 1; on poverty and the Franciscans, 21, 63–7.
16 *Sanctifying Signs*, 99; see also Aers's *Salvation and Sin: Augustine, Langland and Fourteenth-Century Theology*, University of Notre Dame Press, 2009.
17 *Sanctifying Signs*, 31, 34; but see also his early *Chaucer, Langland*, 61.
18 See J. Simpson, reviewing Aers's *Sanctifying Signs* and *Salvation and Sin*, in *YLS*, 24 (2010), 205–9.

NOTES TO PP. 218–21

19 See, for example, L. Bishop, "Will and the Law of Property in *Piers Plowman*," *YLS*, 10 (1996), 23–41; A. Galloway, "Making History Legal: *Piers Plowman* and the Rebels of Fourteenth-Century England," in *William Langland's Piers Plowman: A Book of Essays*, ed. K. M. Hewett-Smith, New York, Routledge, 2001, 7–39.

20 B. J. Harwood, "The Plot of *Piers Plowman* and the Contradictions of Feudalism," in *Speaking Two Languages: Traditional Disciplines and Contemporary Theory in Medieval Studies*, ed. Allen J. Frantzen, Albany, State University of New York Press, 1991, 91–114.

21 A. Cole, "Trifunctionality and the Tree of Charity: Literary and Social Practice in *Piers Plowman*," *ELH*, 62 (1995), 1–27.

22 S. Justice, *Writing Rebellion: England in 1381*, Berkeley, University of California Press, 1994, ch. 3.

23 J. Simpson, *Piers Plowman. An Introduction*, 2nd revised edn., Exeter University Press, 2007, 1–2, 58. Also on the poem's multi-genericism, see Bloomfield, *Fourteenth-Century Apocalypse*, ch. 1; S. Justice, "The Genres of *Piers Plowman*," *Viator*, 19 (1988), 291–306.

24 "'After Craftes Conseil clotheth yow and fede': Langland and London City Politics," in *England in the Fourteenth Century: Proceedings of the 1991 Harlaxton Symposium*, ed. Nicholas Rogers, Stamford, Paul Watkins, 1993, 109–27 (114).

25 "The Power of Impropriety: Authorial Naming in *Piers Plowman*," in *William Langland's Piers Plowman*, ed. Hewett-Smith, 145–65 (153–4, 161, 156).

26 R. Hanna, "Will's Work," in *Written Work*, ed. Justice and Kerby-Fulton, 23–66 (36); "'Meddling with Makings' and Will's Work," in *Late-Medieval Texts and their Transmission: Essays in Honour of A. I. Doyle*, ed. A. J. Minnis, Cambridge, D. S. Brewer, 1994, 85–94 (87, 92–4).

27 K. Kerby-Fulton, "Langland and the Bibliographic Ego," in *Written Work*, ed. Justice and Kerby-Fulton, 67–143 (73).

28 D. Lawton, "The Subject of *Piers Plowman*," *YLS*, 1 (1987), 1–30 (2); Middleton, "Invention of Experience," 101; see also "The Idea of Public Poetry," 107, 109.

29 Lawton, "The Subject of *Piers Plowman*," 10–12, 14.

30 *Ibid.*, 3, 8–9, 21.

31 M. Carruthers, *The Search for St. Truth: A Study of Meaning in Piers Plowman*, Evanston, Northwestern University Press, 1973, 4.

32 W. Rogers, *Interpretation in Piers Plowman*, Washington, DC, Catholic University of America Press, 2002, 6, 18, 27, 25.

33 L. Scanlon, "Personification and Penance," *YLS*, 21 (2007), 1–29 (22, 24). Earlier wholly or partially deconstructive readings include L. Finke, "Truth's Treasure: Allegory and Meaning in *Piers Plowman*," in *Medieval Texts and Contemporary Readers*, ed. L. A. Finke and M. B. Shichtman, Ithaca, NY, Cornell University Press, 1987, 51–68; G. Rudd, *Managing Language in Piers Plowman*, Cambridge, D. S. Brewer, 1994: Rudd both links Langland's "relativistic" attitude to language to that of Paul de Man and yet insists that Langland still believes in a transcendental *logos* (223–31). Compare B. Harwood, who argues that the

poem is about the desire for intuitive knowledge of the object of faith, in *Piers Plowman and the Problem of Belief*, University of Toronto Press, 1992.

34 D. V. Smith, *The Book of the Incipit: Beginnings in the Fourteenth Century*, Minneapolis, University of Minnesota Press, 2001, 23, 7, 31; see also 5–16.

35 Smith, "Negative Langland," 41, 48, 56.

36 S. Tolmie, "Langland, Wittgenstein, and the End of Language," *YLS*, 20 (2006), 115–39 (121).

37 "Langland, Wittgenstein, and the Language Game," *YLS*, 22 (2008), 103–29.

38 "Langland, Wittgenstein, and the End of Language," 132, 136; also Tolmie, "The Book of the World as I Found It: Langland and Wittgenstein's *Tractatus Logico-Philosophicus*," *Exemplaria*, 20 (2008), 341–60.

39 (Formerly) L. O. Fradenburg, "Needful Things," in *Medieval Crime and Social Control*, ed. Barbara A. Hanawalt and David Wallace, Minneapolis, University of Minnesota Press, 1998, 49–69 (49, 52, 55).

40 N. Zeeman, *Piers Plowman and the Medieval Discourse of Desire*, Cambridge University Press, 2006, especially Introduction and ch. 1.

41 *Ibid.*, chs. 2, 4, 5, and 6.

42 D. Aers, "Class, Gender, Medieval Criticism, and *Piers Plowman*," in *Class and Gender in Early English Literature: Intersections*, ed. B. Harwood and G. R. Overing, Bloomington, Indiana University Press, 1994, 59–75; C. Lees, "Gender and Exchange in *Piers Plowman*," in *Class and Gender*, ed. Harwood and Overing, 112–30 (117, 124).

43 S. Trigg, "The Traffic in Medieval Women: Alice Perrers, Feminist Criticism and *Piers Plowman*," *YLS*, 12 (1998), 5–29; E. Fowler, "Civil Death and the Maiden: Agency and the Conditions of Contract in *Piers Plowman*," *Speculum*, 70 (1995), 760–92; K. E. Kennedy, "Retaining Men (and a Retaining Woman) in *Piers Plowman*," *YLS*, 20 (2006), 191–214.

44 H. Cooper, "Gender and Personification in *Piers Plowman*," *YLS*, 5 (1991), 31–48; see also J. J. Paxson, "Gender Personified, Personification Gendered, and the Body Figuralized in *Piers Plowman*," *YLS*, 12 (1998), 65–96 (68–9).

45 E. Robertson, "Souls that Matter: The Gendering of the Soul in *Piers Plowman*," in *Mindful Spirit in Late Medieval Literature: Essays in Honor of Elizabeth D. Kirk*, ed. B. Wheeler, New York, Palgrave Macmillan, 2006, 165–86 (177–8).

46 M. Raskolnikov, *Body against Soul: Gender and Sowlehele in Middle English Allegory*, Columbus, Ohio State University Press, 2009, ch. 5 (173, 190–1, 196). Citations from Schmidt's parallel-text edition.

47 "Gender Personified," 76, 91; also 72–81; J. J. Paxson, "Inventing the Subject and the Personification Will in *Piers Plowman*: Rhetorical, Erotic and Ideological Origins and Limits in Langland's Allegorical Poetics," in *William Langland's Piers Plowman: A Book of Essays*, ed. Hewett-Smith, 195–231.

48 "Inventing the Subject," 201, 210; also 224–31.

49 R. Hanna, "School and Scorn: Gender in *Piers Plowman*," *NML*, 3 (1999), 213–27 (214, 221, 224–7).

50 Middleton, "Commentary," 127, 132, 135.

51 Middleton, "Invention of Experience," 93; Raskolnikov, *Body against Soul*, 13.

52 One exception occurs at A.12.33, when, in her observation that the overly curious dreamer will only see what he wants to see, "as he seyþ, such I am, when he with me carpeþ," Scripture surely provides a succinct analysis of a fundamental Langlandian allegorical technique.
53 Aers, *Sanctifying Signs*, 38.
54 Simpson, *Piers Plowman*, 127.

Introduction: studying Piers Plowman *in the twentieth and twenty-first centuries*

Aers, D., *Piers Plowman and Christian Allegory*, London, Edward Arnold, 1975.

Alford, J. A. (ed.), *A Companion to Piers Plowman*, Berkeley, University of California Press, 1988.

Barney, S. A., "Langland's Prosody: The State of Study," in *The Endless Knot: Essays on Old and Middle English in Honor of Marie Borroff*, ed. M. Teresa Tavormina and R. F. Yeager, Cambridge, D. S. Brewer, 1995, 65–85.

Blanch, R. J. (ed.), *Style and Symbolism in Piers Plowman: A Modern Critical Anthology*, Memphis, University of Tennessee Press, 1969.

Brewer, C., *Editing Piers Plowman: The Evolution of the Text*, Cambridge University Press, 1996.

Cole, A., *The Birth of Theory*, University of Chicago Press, 2014.

Duggan, H. N., "Notes on the Metre of *Piers Plowman*: Twenty Years On," in *The Metres of Alliterative Verse*, ed. J. Jefferson and A. Putter, Leeds Texts and Monographs, ns 17, 2009, 159–86.

Gellrich, J., "Allegory and Materiality: Medieval Foundations of the Modern Debate," *Germanic Review*, 77 (2002), 146–59.

Grady, F. and A. Galloway (eds.), *Answerable Style: The Idea of the Literary in Medieval England*, Columbus, Ohio State University Press, 2013.

Hanna, R., *William Langland*, Authors of the Middle Ages: English Writers of the Late Middle Ages 3, Aldershot, Variorum, 1993.

London Literature, 1300–1380, Cambridge University Press, 2005.

Holsinger, B., *The Premodern Condition: Medievalism and the Making of Theory*, University of Chicago Press, 2005.

Horobin, S., "'In London and opelond': The Dialect and Circulation of the C Version of *Piers Plowman*," *Medium Ævum*, 74 (2005), 248–69.

Hussey, S. S. (ed.), *Piers Plowman: Critical Approaches*, New York, Barnes and Noble, 1969.

The International *Piers Plowman* Society [www.piersplowman.org] [includes information on the *Yearbook of Langland Studies*, plus a searchable annotated bibliography from the annual bibliographies printed in that journal, 1987–].

Justice, S., "Who Stole Robertson?" *PMLA*, 124 (2009), 609–15.

Kane, G., *Piers Plowman: The Evidence for Authorship*, London, Athlone Press, 1965.

Manly, J., "The Lost Leaf of *Piers the Plowman*," *Modern Philology*, 3 (1906), 359–66.

Middleton, A., "Acts of Vagrancy: The C Version 'Autobiography' and the Statute of 1388," in *Written Work: Langland, Labor and Authorship*, ed. S. Justice and K. Kerby-Fulton, Philadelphia, University of Pennsylvania Press, 1997, 208–317.

"William Langland's 'Kynde Name': Authorial Signature and Social Identity in Late-Fourteenth-Century England," in *Literary Practice and Social Change in Britain, 1380–1530*, ed. L. Patterson, Berkeley, University of California Press, 1990, 15–82.

Patterson, L., *Negotiating the Past: The Historical Understanding of Medieval Literature*, Madison, University of Wisconsin Press, 1987.

Rigg, A. G. and C. Brewer (eds.), *William Langland: Piers Plowman: The Z Version*, Studies and Texts 59, Toronto, Pontifical Institute, 1983.

Robertson, D. W., Jr., *A Preface to Chaucer: Studies in Medieval Perspectives*, Princeton University Press, 1962.

Robertson, D. W., Jr. and B. F. Huppé, *Piers Plowman and Scriptural Tradition*, Princeton University Press, 1951.

Vasta, E. (ed.), *Interpretations of Piers Plowman*, University of Notre Dame Press, 1968.

Vaughan, M. F. (ed.), *Piers Plowman: The A Version*, Baltimore, Johns Hopkins University Press, 2011.

Wallace, D., *Premodern Places: Calais to Surinam, Chaucer to Aphra Behn*, Oxford, Wiley-Blackwell, 2006.

Warner, L., *The Lost History of Piers Plowman: The Earliest Transmission of Langland's Work*, Philadelphia, University of Pennsylvania Press, 2011.

Wood, S., *Conscience and the Composition of Piers Plowman*, Oxford University Press, 2012.

THE POEM AND ITS TRADITIONS

1 Major episodes and moments in Piers Plowman B

Adams, R., "Langland's Theology," in *A Companion to Piers Plowman*, ed. J. A. Alford, Berkeley, University of California Press, 1988, pp. 87–114.

Aers, D., *Chaucer, Langland and the Creative Imagination*, London, Routledge and Kegan Paul, 1980.

Aers, D. and L. Staley, *The Powers of the Holy: Religion, Politics, and Gender in Late Medieval English Culture*, University Park, PA, Penn State Press, 2004.

Baker, D., "The Pardons of *Piers Plowman*," *Neuphilologische Mitteilungen*, 85 (1984), 462–72.

Baldwin, A., *The Theme of Government in Piers Plowman*, Cambridge, D. S. Brewer, 1981.

Barney, S. A., *The Penn Commentary on Piers Plowman, Volume 5: C Passūs 20–22; B Passūs 18–20*, Philadelphia, University of Pennsylvania Press, 2006.

Barnie, J., *War in Medieval English Society: Social Values and the Hundred Years' War*, Ithaca, NY, Cornell University Press, 1974.

Birnes, W., "Christ as Advocate: The Legal Metaphor in *Piers Plowman*," *Annuale Mediaevale*, 16 (1975), 71–93.

Burrow, J., "The Action of Langland's Second Vision," *Essays in Criticism*, 15 (1965), 247–68.

Cole, A., *Literature and Heresy in the Age of Chaucer*, Cambridge University Press, 2008.

Crane, S., "The Writing Lesson of 1381," in *Chaucer's England: Literature in Historical Context*, ed. B. Hanawalt, Minneapolis, University of Minnesota Press, 1992, 201–21.

Frank, R. W., *Piers Plowman and the Scheme of Salvation*, New Haven, Yale University Press, 1957.

Galloway, A., *The Penn Commentary on Piers Plowman, Volume 1: C Prologue–Passus 4; B Prologue–Passus 4; A Prologue–Passus 4*, Philadelphia, University of Pennsylvania Press, 2006.

Harbert, B., "Langland's Easter," in *Langland, the Mystics and the Medieval English Religious Tradition: Essays in Honour of S. S. Hussey*, ed. H. Phillips, Cambridge, D. S. Brewer, 1990, 57–70.

Hudson, A., "*Piers Plowman* and the Peasant's Revolt: A Problem Revisited," *YLS*, 8 (1994), 85–106.

Justice, S., *Writing and Rebellion: England in 1381*, Berkeley, University of California Press, 1994.

Kerby-Fulton, K., *Reformist Apocalypticism and Piers Plowman*, Cambridge University Press, 1997.

Lawton, D., "*Piers Plowman*: On Tearing – or Not Tearing – the Pardon," *Philological Quarterly*, 60 (1981), 414–22.

Lees, C., "Gender and Exchange in *Piers Plowman*," in *Class and Gender in Early English Literature*, ed. B. Harwood and G. Overing, Bloomington, Indiana University Press, 1994, 112–90.

Middleton, A., "Narration and the Invention of Experience: Episodic Form in *Piers Plowman*," in *The Wisdom of Poetry: Essays in Early English Literature in Honor of Morton W. Bloomfield*, ed. L. Benson and S. Wenzel, Kalamazoo, MI, Medieval Institute Publications, 1982, 91–122.

"The Audience and Public of *Piers Plowman*," in *Middle English Alliterative Poetry and its Literary Background: Seven Essays*, ed. D. Lawton, Cambridge University Press, 1982, 101–23.

Pearsall, D., "Poverty and Poor People in *Piers Plowman*," in *Piers Plowman: Medieval English Studies Presented to George Kane*, ed. E. Kennedy *et al.*, Cambridge, D. S. Brewer, 1988, 185–207.

Schmidt, A. V. C., *The Clerkly Maker*, Cambridge, D. S. Brewer, 1987.

"The Inner Dreams in *Piers Plowman*," *Medium Ævum*, 55 (1986), 24–40.

Simpson, J., "From Reason to Affective Knowledge: Modes of Thought and Poetic Form in *Piers Plowman*," *Medium Ævum*, 55 (1986), 1–23.

"Grace Abounding: Evangelical Centralisation and the End of *Piers Plowman*," *YLS*, 14 (2001), 49–73.
Piers Plowman: An Introduction, 2nd rev. edn., Exeter University Press, 2007.
Smith, D. V., *The Book of the Incipit: Beginnings in the Fourteenth Century*, Minneapolis, University of Minnesota Press, 2001.
Steiner, E., *Documentary Culture and the Making of English Literature*, Cambridge University Press, 2003.
Stokes, M., *Justice and Mercy in Piers Plowman*, London, Croom Helm, 1984.
Szittya, P., *The Antifraternal Tradition in Medieval England*, Princeton University Press, 1986.
Tavormina, M. T., *Kindly Similitude: Marriage and Family in Piers Plowman*, Cambridge, D. S. Brewer, 1995.
Trigg, S., "The Traffic in Medieval Women: Alice Perrers, Feminist Criticism and *Piers Plowman*," *YLS*, 12 (1998), 5–29.
Waldron, R., "Langland's Originality: The Christ-Knight and the Harrowing of Hell," in *Medieval English Religious and Ethical Literature: Essays in Honor of G. H. Russell*, ed. G. Kratzmann and J. Simpson, Cambridge, D. S. Brewer, 1986, 66–81.
Woolf, R., "The Theme of Christ the Lover-Knight in Medieval English Literature," *Review of English Studies*, 13 (1962), 1–16.
"The Tearing of the Pardon," in *Piers Plowman: Critical Approaches*, ed. S. S. Hussey, London, Methuen, 1969, 50–75.

2 *The versions and revisions of* Piers Plowman

Manuscript facsimiles

Benson, C. D. and L. S. Blanchfield, *The Manuscripts of Piers Plowman: The B-Version*, Cambridge, D. S. Brewer, 1997 [reduced images of a side from each copy; the accompanying text should be approached with caution].
Duggan, H. W. (gen. ed.), *The Piers Plowman Electronic Archive*, various publishers, 1999– [an ongoing project of digitized facsimiles of full manuscripts, on CD-ROM with extensive annotation; to date, limited to B Version copies, F W O L M Hm R = vols. 1–7, respectively].
Matsushita, T., *Piers Plowman: The A Version: Facsimiles of the Twenty Manuscripts with their Diplomatic Texts*, 3 vols., Tokyo, Senshu University, 2008 [full facsimiles of varying quality and scaling].
Piers Plowman: A Facsimile of the Z-Text in Bodleian Library, Oxford, MS Bodley 851, ed. C. Brewer and A. G. Rigg, Cambridge, D. S. Brewer, 1994.
Piers Plowman: Facsimile: Bodleian Library Oxford, MS. Douce 104, ed. D. Pearsall and K. Scott, Woodbridge, D. S. Brewer, 1992.
Piers Plowman: The Huntington Library Manuscript (HM 143) reproduced in Photostat, ed. R. W. Chambers *et al.*, San Marino, Huntington Library, 1936.

Editions (for the Athlone and Schmidt editions, see list of abbreviations)

Knott, T. A. and D. C. Fowler (eds.), *Piers the Plowman: A Critical Edition of the A Version*, Baltimore, Johns Hopkins University Press, 1952.

Pearsall, D. (ed.), *William Langland Piers Plowman: A New Annotated Edition of the C-Text*, 2nd edn., Exeter University Press, 2008.

Rigg, A. G. and C. Brewer (eds.), *William Langland: Piers Plowman: The Z Version*, Studies and Texts 59, Toronto, Pontifical Institute, 1983.

Skeat, Walter W. (ed.), *The Vision of William Concerning Piers the Plowman in Three Parallel Texts . . .*, 2 vols., Oxford, Clarendon Press, 1886 [reformulating work previously published as EETS os 28, 38, 54, 67, and 81].

Vaughan, M. F. (ed.), *Piers Plowman: The A Version*, Baltimore, Johns Hopkins University Press, 2011.

Wynnere and Wastour, in *Alliterative Poetry of the Later Middle Ages: An Anthology*, ed. T. Turville-Petre, London, Routledge, 1989, 38–66.

Discussions

Adams, R., "Editing *Piers Plowman* B: The Imperative of an Intermittently Critical Edition," *Studies in Bibliography*, 45 (1992), 31–68.

"The R/F MSS of *Piers Plowman* and the Pattern of Alpha/Beta Complementary Omissions: Implications for Critical Editing," *TEXT*, 14 (2002), 109–37.

Adams, R. and T. Turville-Petre, "The London Book-Trade and the Lost History of *Piers Plowman*," *RES*, 64 (2013).

Alford, J. A. (ed.), *A Companion to Piers Plowman*, Berkeley, University of California Press, 1988.

Brewer, C., *Editing Piers Plowman: The Evolution of the Text*, Cambridge University Press, 1996.

Davis, B. P., "The Rationale for a Copy of a Text: Constructing the Exemplar for British Library Additional MS 10574," *YLS*, 11 (1997), 141–55.

Donaldson, E. T., *Piers Plowman: The C-Text and its Poet*, New Haven, Yale Studies in English 113, 1949.

Doyle, A. I., "Remarks on Surviving Manuscripts of *Piers Plowman*," in *Medieval English Religious and Ethical Literature: Essays in Honour of G. H. Russell*, ed. G. Kratzmann and J. Simpson, Cambridge, D. S. Brewer, 1986, 35–48.

Doyle, A. I. and M. B. Parkes, "The Production of Copies of the *Canterbury Tales* and the *Confessio Amantis* in the Early Fifteenth Century," in *Medieval Scribes, Manuscripts, and Libraries: Essays Presented to N. R. Ker*, ed. M. B. Parkes and A. G. Watson, London, Scolar, 1973, 163–210.

Fowler, D. C., "A New Edition of the B Text of *Piers Plowman*," *YES*, 7 (1977), 23–42.

Galloway, A., *The Penn Commentary on Piers Plowman, Volume 1*, Philadelphia, University of Pennsylvania Press, 2006 [the only other published volume, the fifth, by Stephen A. Barney, deals with the lightly revised conclusion to the text, extant in only the two later versions].

Hanna, R., *Pursuing History: Middle English Manuscripts and their Texts*, Figurae: Reading Medieval Culture, Stanford University Press, 1996, 195–243, 312–19.

William Langland, Authors of the Middle Ages: English Writers of the Late Middle Ages 3, Aldershot, Variorum, 1993, with supplements, *YLS*, 14 (2000), 185–98; 16 (2002), 169–77.

Horobin, S., "Harley 3954 and the Audience of *Piers Plowman*," in *Medieval Texts in Context*, ed. G. D. Caie and D. Renevey, London, Routledge, 2008, 68–84.

"'In London and opeland': The Dialect and Circulation of the C Version of *Piers Plowman*," *Medium Ævum* 74 (2005), 248–69.

Horobin, S. and L. R. Mooney, "A *Piers Plowman* Manuscript by the Hengwrt/ Ellesmere Scribe and its Implications for London Standard English," *SAC*, 26 (2004), 65–112.

Justice, S., *Writing and Rebellion: England in 1381*, Berkeley, University of California Press, 1994.

Kane, G., *Piers Plowman: The Evidence for Authorship*, London, Athlone Press, 1965.

"The Text," in Alford, 175–200.

"The 'Z Version' of *Piers Plowman*," *Speculum*, 60 (1985), 910–30.

Lawler, T., "A Reply to Jill Mann: Reaffirming the Traditional Relation between the A and B Versions of *Piers Plowman*," *YLS*, 10 (1996), 145–80.

Manly, J. M., "*Piers Plowman* and its Sequence," in *The Cambridge History of English Literature vol. 2: The End of the Middle Ages*, ed. A. W. Ward and A. R. Waller, Cambridge University Press, 1908, 1–42.

Mann, J., "The Power of the Alphabet: A Reassessment of the Relationship between the A and B Versions of *Piers Plowman*," *YLS*, 8 (1995), 21–50.

Middleton, A., "Acts of Vagrancy: The C Version 'Autobiography' and the Statute of 1388," in *Written Work: Langland, Labor, and Authorship*, ed. S. Justice and K. Kerby-Fulton, Philadelphia, University of Pennsylvania Press, 1997, 208–317.

"Making a Good End: John But as a Reader of *Piers Plowman*," in *Medieval English Studies Presented to George Kane*, ed. E. D. Kennedy *et al.*, Woodbridge, D. S. Brewer, 1988, 243–66.

Russell, G. H., "Some Aspects of the Process of Revision in *Piers Plowman*," in *Piers Plowman: Critical Approaches*, ed. S. S. Hussey, London, Methuen, 1969, 27–49.

Samuels, M. L., "Dialect and Grammar," in Alford, 201–21.

Turville-Petre, T., "Putting It Right: The Corrections of Huntington Library MS Hm 128 and BL Additional MS 35287," *YLS*, 16 (2002), 41–65.

Warner, L., "The Ending and End of *Piers Plowman* B: The C-Version Origins of the Final Two Passus," *Medium Ævum* 76 (2007), 225–50.

Weldon, J., "*Ordinatio* and Genre in MS CCC 201," *Florilegium* 12 (1993), 159–75.

Wood, S., *Conscience and the Composition of Piers Plowman*, Oxford University Press, 2012.

3 *Literary history and* Piers Plowman

Bloomfield, M., *Piers Plowman as a Fourteenth-Century Apocalypse*, New Brunswick, Rutgers University Press, [1962].

Bourquin, G., *Piers Plowman: études sur la génèse littéraire des trois versions*, 2 vols., Paris, Librairie Honoré Champion, 1978.

de Deguileville, G., *Le pèlerinage de vie humaine*, ed. J. J. Stürzinger, London, The Roxburghe Club, 1893.

Hamilton, A. C., "Spenser and Langland," *Studies in Philology*, 55 (1958), 533–48.

Hanna, R., "Langland's Ymaginatif: Images and the Limits of Poetry," in *Images, Idolatry, and Iconoclasm in Late Medieval England: Textuality and the Visual Image*, ed. J. Dimmick, J. Simpson, and N. Zeeman, Oxford University Press, 2002, 81–94.

"William Langland," in *The Cambridge Companion to Medieval English Literature, 1100–1500*, ed. L. Scanlon, Cambridge University Press, 2009, 125–38.

Hardwick, P., "'Biddeth Peres Ploughman go to his werk': Appropriation of *Piers Plowman* in the Nineteenth and Twentieth Centuries," in *Film and Fiction: Reviewing the Middle Ages*, ed. T. Shippey and M. Arnold, Cambridge, D. S. Brewer, 2002, 171–95.

Justice, S., "The Genres of *Piers Plowman*," *Viator*, 19 (1988), 291–306.

"Literary History," in *Chaucer: Contemporary Approaches*, ed. D. Raybin and S. Fein, University Park, Penn State University Press, 2010, 199–214.

Kelen, S., *Langland's Early Modern Identities*, New York, Palgrave Macmillan, 2007.

Middleton, A., "Introduction: The Critical Heritage," in *A Companion to Piers Plowman*, ed. J. A. Alford, Berkeley, University of California Press, 1988, 1–25.

"Narration and the Invention of Experience: Episodic Form in *Piers Plowman*," in *The Wisdom of Poetry: Essays in Early English Literature in Honor of Morton W. Bloomfield*, ed. L. Benson and S. Wenzel, Kalamazoo, Medieval Institute Publications, 1982, 91–122.

Salter, E. "*Piers Plowman* and *The Simonie*," *Archiv für das Studium der neueren Sprachen und Literaturen*, 203 (1967), 241–54.

Smith, D. V., *The Book of the Incipit: Beginnings in the Fourteenth Century*, Minneapolis, University of Minnesota Press, 2001.

Steiner, E., *Documentary Culture and the Making of Medieval English Literature*, Cambridge University Press, 2003.

4 *Allegory and* Piers Plowman

Aers, D., *Piers Plowman and Christian Allegory*, London, Edward Arnold, 1975.

Auerbach, E., "Figura," in *Scenes from the Drama of European Literature*, New York, Meridian Books, 1959, 11–76.

Barney, S. A., *Allegories of History, Allegories of Love*, Hamden, CT, Archon Books, 1979.

"Allegorical Visions," in *A Companion to Piers Plowman*, ed. J. A. Alford, Berkeley, University of California Press, 1988, 117–33.

Bloomfield, M., "A Grammatical Approach to Personification Allegory," in Bloomfield, *Essays and Explorations: Studies in Ideas, Language and Literature*, Cambridge, MA, Harvard University Press, 1970, 243–60.

Cervone, C. M., *Poetics of the Incarnation: Middle English Writing and the Leap of Love*, Philadelphia, University of Pennsylvania Press, 2012.

Charity, A. C., *Events and their Afterlife: The Dialectics of Christian Typology in the Bible and Dante*, Cambridge University Press, 1966.

Dronke, P., "Arbor Caritatis," in *Medieval Studies for J. A. W. Bennett Aetatis Suae LXX*, ed. P. L. Heyworth, Oxford University Press, 1981, 207–53.

Frank, R. W., Jr., "The Art of Reading Medieval Personification-Allegory," *ELH*, 20 (1953), 237–50; repr. in Vasta (see below).

Gombrich, E. H., *Symbolic Images*, London, Phaidon Press, 1972 (esp. pp. 123–91).

Gradon, P., *Form and Style in Early English Literature*, London, Methuen, 1971 (chs. 1 and 6).

Griffiths, L., *Personification in Piers Plowman*, Cambridge, D. S. Brewer, 1985.

Hollander, R., *Allegory in Dante's Commedia*, Princeton University Press, 1969.

Jauss, H., "Form und Auffassung der Allegorie in der Tradition der *Psychomachia*," in *Medium Ævum Vivum: Festschrift für Walther Bulst*, ed. H. R. Jauss and D. Schaller, Heidelberg, Winter, 1960, 179–206; slightly expanded version published as "La transformation de la forme allégorique entre 1180 et 1240: d'Alain de Lille à Guillaume de Lorris," in *L'humanisme médiéval dans les littératures romanes du XIIe au XIVe siècle*, ed. Anthime Fourrier, Paris, Librairie Klincksieck, 1964, 107–46.

Katzenellenbogen, A., *Allegories of the Virtues and Vices in Mediaeval Art*, London, Warburg Institute, 1939; repr. New York, Norton, 1964.

Mann, J., "Eating and Drinking in *Piers Plowman*," *Essays and Studies*, 32 (1979), 26–43.

Langland and Allegory, The Morton W. Bloomfield Lectures II, Kalamazoo, MI, Medieval Institute Publications, 1992; reprinted in *The Morton W. Bloomfield Lectures, 1989–2005*, ed. D. Donoghue, J. Simpson, and N. Watson, Kalamazoo, MI, Medieval Institute Publications, 2010, 20–41.

Paxson, J., *The Poetics of Personification*, Cambridge University Press, 1994.

Quilligan, M., *The Language of Allegory: Defining the Genre*, Ithaca, NY, Cornell University Press, 1979.

Raabe, P., *Imitating God: The Allegory of Faith in Piers Plowman B*, Athens, University of Georgia Press, 1990.

Salter, E., "Medieval Poetry and the Figural View of Reality," *Proceedings of the British Academy*, 54 (1968), 73–92.

Schless, H., "The Backgrounds of Allegory: Langland and Dante," *YLS*, 5 (1991), 129–42.

Singleton, C. S., *Dante's Commedia: Elements of Structure*, Baltimore, Johns Hopkins University Press, 1977 [originally 1954].

Journey to Beatrice, Baltimore, Johns Hopkins University Press, 1977 [originally 1958].

Smith, M., *Prudentius' Psychomachia; A Reexamination*, Princeton University Press, 1976.

Spearing, A. C., "*Piers Plowman*: Allegory and Verbal Practice," in *Readings in Medieval Poetry*, Cambridge University Press, 1987, 216–45, 261–4.

Steiner, E., *Documentary Culture and the Making of Medieval English Literature*, Cambridge University Press, 2003.

Tuve, R., *Allegorical Imagery: Some Medieval Books and their Posterity*, Princeton University Press, 1966.

Vasta, E. (ed.), *Interpretations of Piers Plowman*, University of Notre Dame Press, 1968 (essays by Frank Donaldson).

HISTORICAL AND INTELLECTUAL CONTEXTS

5 *The Rokeles: an index for a "Langland" family history*

Adams, R., *Langland and the Rokele Family: The Gentry Background to Piers Plowman*, Dublin, Four Courts Press, 2013.

Barron, C., "William Langland: A London Poet," in *Chaucer's England: Literature in Historical Context*, ed. Barbara Hanawalt, Minneapolis, University of Minnesota Press, 1992, 91–109.

Bennett, M., "William called Long Will," *YLS*, 26 (2012), 1–25.

Hanna, R., *William Langland*, Authors of the Middle Ages: English Writers of the Late Middle Ages 3, Aldershot, Variorum, 1993.

"Emendations to a 1993 'Vita de Ne'erdowel,'" *YLS*, 14 (2000), 185–98.

Kane, G., *Piers Plowman: The Evidence for Authorship*, London, Athlone Press, 1965.

Matheson, L., review of Ralph Hanna, *William Langland*, YLS, 8 (1994), 192–4.

Middleton, A., "William Langland's 'Kynde Name': Authorial Signature and Social Identity in Late Fourteenth-Century England," in *Literary Practice and Social Change in Britain, 1380–1530*, ed. L. Patterson, Berkeley and Los Angeles, University of California Press, 1990, 15–82.

6 *Religious forms and institutions in* Piers Plowman

Aers, D., *Sanctifying Signs: Making Christian Tradition in Late Medieval England*, University of Notre Dame Press, 2004.

Cole, A., *Literature and Heresy in the Age of Chaucer*, Cambridge University Press, 2008.

Duffy, E., *The Stripping of the Altars: Traditional Religion in England, c.1400–c.1580*, 2nd edn., New Haven, Yale University Press, 2005.

Gwynn, A., *The English Austin Friars in the Time of Wyclif*, Oxford University Press, 1940.

Helmholz, R., *The Oxford History of the Laws of England*, vol. 1: *Canon Law and Ecclesiastical Jurisdiction from 597 to the 1640s*, Oxford University Press, 2004.

Knowles, D., *The Religious Orders in England*, 3 vols., Cambridge University Press, 1961–2.

Pantin, W. A., *The English Church in the Fourteenth Century*, University of Toronto Press, 1980.

Platt, C., *The Parish Churches of Medieval England*, London, Secker and Warburg, 1981.

Scase, W., *Piers Plowman and the New Anticlericalism*, Cambridge University Press, 1989.

Simpson, J., *Piers Plowman: An Introduction to the B-Text*, 2nd, rev. edn., Exeter University Press, 2007.

Southern, R. W., *Western Society and the Church in the Middle Ages*, Harmondsworth, Penguin, 1970.

Swanson, R. N., *Catholic England: Faith, Religion, and Observance before the Reformation*, Manchester University Press, 1992.

Church and Society in Late Medieval England, Oxford, Blackwell, 1989.
Warren, A. K., *Anchorites and their Patrons in Medieval England*, Berkeley, University of California Press, 1985.

7 *Political forms and institutions in* Piers Plowman

Alford, J., *Piers Plowman: A Glossary of Legal Diction*, Cambridge, D. S. Brewer, 1988.
Baldwin, A. P., *The Theme of Government in Piers Plowman*, Cambridge, D. S. Brewer, 1981.
Benson, C. D., *Public Piers Plowman: Modern Scholarship and Late Medieval English Culture*, Philadelphia, Penn State University Press, 2004.
Dodd, G., "A Parliament Full of Rats? *Piers Plowman* and the Good Parliament of 1376," *Bulletin of the Institute for Historical Research*, 79 (2006), 21–49.
Giancarlo, M., *Parliament and Literature in Late Medieval England*, Cambridge University Press, 2007.
Harding, A., *Medieval Law and the Foundations of the State*, Oxford University Press, 2002.
Harriss, G., *Shaping the Nation: England, 1360–1461*, Oxford University Press, 2005.
Justice, S., *Writing and Rebellion: England in 1381*, Berkeley, University of California Press, 1994.
Kennedy, K., *Maintenance, Meed, and Marriage in Medieval English Literature*, New York, Palgrave Macmillan, 2009.
Stokes, M., *Justice and Mercy in Piers Plowman*, London, Croom Helm, 1984.

8 *Christian philosophy in* Piers Plowman

Aers, D., *Sanctifying Signs: Making Christian Tradition in Late Medieval England*, University of Notre Dame Press, 2004.
Alford, J. A., *Piers Plowman: A Glossary of Legal Diction*, Cambridge, D. S. Brewer, 1988.
"Langland's Learning," *YLS*, 9 (1995), 1–8.
Bowers, J., *The Crisis of Will in Piers Plowman*, Washington, DC, Catholic University of America Press, 1986.
The Cambridge History of Later Medieval Philosophy: From the Rediscovery of Aristotle to the Disintegration of Scholasticism, 1100–1600, ed. N. Kretzmann, A. Kenny, and J. Pinborg, Cambridge University Press, 1982, 1988.
The Cambridge History of Literary Criticism, vol. 2: *The Middle Ages*, ed. Alastair Minnis and Ian Johnson, Cambridge University Press, 2008.
Carruthers, M., *The Book of Memory: A Study of Memory in Medieval Culture*, 2nd edn., Cambridge University Press, 2008.
Coleman, J., *Piers Plowman and the Moderni*, Rome, Edizioni di storia e letteratura, 1981.
Courtney, W. J., *Schools and Scholars in Fourteenth-Century England*, Princeton University Press, 1987.
Galloway, A., "*Piers Plowman* and the Schools," *YLS*, 6 (1992), 89–107.

"The Rhetoric of Riddling in Late-Medieval England: The 'Oxford' Riddles, the *Secretum philosophorum*, and the Riddles in *Piers Plowman*," *Speculum*, 70 (1995), 68–105.

Gwynn, A., *The English Austin Friars in the Time of Wyclif*, Oxford University Press, 1940.

Hanna, R., "Literacy, Schooling, Universities," in *The Cambridge Companion to Medieval English Culture*, ed. A. Galloway, Cambridge University Press, 2011, 179–84.

Harwood, B. J., *Piers Plowman and the Problem of Belief*, University of Toronto Press, 1992.

A History of the University of Cambridge, gen. ed. C. N. L. Brooke, Cambridge University Press, 1988–2004; esp. vol. 1, D. Riehl Leader, "The University to 1546."

The History of the University of Oxford, gen. ed. T. H. Aston, Oxford, Clarendon Press, 1984–2000; esp. vol. 1, *The Early Oxford Schools*, ed. J. I. Catto (1984); and vol. 2, *Late Medieval Oxford*, ed. J. I. Catto and R. Evans (1992).

Karnes, M., *Imagination, Meditation, and Cognition in the Middle Ages*, University of Chicago Press, 2011.

Lawler, T., "Langland Versificator," *YLS*, 25 (2011), 37–76.

Leff, G., *Bradwardine and the Pelagians: A Study of his "De causa Dei" and its Opponents*, Cambridge University Press, 1957.

Mann, J., "'He Knew Nat Catoun': Medieval School-Texts and Middle English Literature," in *The Text in the Community: Essays on Medieval Works, Manuscripts, Authors, and Readers*, ed. J. Mann and M. Nolan, University of Notre Dame Press, 2006, 41–74.

Schmidt, A. V. C., "Langland and Scholastic Philosophy," *Medium Ævum*, 38 (1969), 134–56.

"Langland's Visions and Revisions," *YLS*, 14 (2000), 5–28.

Smith, D. V., *The Book of the Incipit: Beginnings in the Fourteenth Century*, Minneapolis, University of Minnesota Press, 2001.

"Negative Langland," *YLS*, 23 (2009), 33–59.

Wittig, J., "*Piers Plowman* B, Passus IX–XII: Elements in the Design of the Inward Journey," *Traditio*, 28 (1972), 211–80.

Zeeman, N., *Piers Plowman and the Medieval Discourse of Desire*, Cambridge University Press, 2006.

9 The non-Christians of Piers Plowman

Aers, D., *Salvation and Sin: Augustine, Langland, and Fourteenth-Century Theology*, University of Notre Dame Press, 2009.

Akbari, S. C., *Idols in the East: European Representations of Islam and the Orient, 1100–1450*, Ithaca, NY, Cornell University Press, 2009.

Seeing through the Veil: Optical Theory and Medieval Allegory, University of Toronto Press, 2004.

"The Rhetoric of Antichrist in Western Lives of Muhammad," *Islam and Christian–Muslim Relations*, 8 (1997), 297–307.

Colish, M., "The Virtuous Pagan: Dante and the Christian Tradition," in *The Unbounded Community: Papers in Christian Ecumenism in Honor of*

Jaroslav Pelikan, ed. W. Caferro and D. G. Fisher, New York, Garland, 1996, 43–77.

Daniel, N., *Islam and the West: The Making of an Image*, rev. edn., Oxford, Oneworld, 1993.

Grady, F., *Representing Righteous Heathens in Late Medieval England*, New York, Palgrave Macmillan, 2005.

Iannucci, A. A., "Limbo: The Emptiness of Time," *Studi danteschi*, 52 (1979–80), 69–128.

Iogna-Prat, D., *Order and Exclusion: Cluny and Christendom Face Heresy, Judaism, and Islam*, 1998; trans. G. R. Edwards, Ithaca, NY, Cornell University Press, 2001.

Kinoshita, S., *Medieval Boundaries: Rethinking Difference in Old French Literature*, Philadelphia, University of Pennsylvania Press, 2006.

Metlitzki, D., *The Matter of Araby in Medieval England*, New Haven, Yale University Press, 1979.

Narin van Court, E., "Hermeneutics of Supersession: The Revision of the Jews from the B to the C text of *Piers Plowman*," YLS, 10 (1996), 43–87.

Rogers, W. E., "The C-Revisions and the Crusades in *Piers Plowman*," in *The Medieval Crusade*, ed. S. J. Ridyard, Woodbridge, Boydell, 2004, 145–56.

Southern, R. W., *Western Views of Islam in the Middle Ages*, Cambridge, MA, Harvard University Press, 1962.

Tolan, J., *Saracens: Islam in the Medieval European Imagination*, New York, Columbia University Press, 2002.

Vitto, C. L., *The Virtuous Pagan in Middle English Literature*, Transactions of the American Philosophical Society 79, part 5, Philadelphia, American Philosophical Society, 1989.

Watson, N., "Visions of Inclusion: Universal Salvation and Vernacular Theology in Pre-Reformation England," *Journal of Medieval and Early Modern Studies*, 27 (1997), 145–87.

READERS AND RESPONSES

10 Manuscripts and readers of Piers Plowman

Benson, C. D., *Public Piers Plowman: Modern Scholarship and Late Medieval English Culture*, Philadelphia, Pennsylvania State University Press, 2004.

Benson, C. D. and L. S. Blanchfield, *The Manuscripts of Piers Plowman: The B-Version*, Cambridge, D. S. Brewer, 1997.

Bowers, J. M., *Chaucer and Langland: The Antagonistic Tradition*, University of Notre Dame Press, 2007.

Doyle, A. I., "Remarks on Surviving Manuscripts of *Piers Plowman*," in *Medieval English Religious and Ethical Literature: Essays in Honour of G. H. Russell*, ed. G. Kratzmann and J. Simpson, Cambridge, D. S. Brewer, 1986, 35–48.

Hanna, R., *William Langland*, Aldershot, Variorum, 1993.

Kelen, S., *Langland's Early Modern Identities*, Basingstoke, Palgrave, 2007.

Kerby-Fulton, K. and D. L. Despres, *Iconography and the Professional Reader: The Politics of Book Production in the Douce Piers Plowman*, Minneapolis, University of Minnesota Press, 1999.

Middleton, A., "The Audience and Public of 'Piers Plowman,'" in *Middle English Alliterative Poetry and its Literary Background*, ed. D. Lawton, Cambridge, D. S. Brewer, 1982, 101–23.

Samuels, M. L., "Langland's Dialect," *Medium Ævum*, 54 (1985), 232–47; repr. in *The English of Chaucer and His Contemporaries*, ed. J. J. Smith, Aberdeen University Press, 1988, 70–85.

Scase, W., *Piers Plowman and the New Anticlericalism*, Cambridge, Cambridge University Press, 1989.

Turville-Petre, T., "Sir Adrian Fortescue and his Copy of *Piers Plowman*," YLS, 14 (2000), 29–48.

11 *Plowman traditions in late medieval and early modern writing*

Aston, M., "Corpus Christi and Corpus Regni: Heresy and the Peasants' Revolt," *Past and Present*, 143 (1994), 3–47.

Barney, S. A., "The Plowshare of the Tongue: The Progress of a Symbol from the Bible to *Piers Plowman*," *Mediaeval Studies*, 35 (1973), 261–93.

Barr, H. (ed.), *The Piers Plowman Tradition: A Critical Edition of "Pierce the Ploughman's Crede," "Richard the Redeless," "Mum and the Sothsegger" and "The Crowned King"*, London, J. M. Dent, 1993.

Bowers, J. M., *Chaucer and Langland: The Antagonistic Tradition*, University of Notre Dame Press, 2007.

Chaudhuri, S., "Ploughman and Shepherd: Langland's Legacy to Tudor Pastoral," *Journal of the Department of English* [University of Calcultta], 22 (1986–7), 50–71.

Freedman, P., *Images of the Medieval Peasant*, Stanford University Press, 1999.

Hardwick, P., "Chaucer: The Poet as Ploughman," *Chaucer Review*, 33 (1998), 146–56.

Horobin, S., "Stephan Batman and his Manuscripts of *Piers Plowman*," *Review of English Studies*, 62 (2011), 358–72.

Hudson, A., "The Legacy of *Piers Plowman*," in *A Companion to Piers Plowman*, ed. J. A. Alford, Berkeley, University of California Press, 1988, 251–66.

Jones, M. R., *Radical Pastoral, 1381–1594: Appropriation and the Writing of Religious Controversy*, Farnham, Ashgate, 2011.

Kelen, S., *Langland's Early Modern Identities*, New York, Palgrave, 2007.

King, J. N., *English Reformation Literature: The Tudor Origins of the Protestant Tradition*, Princeton University Press, 1982.

Kirk, E. D., "Langland's Plowman and the Recreation of Fourteenth-Century Religious Metaphor," YLS, 2 (1988), 1–21.

Lawton, D., "Lollardy and the *Piers Plowman* Tradition," *Modern Language Review*, 76 (1981), 780–93.

Little, K. C., "The 'Other' Past of Pastoral: Langland's *Piers Plowman* and Spenser's *Shepheardes Calendar*," *Exemplaria* 21.2 (2009), 160–78.

Transforming Work: Early Modern Pastoral and Late Medieval Poetry, University of Notre Dame Press, 2013.

McCarl, M. R. (ed.), *The Plowman's Tale: The c. 1532 and 1606 Editions of a Spurious Canterbury Tale*, New York, Garland, 1997.

McRae, A., *God Speed the Plough: The Representation of Agrarian England, 1500–1660*, Cambridge University Press, 1996.

Warner, L., *The Myth of Piers Plowman: Constructing a Medieval Literary Archive*, Cambridge University Press, 2014.

Wheatley, E., "A Selfless Ploughman and the Christ/Piers Conjunction in Langland's *Piers Plowman*," *Notes and Queries*, ns 40 (1993), 135–42.

Wilson, E. (ed.), *The Winchester Anthology: A Facsimile of British Library Additional Manuscript 60577 with an Introduction and List of Contents by Edward Wilson and an Account of the Music by Iain Fenlon*, Cambridge, D. S. Brewer, 1981.

INDEX

Aers, David, 174, 217–18
Alford, John, 2, 8–9
allegory, 3, 26, 120, 124–5, 131, *also* chapter 4
alliterative poetry, late medieval efflorescence of, xii
Ancrene Wisse, 26
Aquinas, Thomas, 3, 143, 156, 157, 218
Aristotle, 137, 138, 139, 146, 150, 155, 157, 192
Athanasian Creed, 22, 27, 147
Auerbach, Erich, 66
Augustine and Augustinian thought, 4, 128, 141, 143, 164, 217, 218

Batman, Stephan, 193–4
battle of Poitiers (1356), xii
Beauchamp, Richard, 180
Bennett, Michael, 6
Benson, David, 163
Besford, Joan, 180
Bible
  1 Cor. 1, 136
  1 Cor. 7, 200
  1 Cor. 13, 75
  2 Cor. 3, 77
  2 Cor. 11, 138
  Apoc. 2, 15
  Apoc. 14, 73
  Cant. 4, 69
  Col. 2, 78, 136
  Gal. 4, 73
  Gal. 6, 79
  Hebrews 11, 143
  Isaiah 7, 143
  Luke 1, 69, 73
  Luke 10, 76
  Luke 12, 77
  Matt. 5, 81
  Matt. 6, 77
  Matt. 7, 78
  Matt. 12, 66
  Matt. 21, 26, 69
  Matt. 22, 24, 76, 78
  Prov. 22, 18
Black Death, xii, 21, 149
Blackfriars Council (1382), xiii, 190
Blanch, Robert J., 2, 5, 6
Bloomfield, Morton, 3, 5, 215
Boccaccio, 37
Boethius, 53, 137, 145
Book of Vices and Virtues, 136
Bradwardine, Thomas, 139
Brewer, Charlotte, 5
Brynstan, John, 195, 205, 206, 207, 208
Buriton, John, 205
But, John (continuator of *Piers Plowman*), xiv, 40, 41, 254

Carruthers, Mary, 221
Chadwick, Dorothy, 4
Chatton, Walter, 142, 152
Chaucer, Geoffrey, xii, xiv, 1, 4, 6, 8, 33, 34, 37, 52, 57, 59, 60, 62, 63, 64, 88, 138, 140, 144, 145, 153, 161, 182, 184, 185, 191, 196, 198, 199, 201, 202, 203, 204, 210, 214, 226, 227, 232, 234, 235, 237, 238, 239, 241, 243, 245, 251
Chrysostom, John, 139
Clopton, Sir William, 180
Cloud of Unknowing, 143
Cok, John, 185, 187, 195
Cole, Andrew, 215, 219
conscience (in medieval culture), 98
Cooper, Helen, 225

Cambridge Companions to...

AUTHORS

Edward Albee edited by Stephen J. Bottoms

Margaret Atwood edited by Coral Ann Howells

W. H. Auden edited by Stan Smith

Jane Austen edited by Edward Copeland and Juliet McMaster (second edition)

Beckett edited by John Pilling

Bede edited by Scott DeGregorio

Aphra Behn edited by Derek Hughes and Janet Todd

Walter Benjamin edited by David S. Ferris

William Blake edited by Morris Eaves

Jorge Luis Borges edited by Edwin Williamson

Brecht edited by Peter Thomson and Glendyr Sacks (second edition)

The Brontës edited by Heather Glen

Bunyan edited by Anne Dunan-Page

Frances Burney edited by Peter Sabor

Byron edited by Drummond Bone

Albert Camus edited by Edward J. Hughes

Willa Cather edited by Marilee Lindemann

Cervantes edited by Anthony J. Cascardi

Chaucer edited by Piero Boitani and Jill Mann (second edition)

Chekhov edited by Vera Gottlieb and Paul Allain

Kate Chopin edited by Janet Beer

Caryl Churchill edited by Elaine Aston and Elin Diamond

Cicero edited by Catherine Steel

Coleridge edited by Lucy Newlyn

Wilkie Collins edited by Jenny Bourne Taylor

Joseph Conrad edited by J. H. Stape

H. D. edited by Nephie J. Christodoulides and Polina Mackay

Dante edited by Rachel Jacoff (second edition)

Daniel Defoe edited by John Richetti

Don DeLillo edited by John N. Duvall

Charles Dickens edited by John O. Jordan

Emily Dickinson edited by Wendy Martin

John Donne edited by Achsah Guibbory

Dostoevskii edited by W. J. Leatherbarrow

Theodore Dreiser edited by Leonard Cassuto and Claire Virginia Eby

John Dryden edited by Steven N. Zwicker

W. E. B. Du Bois edited by Shamoon Zamir

George Eliot edited by George Levine

T. S. Eliot edited by A. David Moody

Ralph Ellison edited by Ross Posnock

Ralph Waldo Emerson edited by Joel Porte and Saundra Morris

William Faulkner edited by Philip M. Weinstein

Henry Fielding edited by Claude Rawson

F. Scott Fitzgerald edited by Ruth Prigozy

Flaubert edited by Timothy Unwin

E. M. Forster edited by David Bradshaw

Benjamin Franklin edited by Carla Mulford

Brian Friel edited by Anthony Roche

Robert Frost edited by Robert Faggen

Gabriel García Márquez edited by Philip Swanson

Elizabeth Gaskell edited by Jill L. Matus

Goethe edited by Lesley Sharpe

Günter Grass edited by Stuart Taberner

Thomas Hardy edited by Dale Kramer

David Hare edited by Richard Boon

Nathaniel Hawthorne edited by Richard Millington

Seamus Heaney edited by Bernard O'Donoghue

Ernest Hemingway edited by Scott Donaldson

Homer edited by Robert Fowler

Horace edited by Stephen Harrison

Ted Hughes edited by Terry Gifford

Ibsen edited by James McFarlane

Henry James edited by Jonathan Freedman

Samuel Johnson edited by Greg Clingham

Ben Jonson edited by Richard Harp and Stanley Stewart

James Joyce edited by Derek Attridge (second edition)

Kafka edited by Julian Preece

Keats edited by Susan J. Wolfson

Rudyard Kipling edited by Howard J. Booth

Lacan edited by Jean-Michel Rabaté

D. H. Lawrence edited by Anne Fernihough

Primo Levi edited by Robert Gordon

TOPICS